Democracy despite Itself

Democracy despite Itself

*Liberal Constitutionalism and
Militant Democracy*

BENJAMIN A. SCHUPMANN
Assistant Professor of Political Science, Yale-NUS College, Singapore

OXFORD
UNIVERSITY PRESS

Great Clarendon Street, Oxford, OX2 6DP,
United Kingdom

Oxford University Press is a department of the University of Oxford.
It furthers the University's objective of excellence in research, scholarship,
and education by publishing worldwide. Oxford is a registered trade mark of
Oxford University Press in the UK and in certain other countries

© Benjamin A. Schupmann 2024

The moral rights of the author have been asserted

All rights reserved. No part of this publication may be reproduced, stored in
a retrieval system, or transmitted, in any form or by any means, without the
prior permission in writing of Oxford University Press, or as expressly permitted
by law, by licence or under terms agreed with the appropriate reprographics
rights organization. Enquiries concerning reproduction outside the scope of the
above should be sent to the Rights Department, Oxford University Press, at the
address above

You must not circulate this work in any other form
and you must impose this same condition on any acquirer

Public sector information reproduced under Open Government Licence v3.0
(http://www.nationalarchives.gov.uk/doc/open-government-licence/open-government-licence.htm)

Published in the United States of America by Oxford University Press
198 Madison Avenue, New York, NY 10016, United States of America

British Library Cataloguing in Publication Data

Data available

Library of Congress Control Number: 2024933466

ISBN 9780192873026

DOI: 10.1093/9780191975950.001.0001

Printed and bound by
CPI Group (UK) Ltd, Croydon, CR0 4YY

Links to third party websites are provided by Oxford in good faith and
for information only. Oxford disclaims any responsibility for the materials
contained in any third party website referenced in this work.

The manufacturer's authorised representative in the EU for product safety
is Oxford University Press España S.A. of el Parque Empresarial San
Fernando de Henares, Avenida de Castilla,
2 – 28830 Madrid (www.oup.es/en).

μάχεσθαι χρὴ τὸν δῆμον ὑπὲρ τοῦ νόμου ὅκωσπερ τείχεος (The people must fight for the law as for the city wall)

Heraclitus Fragment DK 22 B 44

Preface

Legal revolution, when democratically elected actors use their legal possession of state power to subvert democratic essentials, poses a distinctive existential threat to democracy, as seen recently in populist 'illiberal democracies' such as Hungary, India, and Turkey. 'Militant democracy', which justifies the defence of constitutional democracy through measures of constitutional entrenchment, including the pre-emptive denial of state power to certain actors, seems to offer an effective counterbalance to legal revolution. However, the use of militant democracy suffers from a crisis of confidence: even its proponents worry that militant democracy may undermine democracy in the process of trying to save it.

This book advances a liberal normative theory of militant democracy by combining John Rawls' political liberalism with Carl Schmitt's state theory—two thinkers rarely thought of as mutually complementary. Rawls' thought provides the substantive *democratic* content of this theory, establishing basic liberal rights as a precondition for a legitimate government. Schmitt's thought provides the *militant* political form, justifying the state's use of proactive militant measures to preserve the political identity of its constitution.

The resulting normative theory justifies adopting three principal mechanisms of militant democracy in democratic constitutions: explicit unamendability, political rights restrictions, and the guardianship of a constitutional court. The 1949 German *Basic Law* exemplifies the constitutional practice of these mechanisms. Because internal enemies and legal revolution pose a perennial threat to democracy, it is crucial to incorporate these defensive measures into future democratic constitutions, following the guidelines of this liberal normative theory of militant democracy.

This book is an outgrowth of my first book, *Carl Schmitt's State and Constitutional Theory*. In it, I argued that Schmitt's anti-positivist jurisprudence is the narrative thread that systematizes his otherwise fragmented writings on the state and constitution. I analysed how, beginning in the mid-1920s, Schmitt warned that the Weimar Republic's constitutional framework left it vulnerable to democratic suicide. The Weimar Constitution's combination of positivist jurisprudence and value-neutral democratic proceduralism inadvertently exposed Weimar democracy to internal antidemocratic forces. Antidemocrats realized they could exploit democracy itself to advance their antidemocratic agenda through legal revolution, as exemplified by Hitler's appointment as Chancellor in 1933.

Schmitt believed his anti-positivist state and constitutional theory offered democracy a better defence against legal revolution. He argued that a constitution by

viii PREFACE

definition had an unamendable super-positive core, whose content was determined by the political identity of its 'people'. Schmitt asserted that basic liberal rights constituted the unamendable core of the Weimar Constitution. Schmitt used that constitutional theory to argue for the banning of Weimar's antidemocratic parties, in particular the Nazi Party and the Communist Party. He also argued that final authority on constitutionality should not rest with the legislature, but instead—building on the ideas of Benjamin Constant—the President of the Republic. Schmitt thus articulated an early version of what his former colleague Karl Loewenstein would later call 'militant democracy'.

Work on Schmitt comes with unique challenges. Soon after Hitler rose to power, Schmitt joined the Nazi party. He used his influence as a public lawyer to defend early Nazi actions. He was an anti-Semite. And he died unrepentant. Not without reason, many have strong opinions about Schmitt. Many are uncomfortable with scholarship that shows that, despite his troubling political views and his flawed character, Schmitt correctly identified some of the most pressing problems of liberal democracy and developed novel solutions to them. Yet for better or for worse, Schmitt made a significant contribution to democratic theory and his ideas influenced the design of many post war democratic constitutions. Although there is more to be gained from Schmitt's thought, persuading others of its value can be a challenge. That challenge can be summed up by one senior colleague's remark that 'Ben, what you argue would sound pretty reasonable if you weren't attributing it to Schmitt'.

In 2016, while I was working on my previous book, Donald Trump was elected President of the United States. That event left many political scientists, like many American voters, wondering 'how did that happen?' His electoral victory, situated within a broader trend of rising populism and corresponding democratic decline, led many to inquire into the nature of populism, its causes, and its relation to democracy.

While those are important issues, I believe there is an even more pressing one. What is most urgent is not understanding the nature of the actor attacking democracy—populist, fascist, communist, whatever. The most urgent questions revolve around how democracy's design allows for its subversion by antidemocrats, whoever they are, and what measures can be taken to better defend democracy against such threats in the future. This book attempts to answer those questions. It builds on the normative arguments of my first book while consciously distancing itself from Schmitt and his controversial legacy.

Unfortunately, the challenges to democracy that framed the writing of my first book are still with us today. Some have gotten worse. Illiberalism in particular seems to be on the rise. Shockingly, at the time of writing, it appears that Donald Trump will be the Republican candidate for President in the 2024 election. This is despite his systematic mismanagement of the United States government, evident from his mishandling of the Covid-19 pandemic, the harm he has done to democratic institutions both domestically and internationally, and his role in instigating the January 6 insurrection. His 2024 campaign platform, documented as Project 2025, includes aggrandizing executive powers, reining in independent agencies such as the Justice Department and Federal Communications Commission, and purging insufficiently loyal civil servants. In addition, there are his vague but troubling pledges at rallies to be 'your retribution', to 'root out vermin', and to purify American blood. Currently, he leads President Biden in several critical polls.

Many other democracies have fared no better than the United States. The 2023 Freedom House report reveals a concerning trend: democratic institutions around the world have been deteriorating for nearly two decades straight. My hope is that this book will help future jurists and legislators in designing more resilient democratic constitutions, thereby avoiding the problems that have plagued so many early twenty-first century democracies.

That I was able to finish this project is thanks to a large number of friends, colleagues, mentors, and interlocutors who have supported me over the years. I am indebted to all of you. Naturally, I bear sole responsibility for its contents and whatever weaknesses there are.

Let me begin by thanking Simone Chambers, Alessandro Ferrara, Alexander Kirshner, Samuel Moyn, Jan-Werner Müller, and Lars Vinx. They participated in a book manuscript workshop hosted by Yale University on 3 January 2023. This project was substantially improved by their comments and criticisms and I was humbled by their engagement with it.

At its early stages, this project benefited from the input of a few scholars. Special thanks are due to Peter Niesen for a very early conversation about militant democracy, which helped frame the project's initial development. I would also like to thank Steven Klein who, after hearing my presentation at the 2018 Prague Colloquium on Philosophy and the Social Sciences, suggested that I turn it into this book. Daniele Santoro and Giuseppe Ballacci also supported its early development by giving me the chance to speak about militant democracy at the University of Minho Centre for Ethics, Politics, and Society.

I am indebted to Luke O'Sullivan for turning his careful eye to the manuscript. His critical feedback and editorial revisions immeasurably improved the final product. He has been an invaluable mentor, discussion partner, and friend since I first arrived in Singapore. My mother, Vivian Schupmann, also saved me from many errors by helping me to copyedit the manuscript.

I thank David Rasmussen for his unwavering encouragement and support over the years. His grasp of the history of philosophy and ability to draw connections across it continue to inspire me. I am also grateful to Martin Loughlin for his support and for his helpful comments on the penultimate draft of the manuscript.

I had the fortune to be a Visiting Fellow at the Yale MacMillan Center. I am grateful to Bryan Garsten, Steven Smith, Steven Wilkinson, Philip Gorski, Hélène Landemore, Samuel Moyn, Giulia Oskian, and Lucia Rubinelli for welcoming me as a colleague during my time there. I am also indebted to Angela Kuhne for

X PREFACE

her assistance with organizing my time at Yale and the manuscript workshop as well as for her direction of the Yale-NUS College New Haven office. Besides the Yale MacMillan Center, this project has also received financial support from the National University of Singapore Humanities and Social Sciences (HSS) Faculty Research Fellowship, as well as my start-up grants from Duke Kunshan University and Yale-NUS College. Without that support, I would not have been able to realize this project. I also would like to thank Jamie Berezin and Lisa Butts of Oxford University Press for their help in shepherding this project throughout the process.

I developed this manuscript through presentations at the Prague Colloquium on Philosophy and the Social Sciences, the American Political Science Association, the International Political Science Association, the University of Helsinki's Eurostorie Conference on Liberalism, the European Political Science Association, the Association for Political Theory, the German Studies Association, the Duke Kunshan University Humanities Centre, and the Yale-NUS College Brown Bag Lunch Seminar.

Far too many friends and colleagues to name have helped me in various ways, but the following merit special acknowledgement: Nida Alahmad, Andrew Arato, Albena Azmanova, Andrew Bailey, William Bain, Nehal Bhuta, Elton Chan, Michelle Chun, Jean L Cohen, Maeve Cooke, John Driffill, Sandra Leonie Field, Pei Gao, Loren Goldman, Bjorn Wee Gomes, Chris Howell, Zach Howlett, Chua Beng Huat, Andrew Hui, Jeannette R Ickovics, Jennie C Ikuta, James Ingram, Samuel Issacharoff, David Jacks, Andreas Kalyvas, Ting Hui Lau, Nomi Claire Lazar, Yu-Hsiang Lei, Jeffrey Lenowitz, Sanford Levinson, Scott MacEachern, Neena Mahadev, Anthoula Malkopoulou, Brett Meyer, James Miller, Brian Milstein, Rohan Mukherjee, Steve Munroe, Terry Nardin, Steven Oliver, Bill Parsons, Anju Mary Paul, Andrew Poe, David Post, Lincoln Rathnam, Joanne Roberts, Rahul Sagar, William E Scheuerman, Patrick Taylor Smith, David Andrew Smith, Alicia Steinmetz, Christina Tarnopolsky, Risa Toha, Nadia Urbinati, Peter Verovšek, Matthew Walker, David Watkins, Xing Xia, Daniel Ziblatt, and the four anonymous reviewers from Oxford University Press.

I do not know where I will be without the support and companionship of my colleagues from Yale-NUS College. I consider myself so fortunate to have had the chance to be a part of Yale-NUS and to have had the chance to contribute to its successes with you. The same goes for my Yale-NUS students. A special thanks goes to Anna Nielsen, who worked as my research assistant in the summer of 2021 as part of the Yale-NUS College Centre for International and Professional Experience (CIPE) Summer Research Programme. I would also like to thank Jadely Seetoh of the Yale-NUS College library, especially for her talent at digging up old and sometimes obscure works of German constitutional theory. Finally, I extend my gratitude to the good people at Alchemist at Khong Guan Building for keeping me well caffeinated throughout the writing process.

I dedicate this book to my wife, Sungmi Lee, who has supported me throughout.

Contents

Introduction	1

PART I

1. Democracy's Problem of Legal Revolution	29
2. Militant Democracy	53

PART II

3. Liberalism and Modern Constitutionalism	81
4. Depoliticization and State Authority	105

PART III

5. Unamendability	137
6. Political Rights Restrictions	155
7. The Guardian of the Constitution	180
Conclusion	204
Bibliography	207
Index	221

Introduction

'Illiberal Democracy' and Militant Democracy

Democracy will always need to defend itself against its enemies.

Some democratic constitutions provide a defence against internal enemies through 'militant democracy'. A militant democracy uses measures of constitutional entrenchment to defend itself against actors bent on revolutionizing it through legal democratic means, including by denying actors access to state power pre-emptively.[1] Legal revolution occurs when formally valid legal procedures are used to alter the substance or identity of the constitution. Measures of militant democracy aim to guarantee that identity. Today, Malkopoulou argues, militant democracy has become synonymous with the party ban.[2] However, older theories discussed other mechanisms of constitutional entrenchment, such as constitutional unamendability and a guardian of the constitution.

The problem of militant democracy is that, at first glance, it can appear to be fundamentally undemocratic itself. Kirshner calls this 'the paradox of militant democracy' (or the paradox of democracy's self-defence).[3] Party bans in particular seem like something right out of an authoritarian playbook. It hardly seems democratic to deny voters the right to choose a party that they think best represents their political identity or to remove policies from the political agenda that they believe best represent their interests. At the same time, it seems as undemocratic for democrats to stand idly by while antidemocrats pursue their political goals using the legislative power of a democracy.

It is up to a normative theory of militant democracy to explain how deploying militant measures of constitutional entrenchment can be consistent with the highest ideals of democracy. Although the discussion of the legitimacy of militant

---

[1] This definition builds on Müller's definition. Jan-Werner Müller, 'The Problem of Peer Review in Militant Democracy' in Uladzislau Belavusau and Aleksandra Gliszczyńska-Grabias (eds), *Constitutionalism under Stress* (Oxford University Press 2020) 259.

The term 'militant democracy' was coined by Karl Loewenstein in a pair of articles entitled 'Militant Democracy'. Karl Loewenstein, 'Militant Democracy and Fundamental Rights, I' (1937) 31(3) The American Political Science Review; Karl Loewenstein, 'Militant Democracy and Fundamental Rights, II' (1937) 31(4) 31 The American Political Science Review.

[2] Anthoula Malkopoulou, 'Militant Democracy and Its Critics' in Anthoula Malkopoulou and Alexander S Kirshner (eds), *Militant Democracy and Its Critics: Populism, Parties, Extremism* (Edinburgh University Press 2019) 2.

[3] Alexander S Kirshner, *A Theory of Militant Democracy: The Ethics of Combatting Political Extremism* (Yale University Press 2014).

Democracy despite Itself. Benjamin A. Schupmann, Oxford University Press. © Benjamin A. Schupmann 2024.
DOI: 10.1093/9780191975950.003.0001

2   INTRODUCTION

democracy dates back to the Weimar constitutional crisis and although many post war constitutions do provide mechanisms for militant democracy, there was no proper normative theory of militant democracy as recently as 2012.[4] There have been significant advances since then, including Kirshner's *A Normative Theory of Militant Democracy* (2014) and Rijpkema's *Militant Democracy: The Limits of Democratic Tolerance* (2018), yet normative theories of militant democracy are still in a relatively early stage of their development.

Building on that emerging literature, this book answers the question, 'What measures of entrenchment may a democracy legitimately adopt to defend itself against illiberal antidemocrats, who revolutionize democracy through legal and democratic methods?' It develops a new 'liberal' normative theory of militant democracy, which explains why future democratic constitutions should be militantly entrenched in order to be able to defend themselves against internal threats.

This liberal normative theory of militant democracy has two basic components. First, a liberal theory of militant democracy holds that basic liberal rights are a *sine qua non* of democratic constitutionalism. A state must guarantee them in order to count as 'democratic' in any meaningful sense of the term. Second, because basic liberal rights are a *sine qua non* of democratic constitutionalism, a liberal normative theory of militant democracy argues that those norms ought to be guaranteed and defended through constitutional entrenchment. A principal role of a democratic state is to ensure that democratic constitutional essentials are perpetuated, so that future generations can live under a legitimate regime. To that end, a liberal normative theory of militant democracy argues that three principal mechanisms offer the best defence of democracy against its legal revolution: explicit constitutional unamendability, political rights restrictions, and a guardian of the constitution. That tripartite set of mechanisms is inspired by the design of the German *Basic Law*, the paradigmatic militant democratic constitution. To date, the German *Basic Law* is the most systematic concrete attempt to preclude the use of legal means to revolutionize the democratic identity of the constitution.

This liberal normative theory of militant democracy draws on the ideas of two thinkers. John Rawls' political liberalism provides the substance of its normative theory. Rawls shows how a democratic society, one that acknowledges the fact of pluralism and what he calls 'the burdens of judgement' (which amounts to a self-conscious epistemological scepticism that denies certainty of transcendent moral truths), can nevertheless conclude that basic liberal rights are authoritative and binding norms. Rawls' ingenuity was finding a way to generate those norms immanently, through an innovation in proceduralism.

Although Rawls did discuss militant forms of the entrenchment of those authoritative norms, including the need to 'contain' antidemocratic threats, justifying

---

[4] Jan-Werner Müller, 'Militant Democracy' in Michel Rosenfeld and András Sajó (eds), *The Oxford Handbook of Comparative Constitutional Law* (Oxford University Press 2012).

institutional forms of entrenchment was never the focus of his work. To complete a liberal normative theory of militant democracy, Rawls' thought needs a more robust justification for its institutionalization. The state and constitutional theory of Carl Schmitt provides that complement. This may seem an odd claim. Schmitt was after all no liberal. Schmitt did, however, justify the constitutional entrenchment of a state's particular 'political' identity. His formal constitutional theory of 'the political' can be appropriated to explain why a democratic state is justified in deploying militant measures to entrench its liberal identity against formally valid legal changes. Schmitt himself did just that in Weimar's twilight, before he opportunistically joined the Nazi party and turned his state and constitutional theory to instead legitimate the Nazi state.[5] Nevertheless, Schmitt's updated Hobbesian project develops the theoretical *form* that measures of militant democracy may take, complementing the *substantive* values generated by Rawls' political liberalism. In other words, Rawls' thought generates its democratic grounding, while Schmitt's thought justifies its militancy.

This alternative liberal theory addresses limitations that existing normative theories of militant democracy have encountered, which I unpack in greater detail in chapter 2. First, they defend an excessively narrow conception of militant *democracy*. Existing normative theories of militant democracy have, almost to a letter, focused solely on threats to political participatory rights, such as the right to vote and to compete to hold public office. As a result, they are unable to detect the threat posed by many contemporary antidemocrats, such as populists who pursue 'illiberal democracy'. Antidemocrats today tend to leave political participatory rights intact (enough), even as they dismantle other democratic fundamentals, including basic liberal rights and the separation and balance of powers. By adopting a minimalistic conception of democracy, existing normative theories are unable to justify a response to what is widely regarded to be the most pressing threat to democracy today.

Second, existing normative theories of militant democracy defend too narrow a conception of *militant* democracy. Almost all focus solely on defending the legitimacy of political rights restrictions, that is, the party ban. In the process, they have overlooked other measures of militant democracy that complement, reinforce, and are even presupposed by measures that restrict political rights—such as constitutional unamendability and the need for a guardian of the constitution.

A liberal normative theory of militant democracy addresses those theoretical limitations. First, a liberal normative theory is able to recognize illiberalism as threat to democracy because it conceives of basic liberal rights as the cornerstone of democratic constitutionalism. Second, a liberal normative theory of militant democracy

---

[5] See Benjamin A Schupmann, *Carl Schmitt's State and Constitutional Theory: A Critical Analysis* (Oxford University Press 2017).

4 INTRODUCTION

resolves the paradox of militant democracy by avoiding it altogether. The paradox emerges through the tension between defending political participatory rights and deploying restrictions on those same rights. A liberal normative theory circumvents that paradox because it subordinates political rights to basic liberal rights. The restriction of the former is justifiable when done for the sake of the latter.

The broader value of a liberal normative theory of militant democracy is that it explains why it is legitimate to build militant mechanisms into the design of democratic constitutions. Why future democratic constitutions should be designed to look more like the German *Basic Law*. This book's argument thus addresses a question of institutional design at the highest level: what kind of mechanisms of entrenchment may be adopted to ensure the survival and continuity of the most basic features of a democratic constitution *at all*. It deals with a first order question of constitutionalism: how a democratic state may best defend itself against antidemocrats attempting to annihilate democratic essentials outright using legal revolutionary methods. To be sure, second order constitutional questions, such as managing the pathologies of judicial review and the entrenchment of elite interests, are also important. But second order questions are only meaningful within the framework of a democratic constitutional order. Something which is unfortunately not a given but which this project attempts to ensure.

'Illiberal Democracy' and Legal Revolution

The reasons for enacting militant measures for democracy's self-defence are as valid today as when the seeds of militant democracy were first sown in Germany in the 1920s and 1930s. Democracy has always had enemies. Some resort to illegal methods in pursuit of their antidemocratic goals. Others adopt legal tactics. A democracy defending itself against illegal or even violent revolutionary tactics is relatively uncontroversial. Existing criminal law is usually adequate for responding to revolution pursued through rebellion, insurrection, armed uprising, sedition, or other forms of treason.

However, democracies face a serious quandary when their enemies include their own citizens who adopt *legal* revolutionary tactics in pursuit of antidemocratic goals. As Capoccia remarks, they pose a distinctive threat because they realize their antidemocratic goals simply by 'playing the game'.[6] What recourse does a democracy have against members who are entitled to the full protection of the constitution yet pursue antidemocratic goals within the bounds of legality and with the support of a majority of voters?

Legal revolution is a perennial threat to democracy.

---

[6] Giovanni Capoccia, *Defending Democracy: Reactions to Extremism in Interwar Europe* (Johns Hopkins University Press 2005) 4–7.

'ILLIBERAL DEMOCRACY' AND LEGAL REVOLUTION 5

Lenin may have been the first to recognize that legal revolution could be used against democracy.[7] He urged his followers to adopt any and all methods to realize a communist state. In particular, Lenin realized the unique vulnerability of 'bourgeois' democracy. Like any other regime, it could be attacked and revolutionized from 'outside', through illegal actions such as strikes, mass violence, and a coup d'état. However, democracy was uniquely vulnerable to attack from within, through legal avenues. By obtaining public power through democratic elections, communist revolutionaries could obstruct government, rewrite the law to promote their political goals, and use parliament itself as a platform to broadcast their ideology.

Building on Lenin's recognition, interwar European antidemocrats on both the right and left formed political parties and competed in elections hoping to overturn liberal democracy from within government. They often paired that tactic with violent revolutionary acts. The NSDAP is an example of this approach. After the failure of the Beer Hall Putsch, the Nazis turned to legal revolution. Their instrumental attitude towards democratic institutions is epitomized by remarks that Hitler and Goebbels made. In 1930, Hitler pledged to his followers that the NSDAP only participated in Weimar democracy in order to bring it down, announcing that 'the [Weimar] constitution dictates the method, but not the goal'.[8] In a similar vein, Goebbels famously remarked that 'the best joke of democracy was that it gives to its enemies the means to destroy itself'.

Even if they fail to subvert democracy outright, antidemocrats can still succeed by adopting legal revolutionary tactics. From within parliament, they can impair both normal democratic government and democracy's ability to defend itself.[9] This is illustrated by the perverse cooperation between the NSDAP and the KPD. They realized that, by cooperating within parliament, they could both decapitate the government using the vote of no confidence and prevent necessary legislation from being passed at the high point of the Great Depression. Deliberate obstructionism was a means to discredit liberal democracy in the eyes of Weimar's electorate, with which they could siphon off voters from Weimar's republican parties and bring themselves closer to realizing their extreme political goals.

Antidemocrats within parliament can also drive democratic parties towards more extreme positions to recover lost votes. This creates a divide between the centre-left and centre-right and makes cooperation between them difficult.[10] As the far-right gained traction in Germany in 1930, centre-right parties like the

---

[7] VI Lenin, 'Left-Wing Communism: an Infantile Disorder' in *Collected Works*, vol 31 (Progress Publishers 1974).

[8] Cited in Lutz Berthold, *Carl Schmitt und der Staatsnotstandsplan am Ende der weimarer Republik* (Duncker & Humblot 1999) 50–51.

[9] Capoccia (n 6) 27–28, 179.

[10] ibid 17–19.

6 INTRODUCTION

Zentrum and the *Deutsche Volkspartei* (DVP) defected from the SPD-led centrist coalition because they could no longer support its centre-left policies.[11] That breakdown within parliament led to the Brüning Chancellorship's rule by emergency decree—which set the precedent for Hitler's rule.

The political goals of twenty-first century antidemocrats differ markedly from the goals of early twentieth-century totalitarian movements. Although their specific political goals may differ, the tactics they use to achieve them overlap in some significant ways. Populists and 'illiberal democrats' today use some of the same legal revolutionary methods as past antidemocrats did.[12] They focus on dismantling institutions associated with liberal constitutionalism, including minority rights, the formal rule of law, and the separation of powers.[13]

Since the end of the Cold War, democracies have only been overthrown through violence in a minority of cases. Since 2000, Svolik shows that *nearly 80 per cent* of cases of democratic backsliding have occurred primarily through legal democratic pathways.[14] Politicians elected with popular support into the executive and legislative branches weaken or subvert democratic norms and institutions through ordinary legislation, the capture of other branches, especially the judiciary, and even constitutional amendment.

In addition to the use of legal revolutionary methods, two other characteristics of democratic backsliding in the post-Cold War period stand out. First, democratic backsliding is not driven solely by elites. Antidemocratic elites often have a significant base of support within the electorate. Democratic backsliding typically occurs today because antidemocrats gain power legally, through free and fair elections with the tacit or explicit support of a majority of voters.[15] Second, antidemocrats often leave political participatory rights broadly intact. They transform democracy into a more direct majoritarian form by removing liberal constitutional freedoms and counter-majoritarian constraints.[16] Constitutions that are not deeply entrenched are especially susceptible to the latter kind of manipulation.

---

[11] ibid 185–87, 192–93.

[12] Although populism is not necessarily illiberal, there does seem to be something of an elective affinity between the two. See Angela K Bourne and Bastiaan Rijpkema, 'Militant Democracy, Populism, Illiberalism: New Challengers and New Challenges' (2022) 18(3) European Constitutional Law Review 378.

[13] Andrew Arato and Jean L Cohen, *Populism and Civil Society: The Challenge to Constitutional Democracy* (Oxford University Press 2022) 124–30.

[14] Milan W Svolik, 'Polarization versus Democracy' (2019) 30(3) Journal of Democracy 20, 21.

[15] ibid 24, 30–31.

[16] Nadia Urbinati, *Democracy Disfigured: Opinion, Truth, and the People* (Harvard University Press 2014) 165; Jordan Kyle and Yasha Mounk, 'The Populist Harm to Democracy: An Empirical Assessment' (26 December 2018) <https://www.institute.global/insights/geopolitics-and-security/populist-harm-democracy-empirical-assessment>; Nadia Urbinati, *Me the People: How Populism Transforms Democracy* (Harvard University Press 2019) 14–20, 94, 192.

The Example of Hungary

The democratic decline of Hungary illustrates how an antidemocratic party can use legal revolutionary tactics to wreak havoc on a democratic public order unentrenched by mechanisms of militant democracy.

The 1989 Hungarian Constitution

The 1989 Constitution of the Republic of Hungary is an example of a minimally entrenched democratic constitution. Essentially a reinstatement of the 1949 Hungarian Constitution, the 1989 Hungarian Constitution was designed to be superseded. Its preamble stated that it was 'to facilitate a peaceful political transition to a constitutional state'. The constitution empowered parliament to adopt a new constitution if the process was initiated by an 80 per cent supermajority.[17] Until that change occurred, Article 19 vested parliament with governmental supremacy, authorizing it to 'ensure the constitutional order of society and define the organization, orientation and conditions of government'. Article 24 set a comparatively low threshold for constitutional amendments of a two-thirds supermajority in its unicameral parliament. The constitution was designed to be flexible deliberately. It was intended to allow the electorate to adapt its constitution according to its will in a time of rapid political change.[18] Every article of the 1989 Constitution legally sat under the reservation of parliament's exercise of the amendment clause. That design effectively authorized Hungary's unicameral legislature to exercise constitutive power, even if it was derived from the constitution.

The 1989 Constitution did contain mechanisms to repress antidemocratic political organizations. For example, under Article 3.1, parties were required by law to 'respect the constitution'. However, Uitz argues that those mechanisms proved 'toothless and ineffective' whenever they were invoked.[19] Part of the reason was the constitution's limited scope for restricting parties and other political organizations. They could only be banned for violent acts, other criminal activities, or for

---

[17] Andrew Arato, 'Regime Change, Revolution, and Legitimacy' in Gábor Attila Tóth (ed), *Constitution for a Disunited Nation: On Hungary's 2011 Fundamental Law* (Central European University Press 2013) 46–47; Gary Jeffrey Jacobsohn and Yaniv Roznai, *Constitutional Revolution* (Yale University Press 2020) 81–82.

[18] Miklós Bánkuti, Gábor Halmai, and Kim Lane Scheppele, 'From Separation of Powers to a Government without Checks: Hungary's Old and New Constitutions' in Gábor Attila Tóth (ed), *Constitution for a Disunited Nation: On Hungary's 2011 Fundamental Law* (Central European University Press 2013) 242; Kim Lane Scheppele, 'The Rule of Law and the Frankenstate: Why Governance Checklists Do Not Work' (2013) 26(4) Governance: An International Journal of Policy, Administration, and Institutions 559, 560.

[19] Renáta Uitz, 'Hungary' in Markus Thiel (ed), *The 'Militant Democracy' Principle in Modern Democracies* (Ashgate 2009) 148–49.

8   INTRODUCTION

violating others' rights.[20] But the 1989 Constitution had nothing in it to prevent a party from legally pursuing antidemocratic political goals.

Article 32 of the 1989 Constitution did grant the constitutional court the authority to review the constitutionality of legislation. In principle, anyone could apply for abstract constitutional review via an *actio popularis* petition.[21] Scheppele notes that in a unicameral parliamentary system, the court plays a disproportionately critical role in guaranteeing democracy.[22] This is because parliamentarism fuses legislative and executive powers and because unicameralism eliminates the internal check of a second legislative chamber. To prevent the court's capture by parliament, the 1989 Constitution required that judicial nominations be approved by a majority of Hungary's parties, rather than just a majority of elected representatives.

The constitutional court's ability to guard the constitution was weakened by the design of the constitution itself, however. One major factor was the supremacy of the amendment clause, which gave parliament final authority over constitutionality. Another was that the constitution gave parliament the mandate to draft and adopt an entirely new constitution. Because of that constitutional design, parliament could argue that it embodied the sovereign will of 'the people' and represented its constituent power.[23] In addition, Arato argues, the constitution itself provided a weak foundation for its defence by the court.[24] The constitution did not explicitly define any substantive constitutional identity. Nor was there much legal precedent that might help establish one. This left the court ill-equipped to rely on anything like a doctrine of implied unamendability to contest procedurally valid amendments. Bánkuti, Halmai, and Scheppele argue further that these design decisions constituted the Achilles' heel of the 1989 constitutional system.[25] They served as the legal-constitutional pathways for parliament to dilute the few checks and balances on its own legislative power and degrade Hungarian democracy.[26]

Despite those inherent weaknesses, Hungary was considered to be a model for the transition from communism to democracy. Independent agencies, such as Freedom House and the V-DEM Institute, consistently rated its elections highly. The 2010 election was no exception.[27] In that election, Fidesz won 53 per cent of the

---

[20]   ibid 162–164, 70.

[21]   Bánkuti, Halmai, and Scheppele (n 18) 243, 250.

[22]   Kim Lane Scheppele, 'Constitutional Coups and Judicial Review: How Transnational Institutions can Strengthen Peak Courts at Times of Crisis (With Special Reference to Hungary)' (2014) 23 Journal of Transnational Law & Contemporary Problems 68; Kim Lane Scheppele, 'Understanding Hungary's Constitutional Revolution' in Armin von Bogdandy and Pál Sonnevend (eds), *Constitutional Crisis in the European Constitutional Area: Theory, Law and Politics in Hungary and Romania* (Hart/Beck 2015) 114.

[23]   Arato (n 17) 49.

[24]   ibid 52–53.

[25]   Bánkuti, Halmai, and Scheppele (n 18) 252.

[26]   Jacobsohn and Roznai (n 17) 88.

[27]   Scheppele, 'Constitutional Coups and Judicial Review' (n 22) 60–61.

vote in coalition with its list partner the KDNP (the Christian Democratic People's Party). However, due to a 1989 election law intended to prevent an excess of small parties from balkanizing and destabilizing parliament, that simple majority enabled the Fidesz-KDNP coalition to take 68 per cent of the seats in parliament.[28] It had the the the two-thirds supermajority it needed to amend the constitution. And Fidesz immediately capitalized on that opportunity.

Fidesz and 'Illiberal Democracy'

Viktor Orbán, the leader of Fidesz, would later argue that he aims to transform Hungary into an 'illiberal democracy'. Liberalism, he argues, is a Western value or even ideology that does not align with the identity and values of the Hungarian people.[29] Orbán argues that, when Western states and institutions such as the European Parliament demand that Hungary adhere to liberal principles and uphold human rights, they are behaving as colonial powers—just as the Soviet Union once did. In his view, Western states use liberal ideology and universalistic institutions to advance their own narrow self-interest at the expense of the Hungarian people, not least of all by constraining its right to democratic self-determination.[30] Ackerman suggests that there is some merit to that claim: foreign powers, including Western liberal democracies, have shaped Hungarian politics and statehood for nearly a century.[31] That experience has, Veročšek argues, affected many Eastern European states' distinctive memory culture and their current policies cannot be divorced from that history, including Hungary's.[32]

From that perspective, the turn to 'illiberal democracy' appears to be a necessary move to reclaim Hungary's sovereignty and its right of democratic self-determination.[33] Veročšek describes how figures like Orbán succeed by exploiting

---

[28] Miklós Bánkuti, Gábor Halmai, and Kim Lane Scheppele, 'Hungary's Illiberal Turn: Disabling the Constitution' (2012) 23(3) Journal of Democracy 138; Scheppele, 'Understanding Hungary's Constitutional Revolution' (n 22) 111–12.

[29] Viktor Orbán, *Speech at the 25th Bálványos Summer Open University and Student Camp* (2014) Viktor Orbán, *Speech at the 29th Bálványos Summer Open University and Student Camp* (2018) Viktor Orbán, *Speech at Conference in Memory of Helmut Kohl* (2018).

[30] Gábor Halmai, 'Populism, Authoritarianism and Constitutionalism' (2019) 20 German Law Journal 296, 299.

[31] A noteworthy case is how the division of the Austro-Hungarian Empire following the First World War left a significant portion of ethnic Hungarians outside its borders. That historical legacy still resonates today and it explains (even if it does not justify) Fidesz's interest in extending the franchise to ethnic Hungarians outside of its borders. I am indebted to Bruce Ackerman for this point.

[32] Peter J Veročšek, *Memory and the Future of Europe: Rupture and Integration in the Wake of Total War* (Manchester University Press 2020); Peter J Veročšek, 'Caught between 1945 and 1989: Collective Memory and the Rise of Illiberal Democracy in Postcommunist Europe' (2020) Journal of European Public Policy.

[33] Laurent Pech and Kim Lane Scheppele, 'Illiberalism Within: Rule of Law Backsliding in the EU' (2017) 19 Cambridge Yearbook of European Legal Studies 4; Halmai (n 30) 300; Jacobsohn and Roznai (n 17) 97.

10   INTRODUCTION

a latent contradiction within the ideal of the 'nation-state', setting the particularistic exclusionary demands of national belonging against the universalistic aspirations of the democratic rule of law.[34] To advance his goal of 'illiberal democracy', Orbán explicitly links Hungarian national identity to the history and traditions of European Christianity.[35] In 2018, Hungary amended its constitution to formalize the state's duty to protect 'Hungary's self-identity and its Christian culture'.[36] Although the constitution continues to acknowledge religious rights, this move seems like a step towards establishing a state religion. Besides weakening constitutional commitments to secularism and the separation of church and state, Plattner describes Orbán as using Christianity and Christian democracy to promote a broader socially conservative agenda. It includes weakening other liberal principles, such as multiculturalism, toleration, refugees and immigrants, and non-traditional families.[37]

In practice, the pursuit of 'illiberal democracy' amounts to what it sounds like: the systematic dismantling of liberal constitutional fundamentals—in particular, institutional checks on governmental power, such as basic rights protections of minorities and the separation and balance of powers.[38] In Hungary, Fidesz managed to remove many constitutional checks and balances on parliament, transmuting Hungarian democracy into a kind of 'radical majoritarianism'.[39] As a result, Uitz argues, Hungary departs from the 'minimum standards associated with constitutionalism and the rule of law'.[40] Halmai goes even further, arguing that 'Hungary (not even a Republic in its name anymore) cannot be considered a liberal constitutional democracy'.[41]

The case of Hungary is particularly noteworthy because its transformation into an 'illiberal democracy' has occurred almost entirely legally, through what the next chapter characterizes as legal revolutionary methods. Scheppele describes how the government remains within the bounds of formal legality to attain its goals, but nevertheless 'achieves a substantively unconstitutional result'.[42] Jacobsohn and Roznai identify Hungary as an exemplary case of this phenomenon, because

---

[34] Peter J Verovšek, '"The Nation Has Conquered the State": Arendtian Insights on the Internal Contradictions of the Nation-State' (2023) Review of International Studies.

[35] Halmai (n 30) 306–08; Renáta Uitz, 'Can You Tell When an Illiberal Democracy Is in the Making? An Appeal to Comparative Constitutional Scholarship from Hungary' (2015) 13(1) International Journal of Constitutional Law 286.

[36] Halmai (n 30) 306–08.

[37] Marc F Plattner, 'Illiberal Democracy and the Struggle on the Right' (2019) 30(1) Journal of Democracy 10–13.

[38] Bánkuti, Halmai, and Scheppele, 'From Separation of Powers to a Government without Checks' 238; Scheppele, 'Understanding Hungary's Constitutional Revolution' (n 22) 112.

[39] Urbinati, *Me the People: How Populism Transforms Democracy* (n 16) 14.

[40] Uitz, 'Can You Tell When an Illiberal Democracy Is in the Making?' (n 35) 280–81.

[41] Gábor Halmai, 'A Coup against Constitutional Democracy? The Case of Hungary' in Mark A Graber, Sanford Levinson, and Mark Tushnet (eds), *Constitutional Democracy in Crisis?* (Oxford University Press 2018) 246.

[42] Scheppele, 'Constitutional Coups and Judicial Review' (n 22) 51–52.

THE EXAMPLE OF HUNGARY   11

it combines 'a signature case of formal legal continuity conjoined with a substantive constitutional rupture'.[43] By adeptly wielding its supermajority in parliament, Fidesz has been able to use formally valid procedures of legal change and constitutional amendment to revolutionize Hungarian democracy.

Fidesz has incrementally pursued a legal transformation of Hungarian democracy since it obtained power in 2010. Some of that transformation unfolded directly in the written constitution. Since 2010, Fidesz has rewritten it repeatedly. Fidesz first amended the 1989 Hungarian Constitution by lowering the threshold to determine the procedure for drafting a new constitution from 80 per cent of parliament to 67 per cent. It then immediately drafted a new constitution, which became the 2011 Hungarian Fundamental Law. Since the Fundamental Law took effect, Fidesz has continued its tinkering. It has amended the 2011 Fundamental Law nine times so far. Besides amending the written constitution, Fidesz has transformed the substance of Hungary's public order in other ways, including by passing a series of 'cardinal acts' (a form of legislation that is procedurally similar to an amendment, because it requires a two-thirds supermajority to be enacted or to be altered) as well as by using ordinary legislation and policies.

Of the structural changes that weakened Hungary's separation and balance of powers, many focused on restricting the powers and independence of the constitutional court—the only significant institutional counterbalance to parliament. The Fourth Amendment to the 2011 Fundamental Law limited the constitutional court's power of judicial review to only considering whether an amendment was procedurally valid; the substance of the amendment was beyond the court's purview. Interestingly, the court itself agreed with the aims of the Fourth Amendment, accepting that it did not have the authority to evaluate the substantive unconstitutionality of procedurally valid amendments.[44] The Fourth Amendment and the court's acceptance of it implies that there is no substantive identity underlying the Hungarian Fundamental Law besides the will of the electorate. The amendment clause now seems to be the supreme clause of the Hungarian Fundamental Law *de jure*, because every other article of the constitution sits under the reservation of its exercise. These changes seem to have resolved any remaining tension between the constitutional court's guardianship of the constitution and parliamentary supremacy.

The constitutional court, along with the ordinary judiciary, were weakened further through a combination of other legal actions by the Fidesz-controlled parliament. These include reducing the court's jurisdiction over the constitution in general, for example by denying its authority to review laws affecting fiscal and tax policy. It also restricted the public's access to the constitutional court, eliminating the *actio popularis* petition. Fidesz also 'colonized' the courts, as Freeman has

---

[43] Jacobsohn and Roznai (n 17) 81.
[44] Scheppele, 'Constitutional Coups and Judicial Review' (n 22) 74.

12   INTRODUCTION

described it, by packing them with loyalists.[45] It did so both by expanding the number of justices on the constitutional court and by tinkering with laws regulating the judiciary, such as the retirement age, the nominating system, and the prior requirement that appointments to the constitutional court be approved by a majority of political parties. All of these actions were designed to subordinate the constitutional court to the legislature and reduce counter-majoritarian checks on legislative power. As a result, Fidesz further consolidated its power.

Fidesz has also weakened other (formerly) independent institutions intended to check and balance the powers of the government. Again, it has done so through colonization and capture, using a combination of legislative changes, which bring those institutions more under the control of the government formally, and appointing loyalists to lead them, thereby aligning them with the governing party informally. Because of that colonization, formerly independent institutions with the power to hold the government accountable, such as the Prosecutor General (which assigns criminal cases to courts), the Media Council (which regulates both public and private mass media), and the State Audit Office (which investigates the misuse of public funds) are now just extensions of the will of the ruling party. Fidesz has used those institutions to advance its agenda and to further entrench its own power.

Besides breaking down the separation of powers, Fidesz has also used its unchecked powers to issue cardinal and ordinary laws that compromise the electoral process itself. Among other things, it has gerrymandered electoral districts, extended the vote to Hungarians living 'near abroad' (a demographic that overwhelmingly favours Fidesz's agenda), and eliminated the second round of voting in single member districts (which allows a candidate with only a plurality of the vote to take a seat in parliament). The overall effect is that Fidesz is extremely unlikely to lose control of parliament in the near future. It can now hold onto its majority in parliament even when it has the support of a minority of voters. And it is more likely to hold onto its two-thirds supermajority. For example, in the 2014 and 2018 elections, it took two-thirds of parliament despite only receiving 45 and 49 per cent of the popular vote.[46] In 2022, 54 per cent of voters supported Fidesz, which again translated to 68 per cent of the seats in parliament, demonstrating Fidesz's successful use of the law to manipulate Hungary's electoral process and ensuring its continued hold on power.

Overall, Fidesz has successfully used legal revolutionary methods to transform Hungarian democracy into a government 'of the ruling party, by the ruling party, and for the ruling party', Bard and Pech write.[47] Its will is now largely unconstrained.

---

[45] Will Freeman, 'Sidestepping the Constiution: Executive Aggrandizement in Latin America and East Central Europe' (2020) 6 Constitutional Studies 41.

[46] Halmai (n 30) 300.

[47] Petra Bárd and Laurent Pech, *How to Build and Consolidate a Partly Free Pseudo Democracy by Constitutional Means in Three Steps: The 'Hungarian Model'* (RECONNECT October 2019) 12.

To get there, Fidesz exploited the fact that Hungarian democracy was comparatively unentrenched and unprotected through counter-majoritarian defences. In turn, it weaponized procedures of democratic legal change, in particular the supremacy of the amendment clause, to entrench and guarantee its own rule.

The Veneer of Democracy

Although Hungary today under Fidesz may be best characterized as antidemocratic, it still claims to be 'democratic'. And it still is democratic, in a narrow sense. It retains the support of a large segment of the electorate and it demonstrates that support through regular elections. That show of support is in fact a defining characteristic of populism, the prevailing form that antidemocrats have assumed in their efforts to backslide democracy over the last couple of decades. Populist regimes tend not to seek to eliminate political participatory rights outright. Instead, they twist liberal democracy into a more direct and simplified majoritarian form.[48] As the constraints of liberal constitutionalism weaken, the formal exercise of political rights becomes a more important source of a regime's legitimation. Urbinati argues that obtaining legitimation through democratic elections is in fact a 'defining dimension of populist regimes'.[49] Populist regimes like Fidesz work hard to demonstrate their democratic credentials and they tend to maintain or, in some cases, even expand institutions of democratic electoral legitimation. They continue to hold regular elections and reassure their critics that they abide by the results of elections. Part of the distinctive appeal of populists is that they promise political inclusion and empowerment to segments of the population who feel they have been ignored, gone unrepresented, or even been excluded from politics by elites and 'outsiders'.[50] For these reasons, many theorists of populism conclude that populism is not totally opposed to democracy. It is closer to democracy's 'shadow'.[51]

---

[48] Benjamin Arditi, *Politics on the Edges of Liberalism: Difference, Populism, Revolution, Agitation* (Edinburgh University Press 2007) 59; Urbinati, *Democracy Disfigured* (n 16) 165; Urbinati, *Me the People* (n 16) 94, 192; Arato and Cohen (n 13) 148.

[49] Urbinati, *Me the People* (n 16) 20.

[50] Cas Mudde and Cristóbal Rovira Kaltwasser, 'Exclusionary vs. Inclusionary Populism: Comparing Contemporary Europe and Latin America' (2013) 48(2) Government and Opposition 147; Albena Azmanova, 'The Populist Catharsis: On The Revival of The Political' (2018) 44(4) Philosophy and Social Criticism 399, 406ff; Anna Grzymala-Busse, 'Conclusion: The Global Forces of Populism' (2019) 51(4) Polity.

[51] Margaret Canovan, 'Trust the People! Populism and the Two Faces of Democracy' (1999) 47(1) Political Studies 3; Arditi (n 48) 7, 49–50; Nadia Urbinati, 'Political Theory of Populism' (2019) 22 Annual Review of Political Science 111, 118.

Theorists who argue that populism rejuvenates democracy, such as Mouffe, Azmanova, and Vergara, obviously see populism as consistent with democratic values. See Chantal Mouffe, *For a Left Populism* (Verso 2018) Azmanova; Camila Vergara, 'Populism as Plebeian Politics: Inequality, Domination, and Popular Empowerment' (2020) 28(2) The Journal of Political Philosophy.

14 INTRODUCTION

In that sense, there is unfortunately something to the idea of 'illiberal democracy', even if it is a problematic concept. In the case of Hungary, Orbán's assertions about the tensions between Hungarian identity and liberalism clearly resonate with a large portion of the Hungarian electorate. Many choose to re-elect Fidesz despite—or even because of—its political platform, preferring to satisfy their partisan interests even if it comes at the expense of democracy. The 2022 Hungarian election gives evidence of this. Scheppele writes that, given the choice between an illiberal autocratic government and democratic renewal with the possibility that a left-leaning party might take power, conservative-leaning voters overwhelmingly preferred the former.[52] Their political identity seems to be defined not by democratic commitments, but such 'conservative' values of ethno-nationalism, anti-Semitism, anti-LGBTQ sentiments, and other illiberal forms of exclusion.

Even when illiberal democrats fall short of outright electoral victory, the popularity of such movements is a disturbing sign that many citizens no longer believe liberal constitutionalism is essential for democracy or an important value in itself. Many voters today openly reject what many political scientists and philosophers agree is a fundamental tenet of democracy and they act on those political beliefs at the ballot box. The popularity of using legal revolutionary methods to pursue 'illiberal democracy' hints at a deeper problem within democratic electorates. Democracies need to contend with this very serious problem.

Although Hungary may be a particularly egregious example of democracy's legal revolution, it is not unique. Freedom House's 2023 edition of its annual 'Freedom in the World Report' found that democracy and freedom in general had declined globally for a seventeenth consecutive year.[53] Many other democratically elected parties and leaders have adopted legal revolutionary methods to pursue their substantively undemocratic goals. In Turkey, Tunisia, Venezuela, Ecuador, and Israel, democracy has been hollowed out either by amending or by entirely replacing the constitution. In these cases, the party in power tends to assert the de facto or de jure power of the government to exercise a derived constituent power and change the constitution.

A more insidious, indirect form of this phenomenon often occurs instead, however. It leaves the written constitution intact but sidesteps its constraints. Such indirect methods of legal revolution have been used in many states, including Poland, Brazil, the Philippines, and even the United States. This approach aims to weaken the separation of powers. In particular, it targets the independence of the judiciary and its authority to review the constitutionality of legislation. By appointing loyalists and passing restrictive legislation, parties in power prevent the judiciary from checking the executive and legislative. They may also erode the judiciary's

---

[52] Kim Lane Scheppele, 'How Viktor Orbán Wins' (2022) 33(3) Journal of Democracy 58.

[53] Freedom House, 'Freedom in the World 2023' (March 2023) <https://freedomhouse.org/sites/default/files/2023-03/FIW_World_2023_DigtalPDF.pdf>.

authority to identify and uphold unenumerated rights or an only implicit constitutional core. Those changes can occur even in states with a history of strong judicial oversight, such as India and Israel. 'Illiberal democratic' parties in power also
weaken other institutions that hold the executive and legislative accountable to the
constitution. They restrict the autonomy of civil society, for example by reining in
academic institutions, the media, private associations, and minorities. They also
turn government agencies, such as the public prosecutor, regulators, and tax officials, into tools for consolidating their power.

Although every case of legal revolution in pursuit of illiberal democracy
is unique, they all share a family resemblance. The driving force today is usually a 'populist' party or coalition. Populists aim to successfully rally a base
strong enough to prevail in free and fair democratic elections, in many cases
by appealing to some form of exclusionary nationalism. Once in power, they
tend to make only minor changes to political participatory rights, through
gerrymandering or voter identification laws. Their real focus is on unleashing
governmental power by eliminating liberal constitutional safeguards, such as
institutional checks and balances, countermajoritarian rights, and independent
often unelected officials. They do so, at least nominally, to re-establish genuine
popular sovereignty.

The danger is deeper than democratic thinkers sometimes acknowledge. Svolik
demonstrates how, for many voters, democracy may be at best a secondary concern.[54] Although voters recognize that they should care about democratic norms
and institutions—such as a legitimate opposition, the separation and balance of
powers, the rule of law, and rights guarantees for minorities and individuals—
these principled concerns are often secondary to more immediate and partisan
ones, such as group identity, material wellbeing and redistribution, and cultural
concerns. Antidemocratic leaders may exploit voters' partisan interests. But they
are not hoodwinking them about their political goals. Too many voters are perfectly willing to set aside democratic values in this way.

The phenomenon of legal revolution in pursuit of illiberal democracy is the
reality facing many democracies around the world. Committed democrats must
recognize that an antidemocratic party can gain power through free and fair elections, particularly when democratic constitutional essentials are unentrenched
and unprotected. In power, antidemocrats can abrogate and revolutionize democracy legally. They often do so by exploiting tensions between formal democratic
procedures and substantive democratic norms, between legality and legitimacy.
When democracies leave constitutional essentials vulnerable to amendment and
other methods of positive legal change, they create greater opportunities for antidemocratic parties like Fidesz to consolidate power. Such parties can incrementally

---

[54] Svolik (n 14) 23–24, 31.

16 INTRODUCTION

eliminate constitutional checks on their legislative and executive authority in order to entrench their rule indefinitely.[55]

Militant Democracy

Most democrats, from radical democrats to classical liberals, agree that 'illiberal democracy' is a contradiction in terms—it is not actually a legitimate form of democracy. Arato and Cohen strengthen this view by convincingly arguing that efforts to separate liberalism from democracy do not improve the quality of democracy, they pave the way to authoritarianism.[56] There is broad recognition that liberal constitutionalism is an integral feature of democracy and that there are normative limits to democratic legal change. And yet, as Moyn writes, reactionaries have proven time and again that *liberalism can die*, leaving behind a hollow shell of democracy.[57] Despite this, the popularity of 'illiberal democracy' and its realization through democratic legal procedures poses an urgent question for democrats: how can a democracy defend itself against members who exploit its own legal procedures to advance antidemocratic political goals?

To be sure, democratic legal procedures usually generate laws and policies that promote fundamental principles of democracy, protect members' basic rights, and promote freedom and equality. However, they are imperfect. The phenomena of illiberal democracy and legal revolution demonstrate that imperfection. They can and have produced profoundly undemocratic outcomes when left unchecked. This raises a question about institutional safeguards: can they be designed to limit the abuse of democratic legal procedures without undermining democracy itself? What mechanisms entrench democracy against its legal revolution?

An analogy with the police may help underscore the need to adopt such mechanisms. To minimize the abuse of police power, democracies require police officers to obtain warrants from independent judges before taking significant actions.[58] That requirement restricts their and the state's potential to violate citizens' basic rights. Similarly, constitutional entrenchment offers an additional layer of oversight that constrains governmental power and mitigates its antidemocratic potential.

Another analogy can be draw from health insurance.[59] Of course, no one wants to have a serious health crisis. But most understand the importance of health insurance—just in case. Similarly, constitutional entrenchment is a kind of

---

[55] Uitz, 'Can You Tell When an Illiberal Democracy Is in the Making?' (n 35) 280.
[56] Arato and Cohen (n 13) 142, 145.
[57] Samuel Moyn, *Liberalism against Itself: Cold War Intellectuals and the Making of Our Times* (Yale University Press 2023) 1.
[58] John Hart Ely, *Democracy and Distrust: A Theory of Judicial Review* (Harvard University Press 1980) 127.
[59] I am indebted to Nadia Urbinati for sharing this analogy with me.

insurance against democratic pathologies. Effective checks and safeguards allow for the early detection and response to problems, preventing them from metastasizing into existential threats.

Drawing on their experience with the rise of totalitarianism, mid-twentieth-century democratic jurists and constitutional designers believed that stronger forms of constitutional entrenchment were necessary in order to foreclose future legal revolutions of democracy. Accordingly, they designed post-war democracies to be 'militant' by installing mechanisms that safeguard their constitutional essentials against those pathologies.

The German *Basic Law* and Militant Democracy

The 1949 German *Basic Law* is arguably the paradigm of militant democracy in constitutional practice.[60] Three principal features define the militant nature of German democracy under the *Basic Law*—explicit constitutional unamendability, political rights restrictions (especially party bans), and designating the Constitutional Court as the guardian of the constitution, effectively placing it at the epicentre of German democracy.[61]

Article 79.3 of the *Basic Law* uses explicit unamendability to entrench the substance of German democracy absolutely.[62] It invalidates any amendments to the principles laid out in Article 1 (human dignity and human rights) and to Article 20 (the constitutional principles and the right of resistance).[63] It also protects

---

[60] For comparative legal analyses of different militant democracies, see Gregory H Fox and Georg Nolte, 'Intolerant Democracies' (1995) 36(1) Harvard International Law Journal 1; Giovanni Capoccia, 'Militant Democracy: The Institutional Bases of Democratic Self-Preservation' (2013) 9 Annual Review of Law and Social Science 207; Svetlana Tyulkina, *Militant Democracy: Undemocratic Political Parties and Beyond* (Routledge 2015).

[61] See Donald P Kommers and Russell A Miller, *The Constitutional Jurisprudence of the Federal Republic of Germany* (Duke University Press 2012) 43.

[62] Unamendability is *explicit* when clauses of the constitution are legally unalterable because they are positively guaranteed through a mechanism like an eternity clause. Unamendability is only *implicit* when the constitutional court may use its power of judicial review to strike down legislation as unconstitutional based on its authority to interpret the constitution. Yaniv Roznai, *Unconstitutional Constitutional Amendments: The Limits of Amendment Powers* (Oxford University Press 2017) 6, 16. See the discussion in chapter 5.

[63] The centrality of the term 'dignity' to the *Basic Law* may seem controversial. For example, Moyn argues that not only is the concept of human dignity a relatively recent innovation and was not considered necessary to get basic liberal rights off the ground historically, it was developed in this form by Catholics to oppose 'secular' appeals to human rights, which they saw as spiritually empty. 'Dignity', he argues, embeds Christian democratic principles in the German Constitution. Samuel Moyn, 'The Secret History of Constitutional Dignity' in Christopher McCrudden (ed), *Understanding Human Dignity* (The British Academy 2013) 96, 106–09.

Despite its origins, framers of the *Basic Law*, such as Schmid and Heuss, chose 'dignity' deliberately because in the twentieth century it served as an ideal compatible with a variety of theological and philosophical traditions. Christoph Goos, 'Würde des Menschen: Restoring Human Dignity in Post-Nazi Germany' in Christopher McCrudden (ed), *Understanding Human Dignity* (The British Academy 2013) 92–93; Aharon Barak, 'Human Dignity: The Constitutional Value and the Constitutional Right'

18 INTRODUCTION

Germany's federal structure. Besides limiting the scope of positive legislation, it also clarifies the constitution's substantive values by signalling them explicitly in positive law.[64]

In the *Basic Law*, human dignity is the only absolute right (rather than a relative right), which means that dignity is not subject to limitations or balancing with other rights or interests.[65] Article 1, which codifies human dignity, trumps all other law. And Article 79.3 ensures that all public authorities are bound to it. The following articles from the 'Basic Rights' portion of the *Basic Law* further concretize and flesh out the meaning of human dignity as relative rights.[66] Although relative rights may be infringed on, it is only after the state adheres to the appropriate procedures to do so and the infringement does not have a disproportionate impact on the rights holder.[67]

Article 79.3 also aligns state authority with the five fundamental principles of German democracy detailed in Article 20: namely, the commitments to a democratic state, a social state, a *Rechtsstaat*, a federal state, and a republic.[68] Those principles are considered valid and binding not simply by being enacted into positive law but because they embody a freestanding 'objective order of values'. That authoritative status explains why those values cannot be validly abrogated, no matter how popular doing so might be with German voters.[69]

Articles 92 and 93 of the *Basic Law* designate the Federal Constitutional Court (FCC) as the guardian of the constitution.[70] The FCC aims to guarantee Germany's democratic public order against both governmental and majoritarian excesses.[71]

in Christopher McCrudden (ed), *Understanding Human Dignity* (The British Academy 2013) 364; Dieter Grimm, 'Dignity in a Legal Context: Dignity as an Absolute Right' in Christopher McCrudden (ed), *Understanding Human Dignity* (The British Academy 2013) 384. They did not intend to invoke Christian democracy but instead liberal fundamentals, such as human autonomy and the opportunity to develop one's own capacity—the very fundamentals that twenty-century phenomena such as totalitarianism and mass society had just demonstrated was highly vulnerable to total annihilation. Goos ibid 89–93.

[64] Werner Heun, *The Constitution of Germany: A Contextual Analysis* (Hart Publishing 2011) 25–26.
[65] Grimm (n 63) 387–88.
[66] Kommers and Miller (n 61) 44.
[67] Mattias Kumm, 'Who's Afraid of the Total Constitution? Constitutional Rights as Principles and the Constitutionalization of Private Law' (2006) 7(4) German Law Journal 348. Kumm summarizes the test of proportionality as a four-step process. A measure or statute infringes *proportionately* on a right if it:

1. Is enacted for a legitimate purpose
2. Actually furthers that legitimate purpose
3. Is necessary (a measure is necessary if no equally effective but less intrusive measure is available)
4. Is proportional in a narrow sense (the benefits of infringing the protected interests must be greater than the loss incurred with regard to the infringed interest).

[68] For an analysis of each of those five principles, see Heun (n 64) 26–48.
[69] ibid 37; See also Kommers and Miller (n 61) 45, 57–58.
[70] Kommers and Miller (n 61) 3, 10; Heun (n 64) 167, 178–79.
[71] Samuel Issacharoff, *Fragile Democracies: Contested Power in the Era of Constitutional Courts* (Cambridge University Press 2015) 138, 145.

The *Basic Law* grants the FCC final authority over the constitution, which trumps that of other branches of government.[72] Kommers and Miller argue the FCC sits at the 'epicentre' of German democracy because of its final authority over constitutionality.[73]

Finally, Article 21 of the *Basic Law* establishes the importance of political parties to German democracy while also regulating them by allowing for the restriction of their rights.[74] Paragraph 1 requires that parties have an internal structure that conforms to democratic principles.[75] Paragraph 2 stipulates that parties are unconstitutional if they 'seek to undermine or abolish the free democratic basic order or to endanger the existence of the Federal Republic of Germany'. (Similarly, Article 9.2 allows political associations to be declared unconstitutional.[76]) Unconstitutionality hinges in particular on whether parties appear to threaten Articles 1 or 20, that is, the articles that codify and signal Germany's basic constitutional identity.[77] Finally, Paragraph 4 establishes that the FCC has the authority to decide on a party's constitutionality. Importantly, although the FCC has that authority, it cannot decide by itself to investigate and dissolve a party. The government, parliament, or a federal state must first initiate the process. This means that the use of political rights restrictions is subject to a system of checks and balances. In addition, as Müller has added, it introduces an element of 'peer review', in that parties play a role in the process by asking themselves whether suspected antidemocrats are sufficiently 'like them' or not.[78]

Militant Democracy as Constitutional Entrenchment

The *Basic Law* helps to illustrate how those three principal features of militant democracy are co-implicating and mutually reinforcing in practice.

---

[72] Heun (n 64) 29, 168–69; Kommers and Miller (n 61) 15.

[73] Kommers and Miller (n 61) 38.

[74] ibid 16.

[75] Kirshner develops a compelling normative theory for why parties must be recognized constitutionally. Parties are the modern institutional bearers of the principle of 'legitimate opposition', ie regularized political competition, which ensures that opposition can effectively participate in governance and make changes to the status quo. Without legitimate opposition, members' formal possession of political rights may be substantively meaningless because they cannot exercise them to choose among different parties and policy goals. In other words, without legitimate opposition, formal political participatory rights may only mask a substantively undemocratic regime. Alexander S Kirshner, *Legitimate Opposition* (Yale University Press 2022).

[76] Associations have been banned to a significantly greater extent in Germany than parties have. See Jan-Werner Müller, 'Individual Militant Democracy' in Anthoula Malkopoulou and Alexander S Kirshner (eds), *Militant Democracy and Its Critics: Populism, Parties, Extremism* (Edinburgh University Press 2019) 20.

[77] Heun (n 64) 96.

[78] Müller, 'The Problem of Peer Review in Militant Democracy' (n 1) 263.

20   INTRODUCTION

Weill argues that unamendability and political rights restrictions are inter-related mechanisms; both perform the same underlying function of constitutional entrenchment.[79] Although it is easy to focus on how measures such as a party ban infringe on members' political rights—which they do—their positive purpose is to defend democratic constitutional essentials against abuses that political rights enable. Political rights restrictions thus entrench the constitution *indirectly*, by denying the legal possession of state power to antidemocratic actors. On the other hand, constitutional unamendability accomplishes entrenchment *directly*, by rendering certain amendments to the constitution invalid.

As measures of entrenchment, unamendability and political rights restrictions are complementary because each focuses on different potential threats to constitutional essentials: unamendability focuses on undemocratic legislative *actions* and containment focuses instead on antidemocratic *actors*. Weill further elaborates on their relationship by framing what they contribute to entrenchment in temporal terms.[80] Political rights restrictions entrench a constitution *proactively*, by preventing antidemocratic organizations access to power in the first place. Unamendability entrenches a constitution *retroactively*, by invalidating amendments and derogations.

Since political rights restrictions and unamendability perform the same underlying function of entrenchment, they naturally complement and reinforce one another. Restrictions on political organizations strengthen unamendability by denying antidemocrats the opportunity to pursue unconstitutional legislation in the first place: even the most committed antidemocrat cannot enact unconstitutional legislation if he cannot hold public office.

Similarly, unamendability bolsters political rights restrictions. Without limitations on constitutional amendment—that is, when the amendment clause is enacted as the supreme clause of the constitution[81]—then the legal rationale for party bans weakens. It seems to defeat the purpose of having political rights if those rights can be infringed after they were exercised legally.[82] What is a (legal) right if not the right to do what is (morally) wrong?[83] It also seems to undermine the rule of law, which stipulates that sanctions should only be applied on the basis of clear,

---

[79] Rivka Weill, 'On the Nexus of Eternity Clauses, Proportional Representation, and Banned Political Parties' (2017) 16(2) Election Law Journal 238.

[80] ibid; Rivka Weill, 'Secession and the Prevalence of Both Militant Democracy and Eternity Clauses Worldwide' (2018) 40(2) Cardozo Law Review 961, 963.

[81] Greenawalt defines a clause as constitutionally supreme when the norms adopted according to it take precedence over norms adopted by any other procedure. Kent Greenawalt, 'The Rule of Recognition and the Constitution' (1987) 85(4) Michigan Law Review 632. When the amendment clause is supreme constitutionally, all ordinary and constitutional law sits under the reservation of its exercise.

[82] See Andrew Arato, 'Multi-Track Constitutionalism beyond Carl Schmitt' (2011) 18(3) Constellations 336.

[83] Jeremy Waldron, 'A Right to Do Wrong' in *Liberal Rights: Collected Papers 1981-1991* (Cambridge University Press 1993).

publicly known and general rules that are applied impartially and equally to all cases.[84]

Because the *Basic Law* installs human dignity as its sole absolute right, it has the status of the supreme clause of the constitution—displacing the amendment clause's status as supreme clause.[85] Moreover, the 'eternity clause' of Article 79.3 serves a dual purpose. Not only does it protect the substantive identity of the *Basic Law*, it also uses the medium of positive law to signal the political identity of the constitution. The constitutional supremacy of human dignity, grounded in the constitution's 'objective system of values', helps to counter criticisms that the use of rights restrictions are politically motivated or based on a legally arbitrary or ungrounded interpretation of the constitution.[86] Finally, it helps to align legality and legitimacy within the constitutional order, reducing potential conflicts between its procedures of legal change and its substantive values.

Müller argues that constitutional courts, acting as the guardian of the constitution, have been instrumental to the rise of militant democracy.[87] A guardian is an essential mechanism of militant democracy for both practical and normative reasons. Arato notes that constitutional entrenchment is not self-enforcing.[88] Neither are political rights restrictions. Some branch of government must have the final authority to interpret and concretize the unamendable articles of the constitution and decide whether laws and policies conflict with them. Similarly, some branch of government must have the final authority to decide whether a political organization holds unconstitutional goals and merits rights restrictions. The guardian of the constitution performs both of those roles.

Besides its functional role in a democracy, constitutional guardianship also plays an important symbolical role. Ackerman writes that the German Federal Constitutional Court's authority and mandate serve as symbols of the state's dedication to liberal democratic principles, in particular limited government and individual freedom.[89] Müller adds that post-war constitutional courts were intentionally designed to check and counterbalance majoritarian procedures, drawing on lessons from the failures of Weimar Germany and the French Third Republic.[90] Courts were designed to correct the imperfections of majoritarian legislative

---

[84] Heun (n 64) 35ff; Judith N Shklar, 'Rights in the Liberal Tradition' (2023) 71(2) Political Studies 279, 280; William E Scheuerman, *The End of Law: Carl Schmitt in the Twenty-First Century* (Rowman & Littlefield International Ltd 2019) 4–5.

[85] Grimm (n 63) 288.

[86] Weill, 'On the Nexus of Eternity Clauses, Proportional Representation, and Banned Political Parties' (n 79) 246.

[87] Jan-Werner Müller, *Contesting Democracy: Political Ideas in Twentieth-Century Europe* (Yale University Press 2011) 147.

[88] Andrew Arato, *The Adventures of the Constituent Power: Beyond Revolutions?* (Cambridge University Press 2017) 368.

[89] Bruce Ackerman, *The Future of Liberal Revolution* (Yale University Press 1992) 104–07.

[90] Müller, *Contesting Democracy: Political Ideas in Twentieth-Century Europe* (n 87) 147–48.

22 INTRODUCTION

procedures that represent the will of 'the people' and their potential for what has been called 'democratic suicide'.

Freeman and Ferrara elaborate on the role of courts, describing how their guardianship offers a different way to represent 'the people', thereby better entrenching society's interest in perpetuating its democratic identity over time.[91] Ferrara argues, for example, that a constitutional guardian can better represent the interests of future generations, who often go unrepresented in legislative bodies but are deeply affected by their decisions. In summary, a constitutional guardian both entrenches and sustains democratic essentials.

A Normative Theory of Militant Democracy

Although militant forms of constitutional entrenchment like the German *Basic Law* install institutional barriers against the legal revolution of democratic constitutional essentials, its normative theory is only in an early stage of development. A little over a decade ago, Müller noted that there was no proper normative theory of militant democracy.[92] In particular, normative theories have so far had difficulty overcoming the paradox of militant democracy (also called the paradox of democracy's self-defence), which is that militant measures, especially the party ban, may be as harmful for democracy as the threats they aim to contain.

Besides the paradox of democracy's self-defence, existing normative theories of militant democracy face other significant normative, practical, and explanatory challenges, which include:

- *A detection problem*: Existing normative theories of militant democracy have some significant blind spots, in particular they tend to say nothing at all about populists and 'illiberal democrats' who attack human rights and other liberal constitutional essentials if they leave political rights mostly intact.
- *Legal indeterminacy*: The conditions or actions that trigger restrictions of political rights may not be clearly defined through positive law; actors who exercise their political rights legally may nevertheless be sanctioned.
- *Discretionary authority*: Related to indeterminacy, state authorities may deploy militant measures at their own discretion, abusing them to consolidate power.

---

[91] Samuel Freeman, 'Constitutional Democracy and the Legitimacy of Judicial Review' (1990) 9 Law and Philosophy; Alessandro Ferrara, *Sovereignty Across Generations: Constituent Power and Political Liberalism* (Oxford University Press 2023).
[92] Müller, 'Militant Democracy' (n 4) 1254.

- *Depoliticization*: Matters that should be left to the electorate to decide are instead taken off the political agenda entirely.
- *Incongruence*: Normative theories of militant democracy focus too narrowly on the party ban, often entirely neglecting other key measures, such as explicit unamendability.

Because of these challenges, scholars and policy makers often doubt the legitimacy of militant democracy. Even advocates of militant democracy seem to lack confidence in it.[93] Most argue that militant measures may be taken only against a narrow subset of antidemocrats, such as those who explicitly invoke symbols of an antidemocratic past (eg the Nazi flag), or that they must be reserved as a last resort against an imminent existential threat. Those normative reservations have practical consequences. By constraining the use of militant measures, we risk allowing antidemocrats to become too strong to stop using legal measures, if they may be stopped by any means at all.

Militant democracy can be more confident. This book develops a new normative theory of militant democracy to give it that confidence. It accomplishes this by focusing on liberalism as the state's constitutional identity. Doing so shifts the focus of what exactly should be defended with militant measures from a minimalistic conception of democracy to liberal democracy. This shift both improves a democracy's ability to detect and counter internal threats and provides a more robust normative foundation for responses to them. In addition, a normative theory re-centred on liberal democracy sidesteps many of the paradoxes that affect existing normative theories of militant democracy, in particular the paradox of democracy's self-defence. By focusing on a richer theory of democracy, this new normative theory allows democrats to be more confident in the deployment of militant measures.

This normative theory also establishes the state's right to defend its democratic identity against its enemies. While it is generally accepted that a democratic state can defend itself against a violent insurrection occurring from without, it is far more challenging to argue for its defense against members using their constitutional rights to destroy it from within. By focusing on the nature of the state and what makes it legitimate, this alternative normative theory provides the basis for the state's self-defence against the threat of internal politicization and civil war.

Argument of the Book

This book unpacks its theory of militant democracy in three parts. Part I, spanning two chapters, outlines the nature of the problem that the book aims to address.

---

[93] I'm indebted to Alex Kirshner for helping me to situate my argument.

24   INTRODUCTION

Chapter 1 examines the challenge of legal revolution, when antidemocrats exploit formally valid legal procedures to amend or derogate a constitution's democratic identity. The chapter develops a typology of legal revolutionary methods, using contemporary examples to illustrate its argument. It highlights the unique existential threat that legal revolution poses to modern constitutional democracy. The chapter concludes with a dilemma: democracy can be turned against itself. That raises the question: what measures can be taken to save democracy from itself, without sacrificing its democratic principles at the same time?

Measures of militant democracy seem to offer an effective way to counteract legal revolutionary threats. At first glance however, those measures appear to be undemocratic themselves. This leads to a crisis of confidence among democrats, who are generally reluctant to embrace militant democracy at all. Even its proponents worry about the legitimacy of militant democracy. Chapter 2 analyses existing normative theories of militant democracy, exploring their limitations and paradoxes. Because of those limitations, this chapter argues that the legitimacy of militant democracy should be re-evaluated, in order to overcome that crisis of confidence and provide democracies with the mechanisms they need to defend themselves.

Part II develops the normative foundations for an alternative theory of militant democracy, intended to address the shortcomings of existing normative theories and better equip democracies to defend themselves against legal revolutionary threats. This alternative normative theory rests on the thought of Rawls and Schmitt, developed in two distinct chapters.

Chapter 3 argues that basic liberal rights are authoritative and binding norms in any democracy. It develops its argument using the thought of John Rawls. It examines how Rawls' political constructivism provides a basis for arguing that basic liberal rights are a conclusion of practical reason. Although there are many ways to demonstrate the authoritative nature of basic liberal rights, Rawls' theory of political liberalism is arguably the most important contribution to political philosophy of the twentieth century and it remains a force to be reckoned with today. Rawls' liberalism helps determine the substance of democracy, explaining why basic liberal rights are the *sine qua non* of a democratic society and must be guaranteed constitutionally, even if popular support for them dissolves due to the spread of unreasonable doctrines within society.

Chapter 4 argues that every state must be able to defend and entrench its constitutional identity, which includes countering internal politicization, internal enemies, and legal revolution. This chapter uses Carl Schmitt's state and constitutional theory to justify the constitutional entrenchment of a state's particular 'political' identity. Schmitt's state and constitutional theory justifies the state's defence of its identity through measures now associated with militant democracy.

Combining the democratic substance of Rawls' thought and the militant form of Schmitt's thought provides the normative foundations for an alternative theory of militant democracy: a democratic state may legitimately adopt and deploy militant mechanisms in order to safeguard democratic constitutional essentials, in particular basic liberal rights, against internal enemies intent on abusing democratic legal procedures for subversive and revolutionary ends.

The final part, Part III, presents arguments for three principal militant mechanisms for entrenching and defending the state's democratic identity against its legal revolution: unamendability, political rights restrictions, and a guardian of the constitution.

Chapter 5 advocates explicit unamendability as a mechanism to entrench the constitution against antidemocratic laws. It argues that explicit unamendability best locks in a state's democratic identity at the constitutional level and defends it against legal change. Explicit unamendability is a crucial device because it denies the legality of antidemocrats' actions directed against constitutional essentials. By tethering the state's democratic political identity to articles of the constitution, unamendability also performs an important signalling and clarifying function.

Chapter 6 theorizes the legitimate use of political rights restrictions, in particular the party ban, as a mechanism for entrenching the constitution against antidemocratic political organizations. To successfully defend democracy against legal revolution, it is, Kirshner writes, necessary to focus on the fact that 'antidemocrats, not just antidemocratic laws, threaten democracy'.[94] Explicit unamendability has its limits to prevent legal revolution. Simply possessing state power legally allows antidemocrats to attack democratic constitutionalism in more indirect ways, for example by derogating the constitution or capturing state agencies responsible for upholding basic rights. Political rights restrictions can pre-emptively cut off those avenues for antidemocrats, denying them the opportunity to acquire state power and turn it against democracy in the first place.

A branch of government must have the final authority to decide on the validity of explicit unamendability and political rights restrictions. Chapter 7 theorizes a guardian of the constitution as the final authority on constitutionality. The guardian has the authority to strike down laws that violate the constitution's unamendable core and to dissolve political organizations that threaten the democratic public order. The constitutional court typically performs this role, serving as a check on the active power of both the legislative and executive branches.

Incorporating these three principal mechanisms of militant democracy into future democratic constitutions would provide them with the means to minimize legal revolutionary threats, in the process improving the chances for a more resilient democratic public order.

This book develops a normative theory to justify a solution to a pressing problem facing democracies today: legal revolution. That abstract focus admittedly means

---

[94] Kirshner, *A Theory of Militant Democracy* (n 3) 4.

26 INTRODUCTION

that other more practical questions go unaddressed. For example, how exactly can these mechanisms be enacted in future constitutions?

In addition, this book focuses only on measures of militant democracy. Those measures can be understood as reactive measures, which respond to internal threats after they have arisen. A democracy can and should adopt other measures that improve its overall quality as a democracy, and in the process minimize the likelihood that internal threats will arise in the first place. Those preventative measures work by addressing grievances that drive members to support antidemocrats. Preventative measures include more robust forms of social democratic redistribution and enhanced civic education.

A crucial lesson for improving democracy's self-defence against internal threats comes from the recent Covid-19 pandemic. States that defended themselves more successfully against Covid-19 used the cumulative act effect, also known as the 'Swiss cheese model' of risk management, to minimize major outbreaks. This approach relies on multiple layers of defense to prevent major catastrophic events. Any single defensive mechanism has its weaknesses and blind spots—much like the holes in a single slice of Swiss cheese—and so, by itself, could allow a threat to pass through. By layering and networking individual defensive mechanisms, their cumulative effect significantly reduces the likelihood of a disastrous outcome.

That layered approach can serve as an effective model for the defense of democracy. Preventative mechanisms and reactive mechanisms constitute the two broad ways of responding to antidemocratic threats. Respectively, they address the grievances of members of the electorate who support antidemocrats' pursuit of public office and they entrench democratic institutions against legal revolutionary attacks. Preventative and reactive mechanisms complement and reinforce one another. The former work upstream, reducing the likelihood that antidemocratic threats will form at all. Those analysed in this book act downstream, halting antidemocratic threats after they have already materialized. They buy a democracy time to address those grievances. The different mechanisms that make up 'militant democracy' thus form an essential set of layers for democracy's self-defense. For that reason, it is crucial to develop a strong normative foundation for the principal mechanisms of militant democracy, in order to better entrench democracy against legal revolutionary challenges. It is to this task that we now turn.

PART I

1

Democracy's Problem of Legal Revolution

Introduction

Populism poses a serious threat to both new and consolidated democracies today. Defined by a Manichean conception of politics and an exclusionary concept of 'the people', populists in power often backslide democratic states toward competitive authoritarianism.[1] They do so by eroding checks and balances on governmental power, crystallizing their control over representative government, and undermining both basic liberal rights and political participatory rights. Because of the gravity of the threat it poses, efforts to better understand populism have dominated political science in recent years.[2]

Yet understanding populism by itself will not be sufficient to defend against democratic backsliding. It also requires analysing the methods and institutional conditions that a malicious actor can exploit, populist or otherwise. A danger uniquely facing democracy is that its elected representatives can exploit the legal powers of public office to realize antidemocratic political goals. The use of formally valid legal procedures to alter the substance or identity of the constitution can be defined as *legal revolution*.

The concept 'legal revolution' was coined in a 1933 article describing the Nazi seizure of power in Weimar Germany. German political and constitutional theorists continued developing the concept, although it remained mostly unknown to English-language scholarship. In response to contemporary populist backsliding, Anglophone constitutional theorists coined a series of related concepts— including 'abusive constitutionalism', 'constitutional capture', 'autocratic legalism',

---

[1] See for example Jan-Werner Müller, *What Is Populism?* (University of Pennsylvania Press 2016); Nancy Bermeo, 'On Democratic Backsliding' (2016) 27(1) Journal of Democracy 5; Steven Levitsky and Daniel Ziblatt, *How Democracies Die* (Crown 2018); Jordan Kyle and Yascha Mounk, 'The Populist Harm to Democracy: An Empirical Assessment' (26 December 2018) <https://www.institute.global/insights/geopolitics-and-security/populist-harm-democracy-empirical-assessment>; Kirk A Hawkins and Cristóbal Rovira Kaltwasser, 'Introduction: The Ideational Approach' in Kirk A Hawkins and others (eds), *The Ideational Approach to Populism Concept, Theory, and Analysis* (Routledge 2019).
    Recent scholarship cautions against overstating this problem. For example, see Brett Meyer, *Over-Diagnosing Democratic Decline* (The Progress Network 2023).
[2] For example, the sense of urgency to respond to the threat of populism and 'illiberal democracy' has influenced if not driven the APSA conference theme statement four years in a row, starting in 2018. The themes for those years were 'Democracy and Its Discontents' (2018); 'Populism and Privilege' (2019); 'Democracy, Difference, and Destabilization' (2020); and 'Promoting Pluralism' (2021). The theme statements clarify that the main goal of each conference was either to problematize or respond to populism and its distinctive attack on democracy.

Democracy despite Itself. Benjamin A. Schupmann, Oxford University Press. © Benjamin A. Schupmann 2024.
DOI: 10.1093/9780191975950.003.0002

'constitutional retrogression', 'democratic erosion', 'populist constitutionalism', and 'constitutional revolution'.[3] These recent concepts all converge on a similar concern: populists distort or eliminate democracy using formally valid legal procedures.[4]

Recent theories have tended to overlook the deeper problem of legal revolution, however. Like other antidemocrats, populists realized that they can achieve their political goals simply by 'playing the democratic game' as Capoccia describes.[5] Legal revolution of democracy is possible because of the way a democratic constitution has been designed. And that constitutional design tends to be rooted in basic democratic values. Defending democracy against legal revolution means assessing whether those constitutional possibilities should exist in the first place.

Democracy, for most theorists, public intellectuals, as well as the general populace, means above all respect for the democratic process rather than a particular outcome. One's loyalty as a democratic citizen lies first with democratic procedures, regardless of how one feels about particular laws or the elected officials that they happen to produce.[6] That respect translates into a public duty to recognize outcomes as politically legitimate simply because they were produced according to the rules of the game.

Most democratic theories recognize that proceduralism extends into the very heart of the constitution. For example, Dahl argued that, for a regime to be fully democratic, its members must have 'final control' over democratic procedures and what they may be used for.[7] Lefort argued that democracy is defined by its being 'instituted and sustained by the dissolution of the markers of certainty': everything is up for grabs as long as a sufficient number of members will it.[8] Finally, Saffon and Urbinati argue that even the most basic decisions must be subject to democratic procedures, if democratic membership is not to be 'trivialized' by being concerned only with issues of marginal importance.[9]

---

[3] David Landau, 'Abusive Constitutionalism' (2013) 47(1) UC Davis Law Review, 189; Jan-Werner Müller, 'Rising to the Challenge of Constitutional Capture: Protecting the Rule of Law within EU Member States' *Eurozine* <https://www.eurozine.com/rising-to-the-challenge-of-constitutional-capt ure/> accessed 21 March 2014; Kim Lane Scheppele, 'Autocratic Legalism' (2018) 85(2) The University of Chicago Law Review; Aziz Huq and Tom Ginsburg, 'How to Lose a Constitutional Democracy' (2018) 78(1) UCLA Law Review; Tom Ginsburg and Aziz Huq, *How to Save a Constitutional Democracy* (University of Chicago Press 2018); Paul Blokker, 'Populism as a Constitutional Project' (2019) 17(2) International Journal of Constitutional Law; Gary Jeffrey Jacobsohn and Yaniv Roznai, *Constitutional Revolution* (Yale University Press 2020).

[4] Nadia Urbinati, 'Political Theory of Populism' (2019) 22 Annual Review of Political Science.

[5] Giovanni Capoccia, *Defending Democracy: Reactions to Extremism in Interwar Europe* (Johns Hopkins University Press 2005) 4–11.

[6] Jan-Werner Müller, *Democracy Rules* (Farrar, Straus & Giroux 2021) 63–64.

[7] Robert A Dahl, 'Procedural Democracy' in Robert E Goodin and Philip Pettit (eds), *Contemporary Political Philosophy: An Anthology* (John Wiley & Sons, Inc 2019) 151–52.

[8] Claude Lefort, 'The Question of Democracy' in *Democracy and Political Theory* (Polity Press 1988) 19; See also Lefort, 'Reversibility' 179; Lefort, 'The Permanence of the Theologico-Political?' 230.

[9] Maria Paula Saffon and Nadia Urbinati, 'Procedural Democracy, the Bulwark of Equal Liberty' (2013) 41(3) Political Theory 461–462.

Yet normative democratic theory rarely discusses the potential for the electorate to use its final control over the political agenda to dismantle democratic essentials, either by removing them from the constitution directly or by using ordinary legislation to derogate the constitution. This is not abstract speculation. In recent years, this is exactly what has happened in many democracies, including in Venezuela, India, Poland, the Philippines, Ecuador, Hungary, and Israel. Whether committed by populists or any other type of antidemocrat, legal revolution occurs because of possibilities inherent in democratic institutions, a design that seems to be normatively mandated by democratic theory.

The problem of legal revolution is that, as long as enemies of democracy are elected to and exercise the powers of public office legally, they obtain the right to use democracy's procedures and institutions to degrade or even completely end democracy. For that reason, the specific nature of the actors disfiguring democracy, populist or otherwise, may matter less than the fact that democracy's legal procedures can be validly turned against its foundational values at all. When that happens, democracy's enemies seem to exploit a feature of democracy—not a bug.

Responding to and preventing legal revolution is a difficult problem. To prevent antidemocrats from using legal revolutionary methods to subvert democracy, democrats first need to confront both the phenomenon of legal revolution and the problem of how it relates to basic values of democracy. This chapter does that in two parts: it first constructs a typology of legal revolution and then analyses how legal revolution is rooted in the ideals and constitutional design of democracy itself.

Theorizing Legal Revolution

Legal revolution occurs when changes are made to the public legal order that are *formally* legal yet appear *substantively* revolutionary. It uses formally valid legal procedures to alter and interrupt the basic structure of the constitution.[10] Recognizing the idea of 'legal revolution' implies that a constitution has an underlying political identity that transcends the series of positive law that make it up, such as the 'basic structure' of the Indian Constitution.[11]

For a non-democracy, legal revolution may have positive potential, as analysed in depth by Preuss and Brunkhorst.[12] Focusing on post-Communist states, Preuss defines legal revolution as a restitutive activity that restores a previously lawful public order or brings about a public order based on the rule of law.[13] From the

---

[10] See Gary Jeffrey Jacobsohn, 'Constitutional Identity' (2006) 68 The Review of Politics.

[11] See Alessandro Ferrara, *Sovereignty Across Generations: Constituent Power and Political Liberalism* (Oxford University Press 2023) 204.

[12] Ulrich K Preuss, *Constitutional Revolution: The Link Between Constitutionalism and Progress* (Humanities Press International 1990); Hauke Brunkhorst, *Critical Theory of Legal Revolutions: Evolutionary Perspectives* (Bloomsbury Academic 2014).

[13] Preuss, *Constitutional Revolution* (n 12) 9.

32 DEMOCRACY'S PROBLEM OF LEGAL REVOLUTION

perspective of many democratic theorists, Ferrara notes, legal revolution can be legitimate when it is progressive and democratizes an authoritarian constitution.[14]

There is, however, nothing that prevents legal revolution from instead being used regressively. For both new and consolidated democracies today, as in 1933, 'legal revolution' can imply that the identity of the state and constitution become somehow less democratic and by extension less legitimate. Democratic legal revolution can take different forms. Eliminating the institutional separation of powers would-be revolutionary because it removes liberal constitutional limitations on the concentration of state power. Altering political participatory rights (such as the right to vote) would-be revolutionary because they are the essential means for citizens to express their interests and values institutionally. And abrogating basic liberal rights (such as freedom of the press) would-be revolutionary because they are the essential means by which citizens can participate effectively and develop their worldviews and conception of the good, as well as their political views.

Conceptual Origins

The concept 'legal revolution' was born almost a century ago. Heinrich Triepel, an early twentieth-century German theorist of public law, coined the term in response to the Enabling Act [*Ermächtigungsgesetz*] of 23 March 1933, which gave Hitler plenary powers and effectively ended the Weimar Republic. Triepel defined the situation as 'legal because what occurred played out according to the forms prescribed by valid statutes [*Gesetzen*]; revolutionary because it transformed law [*Recht*] in a ground-breaking way. Thus, the same act can be both legal and revolutionary'.[15]

Triepel meant for 'legal revolution' to convey a new and different possibility for revolution, one unique to modern democratic constitutionalism. Traditional revolutions had occurred through violent and illegal means, when a new power overthrew the existing government and replaced its constitutional order with an entirely new one,[16] for example, a *coup d'état*. In the phrase 'legal revolution', the

---

[14] Ferrara, *Sovereignty Across Generations* (n 11) 267–68.

[15] Heinrich Triepel, 'Die nationale Revolution und die deutsche Verfassung' *Deutsche allgemeine Zeitung* (2 April 1933); Cf Ivan Ermakoff, 'Law against the Rule of Law: Assaulting Democracy' (2020) 47(1) Journal of Law and Society 173.

Triepel was likely building on Jellinek's 1906 argument that 'constitutional transformation' can completely destroy and rebuild an existing state system without causing any sudden disruption to the state itself. Georg Jellinek, 'Constitutional Amendment and Constitutional Transformation' in Arthur J Jacobson and Bernhard Schlink (eds), *Weimar: A Jurisprudence of Crisis* (University of California Press 2002) 57.

[16] Ivan Ermakoff, *Ruling Oneself Out: A Theory of Collective Abdications* (Duke University Press 2008) 23; see also Jacobsohn and Roznai (n 3) 59ff.

noun 'revolution' describes that same *outcome*, of a radical change having occurred; whereas the adjective 'legal' highlights the different *means* used.[17] It underscores how, although state power could be obtained and exercised within the bounds of the positive law, its exercise and effects could nevertheless transmute the constitution's identity.[18]

Triepel's argument unfolded in the context of an ongoing disagreement in Weimar about juridical methods between positivists and anti-positivists.[19] Part of their basic methodological disagreement was over whether the basic public legal order was reducible to the system of statutes that made up the document called 'the constitution', a position known as monism, or whether state and constitution were something more than the sum of their parts, a position known as dualism.[20] Triepel, an anti-positivist, argued that—even if a change to the law was valid, in a formal–procedural legal sense—certain laws and ordinances and certain constitutional amendments could nevertheless violate the constitution's 'basic ideas' [*Grundgedanken*]. For that reason, they could be substantively illegitimate and unconstitutional.

Triepel intended for 'legal revolution' to describe the use of the legal and constitutional procedures to overthrow the basic values of constitutional democracy. Legal revolution describes the method of revolution, not the goal. One does not need to be a fascist to use legal revolutionary methods. Ermakoff, for example, discusses how the methods employed by populists today are *structurally* similar to methods employed by the Nazi party.[21] To be clear, antidemocrats who use legal revolutionary methods today hold different political goals than mid-twentieth century totalitarians did. Their timeframe is also slower: legal revolution today tends to unfold over years, rather than weeks. Nevertheless, like their predecessors, antidemocrats today use legal revolutionary methods to pursue their political goals.[22] So although populists and totalitarians may have different political goals and operate on different time scales, the structural similarities of their methods are

---

[17] Karl Dietrich Bracher, 'The Technique of the Nationalist Seizure of Power' in *The Path to Dictatorship, 1918-1933; Ten Essays* (Anchor Books 1966) 115.

[18] Christian Hillgruber, 'Deutsche Revolutionen – "Legale Revolutionen"? Über den legitimatorischen Mehr- oder Minderwert (des Anscheins) verfassungskontinuierlicher Legalität' (2010) 49(2) Der Staat 167–69.

[19] Gerhard Dannemann, 'Legale Revolution, Nationale Revolution. Die Staatsrechtslehre zum Umbruch von 1933' in Ernst-Wolfgang Böckenförde (ed), *Staatsrecht und Staatsrechtslehre im Dritten Reich* (CF Müller 1985) 12–15; Michael Stolleis, *A History of Public Law in Germany, 1914–1945* (Oxford University Press 2004) 440ff.; Stefan Korioth, 'Rettung oder Überwindung der Demokratie – Die Weimarer Staatsrechtslehre im Verfassungsnotstand 1932/33' in Christoph Gusy (ed), *Demokratisches Denken in der Weimarer Republik* (Nomos Verlagsgesellschaft 2000) 511ff; Benjamin A Schupmann, *Carl Schmitt's State and Constitutional Theory: A Critical Analysis* (Oxford University Press 2017) 6ff.

[20] On monism and dualism, see for example Hans Kelsen, *General Theory of Law & State* (Transaction Publishers 2008) 182ff.

[21] Ermakoff, 'Law against the Rule of Law' (n 15) 182–83.

[22] ibid 183–84.

34 DEMOCRACY'S PROBLEM OF LEGAL REVOLUTION

noteworthy because it highlights a unique and seemingly perennial problem from which democracies suffer.[23]

A Typology of Legal Revolution

There have been a few contemporary attempts at a typology of legal revolution so far. Ginsburg and Huq identify five pathways that constitutional retrogression can take: constitutional amendment, eliminating institutional checks, centralizing executive power, shrinking the public sphere, and eliminating political competition.[24] Varol identifies a different set of mechanisms for legal revolution (what he calls 'stealth authoritarianism'): changing the make-up of the judiciary, changing electoral laws, and weaponizing libel laws, surveillance, and 'non-political' crimes against the opposition.[25] Finally, Ermakoff distinguishes structural and conjunctural effects of legal revolution.[26] Structural changes revise the 'rules of the political game' by changing how power is allocated and how decisions are made. Conjunctural changes, on the other hand, disadvantage or incapacitate political competitors by creating temporary advantages for power holders.[27]

This section builds on those existing typologies to develop its own account, focusing on how legal revolutionary acts affect the democratic identity of the constitution. Developing an alternative typology underscores Kirshner's argument that focusing primarily on defending against antidemocratic laws may not be enough to prevent legal revolution: antidemocratic actors, not just antidemocratic legislative acts, threaten democracy.[28]

In outline form, this typology of legal revolution is as follows:

I. *Direct legal revolution* (changes to constitutional identity by amendment or referendum)
II. *Indirect legal revolution* (changes to constitutional identity without amendment)
    A. Breach of the constitution by derogation or desuetude
    B. Breakdown of the separation and balance of powers
        1. Weakening other branches

---

[23] The structural similarities can sometimes be uncanny. Hugo Chavez, just like Adolf Hitler, began his pursuit of public power with a failed violent putsch before pivoting to legal revolutionary methods. See Kurt Weyland, 'Latin America's Authoritarian Drift: The Threat from the Populist Left' (2013) 24(3) Journal of Democracy 18.

[24] Ginsburg and Huq, *How to Save a Constitutional Democracy* (n 3) 123.

[25] Ozan O Varol, 'Stealth Authoritarianism' (2015) 100(4) Iowa Law Review 1686.

[26] Ermakoff, 'Law against the Rule of Law' (n 15) 166.

[27] ibid 179.

[28] Alexander S Kirshner, *A Theory of Militant Democracy: The Ethics of Combatting Political Extremism* (Yale University Press 2014) 4.

a. Judiciary
b. Administrative
c. Legislative
2. Aggrandizing the Executive
C. Erosion of civil society and individual rights guarantees
1. Disenfranchise the opposition's base (deny/dilute participatory and membership rights)
2. Weaken independent counterpowers (chill civil liberties and equal protection)

The two principal types of legal revolution are distinguished by their effect on the written constitution. *Direct* legal revolution occurs by amending the constitution itself. *Indirect* legal revolution occurs when actors opposed to the identity of the constitution undermine its practice without altering the text of the constitution directly. Indirect legal revolution can be broken down into three basic subtypes. The first, breach of the constitution, occurs when ordinary law derogates the constitution. Ordinary laws enacted by the legislature are allowed to supersede constitutional articles in practice, even if they should be struck down as unconstitutional. The second type occurs when the separation and balance of powers within government is broken down, for example by the executive branch capturing the authority of a separate and co-equal branch. The third type of indirect legal revolution involves the erosion of the independence of civil society through the infringement of basic liberal rights, rights of membership, the formal rule of law, and equal protection before the law.

Direct Legal Revolution

Direct legal revolution occurs when changes to the written constitution alter its political identity. These could occur for example through amendment, a national assembly, or a referendum. Several recent cases illustrate direct legal revolution.

Fidesz's government in Hungary illustrates direct legal revolution. In 2012, after first ratifying a new constitution, Fidesz then used the amendment procedure systematically to transform Hungary into an 'illiberal democracy'.[29] Among other things, those changes made Hungary less liberal by limiting speech rights, constitutionally privileging Christianity, and undermining the independence of the judiciary.[30]

Another example comes from Turkey. In 2017, the Erdoğan government successfully held a referendum on its constitution and transformed Turkey from

---

[29] Jacobsohn and Roznai (n 3) 92.
[30] Laurent Pech and Kim Lane Scheppele, 'Illiberalism Within: Rule of Law Backsliding in the EU' (2017) 19 Cambridge Yearbook of European Legal Studies 3; Petra Bárd and Laurent Pech, *How to Build and Consolidate a Partly Free Pseudo Democracy by Constitutional Means in Three Steps: The 'Hungarian Model'* (RECONNECT October 2019); Jacobsohn and Roznai (n 3) 89–90.

a parliamentary democracy into a presidential democracy.[31] Although there is nothing wrong with presidentialism per se, Erdoğan's new constitutional order created what some commentators call a 'hyperpresidency', due to the executive's limited accountability to the legislative and other traditional institutional checks and balances.[32] Turkey's new order added other forms of executive aggrandizement, such as longer terms in office and the authority to issue wide-ranging decrees, to its degradation of liberal constitutionalism.[33]

A final recent example comes from Ecuador. In 2008, Correa, as part of his 'Citizen's Revolution', engineered a constitutional referendum.[34] Among other things, the new constitution made amendment significantly easier. These constitutional changes were instrumental in helping Correa to further expand the powers of the executive, including by eliminating the constitution's limits on presidential terms in office (although in a later course correction, term limits were reinstated).

All of the above changes revolutionized their respective constitutions by making them substantively less democratic. Although each revolution was unique, one similarity is the concentration of power in the executive. All these examples involve the breakdown of the separation of powers, weakening competing branches and removing or limiting liberal constitutional guarantees. Yet all of those revolutionary changes were consistent with the positive legal procedures for amending and revising the constitution.

Indirect Legal Revolution

High thresholds for enacting changes to the constitution can prevent antidemocrats from using direct methods of legal revolution to realize their political goals. Even if they cannot legally change the constitution itself, would-be revolutionaries can still disfigure and backslide democracy through *indirect* methods of legal revolution. There are three main subtypes of indirect legal revolution: breach of the constitution, the breakdown of the separation of and balance between powers of government, and the erosion of civil society and individual rights protections.

Breach of Constitution

A breach of the constitution (from the German, *Verfassungsdurchbrechung*) occurs when the legislature passes an ordinary law that contradicts but does not

---

[31] Kemal Kirişci and Amanda Sloat, 'The Rise and Fall of Liberal Democracy in Turkey: Implications for the West' Brookings <https://www.brookings.edu/research/the-rise-and-fall-of-liberal-democracy-in-turkey-implications-for-the-west/> accessed February 2019.
[32] Berk Esen and Sebnem Gumuscu, 'How Erdoğan's Populism Won Again' (2023) 34(3) Journal of Democracy 26.
[33] Scheppele, 'Autocratic Legalism' (n 3) 569.
[34] Bermeo (n 1) 12.

abolish an article of the constitution.[35] It is also called 'amendment by statute'. As long as the ordinary law is not struck down, by judicial review for example, it amounts to a derogation of the constitution. Another form of constitutional breach is what Albert refers to as 'constitutional desuetude', which occurs when political actors either no longer use or publicly repudiate an article of the constitution consciously and over time.[36] In practice, a breach of constitution may not appear to differ significantly from a direct form of legal revolution.[37] Yet when the constitution is only derogated, those unconstitutional ordinary laws can still be struck down in principle.[38] The original democratic constitution remains in effect. As long as it does, that constitution can serve as the basis for a legal restoration of democracy, as in Preuss's and Brunkhorst's progressive conception of legal revolution.

There are many recent examples of breaches of the constitution. Sadurski describes how, in Poland, the Law and Justice Party (PiS) passed a series of laws that redefined the appointment procedures and the retirement age for judges.[39] According to the constitution, the legislature did not have the authority to make those changes. Yet those laws still stand. The result is that both parliament and the president have subordinated the Constitutional Tribunal (Poland's constitutional court) to themselves, eroding the equality of the judiciary and undermining the liberal constitutional separation and balance of powers. Similarly, by passing the Citizenship Amendment Act in December 2019 (when taken in conjunction with the National Register of Citizens), India's BJP-led parliament effectively turned religion into a criterion for citizenship—derogating its liberal constitutional commitment to secularism.[40]

Breakdown of the Separation and Balance of Powers
Breaches of the constitution are more likely to succeed when combined with a second subtype of indirect legal revolution, the breakdown of the separation and balance between the powers of government, which either enhances the power of the executive branch or comparatively weakens the other branches.

---

[35] Horst Ehmke, 'Verfassungsänderung und Verfassungsdurchbrechung' (1953) 79(4) Archiv des öffentlichen Rechts 386, 389. The division within the Weimar methods debates carried over breaches of the constitution: broadly speaking, positivists considered breaches constitutionally permissible while anti-positivists did not.

[36] Richard Albert, 'Constitutional Amendment by Constitutional Desuetude' (2014) 62(3) The American Journal of Comparative Law 643–46. I'm indebted to Alessandro Ferrara for introducing this form to me.

[37] Triepel, who had a dualist approach to the state and constitutionalism, characterized a breach of constitution as 'nothing but a *coup d'état*'. Ehmke (n 35) 390.

[38] Claude Klein, 'On the Eternal Constitution: Contrasting Kelsen and Schmitt' in Dan Diner and Michael Stolleis (eds), *Kelsen and Schmitt: A Juxtaposition* (Bleicher Verlag 1999) 65.

[39] Wojciech Sadurski, 'Constitutional Crisis in Poland' in Mark A Graber, Sanford Levinson and Mark Tushnet (eds), *Constitutional Democracy in Crisis?* (Oxford University Press 2018) 259.

[40] Anmol Jain, 'Citizenship by Religion: The Indian Citizenship Regime 1947–2019' *Verfassungsblog* <https://verfassungsblog.de/citizenship-by-religion/> accessed 29 June 2018.

38 DEMOCRACY'S PROBLEM OF LEGAL REVOLUTION

Indirect legal revolution's success often relies on subordinating the judiciary to the executive, 'colonizing' it, as Freeman puts it.[41] Poland also illustrates this sub-type of indirect legal revolution. Choudhry describes how, after the 2015 elections in Poland, President Duda refused to swear judges into Poland's constitutional court because they had been nominated and elected by the outgoing parliament; they were not explicitly loyal to him.[42] He instead waited for the incoming parliament to nominate and elect a second set of loyalist judges, who he then swore in—consolidating executive control, his control, over the constitutional court.[43] In addition to appointing loyalists to existing vacancies, an executive can pack the judiciary with loyalists in order to subordinate it.[44] Besides capturing the judiciary, Scheppele argues that the autonomy of a constitutional court can instead be weakened, counterintuitively, by expanding its competence. Expanding a court's competence can weaken it by allowing politically insignificant cases to deluge the court, drowning its time and energy and so preventing it from focusing on actually pressing constitutional questions.[45]

The executive's authority to make appointments can also be used to weaken the state administration and bureaucracy, undermining its independence and turning it into an extension of executive will. In many cases, the executive holds some authority over departments of the state, such as the military, police, finance, taxation, election commission, and justice. One critical example is the authority to appoint heads of those departments. Ginsburg and Huq describe how, by dismissing and replacing anyone deemed insufficiently loyal, the executive can transform a relatively autonomous and technocratic department into a 'politicized' extension of its own will.[46]

The Trump Presidency provides an illustration of how administrative appointments can be used to pursue indirect legal revolution. The appointment of William Barr as United States Attorney General politicized the Justice Department and ensured that it was an extension of the President's will, for example by interpreting the Mueller Report as exculpating the President.[47] Barr also quashed prosecution of the President's allies in order to shield the President from criminal exposure. Rather than subordinating a department to a central authority, an appointment

---

[41] Will Freeman, 'Sidestepping the Constiution: Executive Aggrandizement in Latin America and East Central Europe' (2020) 6 Constitutional Studies 40ff.

[42] Sujit Choudhry, 'Will Democracy Die in Darkness? Calling Autocracy by its Name' in Mark A Graber, Sanford Levinson, and Mark Tushnet (eds), *Constitutional Democracy in Crisis?* (Oxford University Press 2018) 574.

[43] Wojciech Sadurski and Maximilian Steinbeis, 'What is Going on in Poland is an Attack against Democracy' *Verfassungsblog* <https://verfassungsblog.de/what-is-going-on-in-poland-is-an-attack-against-democracy/> accessed 11 November 2019; Sadurski (n 39) 259–65; Choudhry (n 42) 576.

[44] Huq and Ginsburg, 'How to Lose a Constitutional Democracy' (n 3) 126.

[45] Scheppele, 'Autocratic Legalism' (n 3) 551.

[46] Huq and Ginsburg, 'How to Lose a Constitutional Democracy' (n 3) 129.

[47] Margaret Talbot, *Trump, Barr, and the Rule of Law* (2019) *The New Yorker* (13 May 2019) <https://www.newyorker.com/magazine/2019/05/13/trump-barr-and-the-rule-of-law> accessed 29 February 2024.

can instead simply cripple it. For example, Scott Pruitt, the appointed Trump Administrator of the Environmental Protection Agency, deliberately hampered its ability to fulfil its mandate and protect the environment.[48]

Indirect methods of legal revolution can also break down the independence of the legislative vis-à-vis the executive. For example, Scheppele describes how Fidesz changed the rules governing discussions on the floor of Hungary's parliament, so that the opposition could not speak there, let alone present bills.[49] As a result, parliament became less deliberative, increasing the Prime Minister's ability to set the legislative agenda and determine its outcomes.

Besides subordinating other branches to itself, the executive can use its legal powers to assert its authority unilaterally. The executive branch typically has the authority to interpret and decide on both matters of international politics and trade as well as the concrete meaning of discretionary concepts like 'danger', 'vital interests', and 'emergency' and issue decrees accordingly. This authority can be used to inhibit other branches' ability to check and balance its power.

For example, frustrated by legislative control over the budget, and its refusal to fund his pet project the border wall, Former President Trump declared a 'national emergency' to obtain that funding. Despite the baldness of his lie (not to mention his admission soon after that there was no emergency at all, he just believed correctly that declaring one would help his cause[50]), Trump obtained the funding successfully. The executive's authority over 'emergencies' and other areas left to its discretion can become a means to bypass the constitutional separation of powers and realize political goals unilaterally.

The Erosion of Civil Society and Individual Rights Guarantees

Indirect legal revolution's third subtype occurs when state power is used to erode civil society and individual rights protections. One way to achieve this is by undermining political participatory rights and membership rights, in order to disenfranchise those who might support the opposition. Another way is by infringing on civil liberties and guarantees of equal protection to limit the autonomy of civil society and its ability to serve as a counter-democratic power.[51]

Political participatory rights are commonly undermined by their outright denial, for example through voter registration laws.[52] In the United States, voter

---

[48] Juliet Eilperin, Brady Dennis, and Josh Dawsey, ' "A Factory of Bad Ideas": How Scott Pruitt Undermined His Mission at EPA' *The Washington Post* (21 April 2018) <https://wapo.st/2Hg8EJh>; Umair Irfan, 'Scott Pruitt Is Slowly Strangling The EPA' *Vox* (8 March 2018) <https://www.vox.com/energy-and-environment/2018/1/29/16684952/epa-scott-pruitt-director-regulations>.

[49] Scheppele, 'Autocratic Legalism' (n 3) 550.

[50] Kim Lane Scheppele, 'Trump's Non-Emergency Emergency, Part II' *Verfassungsblog* <https://verfassungsblog.de/trumps-non-emergency-emergency-part-ii/> accessed 18 January 2024.

[51] See Pierre Rosanvallon, *Counter-Democracy* (Cambridge University Press 2008).

[52] Theodore R Johnson, 'The New Voter Suppression' <https://www.brennancenter.org/our-work/research-reports/new-voter-suppression> accessed 15 February 2021.

40 DEMOCRACY'S PROBLEM OF LEGAL REVOLUTION

registration laws have been and continue to be systematically deployed in order to disenfranchise African American voters. Insofar as they are tolerated, voter registration laws may breach the constitution by violating the Fourteenth and Fifteenth Amendments of the US Constitution.

A less overt method to undermine political participatory rights is calculated dilution. Gerrymandering is a common way to dilute votes. Hungary demonstrates how to use gerrymandering to pursue broader goals of democratic subversion. Following its 2010 electoral victory, Fidesz obtained the authority to appoint the members of Hungary's Electoral Commission. Its appointees gerrymandered electoral districts and ensured that Fidesz would continue to hold a two-thirds supermajority in parliament.[53] (The strategy worked well: in 2018, Fidesz took 67 per cent of seats in parliament despite winning only 53 per cent of the popular vote. Because of gerrymandering, Fidesz was able to hit the threshold for exercising the amendment clause of the constitution, illustrating how indirect legal revolution can be a stepping stone to direct legal revolution.) Whether through outright denial or calculated dilution, the infringement of political participatory rights undermines both political equality and opposition parties' ability to contest the current government's hold on power.

Indirect legal revolution can also occur by infringing on civil liberties, such as rights of speech, the press, and association, and guarantees of equal protection. Varol describes how 'non-political crimes' can be used to harass individuals and organizations and dissuade them from opposing a regime.[54] A regime can exploit legal tools, such as libel and defamation lawsuits, tax evasion lawsuits, and state surveillance, in order to threaten members of opposition parties that it deems to be its enemies.[55] Often, those enemies are journalists, academics, non-governmental organizations, and of course opposition politicians. In addition, it can deny state funding to the media, academic institutions, and other non-governmental institutions in order to punish them for dissent and opposition. Funding can also be used to nudge institutions into harmonizing with government policy or becoming its (uncritical) mouthpieces. Finally, it can impede journalists' access to sources of or the means to transmit knowledge, for example by denying them access to political press conferences or by revoking their broadcasting licences.[56] A regime thus does not need to alter the fundamental rights and protections guaranteed by a democratic legal order directly in order to degrade democracy. There are clearly

---

[53] Gábor Attila Tóth (ed) *Constitution for a Disunited Nation: On Hungary's 2011 Fundamental Law* (Central European University Press 2013) 256; Kim Lane Scheppele, *Hungary and the End of Politics* (6 May 2014) *The Nation* <https://www.thenation.com/article/archive/hungary-and-end-politics/> accessed 29 February 2024; Bárd and Pech (n 30) 17; Gábor Halmai, 'A Coup against Constitutional Democracy? The Case of Hungary' in Mark A Graber, Sanford Levinson, and Mark Tushnet (eds), *Constitutional Democracy in Crisis?* (Oxford University Press 2018) 246.

[54] Varol (n 25) 1705.

[55] Bermeo (n 1) 11.

[56] Huq and Ginsburg, 'How to Lose a Constitutional Democracy' (n 3) 132ff.

many indirect legal methods by which it can chill their exercise—particularly basic liberties, like freedoms of speech and the press, and by extension the effective participation within a democracy that they grant.[57]

Because it is easier to meet the requirements, most legal revolution today tends to occur indirectly. For this reason, indirect legal revolution may be the greater threat. And as Hungary demonstrates, indirect legal revolution may also serve as a stepping stone to direct legal revolution. In any case, indirect legal revolution demonstrates how antidemocrats are able to degrade and harm democracy simply by legally possessing state power.

The above demonstrates how multifaceted the phenomenon of legal revolution is. Antidemocrats can pursue the legal revolution of a democracy through a variety of pathways. Indirect legal revolution in particular underscores how antidemocratic actors can pursue their antidemocratic goals while remaining within the bounds of the law, on the authority of the electorate and democratic elections, and without even overtly targeting the constitution.

Legal Revolution and Democratic Legitimacy

Regardless of whether legal revolution occurs directly or indirectly, it presents a serious challenge to democracies. As populist movements demonstrate today, legal revolution is an extremely effective method of disfiguring and eroding democratic institutions, including the separation and balance of powers, fundamental rights (civil liberties, political participatory rights, membership rights, and due-process rights), and democratic procedures. Without those constitutional essentials, a state becomes unrecognizable as a democracy. It may be tempting to conclude that legal revolution is substantively illegitimate. However, the *legality* of legal revolution within modern democratic constitutionalism complicates that picture.

Modern constitutionalism requires that, in principle, 'the people' has control over the laws that it is subject to, including the most basic aspects of the public order. Although it may delegate its authority to legislate and decide, 'the people' *is* the best judge of its own competence and limits in a democracy.[58] 'The people's' control over those laws must include even those that govern essential features of the democratic process itself. These features include questions about who is entitled to membership, what the rights of membership are, and what the basic structure of the government is. Democratic legal procedures are often assumed to be the principal channel by which the will of 'the people' is most validly represented. And the outcome of those democratic legal procedures cannot be predetermined, if the word 'democracy' is to have any real meaning.

---

[57] Varol (n 25) 1710.
[58] Dahl (n 7) 152.

42 DEMOCRACY'S PROBLEM OF LEGAL REVOLUTION

Insofar as that is the case, then the boundary between legality and legitimacy starts to dissolve. If positive legal procedures are the most authoritative expression of the identity and will of 'the people' and democracy requires 'the people' have final control over the political agenda, then it is less obvious that legal revolution is democratically illegitimate. In that case, legal revolution seems to be an inherent, if undesirable, possibility of modern democracy.

The Paradox of Modern Constitutionalism

Unpacking modern constitutionalism can help clarify the relationship between democracy and legal revolution. Constitutionalism seeks to answer the question 'why is a particular legal order *legitimate* at all?'[59] In other words, 'why should one obey the law, except because it threatens one with a sanction?' It asks whether the law is right. Kelsen framed the question of constitutionalism by asking what makes the state and its laws different from a gang of highway robbers who hold you at gunpoint and demand that you obey their commands?[60]

The modern era complicated answering that question of constitutionalism. Modernity is defined by the break with traditional sources of authority. In particular, modern scepticism began a process of the disenchantment of *transcendent* authorities. Transcendent authority, rooted in normative truths such as the Catholic Church's interpretation of divine law, could no longer be accepted as self-evident. Modern society became characterized by the fact of pluralism, as individuals developed very different perceptions of the world, values, and what was normative truth.[61] Plural beliefs about what was 'right' and 'true' seeded disagreements about what norms and truths should be upheld publicly with the force of law.[62] Different worldviews sometimes collided over what legitimate public order was. At times, those disagreements became violent and erupted into violence and civil war.

Because of that pluralism and disagreement, public order could not be justified by appealing to particular transcendent truths and also remain stable. Any particular transcendent justification would appear illegitimate to at least some subjects. Those who disagreed would obey only because the state threatened them

---

[59] Ernst-Wolfgang Böckenförde, 'The Constituent Power of the People: A Liminal Concept of Constitutional Law' in Mirjam Künkler and Tine Stein (eds), *Constitutional and Political Theory: Selected Writings*, vol I (Oxford University Press 2016) 169.

[60] Hans Kelsen, *The Pure Theory of Law* (Max Knight tr, University of California Press 1970) 44–50; Cf Lars Vinx, *Hans Kelsen's Pure Theory of Law: Legality and Legitimacy* (Oxford University Press 2007) 36–37.

[61] John Rawls, *Political Liberalism* (Columbia University Press 1996) 63 Jeremy Waldron, *Law and Disagreement* (Oxford University Press 1999) 253–54.

[62] Richard Bellamy, *Political Constitutionalism: A Republican Defence of the Constitutionality of Democracy* (Cambridge University Press 2007) 4.

with legal consequences. From their perspective, such a state would at best be akin to a gang of robbers—if not heretical for violating their beliefs. A public order that relies solely on power to maintain itself will be unstable and struggle to survive over time. For those reasons, modern societies needed to find a different way to generate political legitimacy.[63]

Moderns eventually concluded that the only legitimate way to answer the question of constitutionalism was *immanently*, that is, through an internal or closed system in which action begins and ends with the agent. Immanence effectively 'disentangled', as Lefort put it, the relationship between power, knowledge, and constitutionalism.[64]

For constitutionalism, immanence means that the subject of the law is also its author. The law is legitimate not because it codifies a transcendent normative fact but because its subject, 'the people', has in principle also authored the law.[65] Public law merely codifies the will of 'the people'. Moderns thus answer the question of constitutionalism democratically. That is, a public legal order must be attributable, directly or indirectly, to the will of 'the people'.[66] For modern constitutionalism, 'the people' has reason to obey the law because 'the people' authorized it. Subjects of the law have reason to see it as a legitimate institution because it really only expresses their will and they are really only obeying themselves.

In making this argument, modern constitutionalism establishes a hierarchical relationship between 'the people' and its constitution, which reveals important qualities about both. 'The people' is the ultimate political authority. In terms of constitutional theory, 'the people' is a constituting power.[67] It is sovereign. The constitution, on the other hand, merely codifies the will of 'the people'. The constitution is therefore a constituted power. This hierarchical relationship means that 'the people' has both the right and the power to intervene into its legal order at will. If it so desires, modern constitutionalism argues, 'the people' may even *legitimately* recall the legal order in its entirety and issue a different constitution.[68] Because it

---

[63] Simone Chambers, 'Democracy and Constitutional Reform: Deliberative versus Populist Constitutionalism' (2019) 45(9–10) Philosophy and Social Criticism 1116, 1124.

[64] Lefort, 'The Question of Democracy' (n 8) 17–18; see also Hans Kelsen, 'On the Essence and Value of Democracy' in Arthur J Jacobson and Bernhard Schlink (eds), *Weimar: A Jurisprudence of Crisis* (University of California Press 2002) 84.

[65] Simone Chambers, 'Democracy, Popular Sovereignty, and Constitutional Legitimacy' (2004) 11(2) Constellations 154; Andreas Kalyvas, 'Popular Sovereignty, Democracy, and the Constituent Power' (2005) 12(2) Constellations 238; Ulrich K Preuss, 'The Exercise of Constituent Power in Central and Eastern Europe' in Martin Loughlin and Neil Walker (eds), *The Paradox of Constitutionalism* (Oxford University Press 2007) 211; Martin Loughlin, 'The Concept of Constituent Power' (2014) 13(2) European Journal of Political Theory 219.

[66] Frank I Michelman, 'Constitutional Authorship' in Larry Alexander (ed), *Constitutionalism: Philosophical Foundations* (Cambridge University Press 2001) 64–66; Martin Loughlin and Neil Walker, 'Introduction' in Martin Loughlin and Neil Walker (eds), *The Paradox of Constitutionalism* (Oxford University Press 2007) 2; Böckenförde (n 59) 169.

[67] Kalyvas (n 65) 226; Loughlin (n 65) 219.

[68] Böckenförde (n 59) 176.

44 DEMOCRACY'S PROBLEM OF LEGAL REVOLUTION

creates its legal order and has complete authority over it, conceptually 'the people' exists prior to and above that legal order.[69]

There is a problem with the above argument, however. Modern constitutionalism suffers from a paradox. 'The people'—as a sovereign unity, as a deciding and acting being—has no empirical reality.[70] 'The people' is a juristic fiction. It is impossible to locate 'the people' "s an intentional, unitary actor anywhere in the world. Hence the practice of enclosing 'the people' in scare quotes. Who counts as a citizen and what are the boundaries of the electorate, how do we know whether some act expresses 'the people's' will, what rights and duties members have, when elections occur and how, what powers a particular office has, how valid statutes may be enacted—all of these questions are answered by an existing constitutional order. The electorate, the government, and the constitution are all powers ostensibly constituted by 'the people'. Because the answers to those questions are specified by existing law, they presuppose that 'the people' has already authorized them.

De Maistre argued that circularity produces the paradox of modern constitutionalism: 'the people' is 'a sovereign that cannot exercise sovereignty'.[71] Because 'the people' is fictitious, it cannot form intentions or have agency. To act or decide on anything at all, 'the people' must first be represented.[72] Yet any constituted power, if it is to be a valid representative of 'the people', must first have been authorized by 'the people'.

Democrats today tend to solve the paradox of modern constitutionalism through a combination of positive legality and proceduralism. Positive legality ensures that the legal order reflects and is responsive to the legislator's will.[73] For positivism, valid law is co-extensive with the commands of the legislator that have been enacted into statutes according to the legal procedures in effect for doing so (as defined by the constitution).[74] In other words, the validity of a law is determined procedurally. The specific content of a law, for example whether it is *moral*, is not in itself relevant for its validity as long as the legal procedures in effect for making law have been adhered to.[75]

---

[69] Andrew Arato, *Post Sovereign Constitution Making* (Oxford University Press 2016) 4–5; Luigi Corrias, 'Populism in a Constitutional Key: Constituent Power, Popular Sovereignty, and Constitutional Identity' (2016) 12 European Constitutional Law Review 6, 9; Yaniv Roznai, '"We the People", "Oui, the People" and the Collective Body: Perceptions of Constituent Power' in Gary Jacobsohn and Miguel Schor (eds), *Comparative Constitutional Theory* (Edward Elgar 2018) 297.

[70] Andrew Arato, *The Adventures of the Constituent Power: Beyond Revolutions?* (Cambridge University Press 2017) 28–29; Mark Tushnet, 'Peasants with Pitchforks, and Toilers with Twitter: Constitutional Revolutions and the Constituent Power' (2015) 13(3) International Journal of Constitutional Law 651; Chambers, 'Democracy, Popular Sovereignty, and Constitutional Legitimacy' (n 65) 154; Preuss, 'The Exercise of Constituent Power in Central and Eastern Europe' (n 65) 216.

[71] Joseph de Maistre, 'Study on Sovereignty' in Jack Lively (ed), *Works* (Allen & Unwin 1965) 93.

[72] Loughlin and Walker (n 65) 1.

[73] Böckenförde (n 59) 175; Loughlin (n 65) 229.

[74] Stanley L Paulson, 'Statutory Positivism' (2007) 1(1) Legisprudence 5–6.

[75] Carl Schmitt, *Legality and Legitimacy* (Duke University Press 2004) 10, 20–23; Karl Dietrich Bracher, 'Nachwort und Ausblick' in Karl Dietrich Bracher, Gerhard Schulz, and Wolfgang Sauer (eds), *Die nationalsozialistische Machtergreifung Studien zur Errichtung des totalitären Herrschaftssystems in*

LEGAL REVOLUTION AND DEMOCRATIC LEGITIMACY   45

Proceduralism, on the other hand, determines the identity of that legislator and how it may be represented legitimately. Because 'the people' does not actually exist, there must be some codified and publicly recognized way to identify a legitimate representation of 'the people'. Proceduralism establishes whether a representation legitimately expresses the will of 'the people'.[76] Institutions like participatory rights, elections, and representative bodies are all institutions that approximate the identity of the 'the people' and allow it to decide, speak, and act. They distinguish its valid representatives from any other group that purports to represent 'the people'. Democratic procedures thereby circumscribe 'the people's' super-legal constituting power within legally defined institutions, normalizing it.[77]

Democratic theory generally agrees that a procedure must guarantee each member a formally equal chance to see his or her beliefs, values, and interests enacted into public law and public policy.[78] That equal chance is institutionalized by guaranteeing each member equal political participatory rights and the opportunity to compete for state power. Authoritative law is generated immanently by aggregating whatever individual members expressly will using their political rights.

In sum, the combination of positive legality and democratic proceduralism specify, on the one hand, how law reflects and is responsive to the will of the sovereign and, on the other hand, how the sovereign 'people' may be validly represented (who the electorate and elected representatives are and how they as a multitude can nevertheless will a single body of laws to which they are all subject). Modern constitutionalism thus links the need for the dynamism of positive law with a procedure that legitimates it democratically.[79]

Direct Legal Revolution and the Supremacy of the Amendment Clause

Modern constitutionalism's criterion for legitimacy, that the law must reflect the will of 'the people', extends into the constitution itself. As does the paradox: to be valid, the constitution too should dynamically reflect and be responsive to the will of 'the people'. Yet, again, 'the people' must first be constituted.

Deutschland 1933/34 (Springer Fachmedien Wiesbaden 1960) 971; Gotthard Jasper, *Die gescheiterte Zähmung. Wege zur Machtergreifung Hitlers, 1930-1934* (Suhrkamp 1986) 138.

[76] Florian Scriba, *'Legale Revolution'? Zu den Grenzen verfassungsändernder Rechtssetzung und der Haltbarkeit eines umstrittenen Begriffs* (Duncker & Humblot 2008) 96; Arato, *Post Sovereign Constitution Making* (n 69) 280; Roznai (n 69) 313.

[77] Preuss, 'The Exercise of Constituent Power' (n 65) 222.

[78] Hans Kelsen, 'Foundations of Democracy' (1955) 66(1) Ethics 38–39; Kelsen, 'On the Essence and Value of Democracy' (n 64) 108; Schmitt 28–36; Dahl (n 7) 148–49; Saffon and Urbinati (n 9) 459.

[79] Cf Jürgen Habermas, 'On the Internal Relation between the Rule of Law and Democracy' in *The Inclusion of the Other: Studies in Political Theory* (MIT Press 1998) 254–55.

The amendment clause seems to provide a solution to the paradox of how the constitution can be ascribed to the will of 'the people'. It provides a positive legal rule of recognition for whether the constitution reflects 'the people's' will. It determines the conditions and thresholds for when 'the people' wills to change its most fundamental laws.

Like other forms of legislation, the validity of the exercise of the amendment clause is determined by the combination of positive legality and democratic proceduralism. That is, the validity of the exercise of the amendment clause is determined on the one hand by whether the formal, positive procedures for amendment have been adhered to—regardless of the substance of the amendment pursued. On the other hand, its validity is determined by whether 'the people' has been represented validly—itself determined by positive legal procedures and thresholds. In the case of the amendment clause, a more demanding procedural threshold for valid representation usually must be met (most commonly, the support of a super-majority of elected representatives instead of a simple majority).

When there are no formal–legal limits on the range of articles of the constitution to which the amendment clause can be applied, then the amendment clause is considered to be the *supreme clause* of the constitution.[80] When supreme, all other articles of the constitution sit under the reservation of its exercise.[81] Articles of the constitution are valid only because the amendment clause has not yet been used to abrogate them. But in principle any and every article of the constitution may be amended or abrogated validly. Legal and constitutional change are only limited by the amendment clause itself.[82] As long as the amendment clause is supreme, constitutional change is limited only by the will of 'the people' as represented by the electorate.

For example, a prevailing interpretation of the amendment clause of the US Constitution, Article V, is that it is *virtually* supreme because it can be applied to every article of the US Constitution, including the Bill of Rights and other amendments. The sole exception is that 'no state, without its consent, shall be deprived of its equal suffrage in the Senate'. Similarly, the amendment clause of the Fundamental Law of Hungary, Article S, is supreme because it is formally unlimited.

Yet it is the very supremacy of the amendment clause that enables direct legal revolution. When it is supreme, the amendment clause can be used to abrogate any and every aspect of the written constitution. This includes articles that appear to codify the democratic identity of the constitution, be it voting rights, basic liberal rights, or even the amendment clause itself. Through the supremacy of the

---

[80] Kent Greenawalt, 'The Rule of Recognition and the Constitution' (1987) 85(4) Michigan Law Review 625, 632.

[81] Klein (n 38) 66–67; Scriba (n 76) 87.

[82] Scriba (n 76) 102.

amendment clause, it is *in principle* possible for a democracy to be amended, legally and incrementally, into a totalitarian state.

The supremacy of the amendment clause collapses two conceptual distinctions in practice. First, it collapses any distinction between constitutional amendment and legal revolution. When any article of the constitution may be valid amended, then there is no legal criterion to distinguish essential from inessential articles of the constitution. From this perspective, the procedurally valid use of the amendment clause is not a revolutionary act. Moreover, it seems to be democratically legitimate because it ensures that the public order continues to correspond to the will of 'the people'.

Second, the supremacy of the amendment clause collapses any distinction between 'the people' as the constituting power and the electorate (or its elected representatives) as a constituted power. Ferrara defines that conception of sovereignty as 'serial' because it invests full constituent power in the present electorate, treating it as completely separated from both past and future generations of that same 'the people'—not to mention any normative conception of democracy.[83] Serial sovereignty is analogous to a property owner being fully entitled to dispose of that property however they please. Under this conception, because 'the people' is just a juristic fiction, its most authoritative material representative—the present electorate—has the right to wield its constituent power.[84] Arato and Cohen warn this risks 'obliterating' the distinction between extraordinary and normal powers.[85]

Insofar as the amendment clause is supreme, whoever is constitutionally authorized to use it legally and constitutionally wields 'the people's' constitutive power, even if as a secondary or delegated authority.[86] A constituted power with the formal legal power to completely refashion the public order can become sovereign in practice, even if that power is thought to be limited super-positively.[87] The supremacy of the amendment clause thus blurs the distinction between a constituted and a constituting power. Yet, at least at first glance, that blurred distinction seems

---

[83] Ferrara, *Sovereignty Across Generations* (n 11) 4, 9, 209.

[84] Andrew Arato, 'Multi-Track Constitutionalism beyond Carl Schmitt' (2011) 18(3) Constellations 324, 340.

[85] Andrew Arato and Jean L Cohen, *Populism and Civil Society: The Challenge to Constitutional Democracy* (Oxford University Press 2022) 184, 195.

[86] David Dyzenhaus, 'The Politics of the Question of Constituent Power' in Martin Loughlin and Neil Walker (eds), *The Paradox of Constitutionalism* (Oxford University Press 2007) 131; Yaniv Roznai, *Unconstitutional Constitutional Amendments: The Limits of Amendment Powers* (Oxford University Press 2017) 121–33; Scheppele, 'Autocratic Legalism' (n 3) 573–74, 577; Huq and Ginsburg, 'How to Lose a Constitutional Democracy' (n 3) 124ff.

[87] Because of the danger it poses to the public order, Arato argues that 'popular sovereignty' should be reconceived as merely a negative 'blocking' concept, whose function is to convey that 'the people' cannot be adequately represented by anyone: Arato, *The Adventures of the Constituent Power: Beyond Revolutions?* (n 70) 28. In general, see Arato, *Post Sovereign Constitution Making* (n 69). However, as long as the procedural pathways to legal revolution remain open, it is not clear what conceiving of 'the people' as a negative blocking concept will accomplish.

48 DEMOCRACY'S PROBLEM OF LEGAL REVOLUTION

justified on democratic grounds: even if it risks a 'wanton republic', as Ferrara refers to it,[88] it seems like the present electorate must have the best claim to represent 'the people'. Anything else risks authoritarianism.

Many constitutional theorists today seem to at least implicitly believe that the amendment clause should be designed to be the supreme clause in order to reflect the most fundamental normative commitments of modern constitutionalism. This belief rests on a civic republican conception of democracy, namely that *legitimate* democratic order must rest ultimately on a radical democratic foundation.[89] The electorate has the right, as the most valid representative of 'the people', to use the positive legal procedures however it wills, even if it uses them to reconstitute the public order in its entirety.

The supremacy of the amendment clause seems necessary to meet the requirements of modern constitutionalism institutionally. However, that supremacy also seems to challenge the intuition that direct forms of legal revolution might be substantively illegitimate. At least at first glance, if we accept that the amendment clause must be the supreme clause of the constitution for a constitution to be democratic, then it seems to follow that modern constitutionalism requires the possibility of direct legal revolution.

Indirect Legal Revolution and the Legal Possession of State Power

If exercising the amendment clause is not possible, would-be revolutionaries may still be able to use the law to undermine the democratic identity of the constitution indirectly. They can do so by exercising their political rights and competing to hold public office, which would grant them the legal possession of state power and the political premium attached to it if successful. Controlling the main powers of government may be enough for antidemocrats to sidestep the constitution, or at least its democratic substance, without needing constitutional change.

Electoral Victory and the Claim to State Power

A democratic electoral victory authorizes a representative to possess and exercise the legal powers of that office.[90] Taken individually, these powers are usually both eminently reasonable and necessary.[91] Even the more extreme powers, such as emergency powers, are often recognized to be necessary. Lazar, for example, argues

---

[88] Ferrara, *Sovereignty Across Generations* (n 11) 211–16.

[89] Arato, *The Adventures of the Constituent Power: Beyond Revolutions?* (n 70) 366–77.

[90] Ernst-Wolfgang Böckenförde, 'Der deutsche Katholizismus im Jahr 1933. Eine kritische Betrachtung' (Hochland 1961) 215, 236.

[91] See Kim Lane Scheppele, 'The Rule of Law and the Frankenstate: Why Governance Checklists Do Not Work' (2013) 26(4) Governance: An International Journal of Policy, Administration, and Institutions 559.

that the possibility of a genuine emergency threatening the state justifies and legitimates the provision of powers to respond to its urgency and scale.[92]

Holding public office can carry a significant political premium, especially at higher levels.[93] Holders obtain the rational–legal authority to issue directives and commands, which puts at their disposal the entire state administrative machinery along with its civil servants. As long as they remain within the bounds of legality, elected officials can expect passive, if not active, support from civil servants.[94] An elected representative can thereby harness the coordinated power of all of the bureaucrats that serve their particular office to advance their political goals.

That political premium extends into civil society. In a democracy, members' loyalty must rest first and foremost with the outcome of formally valid democratic procedures. Elected representatives can expect each citizen to respect and obey their lawful decisions in office, regardless of whether individual citizens agree with the substance of their decisions.

Finally, that political premium also offers a temporal advantage, by virtue of being able to initiate legal processes. For example, when an elected representative issues a formally valid directive or command, subordinates tasked with executing it may have little legal ground for opposition. Institutional checks and balances on formally valid acts are typically reactive and are often slowed by a lengthy process of judicial review. That dynamic provides a significant temporal advantage to elected representatives in active branches of government, in particular the executive.

Antidemocrats in Power

When antidemocrats win public office, they can use the power of their office and its political premium to undermine democracy indirectly. In particular, they can exploit the tension between the legality and illegitimacy of their actions to advance their political goals.

Elected representatives' rational-legal authority tends to have a particularly strong influence over segments of society committed to 'law and order', including the military and police, civil servants, social conservatives, and the middle classes.[95] The Weimar Republic offers a poignant illustration of this.[96] After the

---

[92] See Nomi Claire Lazar, *States of Emergency in Liberal Democracies* (Cambridge University Press 2009).

[93] The concept 'the political premium of the legal possession of state power' was coined by Schmitt while discussing the threat of the KPD and NSDAP seizing power. See Schmitt 31–32, 98–100; Carl Schmitt, 'The Legal World Revolution' (1987) 72 Telos 73, 76; Carl Schmitt, 'Was bedeutet der Streit um den 'Rechtsstaat'?' in Günter Maschke (ed), *Staat, Großraum, Nomos: Arbeiten aus den Jahren 1916-1969* (Dunker & Humblot 1995) 125–26; Carlo Galli, *La Genealogia della Politica: Carl Schmitt e la crisi del pensiero politico moderno* (Il Mulino 1996) 645, 857.

[94] Frank Hertweck, Dimitrios Kisoudis, and Gerd Giesler (eds), *'Solange das Imperium da ist': Carl Schmitt im Gespräch mit Klaus Figge und Dieter Groh 1971* (Duncker & Humblot 2010) 95–96.

[95] See Ermakoff, 'Law against the Rule of Law' (n 15) 181–82.

[96] Wolfgang Sauer, 'Die Mobilmachung der Gewalt' in Karl Dietrich Bracher, Gerhard Schulz, and Wolfgang Sauer (eds), *Die nationalsozialistische Machtergreifung Studien zur Errichtung des totalitären Herrschaftssystems in Deutschland 1933/34* (Springer Fachmedien Wiesbaden 1960) 710; Bracher,

50 DEMOCRACY'S PROBLEM OF LEGAL REVOLUTION

NSDAP took over the leadership of Weimar's ministries, bureaucrats committed to the republic faced a dilemma: did upholding Weimar democracy mean obeying the lawfully formulated commands of their new superiors, out of respect for the democratic process? Faced with that dilemma and in the absence of any coordinated efforts, many found it difficult to oppose, let alone check, the decisions of those in power. Many chose to respect the formal legality of their decisions, perceiving correctly that the law itself is a normative order and preferring its practical clarity over the ambiguities that other normative orders can present.

A more sinister dimension of the tension between legality and legitimacy involves the sometimes underestimated role that ordinary citizens can play in undermining democracy. Because legality has its own normative power, ordinary citizens may view a conflict between legality and legitimacy as a choice between two equally weighted norms. Svolik describes how antidemocrats exploit that dilemma to advance their political goals.[97] For example, members may have to decide between a candidate who satisfies their immediate partisan interests or one who upholds democratic fundamentals in an election. Antidemocratic politicians may promise to increase material redistribution or to constitutionalize a particular religion—as Chavez and Erdoğan have done. When society is sufficiently polarized, Svolik argues, ordinary citizens privilege their partisan interests as long as a legal pathway to satisfy them exists, even if it means sacrificing democratic norms in the process.

Because of the temporal advantage that comes with the legal possession of state power, it can be difficult to prevent and reverse antidemocrats' use of the powers of their office. In some cases, there may be no legal checks on their exercise. Even when institutional checks do exist, that temporal advantage can nullify them in practice. For example, in 1962 de Gaulle bypassed the constitution and unilaterally convened a constitutional referendum, aimed at strengthening the presidency—his office—at parliament's expense. Although the referendum was unconstitutional, the Constitutional Council, the French Constitution's guardian, interpreted the public's approval of de Gaulle's change as a 'direct expression of national sovereignty' that superseded its illegality.[98] Consider another somewhat hypothetical scenario: in advance of a presidential election, an antidemocratic party manipulates voter registration laws to disenfranchise voters backing the opposition. Were that party's deliberate suppression challenged and then successfully reversed

---

'Nachwort und Ausblick' (n 75) 971; Bracher, 'The Technique of the Nationalist Seizure of Power' (n 17) 126; Hans-Ulrich Thamer, *Verführung und Gewalt: Deutschland 1933-1945* (Siedler 1986) 272, 280; Hillgruber (n 18) 191.

[97] Milan W Svolik, 'Polarization versus Democracy' (2019) 30(3) Journal of Democracy 23–31.
[98] Bruce Ackerman, *Revolutionary Constitutions: Charismatic Leadership and the Rule of Law* (Harvard University Press 2019) 193.

in court only months after the election, the ramifications are unclear.[99] Would it trigger an extraordinary presidential election? Or the nullification of the laws that antidemocratic party passed following its election? These questions could trigger a constitutional crisis. What is clear is that antidemocrats have a significant temporal advantage if they can hold office legally, which they may use to create consequential fait accomplis that advance their revolutionary goals *before* any legal countermeasures can be deployed to undo them—if they can be undone at all.[100]

As the above typology of legal revolution demonstrates, indirect legal revolution can assume many different forms. In contrast with direct legal revolution, which is made possible by the amendment clause, there is no single cause of indirect forms of legal revolution. Moreover, many of the powers of public office that can be abused for indirect legal revolutionary ends seem to have a reasonable and often necessary foundation. Eliminating these powers is thus not a practical solution. The problem of indirect legal revolution is clearest when antidemocrats stitch together reasonable powers of public office to subvert democratic norms. In doing so, they transmute a democracy into what Scheppele terms an autocratic 'Frankenstate'.[101] Poland illustrates this problem.[102] By passing a series of acts that weakened the Polish Constitutional Tribunal's independence (such as the court packing described above), the PiS-led parliament freed itself to cripple basic liberal and political rights. Were the court genuinely independent, it likely would have struck down parliament's laws as unconstitutional. As parliament eroded those rights, PiS further marginalized the opposition, consolidating its power and becoming better equipped to realize its political goals.

At its core, the problem of indirect legal revolution appears rooted in the nature of democracy itself. When representatives win public office in a democracy, they secure a claim to each citizen's obedience to the lawful exercise of their powers. There does not seem to be a way to erect legal guardrails to ensure that every legal power of public office is exercised in the pursuit of substantively 'democratic' ends. Antidemocrats have long recognized that. Even if they are not strong enough to rewrite the constitution directly, they may still be able to undermine democracy using other legal means. Thus, the crux of the problem of indirect legal revolution may be that antidemocrats have the opportunity to compete for and hold public office at all.

---

[99] See Jack M Balkin and Sanford Levinson, 'Understanding the Constitutional Revolution' (2001) 87(6) Virginia Law Review 1045, 1048.

[100] Schmitt, 'The Legal World Revolution' (n 93) 74.

[101] Scheppele, 'The Rule of Law and the Frankenstate' (n 91). Roznai uses Eubulides' paradox, which questions when individual grains become a heap, to convey the same idea. See Yaniv Roznai, 'The Straw that Broke the Back of the Constitution? When Quantity Transforms to Quality' (2021) International Journal of Constitutional Law Blog 559–562. <https://www.iconnectblog.com/the-straw-that-broke-the-back-of-the-constitution-when-quantity-transforms-to-quality/> accessed 17 March 2024.

[102] Sadurski (n 39) 267–71.

Legal Revolution and Democracy

The problem facing liberal democracies is thus not populism or any other ideology per se. The underlying problem is that enemies of democracy have the capability to abuse formally valid legal procedures to alter the democratic substance and identity of the constitution.

The most visible and damaging form of legal revolution occurs directly, when the constitutional supremacy of the amendment clause is used to alter the democratic substance of the constitution itself. If they are unable to exercise the amendment clause directly, antidemocrats can also employ more subtle indirect tactics to harm democracy, such as breaching the constitution, breaking down the separation and balance of powers, and eroding fundamental rights. Preventing legal revolution also requires safeguarding democratic constitutional essentials by ensuring that antidemocrats cannot wield the legal powers of public office against them.

Although democrats may broadly agree that turning democratic legal procedures against democracy is both illegitimate and undesirable, formulating a response to legal revolution is a difficult exercise. The mechanisms that can be exploited for legal revolution seem to be democratic essentials. Normative theory seems to require that democratic institutions be designed that way. For that reason, legal revolution seems to be a kind of shadow of democratic constitutionalism. Legal revolution's roots in the norms of modern constitutionalism place democrats in an awkward and, at first glance, intractable position when it comes to defending democracy against legal revolutionary tactics.

The phenomenon of legal revolution raises two interrelated and pressing questions. First, how can democratic normative theory justify defending democratic essentials against legal revolution without betraying its commitment to democratic values and modern constitutionalism? Second, how exactly should democratic constitutions be designed in order to best safeguard them against internal antidemocrats? The rest of this book answers those questions.

2
Militant Democracy

Introduction

'Militant democracy' offers a defence against the legal revolution of democratic constitutional essentials. It can be defined as mechanisms of constitutional entrenchment that pre-emptively deny antidemocrats the legal democratic means to revolutionize democracy.[1] Many democratic constitutions adopted measures of militant democracy following the Second World War. However, it is only recently that political and legal theorists have begun to fully consider the legitimacy of militant democracy. It is up to normative theories of militant democracy to determine the democratic legitimacy of its mechanisms.

Existing normative theories of militant democracy, without exception, converge on defending a rather narrow conception of 'democracy', understood as the guarantee of formally equal political rights, such as the right to vote and hold public office, and value-neutral majoritarian procedures.[2] In order to entrench that narrow conception of 'democracy', those theories tend to analyse the democratic legitimacy of just a single defensive measure: the party ban. That focus allows normative theories of militant democracy to identify and respond to certain threats to democracy, such as antidemocrats who work to disenfranchise a specific segment of the population.

However, that narrow focus leaves militant democracy ill-equipped to identify and respond to the most pressing threat to democracy today: antidemocratic members who pursue so-called 'illiberal democracy' through legal revolutionary tactics. There are several reasons for that oversight.

First, they are unable to recognize illiberalism as a threat to democracy. Rijpkema has termed this the 'detection problem' of militant democracy.[3] Antidemocrats today, many populists for example, tend to leave political rights intact enough for the state they govern to continue to qualify as a democracy, at least according to

---

[1] See Jan-Werner Müller, 'The Problem of Peer Review in Militant Democracy' in Uladzislau Belavusau and Aleksandra Gliszczyńska-Grabias (eds), *Constitutionalism under Stress* (Oxford University Press 2020) 259.

[2] I am indebted to Alex Kirshner for suggesting this framing of militant democracy.

[3] Bastiaan Rijpkema, 'Militant Democracy and the Detection Problem' in Anthoula Malkopoulou and Alexander S Kirshner (eds), *Militant Democracy and Its Critics: Populism, Parties, Extremism* (Edinburgh University Press 2019).

Democracy despite Itself. Benjamin A. Schupmann, Oxford University Press. © Benjamin A. Schupmann 2024.
DOI: 10.1093/9780191975950.003.0003

a narrow conception of democracy. They instead concentrate on rolling back institutions of liberal constitutionalism, such as the separation of powers and basic rights. Existing theories of militant democracy are generally unable to recognize the dangers of populism and 'illiberal democracy'. As a result, they cannot justify defending democracy against the legal revolutionary tactics of those types of antidemocrats.

Second, existing normative theories suffer from 'the paradox of democracy's self-defence', which also arises from that narrow focus on political rights. When they do identify a party as a threat to democracy, these normative theories defend political rights restrictions, which at first glance seem to compromise the very democratic values that they seek to defend—the formal guarantee of *every* member's political rights. The paradox is thus that the measures taken to defend democratic constitutional essentials seem to degrade democracy itself. Critics, highlighting this potential contradiction, argue that militant democracy leads to problems such as legal indeterminacy, unchecked discretionary authority, and the depoliticization of issues that should be left to 'the people' to decide. Existing normative theories of militant democracy thus seem to rest on a normative contradiction.

Third, advocates of militant democracy, concerned about the legitimacy of deploying militant measures at all, tend to argue that they should only be a last resort—when antidemocrats pose an imminent existential threat to democracy. That hesitation gives rise to a different, practical paradox: by the time militant measures can be deployed legitimately, they may no longer be practically effective against antidemocrats. Existing normative theories reflect a lack of confidence in the legitimacy of militant democracy, which can have consequences for their practical application.

Finally, existing normative theories of militant democracy do not discuss measures besides the party ban, in particular unamendability and a guardian of the constitution. As discussed in the introduction, both unamendability and a guardian of the constitution are crucial for reinforcing as well as tempering the legitimate use of political rights restrictions. That interrelationship is exemplified in the paradigmatic militant democratic constitution: the German *Basic Law*. Existing theories' narrow focus on party bans leaves them disconnected from the real-world practice of militant democracy. Given that disparity, coupled with the interrelationship between political rights restrictions and other entrenchment mechanisms, these theories offer a limited theory of the legitimacy and limits of political rights restrictions.

By analysing those shortcomings in detail, this chapter sets the stage for a radical reassessment of both the legitimacy and limits of militant democracy's capacity to address the problem of legal revolution, topics which will be taken up in the second and third sections of this book.

Normative Theories of Militant Democracy

Normative theories of militant democracy argue that a democracy may entrench itself using measures that pre-emptively deny antidemocrats the legal democratic means to revolutionize democracy.[4] Articulating a normative theory of militant democracy is essential because, at least at first glance, measures of militant democracy may seem antidemocratic themselves.

Normative theories of militant democracy today focus almost exclusively on the party ban. As defined by Niesen, the party ban encompasses 'all juridical forms that effectively prevent the founding and continued operation of political parties, whether in the form of dissolution, substantive registration requirements, temporary suspension, or prohibition of and prosecution for party formation'.[5]

Because of that exclusive focus, Malkopoulou argues, the terms 'militant democracy' and 'party ban' are used almost interchangeably in normative theory today.[6] However, the party ban is only the most visible form of militant democracy. Even political rights restrictions can take a variety of less extreme forms. Some scholars adopt a more expansive view of this dimension of constitutional entrenchment. Müller, for example, explores other targets of political rights restrictions, including associations and individuals.[7] Both Capoccia and Issacharoff identify alternatives to an outright ban. Issacharoff discusses how a democracy can defend itself by temporarily limiting an antidemocratic party's access to the electoral arena—a policy that India has implemented for example.[8] Capoccia adds other milder forms of rights restriction, including on antidemocratic messaging and propaganda, prohibitions of certain symbols, limits on rights of assembly and public demonstration, and controls on the spread of misinformation and fake news.[9] Nevertheless, normative theorizing about militant democracy tends to remain narrowly focused

---

[4] This definition builds on others' definitions of militant democracy. See Patrick Macklem, 'Militant Democracy, Legal Pluralism, and The Paradox of Self-Determination' (2012) 19(4) International Journal of Constitutional Law, 488; Samuel Issacharoff, 'Fragile Democracies' (2007) 120(6) Harvard Law Review, 1406; Jan-Werner Müller, 'Militant Democracy' in Michel Rosenfeld and András Sajó (eds), *The Oxford Handbook of Comparative Constitutional Law* (Oxford University Press 2012) 1253; András Sajó, 'Militant Democracy and Emotional Politics' (2012) 19(4) Constellations, 562; Peter Niesen, 'Banning the Former Ruling Party' (2012) 19(4) Constellations, 540; Alexander S Kirshner, *A Theory of Militant Democracy: The Ethics of Combatting Political Extremism* (Yale University Press 2014) 6–7, 11; Svetlana Tyulkina, *Militant Democracy: Undemocratic Political Parties and Beyond* (Routledge 2015) 185; Anthoula Malkopoulou and Ludvig Norman, 'Three Models of Democratic Self-Defence: Militant Democracy and Its Alternatives' (2018) 66(2) Political Studies 442; Bastiaan Rijpkema, *Militant Democracy: The Limits of Democratic Tolerance* (Routledge 2018) 153–54, 194.

[5] Niesen (n 4) 541.

[6] Anthoula Malkopoulou, 'Militant Democracy and Its Critics' in Malkopoulou and Kirshner (n 3) 2; see also Alexander S Kirshner, 'Militant Democracy Defended' in ibid, 56.

[7] Jan-Werner Müller, 'Individual Militant Democracy' in Malkopoulou and Kirshner (n 3).

[8] Issacharoff (n 4) 1447ff.

[9] Giovanni Capoccia, *Defending Democracy: Reactions to Extremism in Interwar Europe* (Johns Hopkins University Press 2005) 59–63.

56   MILITANT DEMOCRACY

on the party ban. That focus overshadows discussions of other effective methods of constitutional entrenchment against legal revolution, whether alternative forms of political rights restrictions or entirely different mechanisms.

In addition to their narrow focus on political rights restrictions, normative theories of militant democracy also converge on a narrow definition of the essence of 'democracy'. That normative core of democracy is proceduralist, defined by members' formally equal political rights, such as the right to vote and hold public office, and value-neutral majoritarian decision-making.

Some normative theories of militant democracy include value-neutral procedures in their definitions of democracy, arguing that what is essential is not the content of any decision per se, but that whatever decisions are made, they must be in principle reversible through democratic legal procedures. Müller, for instance, draws on Lefort's concept of 'institutionalized uncertainty' to define the normative essence of democracy, which militant measures ought to entrench. That normative core is members' formally equal chance to form a majority and pursue their political goals, whatever those goals may be.[10] Similarly, Issacharoff, Macklem, and Rijpkema all define the essence of democracy in terms of the procedural possibilities for future majorities to reverse or 'self-correct' the decisions of present majorities, whatever those present decisions are.[11] Jovanović also presents his normative theory of militant democracy as a defence of value-neutral proceduralism, arguing that democracy is akin to a game: 'players' may play however they like, as long as they adhere to its formal 'rules'.[12] Tyulkina, by conceiving of democracy in indefinite and inherently plural terms, also seems to endorse definition of democracy similar to Lefort's institutionalized certainty.[13] Whatever their differences, these scholars all agree that militant democracy is about defending formally equal rights playing out in value-neutral procedures whose output may be reversed by future generations.

The 'concentric model' of democracy's self-defence, developed by Rummens, Abts, and Sottiaux, aims to balance value-neutral proceduralism and substantive values (in particular 'liberty' and 'equality').[14] However, that model argues that members themselves must have the final say in deciding and redeciding the concrete

---

[10] See for example Jan-Werner Müller, 'A "Practical Dilemma Which Philosophy Alone Cannot Resolve"? Rethinking Militant Democracy: An Introduction' (2012) 19(4) Constellations 488; Jan-Werner Müller, 'Protecting Popular Self-Government from the People? New Normative Perspectives on Militant Democracy' (2016) 19 Annual Review of Political Science 25–254; Jan-Werner Müller, Democracy Rules (Farrar, Straus and Giroux 2021) 62–64, 71–72.

[11] Issacharoff (n 4) 1411, 1464–65; Patrick Macklem, 'Guarding the Perimeter: Militant Democracy and Religious Freedom in Europe' (2012) 19(4) Constellations, 500, 505; Rijpkema, Militant Democracy (n 4) 11, 37, 134–36, 170.

[12] Miodrag Jovanović, 'How to Justify "Militant Democracy": Meta-Ethics and the Game-Like Character of Democracy' (2016) 42(8) Philosophy and Social Criticism 745, 752.

[13] Tyulkina (n 4) 1, 30.

[14] Stefan Rummens and Koen Abts, 'Defending Democracy: The Concentric Containment of Political Extremism' (2010) 58 Political Studies 650.

meaning of those substantive values.[15] Because it rests on that radical democratic foundation, the concentric model in the end also conceives of democracy as an open-ended and value-neutral proceduralism.[16] In this regard, the concentric model appears to defend the same normative core as the above-mentioned theories.

Normative theories of militant democracy may instead focus their defence of democracy on the entrenchment of members' political rights, rather than value-neutral procedures. Rosenblum and Niesen, for example, both argue that militant democracy defends members' equal political rights, which guarantee that each has a formally equal chance to translate their beliefs, values, and interests into law.[17] Echoing that sentiment, Kirshner argues that every citizen holds an indefeasible equal claim to participate, which again takes the institutional form of political rights.[18] Because they are preconditions for valid democracy, Kirshner argues that those rights must remain inviolable, however members choose to exercise them.[19] Similarly, Vinx conceives of democratic legitimacy in terms of the commitment to 'equal chance', institutionalized through formal political rights and the supremacy of legislative procedures.[20]

Existing normative theories of militant democracy vary in their emphasis on democracy's essence. Some focus on value-neutral procedures and others on members' formally equal political rights. But these really just capture different facets of the same underlying, narrow conception of democracy—one notable in part because it does not mention liberal constitutionalism. Regardless of their emphasis, these normative theories all agree that their role is to justify the use of political rights restrictions to defend that normative core.

The Problem of Detection and Illiberalism

As a result, existing normative theories of militant democracy have some theoretical and practical shortcomings, which leave them poorly equipped to address some of the most pressing problems facing many democracies around the world today.

---

[15] ibid; Stefan Rummens, 'Resolving the Paradox of Tolerance' in Malkopoulou and Kirshner (n 3) 119.

[16] Stefan Sottiaux and Stefan Rummens, 'Concentric Democracy: Resolving the Incoherence in the European Court of Human Rights' (2012) 10(1) Case Law on Freedom of Expression and Freedom of Association' 106, 117.

[17] Peter Niesen, 'Anti-Extremism, Negative Republicanism, Civic Society: Three Paradigms for Banning Political Parties' (2002) 03(07) German Law Journal, 2; Niesen, 'Banning the Former Ruling Party' (n 4) 19; Nancy Rosenblum, 'Banning Parties: Religious and Ethnic Partisanship in Multicultural Democracies' (2007) 1(1) Law & Ethics of Human Rights 21, 60.

[18] Kirshner, A Theory of Militant Democracy (n 4) 5–6, 24, 33, 36, 117.

[19] ibid 35–37, 40–47; Kirshner, 'Militant Democracy Defended' (n 6) 59.

[20] Lars Vinx, 'Democratic Equality and Militant Democracy' (2020) 27(4) Constellations 685, 687–89.

58 MILITANT DEMOCRACY

One significant challenge facing existing normative theories of militant democracy is a significant blind spot regarding genuinely popular movements pursuit of certain goals like 'illiberal democracy'. These movements undermine democracy by legally revolutionizing fundamentals of liberal constitutionalism, in the separation and balance of powers and basic liberal rights. Notably, however, they leave both political rights and procedures of legal change largely intact. Few thinkers would accept majoritarian procedures decoupled from liberal constitutionalism as genuine democracy.[21] Yet, because of the way that they conceive of democracy, existing normative theories fail to recognize 'illiberal democracy' as an existential threat to democracy, let alone provide a justification for militant defences against it.

Rijpkema suggests that militant democracy suffers from a 'detection problem'. The criteria necessary to identify an antidemocratic threat both accurately and in time to prevent it are underdetermined.[22] In order for a democratic state to deploy militant measures to defend itself, some authority, like a judge, must be able to transparently and defensibly determine whether that target genuinely represents an antidemocratic threat. Rijpkema argues—rightly—that the criteria for detection must be as legally determinate as possible.[23] Legal determinacy serves two purposes. First, it deters politically-motivated abuses of militant measures by reducing their discretionary deployment. It helps uphold the rule of law when militant measures are deployed. Second, legal determinacy plays an informative role. It communicates to political parties what actions might trigger sanctions, clarifying the legal limits of political goals.

Existing normative theories of militant democracy only recognize actors who threaten that narrow conception of democracy as genuine threats and therefore as potential candidates for a militant response. They do not recognize other actions, for example infringements on religious liberties or due process, as undemocratic if they may in principle be reversed in the future. The consequence is that, as long as actors acquire state power legally and democratically and as long as they leave democracy's basic procedural components intact enough, normative theories of militant democracy cannot justify responding to them, no matter what else they do.

Due to its blind spots, Rovira Kaltwasser argues that militant democracy is poorly equipped to respond to the most pressing challenge to democracy today: illiberal populist parties.[24] Unlike past antidemocrats, populists do not typically aim to abolish democracy, narrowly construed. To the contrary, they

---

[21] Andrew Arato and Jean L Cohen, *Populism and Civil Society: The Challenge to Constitutional Democracy* (Oxford University Press 2022) 145.
[22] Rijpkema, 'Militant Democracy and the Detection Problem' (n 3) 169.
[23] ibid 177.
[24] Cristóbal Rovira Kaltwasser, 'Militant Democracy versus Populism' in Malkopoulou and Kirshner (n 3) 85.

conceive of themselves as genuinely democratic actors. They generally leave democratic institutions like political rights and majoritarian procedures intact. They are antidemocratic because they procedurally degrade minority rights, civil society's independence, and institutional checks and balances on their power.

To be sure, populists in power may also degrade political rights, using tactics such as gerrymandering and voter registration laws. Yet it is not clear whether those actions merit a militant response under any existing normative theory of militant democracy. Moreover, it is not clear to what extent antidemocratic populists differ from 'normal' democratic parties in that regard. After all, even normal democratic parties gerrymander. And every democracy needs a process for registering voters. So although populists differ from 'normal' democratic parties, that difference seems to be one of degree rather than kind, at least regarding changes to 'democracy' narrowly construed. Existing theories cannot identify contemporary antidemocratic parties and leaders, such as Fidesz, the BJP, the AKP, and Netanyahu, as democratic threats as long as they leave political rights and mechanisms of legal change alone.

Contemporary antidemocrats' use of legal revolutionary methods presents a second type of detection problem for existing normative theories of militant democracy. They backslide democracy by introducing changes that, when viewed individually, may seem both legally and morally unobjectionable. And, although their political end goals may seem obviously undemocratic, contemporary antidemocrats rarely publicize their tactics or the steps employed to achieve their ultimate goals.[25] Instead, they insist on their democratic credentials and strict adherence to the letter of the law. Scheppele argues that the true nature of their threat only becomes evident after analysing their acts as a whole, which create what she has famously called a democratic 'Frankenstate'.[26] Their commitment to formal legality masks that threat and allows them to appear as dedicated to democracy as any other party. That appearance leaves genuine democrats struggling to find a firm basis for the deployment of militant measures.

Despite remaining within legal boundaries, 'illiberal democrats' are widely seen as the most serious threat to democracy in the twenty-first century. This is clearest in the latest Freedom House report, which shows that democracy entered its seventeenth year of decline in 2023.[27] Its authors argue that the leading indicator of democratic decline is the erosion of guarantees of free expression, in particular a free media and free personal expression. The erosion of democracy occurs mainly today through internal legal processes, driven by popularly elected representatives.

---

[25] I am indebted to Jan-Werner Müller for raising this point.

[26] Kim Lane Scheppele, 'The Rule of Law and the Frankenstate: Why Governance Checklists Do Not Work' (2013) 26(4) Governance: An International Journal of Policy, Administration, and Institutions 559.

[27] Freedom House, 'Freedom in the World 2023' (March 2023) <https://freedomhouse.org/sites/defa ult/files/2023-03/FIW_World_2023_DigtalPDF.pdf>.

60 MILITANT DEMOCRACY

Some theorists of militant democracy acknowledge that detection problem. For instance, Rijpkema recognizes that, if a party only eliminated basic liberal rights, it would not be a valid target for measures of militant democracy.[28] Members of a democracy retain their political rights. And the decision to eliminate basic liberal rights could be reversed with democratic procedures in the future. Of course, 'illiberal democrats' exploit that blind spot. By eroding liberal constitutional safeguards, they not only promote their objectives, such as ethno-nationalism, they also consolidate their power. All while maintaining enough of an institutional veneer to proclaim their democratic legitimacy.[29]

The above criticism should not be interpreted to mean that existing normative theories of militant democracy do not have any value for democracy's self-defence. Kirshner convincingly theorizes the role that militant democracy should play when antidemocrats threaten *political* rights, as they did during in the Reconstruction and in the context of the Voting Rights Act in the United States in the nineteenth and twentieth centuries, respectively.[30] In a similar vein, Niesen shows how 'banning the former ruling party', which many post-fascist democracies have done, plays an important stabilizing and symbolic role, which allows a new democracy to move on from a past antidemocratic regime.

Yet, when it comes to contemporary threats to democracy—particularly from populist 'illiberal democrats'—existing normative theories seem to be looking the wrong way. That blind spot underscores the need to reevaluate how normative theories of militant democracy detect threats, as well as to undertake deeper reflection about what must be safeguarded for a democracy to remain a democracy at all.

The Paradox of Democracy's Self-Defence

A second challenge facing existing normative theories of militant democracy is what Müller calls the democratic dilemma or paradox.[31] Kirshner calls this 'the paradox of democracy's self-defence'. At its core, this paradox implies that using militant measures to defend democracy degrades it no less than whatever antidemocratic threats those measures aim to contain. If we believe that political rights are the *sine qua non* of democracy, then a party ban, because it restricts members' political rights, seems to do serious damage to democracy. Democracies thus face a normative dilemma: Refraining from employing militant measures seems to degrade democracy passively, by allowing internal antidemocrats to act unhindered.

---

[28] Rijpkema, *Militant Democracy* (n 4) 154.
[29] Peter J Verovšek, '"The Nation Has Conquered the State": Arendtian Insights on the Internal Contradictions of the Nation-State' (2023) Review of International Studies.
[30] Kirshner, *A Theory of Militant Democracy* (n 4) 144–68.
[31] Müller, 'Militant Democracy' (n 4) 1254.

THE PARADOX OF DEMOCRACY'S SELF-DEFENCE   61

Employing militant measures seems to degrade democracy actively, by directly compromising its core principles. Thus, the paradox is that democracy will be degraded no matter what democrats do.

Criticisms of Militant Democracy

Many criticisms of militant democracy build on the normative problems introduced by this paradox. Critics argue that, because political rights restrictions themselves degrade democracy, militant democracy cannot be justified as a defence of democracy. This criticism centres on the following two concerns:

First, the criteria for deploying repressive measures of militant democracy seem to be legally indeterminate. That indeterminacy deformalizes the rule of law. Whoever has the authority to deploy political rights restrictions may rely on extra- or superlegal criteria to judge what is a threat to democracy. That grants the state undue discretionary authority to decide when to deploy political rights restrictions. (A case in point is their use against religious parties that pose no threat to democracy, such as the case of Refah, which I take up below.)

Second, militant democracy risks depoliticizing issues that should, in a genuine democracy, be left to 'the people' to decide. The use of militant measures to forestall politically popular changes *incorrectly* presupposes that some matters can be settled once and for all and may accordingly be taken off the political agenda.

Critics tend not to distinguish these two issues due to their overlap. They typically focus on the problem of depoliticization. However, legal indeterminacy poses a distinctive problem that should be examined on its own. Addressing one of these concerns does not necessarily resolve the other.

Legal Indeterminacy and State Discretionary Authority

Critics, such as Invernizzi-Accetti and Zuckerman, argue that militant democracy is inherently arbitrary because of the paradox and the difficulty in proscribing what actions may trigger a repression of a party's political rights. The problem with militant democracy, they argue, is that political actors can be deprived of their fundamental rights for using them legally. Militant democracy is legally indeterminate because what actions would trigger a repressive response cannot be specified clearly in advance.[32]

Legal determinacy is a defining feature of the formal rule of law, which is typically considered a cornerstone of democracy. Among other things, the formal rule of law stipulates that sanctions should only be applied on the basis of clear, publicly known and general rules that are applied impartially and equally to all cases and

---

[32] Carlo Invernizzi-Accetti and Ian Zuckerman, 'What's Wrong with Militant Democracy?' (2017) 65(1) Political Studies 187ff.

62   MILITANT DEMOCRACY

promulgated in advance. [33] That general form ensures that like cases will be treated in like ways. The rule of law is essential to democracy because it helps guarantee the accountability of state power, by constraining state actions to those pre-sanctioned by 'the people'. In addition, it offers clarity on what actions might elicit a state response, helping members to remain within the confines of the law without facing unwanted penalties.

Legal indeterminacy presents a normative problem because it frees state authority from those legal guardrails, diminishing its accountability to 'the people'. As law deformalizes, an officeholder's discretion over how to exercise their legal powers increases. Even when done in good faith, that exercise can be unpredictable and inconsistent, creating uncertainty about what acts might trigger a sanction or whether the principle of equality before the law will be upheld. A deeper problem of the deformalization of the rule of law is it can be abused to paint a veneer of legal legitimacy over arbitrary actions taken to advance a powerholder's personal interests.

To reduce the problem of indeterminacy, existing normative theories of militant democracy often minimize what they aim to entrench through political rights restrictions. Defending only a minimal conception of democracy, namely political rights and majoritarian procedures, also narrows what might trigger a militant response. That simultaneously decreases the chance that political rights restrictions can be abused. For example, only organizations that overtly threaten political rights and procedures—such as the NSDAP or postbellum Southern Democrats—would be candidates for militant democracy's repressive measures. The disadvantage of this minimal conception, as discussed in the section above, is that it will fail to detect most contemporary threats to democracy.

When critics of militant democracy worry about discretionary authority, their concerns may stem from the use of repressive measures to uphold vaguely and extralegally defined values, such as 'pluralism', 'freedom', and 'equality'. When restrictions of political rights are not anchored in the violation of a positively defined statute, that indeterminacy does raise valid questions. For instance, who has the authority to decide what counts as democratic 'pluralism', when that may entail depriving others of their political rights? This is particularly problematic when, as militant democracy seems to argue, democratic essentials should not be left to voters to decide.

Of course, the formal rule of law will never be fully determinate. Kirshner points out that ambiguities, especially in the penumbra of a normal public order, allow powerholders to exercise considerable discretion.[34] However, there is a significant difference between, on the one hand, exercising interpretative discretion on

---

[33] Werner Heun, *The Constitution of Germany: A Contextual Analysis* (Hart Publishing 2011) 35ff; Judith N Shklar, 'Rights in the Liberal Tradition' (2023) 71(2) Political Studies 279, 280; William E Scheuerman, *The End of Law: Carl Schmitt in the Twenty-First Century* (Rowman & Littlefield International Ltd 2019) 4–5, 136.
[34] Kirshner, 'Militant Democracy Defended' (n 6) 64–65.

penumbral cases at the fringes of an otherwise determinate public order and, on the other, having the authority to decide what count as fundamental principles. It is one thing to levy a sanction for violating a predefined positive law, which actors can reasonably understand how to avoid violating. It is another to legally authorize an office holder to use repressive measures against a party that threatens a principle that he or she has the power to identify and define.

Critics like Invernizzi-Accetti and Zuckerman worry that, even when there are oversight mechanisms to hold those in power accountable, legal indeterminacy and discretionary authority can be abused to corrupt democracy.[35] In particular, they worry that office holders will be able to use that authority to systematically disenfranchise the opposition, in an intensified form of McCarthyism.

Even were that discretionary authority exercised in good faith, Rosenblum, Malkopoulou, and Norman democracy argue that democracy can still be degraded. With the uncertainty about what exactly could trigger the sanction of political rights restrictions, parties, associations, and even individuals may excessively self-censor their political goals and actions out of an abundance of caution.[36]

The Case of Refah

The potential for abuse of legal indeterminacy and discretionary authority is illustrated by militant democracy's growth into 'militant secularism'. This was exemplified by the Turkish Constitutional Court's 1998 decision to ban the Refah party, a verdict later upheld by the European Court of Human Rights in 2003. The Court argued that Refah threatened the Turkish state's secular integrity, suggesting that Refah's religious orientation hinted at a broader intent to refashion Turkey into an Islamic state governed by Shariah law. Critics of militant democracy, including Macklem and Rosenblum, argue that the Refah ban illustrates how militant democracy can degrade democracy.[37]

Responding to Refah, advocates of militant democracy argue that its mechanisms cannot legitimately be used to advance secularism or to target parties solely for their religious foundations. Discussing Refah, Kirshner writes that its goals, such as permitting women to wear religious attire in public universities or establishing Islamic marital courts did not pose any tangible threat to Turkish democracy.[38] He argues that, unless religious parties threaten political rights or democracy's underlying normative commitments, they are not legitimate targets of militant democracy's repressive measures. If anything, Refah seemed to lean toward expanding liberal values by promoting (religious) plurality in the public sphere. Similarly, other theorists argue that evicting religious parties from the

---

[35] Invernizzi-Accetti and Zuckerman (n 32) 190.
[36] Rosenblum (n 17) 53–55; Malkopoulou and Norman (n 4) 447.
[37] Rosenblum (n 17) 31, 62–64; Macklem, 'Guarding the Perimeter' (n 11) 579–81; see also Müller, 'Militant Democracy' (n 4) 1264–65.
[38] Kirshner, A Theory of Militant Democracy (n 4) 134–35

64 MILITANT DEMOCRACY

political arena based solely on religious identity contradicts the normative foundations of militant democracy.[39]

The underlying problem posed by Refah is that state authorities were able to redefine democracy to encompass secularism. That redefinition enabled them to champion the defence of 'democracy' against imagined incursions by religious parties and associations. Macklem has argued that the case of Refah illustrates the pitfalls of building militant democracy on a legally indeterminate foundation.[40] When state officials have broad discretion to determine what 'democracy' is, they can use that power legally but in bad faith. Militant democracy can thereby become a means for the already powerful to exclude certain segments of society, both by preventing them from participating in government and by symbolically asserting that they are not full members of 'the people'.

Whenever the decision to deploy militant measures is grounded in legal indeterminacy and discretionary authority, the potential for abuse becomes legally possible, as in the Refah case. Yet even well-intentioned authorities could unintentionally repress political rights, undermining the legitimacy of the entire public order. As Invernizzi-Accetti and Zuckerman suggest, those in power might genuinely believe that secularism is a precondition for democracy. Consequently, they may legally repress religious parties, restricting 'democratic membership within a misleadingly democratic guise'.[41] Cases like Refah underscore how legal indeterminacy and discretionary authority can inadvertently widen the scope of militant democracy's application beyond its designers' intentions.

Depoliticization

Besides the problems of legal indeterminacy and discretionary authority, critics worry that by ruling out certain constitutional changes, repressive measures depoliticize fundamental questions of public order. Rovira Kaltwasser argues that, by predefining what values or views constitute antidemocratic goals, militant democracy predetermines the answer to basic political questions.[42] Critics argue that in a genuine democracy, the electorate must have the last word on any decision, advancing a kind of radical democratic foundationalism. Because it takes options off the political agenda, these critics believe that militant democracy risks trivializing democracy.

Taking options off the political agenda, Nitzschner argues, reveals militant democracy's institutional conservativism: at its core, militant democracy embeds

---

[39] Niesen, 'Banning the Former Ruling Party' (n 4) 543; Jan-Werner Müller, 'Militant Democracy and Constitutional Identity' in Gary Jacobsohn and Miguel Schor (eds), *Comparative Constitutional Theory* (Edward Elgar 2018) 425.

[40] Macklem, 'Guarding the Perimeter' (n 11) 585ff.

[41] Invernizzi-Accetti and Zuckerman (n 32) 193.

[42] Kaltwasser 87; see also Invernizzi-Accetti and Zuckerman (n 32) 189.

democratic essentials into the public order.[43] In doing so, critics object, it unduly prevents the electorate from having the right to redecide fundamental political questions—such as who belongs to 'the people', what basic rights and duties members have, or how its institutions should counterbalance one another. Essentially, critics charge that militant democracy prevents the electorate from re-evaluating democracy's basic 'rules of rule-making'.

Weill, among others, argues persuasively that militant democracy is ultimately a theory of constitutional entrenchment.[44] In that regard, Nitzschner's claim holds true: militant democracy does aim to depoliticize democratic essentials and, in that sense, it is indeed institutionally conservative. Political rights restrictions are a *negative* form of constitutional entrenchment, Weill argues. They do not articulate what exactly the identity of the constitution is or protect it against legal change directly. But they can prevent malicious actors from having the legal opportunity to alter the existing constitution in the first place.

Critics argue that depoliticizing democratic constitutional essentials effectively severs democracy from its radical democratic foundations, depriving 'the people' of its voice and will on the most important issues.[45] They worry that it hardly seems democratic to prevent voters from choosing the party or policies that they think best represents their political identity. Depoliticization, as absolute entrenchment, betrays democracy's commitment to institutionalized uncertainty.

---

[43] Patrick Nitzschner, 'On Militant Democracy's Institutional Conservatism' (2023) 0(0) Philosophy and Social Criticism.

[44] Rivka Weill, 'On the Nexus of Eternity Clauses, Proportional Representation, and Banned Political Parties' (2017) 16(2) Election Law Journal 246; Rivka Weill, 'Secession and the Prevalence of Both Militant Democracy and Eternity Clauses Worldwide' (2018) 40(2) Cardozo Law Review 961, 963.

[45] Rosenblum (n 17) 58. For this reason, Malkopoulou argues, militant democracy has structural similarities to technocracy. Both presuppose that there are objectively 'correct' decisions in government and such matters need not be subjected to democratic legal procedures. Anthoula Malkopoulou, 'What Militant Democrats and Technocrats Share' (2023) 26(4) Critical Review of International Social and Political Philosophy.

However, most critics also recognize that democracy does have essential features, defined independent of what a present majority or supermajority happens to want at a given moment. They argue that, without those essential features, a government cannot be described as a 'democracy'—no matter how many voters openly support that government. 'Illiberal democracy' is a case in point. Still, many of those critics also argue that the right to determine what is 'democracy' should nevertheless be left to 'the people', ie the electorate, to decide. In effect, these critics seem to argue, democrats have to trust the present generation of voters not to commit democratic suicide. Or they may believe that 'the people' is inherently good and that history is teleologically progressive, so that democratic freedoms will be bear fruit over a long enough timeline.

Keynes famously argued, however, that in the *long run* we are all dead. To surrender society to natural processes and hope that an assumed inherent goodness will prevail over time, effectively giving up on both human agency and reason in the process, would be a different kind of depoliticization.

Here, Schmitt's famous remark that one can classify all state and political theory according to its philosophical anthropology seems on point. Carl Schmitt, *The Concept of the Political* (University of Chicago Press 1996) 58. What distinguishes militant democracy from many other democratic theories is its assumption that human nature is not fundamentally good, but that better political outcomes can be brought about through human reason and agency.

66   MILITANT DEMOCRACY

Critics' concerns about depoliticization tend to overlap with their concerns about legal indeterminacy. Both seem to sever democratic procedures from their radical democratic foundations. Although they may be related to one another and have a kind of elective affinity, it is important to flag that addressing one problem will not necessarily address the other. That is, even if the deployment of political rights restrictions can be made legally determinate, the problem of depoliticization can still present a normative problem for militant democracy. Conversely, even if depoliticization were resolved, the shadow of legal indeterminacy remains. Legal indeterminacy and depoliticization each pose a distinct and serious normative challenge to theorizing militant democracy.

Responses to the Paradox

Normative theories of militant democracy respond to the paradox of democracy's self-defence. Although each theory develops its own idiosyncratic response, they generally break down into one of two broad types.

The first bites the bullet regarding the paradox. It accepts that political rights restrictions are not democratically legitimate. However, it justifies their ad hoc and exceptional use, invoking what is essentially reason of state. It concludes that militant measures are valid as a last resort against an imminent threat to a democratic state's survival.

The second type argues that political rights restrictions can be reconciled with democratic norms. It argues that, by participating in a democratic society and its institutions, members have implicitly contracted into democratic norms. Pursuing antidemocratic goals violates that social contract. It amounts to self-disenfranchisement, which justifies the state's repressive reaction.

However, the underlying issue—the tension between political rights restrictions and democratic values—remains unresolved in both. In either case, advocates of militant democracy seem to lack confidence in the legitimacy of political rights restrictions. That unresolved paradox presents a significant obstacle, both integrating militant democracy into constitutions and for its practical deployment when democracies must defend themselves.

Illegitimate but Practically Necessary

The first response to the paradox concedes that there is no way to overcome it: political rights restrictions cannot be reconciled with democratic values. They are a grave violation of members' inalienable rights. Nevertheless, this response argues, militant democracy can be justified in exceptional situations, especially in response to an imminent existential threat to democratic essentials.

Kirshner's theory of militant democracy exemplifies this type of response. Kirshner defends the inviolability of members' political rights. The 'first participatory principle' of his normative theory of militant democracy is that political rights are the *sine qua non* of any democratic regime. Their infringement would damage not only the rights-holder but also the legitimacy of the public order.[46] For that reason, he accepts that political rights restrictions are democratically illegitimate.[47] Yet, in the face of an imminent credible threat, Kirshner recognizes that it may nevertheless be necessary to restrict some members' political rights in order to safeguard others' political rights and maintain democratic principles in the future.[48] For that reason, Kirshner acknowledges that political rights restrictions may be deployed on an ad hoc, albeit illegitimate basis in exceptional situations.

Niesen's theory of 'negative republicanism' is another example of this type of response to the paradox. Negative republicanism also argues that political rights are integral to democracy and may not be infringed legitimately.[49] However, it recognizes that other, contextual considerations matter. For example, the case of a new democracy grappling with its recent undemocratic history. Such a state may need to protect itself against antidemocrats who appropriate and weaponize symbols from its past, with the intent of undermining the new and still fragile democratic order. To consolidate its nascent democratic institutions, Niesen argues, a new democracy may erect a 'backwards-looking barrier' that restricts the political rights of parties and associations that draw on its particular antidemocratic past.[50] Echoing that sentiment, Rosenblum suggests that a democracy may adopt tailored restrictions to limit 'our' extremists in light of its unique history.[51]

Rijpkema theorizes militant democracy as a defence of 'democratic self-correction'. According to his approach, because political rights restrictions impose significant 'democratic costs', a state acts illegitimately when deploying them.[52] Therefore, he argues, they should be deployed with extreme caution: they may only target actors who either infringe on others' political rights or threaten democratic legal procedures, such as the amendment clause. (At points, Rijpkema also suggests that the possession of political rights hinges on every member's tacit consent to all members' participation in democratic institutions. If some members try to use their political rights against that commitment to democratic self-correction, they may in effect forfeit them.[53])

While all these theorists argue that political rights restrictions lack legitimacy, they all also recognize that circumstances, such as an emergency or an undemocratic history, can threaten democracy sufficiently to mitigate that illegitimacy and

---

[46] Kirshner, *A Theory of Militant Democracy* (n 4) 36, 55.
[47] Ibid 109–11, 121–33.
[48] Ibid 130.
[49] Niesen, 'Anti-Extremism, Negative Republicanism, Civic Society' (n 17) 2, 13, 17–18.
[50] Ibid 2, 7–8; Niesen, 'Banning the Former Ruling Party' (n 4) 540, 542, 555–56; Samuel Issacharoff (n 4) 30.
[51] Rosenblum (n 17) 39–40.
[52] Rijpkema, *Militant Democracy* (n 4) 155–56.
[53] Ibid 134, 140, 169; Rijpkema, 'Militant Democracy and the Detection Problem' (n 3) 172–73.

68 MILITANT DEMOCRACY

justify restrictions on an ad hoc basis. This approach thus acknowledges an uncomfortable reality: exceptional, undemocratic measures may be the only way to safeguard democracy's future.

Given the concerns about the illegitimacy of restricting political rights, this response typically limits the use of political rights restrictions to a measure of last resort. Kirshner emphasizes that even antidemocratic citizens have a legitimate interest in exercising political rights. He argues that political rights restrictions should be deployed only when antidemocrats are either actively violating others' political rights or are may do so imminently.[54] Similarly, Rijpkema believes that since militant democracy deprives members of their core rights, it should only be a measure of last resort.[55] He adds that rights restrictions should be governed by procedural safeguards, including judicial review and international oversight (such as by the European Court of Human Rights).[56] Issacharoff argues that political rights restrictions should only be deployed if antidemocrats pass a 'clear and present danger' test.[57] Niesen's negative republicanism limits their use to a very narrow subset of antidemocrats: those who appeal to their country's antidemocratic past. Antidemocrats who do not use that history or creatively skirt it have the right to form parties and pursue their political goals.

A Democratic Social Contract

The second response to the paradox asserts that, appearances aside, the infringement of political rights can be consistent with democracy. This approach argues that the possession of positive political rights is contingent on one's prior consent to democratic public order. Because these rights are contingent, they are neither inalienable nor immune from infringement. If members violate the basic norms of democracy, it signals a withdrawal of their consent. In doing so, they surrender any claim to enjoy the rights and privileges that come with membership in that democracy. The state may legitimately restrict their political rights, because in effect those members already renounced them.

One form of this second response posits that a democratic state is the product of an implicit social contract. Vinx, for example, argues that membership in a democracy presupposes that one has at least implicitly contracted into its commitment to equal chance.[58] The political rights one enjoys hinge on upholding the tenets of that democratic social contract. That means recognizing and respecting the political rights of other members and, by extension, their ability to form a majority. It also highlights a corresponding duty of loyalty to valid democratic legislation, however one feels about it personally. If citizens renege on their democratic obligations,

---

[54] Kirshner, *A Theory of Militant Democracy* (n 4) 95, 130–33, 165.
[55] Rijpkema, *Militant Democracy* (n 4) 155–56.
[56] Ibid 194–98.
[57] Issacharoff (n 4) 1436–37.
[58] Vinx (n 20) 690–91.

for example by using their political rights to deprive others of political rights, the state may legitimately restrict their political rights, in the process guaranteeing the democratic social contract for those still committed to it.

Jovanović likens democracy to a 'game' governed by fixed rules.[59] By deciding to 'play', one agrees to play by its rules. Jovanović writes that, just as 'no game is designed to allow its participants to fundamentally challenge the very objectives, rules, and means of the game', members who refuse to adhere to norms of democracy may be excluded from participation.[60] Refusing to play by the rules undermines the game not just for that individual, but for everyone. Similarly to Vinx's approach, members who oppose democratic fundamentals may lose their political participatory rights because they violate the preconditions for participation.

Finally, the 'concentric model of containment' also argues that political rights hinge on members' adherence to democratic norms. Also using the game metaphor, Rummens and Abts argue that citizens must 'unconditionally endorse the full set of procedural and substantive presuppositions of the game they want to play'.[61] Those who refuse to play by the rules become democracy's 'enemies' and may face exclusion.[62] The concentric model stands out by advocating that even democracy's enemies should retain limited political rights. However, it only allows them to exercise those rights at the 'periphery' of democracy.[63] Allowing their participation at the periphery balances the need to take into account each member's interests with safeguarding against undemocratic and destabilizing agendas.

In these examples, the paradox is resolved because citizens' political rights are grounded on a prior, implicit commitment to democratic principles. Democratic public order holds greater normative significance than individual members' exercise of their political rights. Hence, actions that contravene its principles can result in the loss of political rights for those who break the underlying democratic social contract.

Although theorists who advocate this second response argue that antidemocrats forfeit their political rights, they seem reluctant to fully commit to the implications of that view. Much like proponents of the first response, they tend to argue that restricting political rights should be a measure of last resort, reserved for imminent existential threats to democracy. For instance, although Jovanović defines anyone who violates 'the rules of the game' as an enemy of democracy, he argues that political rights restrictions should only be used when the game itself faces an imminent danger.[64] The concentric model uses a 'sliding scale' to determine whether to use political rights restrictions. It argues that, despite their goal of subverting

---

[59] Jovanović (n 12) 753; Rummens and Abts (n 14) 655; Kirshner, *A Theory of Militant Democracy* (n 4) 154–58.

[60] Jovanović (n 12) 755.

[61] Rummens and Abts (n 14) 655; cf Sottiaux and Rummens (n 16) 116.

[62] Rummens and Abts (n 14) 653.

[63] Ibid 652–54; Sottiaux and Rummens (n 16) 116; Rummens (n 15) 120.

[64] Jovanović (n 12) 753–54.

70   MILITANT DEMOCRACY

democracy, antidemocrats who pose only a marginal threat and operate at society's fringes should be given wide latitude to act. It reserves the party ban for only the most existentially significant threats.[65]

Vinx departs from this second response by arguing that his theory allows for the use of political rights restrictions against any antidemocrat, regardless of whether the threat is imminent.[66] However, in widening the scope of its application, his theory seems to expose itself to other normative problems of militant democracy, namely the deformalization of the rule of law and discretionary authority. For example, Vinx argues that militant measures could be deployed against even a superlatively legalistic Nazi. Yet there seems to be something deeply problematic about allowing the state to curtail the rights of marginal political actors who have not broken any laws. Again, if the basis for rights restrictions does not stem from the violation of positive law, then it implies the use of extralegal criteria. But relying on extralegal criteria to justify depriving members of basic rights would seem to corrupt democratic essentials. In particular, it seems to compromise its commitments to both proceduralism and the rationality of the formal rule of law. Thus, to avoid degrading democracy in that way, existing normative theories of militant democracy tend to treat political rights restrictions as a measure of last resort.

Militancy as a Last Resort

Because of its normative problems, theorists of militant democracy generally discourage the use of political rights restrictions—except as a last resort against imminent, existential threats. They also argue that the scope of their use should be limited to only groups that threaten political rights or basic democratic legal procedures. That reluctance underscores just how pervasive uncertainty about the broader legitimacy of militant democracy is. Some advocates, Kirshner for example, openly express their reservations. In any case, even amongst defenders of the legitimacy of militant democracy, it seems that its measures should be avoided wherever possible.

Reservations about using measures of militant democracy have practical consequences, however. By limiting them solely to immediate existential threats, there is an increased risk that, by the time militant measures can be deployed legitimately, they will be no longer be capable of halting an antidemocratic party's rise to power.

Building on Christoph Möllers' argument, Müller problematizes that risk as a practical paradox, writing that 'countries that can have militant democracy probably do not need it; whereas those that need it, cannot have it'.[67] By the time a

---

[65] Rummens and Abts (n 14) 653; Sottiaux and Rummens (n 16) 117–18.
[66] Vinx (n 20) 696–97.
[67] Müller, 'Militant Democracy and Constitutional Identity' 419.

democracy can justify repressing an antidemocratic party, it may find it difficult to muster the means to actually do so. If a party is in a position to turn democratic legal procedures against democracy, it probably already enjoys substantial electoral support. Even if the government can deny an antidemocratic party the legal pathways to revolutionize democracy, that party may recognize its strength and just resort to extralegal measures. Until that point, restricting a party's political rights will likely be illegitimate according to militant democracy's criteria for deployment. For that reason, resolving the paradox of democracy's self-defence by reserving political rights as a measure of last resort could leave militant democracy too weak and its measures too untimely to effectively prevent antidemocrats' seizure of power.

Besides those normative issues, there are practical consequences to hesitating and delaying in the face of antidemocrats using legal revolutionary methods. As antidemocrats gain seats in parliament, they not only become more capable of achieving their political goals by themselves. Capoccia analyses how their mere presence can also impair democrats' ability to coordinate an effective response.[68] It has a centrifugal effect within representative institutions. Moderate, centrist parties on the left and right will adopt more fringe positions to recover lost votes, making the formation of a centrist coalition that actually supports democracy more difficult. Beyond the visible issue of growing antidemocratic strength, delaying may mean that democrats can no longer coordinate to defend democracy at all.

Even when there are legitimate grounds to deploy political rights restrictions, existing normative theories of militant democracy may be incapable of countering an antidemocratic threat, due to constraints on their deployment. Both Schwartzberg and Müller have expressed scepticism that measures of militant democracy might actually save a distressed democracy. Müller describes the idea that a militant constitution could have safeguarded the paradigmatic struggling democracy, the Weimar Republic, as a 'useful fiction'.[69] Similarly, Schwartzberg argues that if the only bulwark against dedicated antidemocrats are legal measures, then it may already be too late to save that democracy.[70]

Historical context may help illuminate their concern. To deploy a party ban against the NSDAP in 1932, when it took a plurality of the vote, would have triggered a popular backlash. By then, Weimar may have been a republic without any republicans. Even if the party could have been banned successfully, Nazism was a genuinely popular movement resting on a solid organizational foundation. It might simply have resorted to illegal revolutionary tactics in its bid for power. This highlights the heart of the practical paradox: political rights restrictions must be

---

[68] Capoccia (n 9) 16–19.
[69] Müller, 'Militant Democracy' (n 4) 1263–64.
[70] Melissa Schwartzberg, *Democracy and Legal Change* (Cambridge University Press 2007) 157–58.

72 MILITANT DEMOCRACY

deployed early to be practically effective, but their deployment can only be justified as a last resort due to doubts about their legitimacy.

Otto Kirchheimer, a jurist associated with the Frankfurt School, underscored additional practical challenges from delaying using political rights restrictions against antidemocrats.[71] Delays enable a party to expand and fortify its base. As a party grows in popularity, amassing funding and better organizing itself, it becomes significantly more difficult to suppress through ordinary legal channels. Moreover, if such a party actually becomes an imminent existential threat, then normal legal channels procedures, normal police, and a normal pace may move far too slowly to respond in time. It will most likely be necessary to resort to a state of emergency, which risks significant damage to democracy even if successfully represses that threat. Apart from the risk of damaging democracy from the top down, it also increases the likelihood of a negative reaction from the bottom up, as the government attempts to defend democracy.

Drawing on their study of democratic backsliding in Poland and Hungary, Pech and Scheppele argue that curbing the legal erosion of democratic constitutional essentials requires 'acting fast as soon as the danger signals are clear'.[72] Swift action is paramount because delays benefit 'illiberal democrats' and other antidemocratic actors. Democrats often prefer to wait, hoping that constitutional measures designed to allow 'cooler heads to prevail' such as time delays and institutional checks will hold the line, so to speak. However, Pech and Scheppele find that delays work to the advantage of contemporary antidemocrats, who can continue consolidating their possession of state power. Speed and timing matter in defending democracy.

The detection problem and the paradox of democracy's self-defence cast a shadow over the legitimacy of political rights restrictions, leading many to harbour deep reservations about their use. Even theories advocating for militant democracy are not confident in them and severely limit their legitimate deployment. That in turn can undermine the efficacy of political rights restrictions, raising doubts about whether they should ever be used in practice.

The above arguments suggest that the imminence of the threat posed by antidemocrats may not be the best criterion for deciding to deploy political rights restrictions. Timing matters in the deployment of militant measures, in a way that runs contrary to how advocates have considered militant democracy so far. There are clear tactical reasons to deploy political rights restrictions against antidemocrats sooner rather than later—as soon as possible, in fact. Moreover, Kirchheimer suggests that there may be normative reasons as well: an inefficient

---

[71] Otto Kirchheimer, *Political Justice: The Use of Legal Procedure for Political Ends* (Princeton University Press 1961) 150–59.
[72] Laurent Pech and Kim Lane Scheppele, 'Illiberalism Within: Rule of Law Backsliding in the EU' (2017) 19 Cambridge Yearbook of European Legal Studies 3, 7.

An Incongruence between Theory and Practice

Another limitation of existing normative theories of militant democracy is their narrow focus on the party ban. While the party ban is one important measure of militant democracy, many constitutions make use of other measures of constitutional entrenchment to pre-emptively deny antidemocrats the legal democratic means to revolutionize democracy. The discrepancy between normative theories of militant democracy and actual militant democratic constitutions, such as the German *Basic Law*, limits the legitimating force of those theories.

As discussed in earlier chapters, Weill argues that unamendability and political rights restrictions are interrelated and complementary mechanisms of constitutional entrenchment.[73] Both mechanisms ultimately perform the same function of entrenching democratic constitutional essentials against legal revolutionary actions. They just differ in how they accomplish that entrenchment.

Political rights restrictions, exemplified by measures like the party ban, entrench democratic constitutional essentials *indirectly*. They prevent antidemocrats from obtaining the legal possession of state power, with which they can pursue their legal revolutionary goals by focusing on antidemocratic *actors*. Political rights restrictions entrench a constitution *proactively*, by denying the legal possession of state power to actors who might pose a threat to its core principles.[74]

Constitutional unamendability complements political rights restrictions by realizing constitutional entrenchment *directly*. It denies the constitutionality of changes made using formal democratic legal procedures, most notably the amendment clause. Unamendability focuses on antidemocratic legal *actions*. It entrenches democratic constitutional essentials *retroactively* by invalidating amendments and derogations of the constitution. It does so through liberal constitutional checks and balances, most notably judicial review.

Weill argues that political rights restrictions and unamendability are more than just complementary and reinforcing. She argues that they are mutually presupposing: a constitution that explicitly adopts one mechanism at least implicitly adopts the other, even if it is not contained in the written constitution.

---

[73] Weill, 'On the Nexus of Eternity Clauses' (n 44) 238.
[74] Ibid 242; Weill, 'Secession and the Prevalence of Both Militant Democracy and Eternity Clauses Worldwide' (n 44) 961.

74 MILITANT DEMOCRACY

Kirshner argues that antidemocratic legislation may just be a lagging indicator of antidemocrats' de facto power.[75] If invalidating antidemocratic legislation is the only means to defend democracy, then antidemocrats who successfully obtain power will have ample time to consolidate it and find other avenues to pursue their legal revolutionary goals, avenues that might succeed. In addition, focusing solely on antidemocratic legislation gives antidemocrats in power the opportunity to engineer political *fait accomplis* with which they can degrade democracy, even if a court can retroactively invalidate those actions. It is therefore imperative, Kirshner argues, to broaden the focus of democracy's self-defence to include antidemocrats who legally possess state power (or threaten to do so).[76]

Restricting the political rights of antidemocratic organizations functionally reinforces unamendability. This is because antidemocrats will have fewer opportunities to pursue unconstitutional legislation. Without the legal possession of state power, they cannot put the fabric of the democratic public order to stress. Neither can they pursue their antidemocratic goals piecemeal, by cobbling together a 'Frankenstate'. Simply put, an antidemocrat cannot enact antidemocratic legislation without first holding public office.

Today's near-exclusive focus on the party ban suggests that normative theories may have gone too far in addressing Kirshner's concern. Although nothing about existing normative theories precludes other mechanisms of militant democracy, they do not take up those other measures of militant democracy, in particular unamendability.[77] That silence creates a conspicuous gap in the discussion.

Implementing a party ban arguably presupposes that certain features of the democratic constitution are unchangeable. Without any constitutionally recognized limits to legal change, the constitutionality of restricting actors for pursuing particular changes seems weak. To deprive an actor of their political rights when that actor adhered to the letter of the constitution is democratically suspect, no matter how the infringement is spun.[78] Unamendability strengthens the case for political rights restrictions by constitutionally defining the scope of changes permitted through democratic legal procedures. It not only clarifies what is constitutional, it also expressly signals the political identity of the constitution. In doing so, it provides a clearer constitutional basis for political rights restrictions.

Furthermore, since neither unamendability nor political rights restrictions are self-enforcing, militant democracy presupposes that a branch of government have the authority to guard the constitution and oversee the constitutionality of elected representatives' actions and goals.

---

[75] Kirshner, *A Theory of Militant Democracy* (n 4) 14.
[76] Ibid 4.
[77] Kirshner, for example, recognizes the importance of judicial review. See ibid 9–21.
[78] See Andrew Arato, 'Multi-Track Constitutionalism beyond Carl Schmitt' (2011) 18(3) Constellations 336.

Most existing normative theories of militant democracy overlook both unamendability and the guardian of the constitution, particularly their complementary and mutually reinforcing interrelationship. That oversight leads to analytic gaps in their normative analyses. It affects actual militant democratic constitutions. There is an incongruity between the sole mechanism that existing normative theories of militant democracy analyse today and the mechanisms that militant democracies actually install to entrench constitutional essentials. Consequently, they fall short in providing a normative theory for the constitutional form that militant democracy actually takes.

Alternatives to Militant Democracy

Given that even advocates of militant democracy have reservations about its legitimacy, and that those normative concerns have practical consequences, this raises the question of what alternatives there are to militant democracy when it comes to addressing *actors threatening the legal revolution of democratic constitutional essentials*.

Like its advocates, explicit critics of militant democracy tend to agree that political rights and democratic legal procedures are the *sine qua non* for a legitimate democracy.[79] Although both critics and advocates broadly agree on the fundamentals of democracy, they diverge on the issue of the paradox of democracy's self-defence. Critics argue that, even if an organization poses an existential threat to the survival of democracy, infringing on members' political rights cannot be legitimate. Such an action would proactively undermine democracy itself. Therefore, critics seize the other horn in the dilemma over the deployment of militant measures: political rights restrictions have no legitimate place in a democracy.

When critics do discuss other ways to defend democracy, they tend to focus on ways to inoculate and strengthen civil society against the allure of antidemocrats. Malkopoulou, for instance, argues that the best defence of democracy is improved social democratic redistribution (along the lines of a capabilities approach). In her collaboration with Norman, Malkopoulou defends ensuring that 'the needy' are protected by the state through 'equal access to education, legal system and natural environment, and a system of protection of social, medical and judicial security'[80] in order to create a more robust level of material welfare. Doing so may undercut

---

[79] For example, see Invernizzi-Accetti and Zuckerman (n 32); Malkopoulou, 'What Militant Democrats and Technocrats Share' (n 45); Rune Møller Stahl and Benjamin Ask Popp-Madsen, 'Defending democracy: Militant and Popular Models of Democratic Self-Defense' (2022) 29(3) Constellations 311–12.
[80] Malkopoulou and Norman (n 4) 454.

the appeal of some antidemocrats, in particular populists who make similar so-cialistic promises.[81] Ideally, this strategy would effectively deny antidemocrats a significant enough base to gain power through elections.

Another strategy to undercut the appeal of antidemocrats is through improved civic education, which Scheppele discusses.[82] Civic education should help citizens to appreciate why liberal constitutionalism is an integral part of democracy, in par-ticular its countermajoritarian aspects. That may inoculate them against the allure of the radical majoritarianism forms of government that populists, for example, promise to realize.

Improved social democratic redistribution and civic education will undoubtedly improve the quality of a democracy and help bolster citizens' loyalty to democratic institutions. And both strategies are compatible with the entrenchment mechan-isms of militant democracy. They can help fortify a democratic society against an-tidemocratic worldviews. However, it would be misleading to label policies that improve democracy as such as 'militant democracy'. While important, policies ex-panded economic redistribution and civic education cannot directly address the problem of legal revolution.[83] Broadening the definition of militant democracy in this way dilutes the concept, and risks collapsing 'militant democracy' into 'democ-racy' itself. In addition, Feisel argues that an advantage of a narrower definition of militant democracy, one for example that focuses on defending against legal revo-lution, is that it provides a sharper analytic lens—which is especially important as democracy confronts novel legal and political contexts.[84]

When it comes to the distinctive problem of the legal revolution of demo-cratic constitutional essentials, critics of militant democracy are *quietistic*. From this perspective, antidemocrats appear to be constitutionally and politically le-gitimate as long they pursue and realize their political goals through democratic

---

[81] Møller-Stahl and Ask Popp-Madsen radicalize the idea that defending democracy requires at-tenuating socio-economic inequality by arguing for what they call 'popular republicanism', modelled on ideas developed by John McCormick. 'Popular republicanism' differs from current democratic in-stitutions in two fundamental ways. First, certain appointments should be made through sortition, mitigated the advantages in the elections that the wealthy might have; second, 'the use of class-specific offices and wealth-excluding institutions': Stahl and Popp-Madsen (n 79) 318–19.

Approaches like these seem normatively troubling because they openly defend policies that would deformalize the rule of law, arguing that citizens who obtain an undefined level of material wealth should *automatically* be deprived of their political rights. In doing so, they seem to walk into the paradox of democracy's self-defence. Despite criticizing militant democracy for the illegitimacy of pol-itical rights restrictions, they defend the exact same thing—just by targeting a different segment of the electorate. Because they do not acknowledge or resolve this tension in their argument, it is not obvious why their automated disenfranchisement would not be as destructive of democratic principles.

Moreover, these approaches also seem to presuppose that internal threats to democracy can only come from the wealthy. It offers no explanation for why other segments of the electorate cannot threaten democracy, despite empirical evidence to the contrary.

[82] Kim Lane Scheppele, 'Autocratic Legalism' (2018) 85(2) The University of Chicago Law Review.

[83] Capoccia (n 9) 48.

[84] Franca Maria Feisel, 'Thinking EU Militant Democracy beyond the Challenge of Backsliding Member States' (2022) 18(3) European Constitutional Law Review 385, 390.

legal procedures. Antidemocrats' adherence to formal legality collapses any distinction between their political goals and genuinely democratic ones. These critics' orientation thus seems to leave the state with no valid recourse against popular antidemocrats who are successfully amassing a base large enough to revolutionize democracy legally. Yet this is exactly how populists like Modi, Erdoğan, Netanyahu, and Chavez, among other antidemocrats, have obtained power and undermined their democracies in recent years.

This quietist view is exemplified by arguments Kelsen made in his 1932 work *Verteidigung der Demokratie*.[85] There, Kelsen argued that a state ceases to be a democracy if it opposes the legally expressed will of a majority. A democracy may not validly stand against its own electorate by denying their will, even if that means its own annihilation. Instead, Kelsen argued, democrats must remain committed to democratic legal procedures no matter the outcome, famously stating that a democrat 'must remain true to his colors, even when the ship is sinking, and can take with him into the depths only the hope that the ideal of freedom is indestructible and that the deeper it has sunk, the more passionately will it revive'.[86]

The underlying issue with the quietist response is that it removes any distinction between legality and legitimacy: *legality is legitimacy*. Essentially, any political goal at all is legitimate if pursued through formal democratic legal procedures, whatever its substantive implications. Moreover, eliding legitimacy and legality aggravates the detection problem described by Rijpkema. A democracy can only detect threats to itself when they are illegal and criminal, such as violent insurrection. Elected representatives who use the powers of their office to overturn an election, for example by refusing to certify the results of a democratic election, simply do not register legally as threats. Not that it matters if they could detect them because, denied measures of militant democracy, democracies have no means to remove popular legal revolutionaries from office anyway. Antidemocrats take advantage of democracies that collapse that distinction.

Besides being unable to detect and respond to the legal revolution of democratic constitutional essentials, quietist alternatives seem only to invert the challenges that militant democracy faces in resolving the paradox of democracy's self-defence. If militant democracy prioritizes the future of democracy at the expense of the present, the alternative seems to sacrifice democracy's future to maintain it in the present.

---

[85] Kelsen's argument is in line with the prevailing positivist jurisprudence of the interwar period, such as that espoused by Anschütz and Thoma. See for example Richard Thoma, 'The Reich as Democracy' in Arthur J Jacobson and Bernhard Schlink (eds), *Weimar: A Jurisprudence of Crisis* (University of California Press 2002) and Gerhard Anschütz, 'Three Guiding Principles of the Weimar Constitution' in Arthur J Jacobson and Bernhard Schlink (eds), *Weimar: A Jurisprudence of Crisis* (University of California Press 2002).

[86] Hans Kelsen, *Verteidigung der Demokratie* (2006), quoted from Clemens Jabloner, 'Introduction to Hans Kelsen' in Arthur J Jacobson and Bernhard Schlink (eds), *Weimar: A Jurisprudence of Crisis* (University of California Press 2002) 74.

In the end, quietism does not resolve the paradox of democracy's self-defence either. Kirshner summarizes quietism's limits well, writing that it would be naïve to believe that 'a world in which militant policies were not on the books would be a world in which malign actors would be *less likely* to undermine the rights of their fellow citizens'.[87]

An Alternative Normative Theory of Militant Democracy

There will always be a need for democracies to defend themselves. The challenges facing democracy today, such as populism, 'illiberal democracy', and legal revolution, demonstrate the perennial nature of that problem. Constitutional entrenchment through 'militant democracy' provides one vital set of mechanisms for democracy to defend itself against its enemies.

Existing normative theories of militant democracy face several fundamental challenges, both normative and practical. One is the detection problem: normative theories of militant democracy struggle to identify today's antidemocrats as such, leaving them unable to justify a militant response. A second is the paradox of democracy's self-defence: the act of restricting political rights itself seems antidemocratic, creating an additional difficulty in justifying militancy. Most normative theories mandate that rights restrictions be used solely as a last resort to help resolve that paradox. But this creates a series of other practical, tactical problems for their use, including the apparent practical paradox that they may only be used legitimately *after* it is too late to save a democracy. A final challenge is the gap between existing normative theories and the actual constitutional practice of militant democracy. Because of their shortcomings, existing theories seem to lack confidence or to be overly cautious. That theoretical squeamishness in turn has repercussions for the actual practice of militant democracy.

Addressing these limitations makes it is possible to provide a stronger normative foundation for democracies to deploy militant measures to defend themselves against their enemies. The following chapters introduce and develop that alternative normative theory of militant democracy.

---

[87] Kirshner, 'Militant Democracy Defended' (n 6) 65.

PART II

3
Liberalism and Modern Constitutionalism

Introduction

Existing normative theories of militant democracy face significant challenges, including detecting contemporary threats to democracy and navigating the paradox of democracy's self-defence. An alternative normative theory of militant democracy, one grounded in Rawls' thought, can address and overcome those challenges.

Central to that theory are two aspects of Rawls' thought. First is Rawls' political constructivism, which asserts that certain constitutional norms, such as basic liberal rights, are authoritative and binding for a democratic people. Second is Rawls' approach to defending the entrenchment of those norms, which encompass constitutional unamendability, the 'containment' of antidemocratic threats, and judicial guardianship.

Rawls' political constructivism uses a thought experiment to identify foundational norms for democracy. It tasks rational representatives with deciding on collective norms under structural conditions of uncertainty, which mirror modern epistemological limitations. The outcome of that hypothetical procedure distils an essential part of the democratic identity of 'the people', applicable to all democracies due to the universality of the practical reasoning it models. Crucially, this approach distinguishes 'the people' from the electorate. The latter is only a limited representation of the political identity 'the people'. That distinction leads to two important normative conclusions: first, that constitutional essentials, especially basic liberal rights, are implicitly unamendable; and second, that restricting the rights of antidemocrats is justifiable, an idea encapsulated in Rawls' concept of 'containment'.

Other liberal philosophies may also successfully navigate the practical and normative issues facing militant democracy and establish a robust democratic constitutional identity. The aim here is not to defend the superiority of Rawls' philosophy per se. Instead, it is to establish the normative foundation for an alternative theory of militant democracy. Given its enduring influence on democratic theory, Rawls' political liberalism seems to provide a solid foundation for that theory.

Democracy despite Itself. Benjamin A. Schupmann, Oxford University Press. © Benjamin A. Schupmann 2024.
DOI: 10.1093/9780191975950.003.0004

Unreasonability and the Deterioration of an Overlapping Consensus

In *Political Liberalism*,[1] Rawls argued that a legitimate public order emerges from an overlapping consensus among its members, who recognize those fundamentals as 'the most reasonable for us'. In addition, he argues that those fundamentals should be articulable independently of any particular worldview or comprehensive doctrine, through a method he calls political constructivism.

In his work, Rawls' focus was on how an overlapping consensus could emerge out of a *modus vivendi*. That emergence occurs when a plural society transitions to de jure stability from a condition of de facto stability, in which public order is the result of an unstable and temporary balance of power among groups, none able to definitively impose their own worldview using the coercive power of public law. Under de jure stability or 'stability for the right reasons', members accept the public order as legitimate even if their group does not possess state power.[2] Rawls believed that, by creating the public space in which members would have to interact with others who did not share their worldview, a *modus vivendi* has the potential to evolve into a more robust constitutional consensus, and eventually into an overlapping consensus.[3]

The reverse situation is also possible, however. A democratic society enjoying de jure stability can deteriorate, as for example when a sufficient number of members hold 'unreasonable' beliefs, beliefs that reject a democratic overlapping consensus. They can work to overwhelm and replace that consensus using legal and illegal revolutionary methods. The deterioration of a legitimate public order does not just risk transforming an overlapping consensus into a *modus vivendi*.[4] A *modus vivendi* itself can deteriorate further in the presence of a critical mass of unreasonable members because they are more likely to see the law as a coercive means of domination, something merely instrumental for advancing the interests of powerholders. That perspective can become infectious. Under the pressure of unreasonable members, even a *modus vivendi* can erode over time.

Furthermore, when a state's domestic affairs are characterized as no more than a *modus vivendi*, it fails to answer the question of constitutionalism: what makes the law legitimate; why do subjects have reason to obey it, besides the threat of coercive force? And when social relations are characterized only by a temporary balance of power among factions with opposed worldviews, a perceived shift in that balance may precipitate a competition among those factions to seize power and advance

---

[1] John Rawls, *Political Liberalism* (Columbia University Press 1996) 145.

[2] ibid 145; Vicente Medina, 'Militant Intolerant People: A Challenge to John Rawls' Political Liberalism' (2010) 58(3) Political Studies 556, 560; Leif Wenar, 'John Rawls', *The Stanford Encyclopedia of Philosophy 2021*, <https://plato.stanford.edu/archives/win2013/entries/rawls/> accessed 31 January 2023.

[3] ibid 164.

[4] Jonathan Quong, 'The Rights of Unreasonable Citizens' (2004) 12(3) The Journal of Political Philosophy 320; Medina (n 2) 561–62.

their idiosyncratic worldviews and their narrow self-interests. 'Unreasonable' members can thus pose an existential threat to both legitimate democratic order as well as peace and stability. Because they can unravel an overlapping consensus, it makes sense to specify what exactly defines a member as 'unreasonable'.

Building on Rawls' account, Quong defines unreasonability as the rejection of the fundamental tenets of liberal democracy.[5] Two principal features define 'unreasonable' members: they reject fair terms of cooperation, rejecting the idea that other members deserve freedom and equality, and they reject the burdens of judgment, rejecting the fact of pluralism and the possibility of reasonable disagreement on normative truth.[6] Given the opportunity and if it is advantageous, unreasonable members will violate fair terms of cooperation.[7] They insist on the truth of their particular comprehensive doctrine and believe in imposing their idiosyncratic values on society. Medina argues that, because of their hostile views, unreasonable members may even see other members as their 'enemies', in the state of nature-like relationship Schmitt described.[8]

No democracy can prevent unreasonable beliefs from arising. They are a natural consequence of democratic toleration and the fact of pluralism. As long as unreasonable members remain a minority and remain within the private sphere, they do not threaten a legitimate constitutional consensus.[9] They will tend to abide by the rules of a liberal public order, even if only out of self-interest. They become a problem when their numbers reach a critical mass. They can then infiltrate the public sphere, and become more capable of destabilizing a democratic constitutional consensus to advance their own worldview.[10]

One way to destabilize a democratic constitutional consensus is of course through violence. However, as discussed in chapter 1, legal revolutionary methods can have the same deleterious effect on a democratic constitution as violent insurrection. By possessing state power legally, unreasonable members can use the coercive power of public law to impose their comprehensive doctrine across society and deny fair terms of cooperation to other members. And because legal revolution plays by the rules of the democratic game, it may be more likely to succeed in democracies ill-equipped to defend themselves against organized members who

---

[5] ibid 323.

[6] Rawls, *Political Liberalism* (n 1) 49–50; cf Quong (n 4) 315; Medina (n 2) 559; Roberta Sala, 'The Place of Unreasonable People beyond Rawls' (2013) 12(3) European Journal of Political Theory 255–56; Andrew Reid, 'How Can Political Liberalism Respond to Contemporary Populism?' (2022) 21(2) European Journal of Political Theory 303; Benedetta Giovanola and Roberta Sala, 'The Reasons of The Unreasonable: Is Political Liberalism Still An Option?' (2022) 48(9) Philosophy and Social Criticism 1227, 1236; Gabriele Badano and Alasia Nuti, 'Under Pressure: Political Liberalism, the Rise of Unreasonableness, and the Complexity of Containment' (2018) 26(2) The Journal of Political Philosophy 145, 150.

[7] Rawls, *Political Liberalism* 60–61, 138; Giovanola and Sala (n 6) 1236.

[8] Medina (n 2) 558.

[9] Quong (n 4) 321.

[10] Rawls, *Political Liberalism* (n 1) 126.

turn positive legal procedures and participatory rights against democratic constitutional essentials.

Populist 'illiberal democrats', Fidesz for instance, fall under Rawls' category of 'unreasonable'. On the one hand, as Ferrara argues, such parties tend to conceive of 'the people' as a homogenous entity and seek to dismantle institutions that legally guarantee pluralism.[11] As a result, they transform the public from a sphere of communicative interaction and reason-giving into a space of factionalism and even enmity. On the other hand, as Badano and Nuti argue, they insist that only those members who belong to the 'authentic' people deserve equal membership.[12] For that reason, they believe that minorities and other 'outsiders' do not deserve the same set of membership rights and protections. Illiberal populists that have successfully obtained power have sought to enact antipluralist policies and demote the status of minorities.

Constructivism and the Authority of Constitutional Norms

In their 1992 overview of debates in metaethics, Darwall, Gibbard, and Railton articulated the canonical definition of constructivism. They define it as a unique kind of proceduralism that determines authoritative and binding norms without resorting to transcendent normative facts.[13] The authoritative nature of those constitutional norms has implications for democratic constitutionalism. They bind independently, regardless of the legally expressed will of the electorate.

Constructivism's virtue is that sets the foundations for any democracy. It also sets normative limits on the changes that can be made to it, which in turn limit what a majority—reasonable or unreasonable—can legitimately accomplish using the law. However, at the same time, constructivism raises complications. First, it is not clear that its freestanding values can be reconciled with the requirements of modern constitutionalism. Second, it is not clear how positing the existence of authoritative constitutional norms can be called 'democratic'.

The following section argues that political constructivism, as theorized by Rawls, provides answers to those problems. It analyses how constructivism generates authoritative constitutional norms and how those norms can be reconciled with the requirements of modern constitutionalism.

---

[11] Alessandro Ferrara, 'Can Political Liberalism Help Us Rescue "The People" from Populism?' (2018) 44(4) Philosophy & Social Criticism 467–71.

[12] Badano and Nuti (n 6) 150–51.

[13] Stephen Darwall, Allan Gibbard, and Peter Railton, 'Toward Fin de siècle Ethics: Some Trends' 101 The Philosophical Review 115, 140; see also Kenneth Baynes, 'Constructivism and Practical Reason in Rawls' (1992) 14 Analyse & Kritik 19; TM Scanlon, 'The Appeal and Limits of Constructivism' in James Lenman and Yonatan Shemmer (eds), Constructivism in Practical Philosophy (2012) 233.

Hypothetical, 'Second-Order' Proceduralism

Ideally, democratic constitutional essentials are accepted as legitimate because they rest on an overlapping consensus within the electorate, who recognize those essentials as 'the most reasonable doctrine for us'.[14] Ferrara unpacks this concept by arguing that members believe that the constitutional order's basic principles and its historical and cultural features best correspond with the liberal principles determined by constructivism.[15] Those basic principles should also embody what the terms and values that uniquely and authentically define a particular 'people'.

However, phenomena such as populism, illiberal democracy, and democratic backsliding highlight the fragility and reversibility of an overlapping consensus. A just public order is unfortunately not a once and for all achievement. It needs continual upkeep. Even with upkeep, it can still come under attack and deteriorate. When unreasonable members attack the status quo using legal revolutionary methods, what kind of a response does Rawls' thought offer?

Political liberalism's other pillar of legitimacy seems to provide an answer. Even when an overlapping consensus has deteriorated and unreasonable members threaten to legally revolutionize the constitution, the constitutional essentials determined by political constructivism still stand. That is, even if unreasonable members are a supermajority and can use democratic legal procedures to fundamentally alter the democratic essence of the constitution, Rawls' approach identifies authoritative and binding constitutional norms that justify rejecting their political will.[16]

Despite determining authoritative norms, political constructivism is still a form of democratic proceduralism.[17] For that reason, political constructivism has several noteworthy structural similarities to other proceduralist theories.[18] Those similarities show how constructivism remains within the normative framework set by modern constitutionalism.

First, constructivism generates legitimate law *immanently*. The appeal to immanent justifications is essential because of the constraints of modern constitutionalism, discussed in chapter 1.[19] Constructivism satisfies those constraints because

---

[14] John Rawls, 'Kantian Constructivism' in Samuel Freeman (ed), *Collected Papers* (Harvard University Press 1999) 306–07.

[15] Alessandro Ferrara, *Sovereignty Across Generations: Constituent Power and Political Liberalism* (Oxford University Press 2023) 133–34.

[16] See Samuel Freeman, 'Political Liberalism and the Possibilty of a Just Democratic Constitution' (1994) 69(3) Chicago-Kent Law Review 643.

[17] Rawls, *Political Liberalism* (n 1) 97. See also Darwall, Gibbard, and Railton (n 13).

[18] Rawls, *Political Liberalism* (n 1) 93ff; Rawls, 'Kantian Constructivism' 310ff; John Rawls, *Justice as Fairness: A Restatement* (The Belknap Press 2003) 88.

[19] The question of constitutionalism asks 'why do we have reason to obey public law, beyond its threat of coercion?' Modern constitutionalism answers that question by arguing that law's legitimacy stems from its democratic nature. 'The people' is autonomous, so it really only follows its own will when it obeys public law. The democratic turn of constitutionalism is rooted in the modern disenchantment

86   LIBERALISM AND MODERN CONSTITUTIONALISM

it recognizes no independent, *transcendent* criteria for determining legitimacy. The only criterion for legitimacy is whether the output is the product of participants acting within the closed proceduralist system. Second, participants within the constructivist procedure all possess formally equal participatory rights, which guarantee them equal consideration as they participate in its decision-making procedures. Third, participants are free to exercise their political rights in whatever way they believe will best realize their goals. Finally, the output of the procedure is majoritarian: the procedure aggregates the interests expressed by individual participants. However, constructivism departs from other proceduralist accounts in two significant ways, which allow it to generate authoritative constitutional norms.

Constructivism's first significant departure is who participates in the procedure. Unlike in other proceduralist theories, in which members of society participate directly, constructivism employs a hypothetical procedure.[20] It is a thought experiment, intended to idealize salient features of an otherwise complicated reality. As a thought experiment, constructivism neither reflects actual historical events nor provides a blueprint for designing real-world democratic legislatures.[21] Instead, it functions as an independent heuristic device for assessing the legitimacy of a democratic constitution.[22] As long as a democracy's actual legislative procedures operate within the constitutional framework determined by the constructivist procedure, then it satisfies the requirements of modern constitutionalism. In other words, that hypothetical procedure generates a yardstick with which to measure an actual democracy's institutions, including its constitution.

In this hypothetical procedure, actual members of society do not represent themselves or participate directly in the decision-making process. Instead, they are represented in a fiduciary relationship by artificial, rational agents.[23] 'Rational' means instrumentally rational: agents will select the most efficient means to realize their given goals.[24] In the procedure, the goal of each rational agent is to secure the interests of a discrete individual member of society. Like the procedure, those agents are rational constructs, designed to distil practical reason.

---

of *transcendent* sources of legitimation, such as the Catholic Church, which gave rise to modern skepticism and the fact of pluralism. It necessitated a different *immanent* source of political and legal legitimacy. Democracy provides that immanence because the law's subjects are also thought to be its authors in a democracy. Democratic public order is legitimate not because it enacts transcendent norms but because it embodies the will of 'the people'. It also allows the law to evolve dynamically with 'the people', giving them continuous reasons to respect and view it as legitimate.

[20] Sharon Street, 'What is Constructivism in Ethics and Metaethics?' (2010) 5(5) Philosophy Compass 366.

[21] Rawls, *Political Liberalism* (n 1), 'Justice as Fairness: Political not Metaphysical' in Samuel Freeman (ed), *Collected Papers* (Harvard University Press 1999) 394, 400, 410; Street (n 20) 366.

[22] Amy Gutmann, 'Rawls on the Relationship between Liberalism and Democracy' in Samuel Freeman (ed), *The Cambridge Companion to Rawls* (Cambridge University Press 2003) 188–89.

[23] Rawls, *Political Liberalism* (n 1) 104; Rawls, 'Kantian Constructivism' in Samuel Freeman (ed), *Collected Papers* (Harvard University Press 1999) 311, 316.

[24] Rawls, *Justice as Fairness: A Restatement* (n 18) 87.

CONSTRUCTIVISM AND THE AUTHORITY   87

Constructivism's second significant point of departure is a constraint built into the structure of the procedure. In the constructivist procedure, each rational representative is placed under a 'veil of ignorance', which blinds it to the concrete identity of whichever individual member that rational agent actually represents.[25] It cannot be certain of who the represented is, exactly, or what their idiosyncratic political goals and interests might be.

That veil of ignorance structurally embeds in constructivist proceduralism the actual limitations on a democratic society imposed by modern epistemology, which gave rise to the fact of reasonable pluralism and motivated constitutionalism's turn to democratic legitimation in the first place. Paralleling our own inability to establish normative truth in the real world, rational representatives in the thought experiment cannot know with any certainty the identity of whoever they represent. The uncertainty produced by the veil of ignorance negates any potential bargaining advantages that would come from knowledge about the world, such as the proportion of members who share one's interests. For example, a rational representative cannot know whether the represented member is part of a religious majority or an extremely marginal religious minority. At best, a rational agent knows the complete range of possible interests that a represented member might hold.

Building epistemic uncertainty directly into the procedure derails the ability of agents to use their political rights to realize the goals of whoever they represent rationally. Not knowing anything concrete about who exactly it represents, no rational agent would try to use the procedure to secure the beliefs, values, and interests of whoever it represents *directly*. Rational agents would recognize that enacting laws that advance a particular set of interests would be an arbitrary and baseless decision, a dice roll over whether they would actually secure the interests of the represented.[26] Random legislation could be antithetical to those interests. Constructivism's two significant departures work together to put rational agents in a performative bind. Within the constraints of the procedure, any rational agent would be averse to using its political rights to pursue substantive policy goals directly.

Although the constraints of the constructivist procedure deny them the confidence to pursue substantive legislative goals directly, rational agents would also recognize that there is still a way to rationally secure the interests of whoever they represent—they can do so *indirectly*.[27] Each agent would recognize that it could enact formal legal guarantees that ensure each member has the freedom from interference that allows them to pursue their idiosyncratic interests by themselves, within the widest range compatible with other reasonable interests.[28]

---

[25] Rawls, 'Kantian Constructivism' (n 14) 310ff; Rawls, 'Justice as Fairness: Political not Metaphysical' (n 21) 400.

[26] Rawls, *Political Liberalism* (n 1) 311.

[27] ibid 307.

[28] ibid 181, 187; Rawls, 'Kantian Constructivism' 313–15; Rawls, *Justice as Fairness: A Restatement* (n 18) 58–59.

The legislative output of constructivist proceduralism is distinctive because it is *second-order* and *negative*. It is second-order because it does not produce any first-order laws that would regulate society directly. It only determines 'the rules of rule-making'. It is negative because the laws it produces limit the output of actual legislative institutions—circumscribing the coercive power of law and the state.

The uncertainty embedded into the hypothetical procedure by the veil of ignorance represents the actual epistemological uncertainty that a constitutional legislator must accommodate in founding a modern public order. Democratic laws can be legitimate only when the public order guarantees every member the constitutional resources necessary to pursue their unique interests and their own conception of 'the good'. In other words, members have reason to see a democratic public order as legitimate because it ensures that each retains rights that safeguard their pursuit of their own conceptions of the good, regardless of whether they hold public power.

The methodology of political constructivism sets its output apart from other forms of proceduralism. It concludes that a legitimate public order should not grant its members full control over the agenda. Considering the structural conditions of epistemic uncertainty and the fact of pluralism, some second-order 'rules of rule-making' must not be left to the discretion of the electorate to dilute or discard entirely—if a state is to maintain its democratic integrity. To be legitimate, it must secure the background conditions generated by the constructivist procedure. While constructivism only removes a narrow set of options from the agenda, it does stipulate that those background conditions must be guaranteed for a state to be legitimate. Moreover, constructivism also offers reconciliatory potential.[29] It can clarify why members should acknowledge the authority of the basic principles of democratic public order, even if those principles do not align with or advance their immediate political and legislative interests.

Constructivism's Formal Output: Normative Truth

The constructivist procedure generates an output with both formal and substantive components. Formally, constructivism argues that the output of its procedure consists of binding and authoritative constitutional norms that are applicable to any democratic society.

Those norms obtain their authority from the design of the constructivist procedure: how it isolates and abstracts the process of practical reasoning as rational agents attempt to design a democratic public order under modern conditions of

---

[29] Rawls, *Justice as Fairness: A Restatement* (n 18) 3–4; Rawls, 'Kantian Constructivism' (n 14) 356.

epistemic uncertainty and the fact of pluralism.[30] The two structural constraints described above, namely the artificial rationality of the agents and the veil of ignorance, distil how practical reason operates when norms cannot be publicly legitimated by appealing to transcendent truths.

Under the epistemic constraints established by constructivism, a rational agent would conclude that it can perform its role best by guaranteeing that whoever it represents has the legal means to pursue their interests autonomously. Furthermore, given that any agent within the constructivist procedure could represent *any* member of society, an agent would choose the set of means that could in principle serve *every* member to pursue their interests themselves. Between the formal equality of every rational agent and the structurally determined need to represent every member of society, rational agents would reach a unanimous agreement on those institutional guarantees.[31] The unanimity of their decision signals that practical reason has been successfully distilled.[32]

Rawls assumes that practical reasoning is a universal human capability.[33] Given that assumption, and taking it against the backdrop of epistemic uncertainty in democratic societies, Rawls held that the conclusions of those rational agents apply universally to any actual democratic society. Essentially, any member of a democratic society can employ practical reasoning. Its universality endows that constructivist procedure with its normative authority.

Although constructivism does generate authoritative norms, those norms fundamentally differ from norms derived from transcendent normative facts, such as divine law or natural right. That distinction matters. Responding to the question of constitutionalism, Claude Lefort had argued that power, knowledge, and law have been 'disentangled' in modern democratic societies, so they could no longer rely on transcendent reason and justice to inform secular affairs.[34] In contrast, constructivism argues that *markers of normative certainty can still be found in modernity*. They can be determined without entangling law in claims of absolute knowledge or the whims of arbitrary power. Instead, the value pluralism inherent in modern democratic societies can itself become a source of normative authority.

---

[30] Rawls, *Political Liberalism* 90, 273–77; See also Baynes (n 13) 19; Carla Bagnoli, *Constructivism in Metaethics* (Metaphysics Research Lab, Stanford University 2021).

[31] Rawls, *Political Liberalism* 383–84; Rawls, 'Kantian Constructivism' (n 14) 339; Freeman 'Political Liberalism' (n 16) 634. In response to an objection from Habermas, Rawls characterizes this deliberating process as an 'omnilogue' (in contrast to a monologue) because any reasoning person is capable of taking part in it.

[32] Rawls, *Political Liberalism* xxii, 93, 274; Rawls, 'Kantian Constructivism' 339; Rawls, 'Justice as Fairness: Political not Metaphysical' (n 21) 401; Bagnoli; Street (n 20) 368, 373.

[33] Rawls, *Political Liberalism* (n 1) 19, 81; See also Baynes (n 13) 20.

[34] Claude Lefort, 'The Question of Democracy' in *Democracy and Political Theory* (Polity Press 1988) 17–19.

Constructivism's Substantive Output:
The Authority of Basic Liberal Rights

What exactly are those markers of normative certainty? Their substantive content consists in the liberal principles of legitimacy, which take the form of classic basic liberal rights when it comes to the constitution.

At the most abstract, Rawls argued that constructivist procedure yields two principles of justice.[35] The first principle states that 'each person has the same indefeasible claim to a fully adequate scheme of equal basic liberties, which scheme is compatible with the same scheme of liberties for all'.[36] The second principle states that 'social and economic inequalities are to satisfy two conditions: first, they are to be attached to positions and offices open to all under conditions of fair equality of opportunity; and second, they are to be to the greatest benefit of the least advantaged members of society'. These principles serve as normative guidelines that establish the minimal guarantee for individuals to autonomously pursue their interests.

Although constructivism yields two principles of justice, Rawls argued that only the first can be constitutionally enacted.[37] The second principle is a measure of the legitimacy of 'the background institutions of society'.[38] It requires balancing liberal property rights with social rights. It also imposes positive duties on members. And its form may depend on a society's prevailing economic conditions. For those reasons, the distribution of goods will be the subject of sufficient reasonable disagreement that it cannot be entrenched in public law. Given those issues, Rawls concluded that members should be able to decide on its concrete form through ongoing democratic deliberation. So, although both principles specify what a democracy should provide for its citizens, only the first principle could be installed in a democratic constitution.

The first principle takes the constitutional form of basic liberal rights. Rawls unfortunately did not provide a comprehensive list of the basic liberal rights that it generates. He wrote that among them are 'freedom of thought and liberty of conscience; the political liberties and freedom of association, as well as the freedoms specified by the liberty and integrity of the person; and finally, the rights and liberties covered by the rule of law'.[39] While Rawls did not enumerate the exact content of this set of basic liberal rights, it was clearly modelled on rights traditionally recognized as classical liberal rights and the liberal rule of law.[40]

---

[35] John Rawls, *A Theory of Justice* (Belknap Press 1999) 52; Rawls, *Political Liberalism* (n 1) 309.

[36] Rawls, *Political Liberalism* (n 1) 5–6; See also Rawls, *Justice as Fairness: A Restatement* (n 18) 42–43.

[37] Rawls, *Justice as Fairness: A Restatement* (n 18) 47–48.

[38] ibid 46.

[39] Rawls, *Political Liberalism* (n 1) 291; See also Rawls, *Justice as Fairness: A Restatement* (n 18) 45.

[40] Based on remarks in the *The Law of Peoples*, the case could be made that Rawls believed the set of basic liberal rights are Articles 3 to 20 of the *Universal Declaration of Human Rights*. On the one hand, Rawls argued that a state must recognize Articles 3 through 18 in order to qualify as 'decent'. John Rawls, *The Law of Peoples* (Harvard University Press 1999) 80 Article 19 (speech rights) and Article 20 (right

CONSTRUCTIVISM AND THE AUTHORITY   91

In contrast to some other democratic theories, Rawls's theory defines basic liberal rights as essential for democratic legitimacy. They lay the foundation that makes democracy possible at all.[41] Without them, the exercise of political rights is hollow. Consequently, they hold a prior normative status. They normatively trump the exercise of political rights.

Defending the authoritative and binding nature of basic liberal rights does not rule out the constitutional enactment of *other* rights—nor their revocation, for that matter. Constructivism sets a constitutional minimum. It cannot determine an exhaustive set of constitutional rights or a comprehensive constitution. Because of its design, constructivism only establishes second-order rules of rule-making. These rules limit the exercise of public power, thereby allowing each member to see the public order as legitimate in principle. That legitimacy comes about because the public order guarantees each the means to realize their unique conception of the good through liberal basic rights. For other constitutional and ordinary legislation, the authority to decide rests with members themselves. They should determine which laws best realize their political identity. That determination includes how best to codify the difference principle. While other articles of the constitution do not hold the same distinctive normative status as basic liberal rights, incorporating them into the constitution would offer them the status of rights and a layer of protection against legal change that ordinary laws do not have. And although constructivism establishes a narrow set of immutable constitutional norms, it still leaves wide latitude for members to introduce or remove other norms from their constitution.

'The People' Versus the Electorate

Modern constitutionalism argues that, for the law to be legitimate, it must reflect the identity and will of 'the people'. Yet, defining what precisely constitutes the identity and will of 'the people' and who has the authority to represent 'the people' is far from clear.

---

to assembly) seem to be the additions necessary to make that set of rights 'liberal'. On the other hand, those rights correspond to the minimum set necessary to create the sphere of negative liberty necessary to pursue one's own conception of the good.

From his discussion of implied unamendability in Rawls' thought, Ferrara suggests that the constructivist procedure may generate content more expansive than just the canonical basic liberal rights. It would consist of five broad elements: 1. Democracy's basic structure, which includes basic liberal rights 2. General legal principles and presuppositions of the rule of law 3. Implicit democratic principles 4. Binding international law and treaties 5. The shared background assumptions that make any meaningful human activity possible. Ferrara, *Sovereignty Across Generations* (n 15) 12.

[41] Samuel Freeman, 'Constitutional Democracy and the Legitimacy of Judicial Review' (1990) 9 Law and Philosophy 327, 338.

92 LIBERALISM AND MODERN CONSTITUTIONALISM

Ferrara discusses the normative problems raised by equating the identity of 'the people' with the procedurally expressed will of the electorate, an argument made by some populists, for example.[42] By collapsing any distinction between 'the people' and the electorate, actions popular with voters that would revolutionize a legitimate democratic order can be portrayed as a legitimate exercise of constituent power.

Rawls critically delineates 'the people', as a constituent power, from the electorate, as a constituted power.[43] While Rawls acknowledged that majoritarian procedures can legitimately represent the will of 'the people' in most cases, he argued that the electorate is at best only a representation of the will and identity of 'the people'. The two are not identical.

Scholars have elaborated on the implications of Rawls' distinction, suggesting that 'the people' is more akin to a normative ideal than a material reality. For example, Freeman argues that 'the people' is 'an ideal of democratic politics' when it comes to democratic constitutional essentials and it cannot be located in any concrete body in society.[44] Essentially, 'the people' is closer to the ideal of public reason, which free and equal persons realize through an act of constituent power. That conception sets substantive limits on what a majority or even a supermajority of the electorate can legitimately achieve. Similar to Freeman's discussion, Michelman and Ferrara analyse how 'the people' is 'always under law', so that even acts of constituent power are subject to a 'higher' normative authority.[45]

Continuing that discussion, Ferrara argues that, within a Rawlsian framework, the identity of 'the people' emerges from the agreement between those freestanding principles, determined by the constructivist approach on the one hand, and the unique qualities that differentiate a people within its particular cultural and historical context on the other.[46] The boundaries of 'the people' are not defined by the electorate.[47] Instead, Ferrara argues for an intergenerational or 'sequential' conception of 'the people'. This approach conceives of 'the people' as a body that extends from the founders into future generations. From this perspective, just as democracy requires extending fair terms of cooperation horizontally to other members of the present generation, it also obliges extending fair terms of cooperation vertically.[48] They must respect the rights and interests of past and future generations who are also members of that same 'the people'.

Setting aside the concept of 'verticality' for a moment, equating 'the people' with the electorate overlooks how the boundaries of the electorate are contingent. For

---

[42] Ferrara, *Sovereignty Across Generations* (n 16) 66–90, 219–22.
[43] Rawls, *A Theory of Justice* (n 35) 313; Rawls, *Political Liberalism* (n 1) 233.
[44] Freeman, 'Political Liberalism' (n 16) 664–65.
[45] Alessandro Ferrara and Frank I Michelman, *Legitimation by Constitution: A Dialgoue on Political Liberalism* (Oxford University Press 2021).
[46] Ferrara, *Sovereignty Across Generations* (n 15) 130ff.
[47] ibid 201ff.
[48] ibid 248–52.

example, until rather recently, eligibility for membership in the electorate in many states depended on one's sex and ethnicity. Few today would take seriously the idea that the mid-nineteenth-century US electorate was identical with 'the people'. However, that is the implication of collapsing 'the people' into the materially existing electorate. Even today, the boundaries of the electorate are contested. Despite the aspiration for universal suffrage, groups such as the young, criminals, migrants and refugees, and foreign workers tend to fall outside the boundaries of the electorate. They are certainly subject to the laws of 'the people'.[49] They may, however, also become a part of that 'people'.

There are thus compelling reasons for accepting Rawls' distinction between 'the people' and the electorate. While majoritarian procedures are generally the best and most expedient way to represent the identity and will of 'the people', they are only a representation. As such, they have limits. But the electorate is an imperfect representation and should not be uncritically equated with 'the people'. Distinguishing 'the people' from the electorate entails several normative consequences:

First, although 'the people' may not have a concrete material existence, the output of its constitutive decision does. Its most authoritative representation seems to be the consequence of its decision to self-constitute in the first place: its constitution. From this perspective, constitutional essentials are the most authoritative expression of the political identity of 'the people'.

Second, because basic liberal rights count as constitutional essentials and are integral to its political identity and existence, 'the people' would never authorize their abrogation. Doing so would be to authorize the destruction of its own political identity and existence.[50]

Third, the electorate is a derivative, constituted power. The constitution delegates legal powers to the electorate—just like any other constituted power. As such, the electorate may not legitimately assume 'the people's' constituent power by sidestepping the constitution. Any attempt by the electorate to overstep those limits and exercise constituent power would be substantively unconstitutional, regardless of whether legal pathways to do so are available. For example, even if the amendment clause is the supreme clause of the constitution and it appears valid to abrogate basic liberal rights, it would still not be a legitimate constitutional change.[51]

Fourth, the identity and will of 'the people', expressed through constitutional essentials, may conflict with the legally expressed will of the electorate.[52] In such

---

[49] On this, see Dahl's seminal discussion of the criterion of inclusiveness and what it means for a procedural account of democracy Robert A Dahl, 'Procedural Democracy' in Robert E Goodin and Philip Pettit (eds), *Contemporary Political Philosophy: An Anthology* (John Wiley & Sons, Inc 2019) 157–60.

[50] Rawls, *Political Liberalism* (n 1) 337, 365–66; Rawls, 'The Idea of an Overlapping Consensus' in Samuel Freeman (ed), *Collected Papers* (Harvard University Press 1999) 439; Freeman, 'Political Liberalism' (n 16) 663.

[51] Preuss arrives to this conclusion by taking a different path. See Ulrich K Preuss, 'The Implications of "Eternity Clauses": The German Experience' (2011) 44(3) Israel Law Review 429, 430.

[52] Freeman, 'Political Liberalism' (n 16) 659.

94 LIBERALISM AND MODERN CONSTITUTIONALISM

cases, constitutional essentials take precedence and legitimately trump the legally expressed will of the electorate.

Although basic liberal rights are integral to the identity of any democratic people, they are not and cannot exhaust that identity. This distinction matters because modern constitutionalism also aims to enable a particular manifestation of 'the people' to express its authentic political identity.[53] Ferrara writes that a constitution will include the distinctive commitments that 'the people' has codified as its 'irrecusable, identity-defining' self.[54] Aspects of that 'people's' identity may change over time. A key challenge of constitutionalism is how to balance those static democratic essentials, which enable 'the people' to develop its authentic identity through law in the first place, with the laws enacted by those procedures, which concretize and particularize that identity.

Recognizing the conceptual and ultimately normative distinction between 'the people' and the electorate is a critical step toward creating that balance. Constructivism provides the theoretical basis that demonstrates how the electorate might illegitimately assume 'the people's' constituent power and turn it against democracy. In order to safeguard the democratic identity of 'the people', Rawls argues that democratic constitutional essentials, namely basic liberal rights, should be taken 'off the political agenda' entirely.[55] Rawls argues they should be depoliticized.

Measures to Entrench Constitutional Norms

Given that basic liberal rights are authoritative constitutional norms that underpin legitimate democratic order, it makes sense to entrench them against positive legal change. So what measures can a democratic state adopt to accomplish that without compromising its democratic legitimacy?

Rawls never directly addressed this question. However, within his broader political philosophy, he did make arguments for institutions that resemble two principal measures of militant democracy. The first is *implied unamendability*, which Rawls argues is a mechanism that 'fixes' basic liberal rights 'once and for all' against legal change. The second is '*containment*', which Rawls argues restricts the political participatory rights of 'unreasonable' actors, effectively denying them the legal possession of state power. This section delves into Rawls' discussion of those two

---

[53] See Bruce Ackerman, *Revolutionary Constitutions: Charismatic Leadership and the Rule of Law* (Harvard University Press 2019) 18–21.

[54] Ferrara, *Sovereignty Across Generations* (n 15) 163.

[55] Rawls, *Political Liberalism* (n 1) 161; Rawls suggests and at times openly advocates taking liberal principles 'off the political agenda' in many places, such as ibid 151–52 (note 16); Rawls, *Justice as Fairness: A Restatement* (n 18) 116, 145–46, 194; Rawls, 'The Idea of an Overlapping Consensus' (n 50) 435–36, 439, 442; Rawls, 'The Domain of the Political and Overlapping Consensus' in Samuel Freeman (ed), *Collected Papers* (Harvard University Press 1999) 494, 496.

measures of entrenchment. It also explores how they relate to the idea a constitutional guardian.

Unamendability: Fixing Basic Liberal Rights 'Once and for All'

Roznai shows that unamendability as a method for entrenching constitutional norms takes either of two forms: explicit or implicit.[56] *Explicit* unamendability occurs when certain clauses of the constitution are legally unalterable.[57] It defines entrenched clauses as constitutionally supreme. For example, Article 79.3 of the German *Basic Law*, the 'eternity clause', renders any amendment to the principles outlined in Articles 1 and 20, as well as to Germany's federal structure, invalid.[58] Those codified and entrenched principles are binding not simply because they are explicitly unamendable; instead, they are thought to codify higher law—an independent 'objective order of values'.

When the amendment clause is positively the supreme clause of the constitution and other articles sit under the reservation of its exercise, then unamendability can at best be *implicit*. Despite the positive supremacy of the amendment clause, some amendments may nevertheless be deemed unconstitutional if they clash with higher, extralegal constitutional norms. Another approach holds that a constitutional amendment by its nature can only modify, but not annihilate, the constitution itself.[59] Implicit unamendability hinges on the assumption that a branch of government—typically the judiciary—holds final authority to determine constitutionality and to review law accordingly.[60] The Basic Structure Doctrine of India illustrates implicit unamendability well. In its landmark case *Kesavananda Bharati Sripadagalvaru v State of Kerala*, the Supreme Court of India asserted that the power to amend the constitution did not include altering its fundamental identity.[61] Through that ruling, the Court affirmed its role as guardian of the democratic identity of the Indian 'people', superseding both the electorate and their representatives in parliament.

---

[56] Yaniv Roznai, *Unconstitutional Constitutional Amendments: The Limits of Amendment Powers* (Oxford University Press 2017).

[57] ibid 16.

[58] Werner Heun, *The Constitution of Germany: A Contextual Analysis* (Hart Publishing 2011) 25–48; Donald P Kommers and Russell A Miller, *The Constitutional Jurisprudence of the Federal Republic of Germany* (Duke University Press 2012) 44–45, 57–58.

[59] Carl Schmitt, *Constitutional Theory* (Duke University Press 2008) 147–58.

[60] Roznai (n 56) argues that implicit unamendability is the result of the court's authority to interpret. However, there is no reason why that authority must be held by the judiciary. Freeman argues that the authority of that branch is distinct from the three ordinary branches of government. Although that authority is typically held by the constitutional court, Freeman discusses the alternative model of a tribunate, as developed by Rousseau. Freeman, 'Constitutional Democracy' (n 41) 359. See the discussion in chapter 7.

[61] See Roznai (n 56) 44ff; Ferrara, *Sovereignty Across Generations* (n 15) 204.

96   LIBERALISM AND MODERN CONSTITUTIONALISM

Although Rawls did not explicitly refer to 'implicit unamendability' in his writings, his views fall under that type.[62] Rawls argued for removing basic liberal rights from the political agenda, writing that they must be 'fixed, once and for all, and assigned special priority' because 'leaving the status and content of those rights and liberties still unsettled [would] subject them to the shifting circumstances of time and place [and greatly raise] the stakes of political controversy, dangerously [increasing] the insecurity and hostility of public life'.[63] At first glance, this argument may seem undemocratic. However, Rawls showed that any serious conception of democracy must be grounded on basic liberal rights. According to political constructivism, they are a freestanding precondition for legitimate public order. His insistence on 'fixing' them raises an important question: how can basic liberal rights be legitimately guaranteed, or are there any circumstances under which they may be legitimately amended?

Two related arguments stem from Rawls' argument that basic liberal rights should be fixed and assigned a special priority. First, by insisting that those rights be 'fixed', Rawls emphasizes their unique status as constitutional essentials. Abrogating those rights would not only undermine the legitimacy of the public order, but would also jeopardize its stability by increasing the risk of regressing back into a *modus vivendi*. As such, any democratic society should therefore aim to guarantee those rights for its members.

Second, Rawls argued that basic liberal rights should be assigned a 'special priority', defined by their fixed status and specific content. By insisting on their special role status within democratic constitutionalism, Rawls can be read as arguing that democratic constitutions should have two distinct procedures—or 'tracks'—for constitutional legislation. That is, basic liberal rights should be governed by a special legislative track, distinct from other articles of the constitution. In making this case, Rawls' argument may have anticipated Arato's theory of 'multitrack constitutionalism'.[64]

Multitrack constitutionalism is best understood when contrasted with dual-track constitutionalism. The latter, exemplified by both the Hungarian *Fundamental Law* and *The US Constitution*, recognizes only two legislative tracks: laws passed by a simple majority ('ordinary' law) and laws that require a higher threshold to pass (constitutional law). That simplicity can create problems for constitutional amendment. On the one hand, the legal revolution of constitutional essentials could be too easy because the thresholds for amendment are too low—for instance, requiring only a two-thirds supermajority in a single chambered legislature, as the Hungarian *Fundamental Law* does. On the other hand, amending non-essentials

---

[62] Roznai (n 56) 145–46.

[63] Rawls, *Political Liberalism* (n 1) 161.

[64] Andrew Arato, 'Multi-Track Constitutionalism beyond Carl Schmitt' (2011) 18(3) Constellations 324–25; Andrew Arato, *The Adventures of the Constituent Power: Beyond Revolutions?* (Cambridge University Press 2017) 388ff.

articles may be overly cumbersome if the amendment thresholds are too high or convoluted—for instance, requiring a two-thirds supermajority in two legislative chambers, followed by ratification by three-quarters of state legislatures, as in the United States.

In contrast, multitrack constitutionalism introduces at least a second track for constitutional legislation, which distinguishes essential from non-essential constitutional articles. For essentials, it may set an extremely high threshold for their amendment. Or it may make them legally impossible to amend. Meanwhile, although amendments to other articles must still meet higher thresholds for change than ordinary legislation, non-essential constitutional articles are still easier to change than constitutional essentials. Introducing a separate track for constitutional essentials signals their special status through positive law and better entrenches them, while allowing the rest of the constitution to be more responsive to the will of the electorate.

Multitrack constitutionalism provides a framework for institutionalizing the normative claims of Rawls' liberalism. As described above, constructivism determines a set of authoritative constitutional norms—basic liberal rights—that should bind any democratic 'people'. In Rawls' approach, not only are they preconditions for democratic legal procedures, they are part of the identity of any democratic 'people'. They are, however, only a constitutional minimum. While they should be entrenched, nothing about them precludes or excludes introducing other constitutional norms. That flexibility allows each 'people' the autonomy to develop its own unique political identity—one that is both authentic, because specific values resonate with its members, and distinct, since it differs from the identities of other 'peoples'. That variability also ensures that the electorate can represent and codify that dynamic and evolving identity of 'the people', as its political identity changes over time. Multitrack constitutionalism, which I return to in chapter 5, clarifies how balancing democracy with authenticity is legally feasible. Establishing a distinctive legislative track for constitutional essentials allows basic liberal rights to be depoliticized and protected against illegitimate change, while also ensuring that 'the people' has wide latitude to introduce and modify other articles of the constitution, so its constitution matches its broader identity.

Defining basic liberal rights as unamendable places an implicit restriction on the exercise of legislative power. Rawls argued that 'the reasonable frames and subordinates the rational' at every legislative stage, setting normative limits on what positive legislation can accomplish.[65] That limitation stems from the constructivist procedure, which works at the highest level of legislation, in which 'the people' exercise their constituent power. There, the reasonable subordinates the rational by determining an essential aspect of a democratic society's political identity, as

---

[65] Rawls, *Political Liberalism* (n 1) 339; See also Gutmann (n 22) 183.

98 LIBERALISM AND MODERN CONSTITUTIONALISM

represented by rational agents operating under the veil of ignorance. The outcome of that procedure determines constitutional essentials, which in turn structure what the government and the electorate can accomplish. It leaves them, as Rawls wrote, with 'far less leeway' in how they may exercise state power and their political participatory rights.[66]

The case for unamendability hinges on distinguishing between 'the people' as a constituting power and the electorate as a constituted power. As described above, Rawls argued that no democratic iteration of 'the people' would grant the electorate, or any other constituted power for that matter, the authority to alter its basic liberal rights because doing so would effectively dismantle its democratic identity. Ferrara argues that Rawls' criterion of reciprocity also shapes constitutional amendment *vertically*: amendments are valid only if they uphold a standard of reasonability *across generations*.[67] Unamendability is implied when basic liberal rights are established as authoritative constitutional norms.

If positive legal procedures can be used to abrogate democratic constitutional essentials, the electorate or its elected representatives may incorrectly believe that it has the discretion to do so, mistaking its amendment power for constitutive power. That misunderstanding could in turn be exploited by unreasonable members, such as advocates of 'illiberal democracy'. Identifying basic liberal rights as unamendable clarifies both the limits of the electorate's powers and the special role that constitutional essentials play in enabling democratic order. Their depoliticization helps to guard against a democracy's descent into a mere *modus vivendi*.

Of the three roles that Rawls assigned to the constitutional court in *Political Liberalism*, the first is to guard the constitution.[68] This is achieved through the court's power of judicial review, which allows it to invalidate efforts to undermine democratic constitutional essentials. Judicial review is a countermajoritarian institution, so it may appear antidemocratic at first glance. After all, it empowers an elite minority to thwart the legally expressed will of a present majority. However, characterizing the constitutional court's guardianship as merely 'antidemocratic' is overly simplistic. Rawls argued that the court plays an invaluable supporting role in establishing the background conditions that allow for democracy to exist in the first place. He believed that judicial review played an essential role in guaranteeing democracy.

Expanding on Rawls' views on the role of constitutional guardianship, Freeman writes that majoritarian legislative procedures, while the primary means for democracy, are imperfect by themselves.[69] Without checks, they too can be antidemocratic—especially if they lose the capacity for self-correction.[70] That can occur, for example, when the legislative branch and other institutions are taken over

[66] Rawls, *Political Liberalism* (n 1) 340.
[67] Ferrara, *Sovereignty Across Generations* (n 15) 273ff.
[68] Rawls, *Political Liberalism* (n 1) 233ff.
[69] Freeman, 'Constitutional Democracy' (n 41) 354.
[70] ibid 361.

by 'unreasonable' elected representatives intent on subverting democratic constitutional fundamentals. The guardian's authority over constitutionality thus serves as a corrective on pathologies of democratic legal procedures. It helps guarantee that all can live freely and equally and can pursue their unique conceptions of the good. As a corrective, the guardian is not just democratically legitimate, it is a practical necessity. Without it, the imperfections of the legislative branch can spin out of control, particularly under the strain of antidemocratic ideologies. By representing those left out of majoritarian institutions and enforcing the unamendability of democratic essentials, the guardian of the constitution actually enhances democracy.[71]

Political Rights Restrictions: 'Containing' Unreasonable Actors

By itself, unamendability may not be sufficient to entrench constitution essentials. An electoral victory grants even unreasonable members the legal possession of state power. Even if they are unable to meet the thresholds necessary to amend democratic essentials out of the constitution, they can still pursue their goals using other legal means. For example, by stringing together democratic an electoral victory, the power of judicial appointment, and ordinary legislation, antidemocrats might be able to successfully derogate or 'breach' the constitution. With loyalists installed in the constitutional court, antidemocrats can be confident that their unconstitutional laws will not be invalidated. Antidemocrats can combine multiple legal acts to pursue their illegitimate political goals, a tactic Scheppele characterizes as stitching together a 'Frankenstate'.[72] Tactics like that demonstrate how the mere presence of antidemocrats in government can become an existential threat to democracy. In addition to mechanisms that invalidate antidemocratic legislation, effective constitutional entrenchment must include mechanisms that can prevent antidemocrats from legally possessing state power.[73]

Rawls provides a normative framework for using political rights restrictions to entrench the constitution, although only indirectly. He argued that, although no democratic state can prevent unreasonable beliefs and actors from emerging, it can aim 'to contain them so that they do not undermine the unity and justice of society'.[74] Rawls unfortunately did not elaborate on the term 'containment', but hinted that legal means might be used to 'force the intolerant to respect the liberty

---

[71] Rawls, *Political Liberalism* (n 1) 232–33.

[72] Kim Lane Scheppele, 'The Rule of Law and the Frankenstate: Why Governance Checklists Do Not Work' (2013) 26(4) Governance: An International Journal of Policy, Administration, and Institutions 559.

[73] Alexander S Kirshner, *A Theory of Militant Democracy: The Ethics of Combatting Political Extremism* (Yale University Press 2014) 4.

[74] Rawls, *Political Liberalism* (n 1) xviii–xix, 64 (note 19); John Rawls, 'The Idea of Public Reason Revisited' (1997) 64 The University of Chicago Law Review 614; See also Freeman, 'Political Liberalism' (n 16) 643.

of others, since a person can be required to respect the rights established by principles that he would acknowledge in the original position'.[75] Gutmann adds that such intolerance could be justifiable and attributable to public reason, if it serves to protect more critical freedoms.[76] Rawls' containment thus seems to restrict political rights for the sake of the more essential basic liberal rights.

Quong fleshes out a convincing interpretation of Rawls's argument for containment. According to Quong, for 'containment' to be conceptually meaningful, it cannot merely be reduced to enforcing the positive law—such as preventing violent hate crimes by racist extremists.[77] If containment only meant enforcing the law, it would be redundant, since a well-ordered state would already punish violations of the law. Instead, Quong argues, containment gains its conceptual significance in circumstances where 'no law is being broken and no harm will directly follow'.[78] In this sense, containment serves as a guideline for how a democracy should handle unreasonable members who threaten a stable and legitimate public order within the bounds of legality.

Quong defends several cases in which containment is legitimate. He argues the most compelling case as that of Nazis using their speech rights to incite the suppression of minorities' rights and otherwise harm them.[79] Quong argues that containment would be legitimate neither because of the offensiveness of the Nazis' views nor because their speech's potential to cause harm indirectly. Rather, containment is legitimate because their use of their speech rights undermines the very basis of a society committed to a fair system of social cooperation among free and equal citizens.

Basic rights protect members' fundamental interests in freedom by imposing legally enforceable obligations on the state and other members to refrain from interfere with them. However, Quong argues, when the interest pursued is fundamentally unreasonable and undermines the rights of others, then appealing to one's rights fails. In such cases, the state may legitimately restrict or 'contain' the exercise of those rights.

If it is legitimate to limit the rights of Nazis who threaten to use their speech rights to degrade democratic fundamentals, then the case for containment should be even stronger against individuals who threaten to use their political rights to undermine democracy directly. If any circumstances justify containment, the most compelling should be the attempt to legal revolutionize democratic constitutional essentials. In such cases, antidemocrats are not merely asserting that their basic rights trump the rights of others. They are arguing that their political rights give them the authority to annihilate liberal democracy altogether. In essence, legal revolution attempts to constitutionalize unreasonability.

---

[75] Rawls, *A Theory of Justice* (n 35) 192.
[76] Gutmann (n 22) 183.
[77] Jonathan Quong, *Liberalism without Perfection* (Oxford University Press 2011) 299.
[78] ibid 300.
[79] ibid 305, 308–11.

'Containment' thus refers to restricting political rights when they may be used to revolutionize democracy legally. It entrenches constitutional essentials by disqualifying political organizations from participating in democratic elections and procedures, as even their participation could undermine democracy through ordinary legal means.

Three considerations may assuage concerns about the undemocratic nature of containment. First, when theorized more narrowly as a mechanism of constitutional entrenchment, containment only justifies restricting *political* rights. Because it leaves basic liberal rights intact, containment aligns with the legitimation requirements of constructivist theory, which mandates that basic liberal rights be guaranteed institutionally. Individuals subjected to containment still retain the freedom to pursue their unique if also unreasonable conceptions of the good and their fundamental interests *privately*, with the full protection of their basic liberal rights. In that way, containment can be reconciled with the legitimation requirements of modern constitutionalism.

In this regard, Rawls' theory provides militant democracy with a normative framework for sidestepping the paradox of democracy's self-defence—which normative theories of militant democracy have so far struggled to address. Based on liberal theory, members' political rights may be legitimately infringed upon in order to defend the more critical basic liberal rights, as determined by constructivism. 'Containment' prevents political rights from being turned against basic liberal rights, which are more fundamental .

Second, while containment keeps basic liberal rights intact, it does restrict organizations' political rights, thereby limiting electoral options and potentially harming democracy. For this reason, Quong argues, containment should not be automated or irreversible.[80] Elected representatives bear the responsibility to decide whether to contain a party demonstrating antidemocratic inclinations. Importantly, a contained party may have its political rights reinstated after demonstrating that it has rehabilitated, allowing reformed antidemocrats to rejoin the democratic community. Organizations affected by political rights restrictions should therefore have the legal means to appeal.

Third, and related to the previous point, a militant democracy must adhere to the rule of law when executing containment. A government should present compelling reasons and evidence for restricting an organization's political rights. The process should be transparent and subject to both oversight and a robust system of checks and balances.

In summary, as fleshed out by Quong, Rawls' concept of containment provides a normative justification for restricting political rights as a means to entrench democratic constitutional essentials. Containment is a crucial complement to

---

[80] ibid 311.

102 LIBERALISM AND MODERN CONSTITUTIONALISM

unamendability, better safeguarding the essential background conditions of democratic society.

'A Practical Dilemma'? The Limits of Rawls for Militant Democracy

This chapter has analysed how elements of Rawls' liberalism provide the foundation for an alternative 'liberal' normative theory of militant democracy. As a contribution to a liberal theory of militant democracy, Rawls' thought first shows that there are authoritative constitutional norms of democracy, namely basic liberal rights. Second, it determines that, in order to entrench those norms, a democratic state may legitimately adopt militant measures, namely unamendability and political rights restrictions, supplemented by a guardian of the constitution.

Political constructivism shows that basic liberal rights are freestanding democratic constitutional essentials because they are the product of practical reason, worked out through constructivism's hypothetical proceduralism. It shows that those norms are authoritative and binding for a pluralistic, democratic society, even if an unreasonable segment of the electorate rejects them using legal democratic procedures. No democratic 'people' would authorize their abrogation because doing so would annihilate its democratic identity.

Because they are essential, basic liberal rights should be entrenched and protected against illegitimate change. This includes protection against forms of otherwise legal change, such as constitutional amendment. To entrench essential norms, Rawls advocated 'fixing' basic liberal rights against legal change through implied unamendability and assigned the constitutional court the duty of guarding them. Rawls also advocated 'containing' unreasonable members who threaten the stability and the justness of democratic society even if the abrogation of constitutional essentials is not legally possible. Although Rawls himself did not fully elaborate what 'containment' meant exactly, there are reasons to believe that Rawls meant something like political rights restrictions.

In the end, however, Rawls seemed to back away from endorsing those militant measures of entrenchment, in particular containment. In a section in A Theory of Justice on democracy's self-defence, Rawls discussed how a democracy might respond to an explosive growth of unreasonable members who threaten to destabilize democracy. After outlining the situation, he concluded that the answer to the question of whether a democracy should actually deploy militant measures in response to internal threats was a 'practical dilemma which philosophy alone cannot resolve' and depended on specific circumstances.[81]

---

[81] Rawls, A Theory of Justice (n 35) 193; See Jan-Werner Müller, 'A "Practical Dilemma Which Philosophy Alone Cannot Resolve"? Rethinking Militant Democracy: An Introduction' (2012) 19(4) Constellations 537.

Part of the reason for Rawls' ambivalence about deploying militant measures may have been because the institutional design of democracy's self-defence was too far beyond the scope of political philosophy for him to discuss it further. Gutmann writes that Rawls conceived of his work as 'normative', rather than 'empirical'.[82] As a normative thinker, Rawls may not have thought himself qualified to discuss matters of democratic practice and institutional design. At the same time, the implications of deploying measures of unamendability and containment may have given him pause. Although Rawls was unambiguous that basic liberal rights were authoritative constitutional norms, he seemed at best uncomfortable when it came their entrenchment.

There are good reasons for his discomfort. As discussed in previous chapters, even advocates of militant democracy are squeamish about militancy because of the normative issues it presents. Not the least of these is that, as Kirshner argues, infringing on political rights damages members' basic interests. No matter how legitimate it may be to infringe on members' political rights, doing so still causes harm. For that reason, a democracy must have good reasons for taking such militant action. Although Rawls did discuss the problems of unreasonability and democratic degradation, his focus lay elsewhere, and the theoretical apparatus he constructs may not be sufficient by itself to get an alternative, liberal normative theory of militant democracy off the ground.

On the one hand, Rawls seemed unsure of how to resolve the potential tension between an electorate genuinely opposed to constitutional essentials. In his debate with Habermas, he seemed to accept that the electorate could legitimately amend *any* article of the constitution—so long as its decision to do so is 'considered'.[83] Rawls' normative qualification is important. It reveals a reluctance to commit to the positive legal codification of the moral limits to constitutional change that his philosophy described. Perhaps Rawls was not convinced that political liberalism provided the state with the normative authority to enforce unamendability, despite the rest of the normative framework he had developed. Something more is needed to justify installing unamendability.

On the other hand, Rawls himself was vague about what containment meant, perhaps because he hoped a democracy would never have to seriously consider deploying those measures. He left it up to others to flesh that concept out. Although Quong develops the potential implications of Rawls' theory, even Quong's approach stops short of linking it directly to entrenchment through the restriction of political rights. To be sure, 'containment' points in that direction, but it stops too far short.

---

[82] Gutmann (n 22) 168. Rosenblum echoes Rawls on this point. When it comes to party bans, she argues that 'I doubt that this subject is amenable to a sharp analytic framework or stable regulative principles except in the broadest sense'. Nancy L Rosenblum, *On the Side of Angels: An Appreciation of Parities and Partisanship* (Princeton University Press 2008) 415.

[83] Rawls, *Political Liberalism* (n 1) 396–99.

104 LIBERALISM AND MODERN CONSTITUTIONALISM

Although Rawls' liberal theory contributes significantly to the foundations of an alternative, liberal theory of militant democracy, then, it has its limits. It determines the authority of basic liberal rights for a democracy, which set objective normative limits on procedures of legal change, but it does not fully explain the legitimacy of deploying 'militant' measures in order to entrench and guarantee authoritative norms.

Despite its limits, Rawls' thought shows that a liberal normative theory of militant democracy might successfully navigate some of the obstacles facing other such normative theories. First and foremost, a liberal approach seems to circumvent the paradox of democracy's self-defence. Insofar as basic liberal rights normatively precede political rights, basic liberal rights circumscribe the legitimate exercise of political rights and act as 'trumps' if the electorate attempts to turn them against more essential democratic constitutional norms. When there is a conflict between the two—for example, if an illiberal democratic party sought to abrogate basic liberal rights and legally revolutionize the constitution's democratic identity—Rawls' theory offers a normative basis for both invalidating that legislation and taking measures against those seeking to adopt it. This Rawls-inspired approach avoids that paradox. First, it shows that basic liberal rights can be generated independently of the will of the electorate, so that their normative authority is freestanding and binds a democratic electorate regardless. Second, it explains why there is no logical tension between the rights suspended and the underlying theory of legitimacy it adopts. Political rights are categorically distinct from basic liberal rights.

Normative theories of militant democracy so far have typically conceived of militant democracy as a defence of political participatory rights through the deployment of party bans. The problem of the paradox emerges from the obvious tension between infringing on some members' political rights for the sake of upholding political rights. These theories then offer a variety of ways to resolve that paradox. However, a liberal theory of militant democracy has the advantage that it simply does not raise the paradox in the first place. Infringements on political rights are predicated on the defence of basic liberal rights, which political liberalism argues have a special and prior normative status.

4

Depoliticization and State Authority

Introduction

John Rawls' political constructivism shows how authoritative and binding liberal norms can be established in a way that accommodates the constraints of modern epistemology and the fact of pluralism. Rawls defended the constitutional entrenchment of basic liberal rights, arguing that they should be taken off the legislative agenda and that antidemocrats should be politically contained. However, Rawls stopped short of endorsing or justifying the use of militant measures, arguing that democracy's self-defence was a 'practical dilemma that philosophy cannot resolve'.

Pace Rawls, the problem of democracy's self-defence can be resolved philosophically by theorizing the state's right to defend its constitutional identity. This chapter argues for the legitimacy of defending its constitutional identity by building on Carl Schmitt's state and constitutional theory. Schmitt theorized that every state was constituted by its 'political' identity, and a state could legitimately use militant measures to defend that identity against legal and extralegal threats.

Schmitt revised Hobbes' response to the problem of civil war to address the challenges of modern democracy. He argued that rational actors would recognize that their mutual insecurity stems from the individuated right to decide and enforce what was 'political', ie what values were so existentially significant they should bind the community and were worth dying for. They would further recognize that they could overcome that insecurity, and the threat of civil war, by ceding that right to the state, in the process authorizing the state to guarantee their collective political identity. Schmitt thus used Hobbes to argue that preventing internal politicization and civil war required curbing the inherent centrifugal forces of democracy itself. This involved, among other things, establishing absolute albeit implicit limits on democratic legal change and the formation of anticonstitutional parties. Schmitt defended the state's prerogative to defend its political identity even against popular legal revolutionary threats.

While essential for developing a normative theory of militant democracy, Schmitt's state and constitutional theory presents limitations that democrats must take into account. If Rawls really only provides the *democratic* dimension of a normative theory of militant democracy, because he was unable to resolve that 'practical dilemma', then Schmitt's thought really only provides its necessary complement, the *militant* dimension. Schmitt was able to justify the state's right

---

Democracy despite Itself. Benjamin A. Schupmann, Oxford University Press. © Benjamin A. Schupmann 2024.
DOI: 10.1093/9780191975950.003.0005

106 DEPOLITICIZATION AND STATE AUTHORITY

to defend its constitutional identity, but because he was at best agnostic about liberalism and democracy, he offered no real guidance on what that identity ought to be. Therefore, a liberal normative theory of militant democracy emerges from the combination of the substance of Rawls' political liberalism and the form of Schmitt's state and constitutional theory. The liberal theory of militant democracy lays the foundation for the mechanisms of constitutional entrenchment analysed in subsequent chapters.

A Preliminary on Schmitt and Democracy

Rawls and Schmitt are obviously an uncomfortable pairing. Their values and methods are not only radically different, they are fundamentally opposed in many regards.

Schmitt embraced and acted on ideas that many consider deplorable. Among other things, he theorized and publicly defended the constitutionality of the Nazi's early actions, including the extralegal assassinations of the Night of Long Knives in 1933.[1] His actions helped to normalize the Nazi regime in its infancy. Moreover, Schmitt's anti-Semitism became evident as helped to expel Jewish jurists from German universities. To his death, Schmitt remained unrepentant for his actions.[2] Modern day antidemocrats, from Jarosław Kaczyński (the chairman of Poland's right-wing populist party Prawo i Sprawiedliwość) to Richard Spencer (the American neo-Nazi), draw inspiration from Schmitt.

However, Schmitt also theorized the legitimacy of mechanisms of constitutionalism entrenchment associated with militant democracy, including implied unamendability, bans of unconstitutional parties, the 'constructive' vote of no confidence, and the need for a guardian of the constitution (although he problematically argued that the President should play that role). Schmitt theorized these measures to contain what he considered to be Weimar's two principal enemies: the Nazi and Communist parties. He was troubled by the fact that both participated in Weimar democracy solely to revolutionize its constitution legally. The fact that Schmitt theorized mechanisms to entrench the Weimar Constitution, in particular its system of basic rights, makes it difficult to depict Schmitt as merely an antidemocrat or fascist. The story is more complicated.

As I argue elsewhere, that apparent inconsistency or 'occasionalism' in Schmitt's thought can be explained by his conservatism, his Hobbesianism, and his realism.[3] At their core, these converge on the idea that stability is the most fundamental

[1] Carl Schmitt, 'Der Führer schützt das Recht' (1934) 15(39) Deutsche Juristen-Zeitung.
[2] Reinhard Mehring, *Carl Schmitt: Aufstieg und Fall* (CH Beck 2009) 358–80.
[3] Benjamin A Schupmann, *Carl Schmitt's State and Constitutional Theory: A Critical Analysis* (Oxford University Press 2017).

political value. In his jurisprudence, Schmitt tended to focus narrowly on the formal need for a decision on the political identity of a public order, rather than on the substantive legitimacy of a particular decision. His state and constitutional theory was intended to describe a pathology of human nature. He believed they described a universal problem facing states, regardless of the specific commitments of the public order. This is not to say that Schmitt was totally agnostic about values. Instead, his primary concern was with securing the public order that he happened to live under—or at least his interpretation of it.

That realism put Schmitt in a peculiar position. Although he never really embraced either liberalism or democracy, he nevertheless employed his conservative state theory to address the political and legal challenges facing the Weimar state. In the process, he helped to create the mechanisms now identified with militant democracy. Those mechanisms have since been incorporated into many post-war democratic constitutions. Democrats today would be remiss to ignore Schmitt's contributions because of his moral failures, particularly when they address some of democracy's most pressing problems.

Similar to the preceding one on Rawls, this chapter does not intend to vindicate Schmitt's thought per se. Nor does it intend to rehabilitate his reputation. Rather, it lays a normative foundation for militant democracy. Schmitt's theory provides a rationale for the state's defence of its political identity, particularly through the adoption of militant constitutional measures such as unamendability and political rights restrictions.

The Problem of Politicization

Schmitt's concept of 'the political' can be interpreted as a diagnosis of a fundamental problem of modern society: the potential for unregulated social pluralism to 'politicize' and in the process destabilize the state and constitution.[4] Under this interpretation, 'the political' is not a normative argument that valorises political violence and enmity.[5] It is descriptive. In this descriptive sense, the concept draws attention to a pathology of human relations. By identifying and conceptualizing

---

[4] Böckenförde argues that Schmitt's *The Concept of the Political* should be read in the context of its late Weimar origins and as a kind of conceptual key that unlocks the themes of his *Constitutional Theory* (and vice versa). Ernst-Wolfgang Böckenförde, 'The Concept of the Political: A Key to Understanding Carl Schmitt's Constitutional Theory' in David Dyzenhaus (ed), *Law as Politics: Carl Schmitt's Critique of Liberalism* (Duke University Press 1998). See also John P McCormick, 'Fear, Technology, and the State; Carl Schmitt, Leo Strauss, and the Revival of Hobbes in Weimar and National Socialist Germany' (1994) 22(4) Political Theory 626; John P McCormick, *Carl Schmitt's Critique of Liberalism: Against Politics as Technology* (Cambridge University Press 1997) 254; Bernard Willms, 'Politics as Politics: Carl Schmitt's "Concept of the Political" and the Tradition of European Political Thought' (1991) 13(4) History of European Ideas, 378; Martin Loughlin, 'Politonomy' in Jens Meierhenrich and Oliver Simons (eds), *The Oxford Handbook of Carl Schmitt* (Oxford University Press 2015) 575–76.
[5] Richard Wolin offers one example of this interpretation of Schmitt.

108 DEPOLITICIZATION AND STATE AUTHORITY

'the political', Schmitt intended to draw attention to what he thought was a major oversight in Weimar's positivist jurisprudence and democratic politics, which had inadvertently exacerbated its problems.[6] He turned to Hobbes to reinforce the state against the centrifugal forces of mass democracy and to stave off civil war.[7]

Schmitt defined 'the political' as those norms or ideas that are so existentially significant that their holders believed they ought to determine the public order and be upheld with force.[8] Any belief- or value-system has the potential to politicize.[9] Religion, ethnicity, and economics were all examples of politicized belief from the last century.

Like many of his contemporaries, Schmitt accepted that modern epistemology, beginning with the scepticism of the Enlightenment, unleashed a process of the disenchantment of transcendent authority. Transcendent authority rooted in metaphysical truths, such as the Catholic Church's interpretation of divine law, was no longer accepted as self-evident.[10] Without a single authoritative truth, belief and value systems pluralized as individuals formed distinct understanding of truth and right.

Disenchantment and the fact of pluralism had political consequences.[11] Subjects began to question the basis and legitimacy of secular authority. Disagreements about the sources of normative authority and what norms were objectively right turned into disagreements about which norms should be upheld with the force of law. Some of those disagreements *politicized*, as subjects resorted to violence in order to realize and uphold publicly what they believed to be objective right. The Confessional Civil Wars that ravaged Europe exemplify the consequences of politicization.

Politicization thus is a problem when one group's political beliefs, about what public 'right' consists in, become fundamentally opposed to another's.[12] Political pluralism leads to outbreaks of violence as groups compete and fight over those beliefs. Adherents may organize into militias or other militant armed groups in order to defend their beliefs. They may feel threatened by the existence of other

---

[6] On the antipositivist origins and orientation of Schmitt's state and constitutional theory, see Schupmann (n 3).

[7] Jan-Werner Müller, 'Re-Imagining Leviathan: Schmitt and Oakeshott on Hobbes and the Problem of Political Order' (2010) 13(2-3) Critical Review of International Social and Political Philosophy 318.

[8] Carl Schmitt, *The Concept of the Political* (The University of Chicago Press 1996) 44–45.

[9] Carl Schmitt, *Constitutional Theory* (Duke University Press 2008) 259–63; Schmitt, *The Concept of the Political* (n 8) 37.

[10] Renato Cristi, *Carl Schmitt and Authoritarian Liberalism: Strong State, Free Economy* (University of Wales Press 1998) 55; Carlo Galli, 'Schmitt and the State' in *Janus's Gaze: Essays on Carl Schmitt* (Duke University Press 2015) 6; Carlo Galli, 'Schmitt's Political Theologies' in *Janus's Gaze: Essays on Carl Schmitt* (Duke University Press 2015) 39.

[11] This is of course a central feature of Schmitt's theory of 'political theology'. I find that concept can be obfuscating at times. Because I do not intend to engage in full discussion of political theology, I have avoided using it here.

[12] Schmitt, *The Concept of the Political* (n 8) 27–32.

worldviews. They may feel that they can only defend their beliefs by suppressing or eliminating the public expression of those other opposed worldviews.

Politicization explains how ideas and ideals can supersede material interests, even an interest in one's own self-preservation.[13] It explains how collective identity can supersede the individual. Ideas, such as spiritual values and the survival of one's immortal soul, are treated as more important than avoiding violent death to preserve one's material life. 'The political' identifies and helps to explain features of human behaviour that, from an external and individualistic perspective, would otherwise appear to be irrational.

When it occurs within a single legal community, politicization is civil war. Schmitt concept of 'the political' repackaged the conditions of Hobbes' state of nature: individuals, asserting their 'right of nature' and, based on the strength of their convictions about what was right, decide for themselves what actions were necessary to uphold right and wrong publicly.[14] Individuals competing to advance conflicting convictions about what is right can shatter public order, peace, and stability.[15] Internal politicization undermines the state's ability to protect anyone.[16] It undermines the state by creating a state of exception, in which the rule of law may not be able to operate and normalize relations at all. For Schmitt, as for Hobbes, the existential insecurity caused by domestic politicization was to be avoided at all costs.

Democratization and Politicization

Schmitt believed that the constitutional form of modern 'mass' democracy had created new and accelerated pathways for politicization.[17] Twentieth-century democracy had inadvertently created a competitive forum for *politically* opposed worldviews to compete to legally possess state power and use procedures of popular sovereignty in order to impose their values on one another with the full force of public law. As they competed, oppositions among the groups intensified. In the process, the state and public law risked being delegitimized, as members began to see both merely as instruments of domination wielded by whichever party held power.

---

[13] ibid 48–49.

[14] ibid 65–66; Carl Schmitt, 'Die vollendete Reformation' (1963) 4(1) Der Staat 61; Ulrich K Preuss, 'Political Order and Democracy: Carl Schmitt and His Influence' in Chantal Mouffe (ed), *The Challenge of Carl Schmitt* (Verso 1999) 160–61; Galli, 'Schmitt and the State' 7; McCormick, 'Fear, Technology, and the State' (n 4) 624.

[15] Carl Schmitt, *The Leviathan in the State Theory of Hobbes: Meaning and Failure of a Political Symbol* (University of Chicago Press 2008) 45. Schmitt see this as a kind of reappropriation of the Hobbesian 'right of nature' because it dealt with individuals deciding how to preserve 'their nature' in a spiritual as well as material sense.

[16] Timothy Stanton, 'Hobbes and Schmitt' (2011) 37 History of European Ideas 161.

[17] Carl Schmitt, *The Crisis of Parliamentary Democracy* (Ellen Kennedy tr, The MIT Press 1988) 16.

110 DEPOLITICIZATION AND STATE AUTHORITY

The pursuit of value-neutral, procedural democracy was well-intentioned. In Schmitt's time, leading jurists including Anschütz, Thoma, and Kelsen argued that a legitimate democracy, one that answered the question of constitutionalism, was a full procedural democracy in which the electorate possessed collective autonomy and decided on the laws that it was subject to, even if only indirectly via elected representatives.[18] Among other things, realizing a full procedural democracy required neutralizing the state as an *independent* authority. Independent state authority was a potentially arbitrary source of power and domination over its members. Confining state power to what was legally prescribed by the positive rule of law, ultimately determined by the will of the electorate, would reduce the extralegal opportunities for state authorities to abuse their power.[19]

Weimar positivists thus aimed to close the gap between ordinary legislation and constitutional amendment, in particular by reducing barriers to constitutional change.[20] They defended guaranteeing formally equal political rights to the electorate, to ensure each member had an equal chance to realize their beliefs and values legally. To fully realize the reduction of the state to its positive legal components, they also defended enacting the amendment clause as the supreme clause of the constitution, which ensured that all law sat under positive legal procedures. They reduced public order to merely the product of positive legal procedures and the state to merely the sum of the positive laws. Kelsen's theory of monism, for example, challenged the 'hypostasisation' of the 'state' through state-theoretic dualism. Their goal was to sublimate state power into a legal, rational form.

However, in societies characterized by the fact of pluralism, the combination of value-neutral democracy and juridical positivism produces an unintended outcome. When any belief, value, and interest had the formally equal opportunity to become public law, Schmitt argued, some groups could organize into parties and seek to enact laws that realize their most existentially defining commitments, which could include beliefs and values fundamentally opposed to those of other groups within society.[21] Politicized legislation could become a flash point. When

---

[18] Ulrich K Preuss, 'The Implications of "Eternity Clauses": The German Experience' (2011) 44(3) Israel Law Review 429, 437; Duncan Kelly, *The State of the Political: Conceptions of Politics and the State in the Thought of Max Weber, Carl Schmitt, and Franz Neumann* (Oxford University Press 2003) 237; David Dyzenhaus, ' "Now the Machine Runs Itself": Carl Schmitt on Hobbes and Kelsen' (1994–1995) 16(1) Cardozo Law Review 13, 17.

The fundamentals of the republican theory developed by Weimar jurists map onto contemporary republican theory—as do Schmitt's criticisms. On this, see Larry Alan Busk, 'Schmitt's Democratic Dialectic: On the Limits of Democracy as a Value' (2021) 47(6) Philosophy & Social Criticism, 687ff.

[19] Carl Schmitt, 'Strong State and Sound Economy' in Renato Cristi (ed), *Carl Schmitt and Authoritarian Liberalism* (University of Wales Press 1932) 218–21. Schmitt challenges monistic state theories, such as Kelsen's. For a recent discussion of this, see Benjamin A Schupmann, 'Hans Kelsen's Political Theology: Science, Pantheism, and Democracy' (2022) 51(3) Austrian Journal of Political Science 42.

[20] See Preuss, 'The Implications of "Eternity Clauses" '(n 18) 436–39.

[21] Schmitt, *The Concept of the Political* (n 8) 32, 49; Carl Schmitt, *Legality and Legitimacy* (Duke University Press 2004) 34–35, 48, 94.

one party used the law to enact the fundamentals of its narrowly held worldview, adherents of opposed worldviews became more likely themselves to organize into political parties, both in order to defend their worldviews against its repression by public power and to enact those worldviews into public law. Schmitt recognized that politicized groups were competing in democratic institutions in order to seize the state's legal apparatus and impose their own factional worldviews.[22] Parliament was becoming an agglomeration of different politicizing parties.

That could trigger a vicious cycle. As political antagonisms sharpened among groups, members retreated into the comfort and security of only associating with other likeminded members. One's political associations, especially the party, played a larger role in members' lives and—at the most extreme—became 'total'. Party members become less likely to believe they have anything in common with members of other parties, in particular that they share any common political identity. A party becomes total as it becomes an all-encompassing community and the only source of its members' existentially determining beliefs, values, and interests.[23] Schmitt argued that a total party constituted its own social microcosm, providing members with a media ecosystem, communal associations (churches, clubs, and bars), schools, and even gangs and private militias to defend them and their community. That microcosm would also increasingly become an echo chamber that created and reinforced its factional political identity.

Schmitt's concern was that, by facilitating members' isolation in now politicizing subcommunities, total parties saw away at the ties that hold society together. That social disintegration has political psychological effects. As different political microcosms realize that they have little or nothing in common with one another, they will start to perceive one another as strangers or foreigners competing for public power. When another total party is in power, its legislation may feel like a foreign imposition, something divorced from and unrepresentative of one's own worldview.

As control over the state vacillates among different total parties, each of which uses the state to enact its factional worldviews and reverse laws passed by other total parties, the areas of society subject to politicized legislation expand. As that happens, the distinction between the state (the public political sphere) and society (the private apolitical sphere) begins to break down.[24] Once the majority begins

---

[22] McCormick, *Carl Schmitt's Critique of Liberalism* (n 4) 276; Dyzenhaus (n 18) 10; Mattias Kumm, 'Who's Afraid of the Total Constitution? Constitutional Rights as Principles and the Constitutionalization of Private Law' (2006) 7(4) German Law Journal 341–42.

[23] Schmitt, *Legality and Legitimacy* (n 21) 8; Kelly, *The State of the Political* (n 18) 198; Ulrich K Preuss, 'Schmitt and the Weimar Constitution' in Oliver Simons and Jens Meierhenrich (eds), *The Oxford Handbook of Carl Schmitt* (Oxford University Press 2014) 472, 481.

[24] Schmitt refers to this state form as the 'quantitatively total state' (although he qualifies that the quantitatively total state is really a depoliticized state populated by total parties).

I try to avoid using Schmitt's jargon here and elsewhere because I find some of his terms unhelpful. In this case, for example, Schmitt's counter concept to the *quantitatively* total state is the *qualitatively* total state. He adopted those concepts from the work of a Czech jurist, Heinz O Ziegler, before the idea of totalitarianism (not to mention its negative connotation) developed.

112   DEPOLITICIZATION AND STATE AUTHORITY

using its legal possession of state power to enact its worldview, the state itself feels increasingly totalitarian for those groups out of power because of the broader and deeper role it assumes in regulating its subjects' lives.[25] Schmitt lived through an instance of that; he believed that designing a constitution along positivist, proceduralist lines had inadvertently accelerated the social conditions leading to civil instability and the breakdown of public order.

The Illegitimacy of the State and the Law

The devolution of the right to decide what is 'political' to society, coupled with the emergence of total parties, triggers a qualitative shift in how members perceive both the state and public law in general.

Schmitt argued that members will increasingly see public law in strategic-instrumental terms as societal oppositions politicize and total parties vie to use the law to advance their factional worldview. They will regard the law solely as a coercive instrument wielded by those in power to further their interests and worldview.[26] Indeed, public law does possess a coercive aspect. However, to be

---

Schmitt thought that a 'total' state, in his particular sense of the word 'total', was unavoidable. 'Total' seems to refer to the interrelationship among state, society, and 'the political'. The modifiers 'quantitative' and 'qualitative' seem to refer to the causal direction of that relationship. In Schmitt's vernacular, when the state is *quantitatively* total, 'the political' is determined first by society. The state itself is neutralized as a political actor. Parties compete to enact their political values, beliefs, and interests totally into law. The political identity of the state is dynamic and vacillates according to whichever party prevailed in the most recent election.

When the state is *qualitatively* total, on the other hand, 'the political' is determined first by the constitution and upheld by the state. Society is politically neutralized, in the sense that the state actively upholds a static political identity and prevents other oppositions from politicizing. This means, as I discuss below, that the state liberalizes society by maintaining a firm public/private distinction.

Schmitt's 'quantitatively total state' most closely aligns with what we would today call a totalitarian state because of its complete penetration of and control over the private sphere. His 'qualitatively total state' most closely corresponds to an authoritarian state because of its authority over political autonomy. A key axis in this distinction is the presence of value-neutral democratic procedures.

Some might find it surprising that Schmitt sees democracy and totalitarianism as potentially aligned. But there is a tradition of interpreting a consequence of democratization in that way. And Schmitt's understanding here has strong affinities with Tocqueville's concerns about democratic despotism. This is, in my reading, one of Schmitt's principal arguments in his *Crisis of Parliamentary Democracy*. See chapter 2 of Schupmann, *Carl Schmitt's State and Constitutional Theory: A Critical Analysis* (n 3).

[25] Günter Maschke, 'Zum "Leviathan" von Carl Schmitt' in Günter Maschke (ed), *Der Leviathan in der Staatslehre des Thomas Hobbes: Sinn und Fehlschlag eines politischen Symbols* ('Hohenheim' Verlag 1982) 219–20, 230–31.

[26] Schmitt uses the concept *Gehorsamerzwingungschance*, taken from Weber's definition of 'rational-legal authority' in *Economy and Society*. Max Weber, *Economy and Society: An Outline of Interpretive Sociology* vol 1 (Guenther Roth and Claus Wittich eds, University of California Press 1978) 215. There, Weber defined rational-legal authority as authority obtained because it has been bequeathed by the law, by procedures. Schmitt's point is that the destabilizing behaviour he describes resulting from political power obtained through formally neutral legal procedures is structural. In other words, these problems are intrinsic to *value-neutral* democratic legal procedures.

considered 'law', that coercive facet must be complemented by legitimacy.[27] In the absence of a corresponding appeal to its rationality or legitimacy, law is impoverished. When members harbour irreconcilable politicized worldviews, parliament will struggle to convince them that its legislation embodies public reason or the common good.[28]

To illustrate, Nazis will not be swayed by public debate on the legitimacy of laws issued by a liberal democrat-controlled parliament, such as laws that guarantee equality and human rights for all ethnic groups within the community. (Similarly, liberal democrats will not be persuaded of the legitimacy of Nazi law.) Their compliance with such laws will stem from the state's coercive power and a strategic calculation that disobedience is, for the moment, more disadvantageous.

Cynically, a political faction out of power might play by the rules of the democratic game solely in anticipation of one day being able to seize state power and impose its own worldview. In a sufficiently politicized society, law will only appear legitimate as long as one's party possesses state power; otherwise, it is nothing more than raw power.

That altered perception of the legitimacy of public law inevitably reflects onto the state, both as the source and enforcer of public law and as a symbol of the unity of the public order. Kelsen's question, 'what makes the state different from a highway robber?' becomes increasingly difficult for members of society to answer—except in the above cynical sense. That perception fuels a vicious cycle: just as they increasingly see the state in strategic-instrumental terms, members will increasingly see the state itself merely as an extension of the political interests of whoever happens to control it. They acknowledge its legitimacy only when they hold the reins of power. As if responding to Kelsen directly, Schmitt remarked that when public law is so normatively impoverished, the state is nothing more than a '*magnum latrocinium*', a giant robber.[29]

When members see the state merely as a vehicle for advancing or inhibiting the *politicized* beliefs of a total party, legal possession of state power becomes an existential matter. Those in power may attempt to entrench their control by 'kicking down the ladder' of democratic access to state power, perhaps through extensive gerrymandering or legally curtailing the opposition's political participatory rights.[30] Positive legal procedures, including the amendment clause, can thus be twisted into the constitutional mechanisms for a current majority to perpetuate its

---

[27] For an analysis of law's two faces, see Jürgen Habermas, 'On the Internal Relation between the Rule of Law and Democracy' in *The Inclusion of the Other: Studies in Political Theory* (The MIT Press 1998) 254–56.

[28] Ulrich K Preuss, 'The Critique of German Liberalism: Reply to Kennedy' (1987) 71 Telos 99–100.

[29] Carl Schmitt, 'Ethic of State and Pluralistic State' in Chantal Mouffe (ed), *The Challenge of Carl Schmitt* (Verso 1999) 195.

[30] Schmitt, *Legality and Legitimacy* (n 21) 51–52. They engage in *indirect* legal revolution, a consequence of the republican normative conclusion that legitimate law requires determining and redetermining 'the rules of rule-making' through procedures of popular sovereignty.

114   DEPOLITICIZATION AND STATE AUTHORITY

rule indefinitely.[31] As members start to view the state as merely an instrument for their factional political interests, they are more likely to conceive of it as akin to a peace treaty or a weak *modus vivendi*—a voluntary contract that they can abandon when a better opportunity presents itself.[32]

Schmitt saw parallels between the politicization occurring in twentieth-century European democracies and that of sixteenth- and seventeenth-century Europe.[33] There were of course some significant differences: in twentieth-century democracy, politicization occurred directly though state institutions like the legislature in addition to outside of them. Opposing factions were no longer primarily religious in nature, but instead comprised secular worldviews such as Nazism, Stalinist Communism, and liberal democracy. Despite their differences, both eras grappled with the same underlying issue: the existential opposition among total worldviews and their adherents' increasing willingness to suppress competing worldviews and assert their own by any means. As total parties exploited democratic legal procedures to advance their political worldviews in the twentieth century, both law and the state were delegitimized, paving the way for the outbreak of a *bellum omnium contra omnes*.[34] The state was losing its ability to contain political heterogeneity and forestall civil war.[35]

Hobbes and Political Authority

To counteract the politicization within twentieth-century democracies, Schmitt believed that it was necessary to find an authoritative basis from which it was possible to settle the basic existential-political disagreements about public order. Only with the authority to define 'the political', Böckenförde argued, can the state fulfil its original purpose: 'to relativize domestic antagonisms, tensions, and conflicts so

---

[31]   Preuss, 'The Implications of "Eternity Clauses"' (n 18) 435.

[32]   Carl Schmitt, *Der Hüter der Verfassung* (Dunker & Humblot 1931) 141; Schmitt, 'Ethic of State and Pluralistic State' (n 29) 207. See Schmitt's discussion of *pacta sunt servanda* Schmitt, *Constitutional Theory* (n 9) 119–20; cf Schupmann, *Carl Schmitt's State and Constitutional Theory* (n 3) 64–67. Schmitt argued that, within a delegitimized state, members would be increasingly likely to conceive of their obligations to it and one another in terms of *pacta sunt servanda* ('agreements must be kept', ie if one signs a treaty ought to perform it in good faith, a relationship that is thought to define international relations). Under those conditions, participants conceive of one another not as members of a single public order equally subject to its laws but as equals in a business-like contract, who may exercise options to exit from the contract. They do not recognize the state's right to legislate per se. Schmitt thought that shift in perspective indicated the degree to which the state and constitution had weakened and were failing in their ability to overcome the problems of civil war.

[33]   John P McCormick, 'Teaching in Vain: Thomas Hobbes, Carl Schmitt and the Crisis of the Sovereign State' in Oliver Simons and Jens Meierhenrich (eds), *The Oxford Handbook of Carl Schmitt* (Oxford University Press 2014) 274–75.

[34]   Schmitt, *Der Hüter der Verfassung* (n 32) 79; cf Maschke (n 25) 230–31.

[35]   Kelly, *The State of the Political* (n 18) 222; Monica Garcia-Salmones Rovira, 'On Carl Schmitt's Reading of Hobbes: Lessons for Constitutionalism in International Law?' (2007) 4 No Foundations: Journal of Extreme Legal Positivism 63.

as to facilitate peaceful debates as well as solutions and ultimately decisions that are in accordance with procedural standards of argumentation and public discourse.[36] That authority had to be something that, in principle, all members had reason to accept as legitimate. Otherwise politicization would just deepen. Schmitt's pressing question was, as Bhuta writes, how can state authority be generated in such circumstances?[37]

To generate that authority, Schmitt turned back to the origins of modern state theory in the thought of Thomas Hobbes. Hobbes' state theory aimed to forestall the chaos and insecurity that comes about when groups politicize and confront one another as enemies. By updating Hobbes' thought to meet twentieth-century conditions, Schmitt hoped to demonstrate that the state could still possess the authority to uphold its political identity—even as a modern democracy. That authority over the political would in turn justify its entrenchment through measures of militant democracy.

Schmitt turned back to Hobbes because he believed that Hobbes had discovered a way to generate political authority despite modern value pluralism. Hobbes had theorized the state in response to a crisis of authority fuelled by domestic politicization. Recognizing the deep religious pluralism of his time, Hobbes understood that legitimate and binding law could not be generated by appealing directly to religious truths, ecclesiastical authority, or transcendent values. Such appeals would only intensify and deepen political divisions within society. Instead, Hobbes sought to ground political authority immanently in practical reasoning, situating rational actors in a hypothetical 'state of nature'. That counterfactual framework allows Hobbes to analyse how practical reasoning could overcome the problems of value plurality and the ensuring anarchy. Schmitt believed that updating Hobbes' thought could offer a solution to the challenge of politicization in the twentieth-century democracy.

Schmitt described Hobbes' *Leviathan* as an ahistorical myth.[38] At first glance, myth may seem like an unconventional way to ground political authority. Yet Hobbes had used a mythical allegory about monsters, fear, the state of nature, and individual conviction about right under conditions of epistemic uncertainty, could provide a compelling legitimation for state authority. Based on its success, Schmitt too believed that myth could demonstrate that state authority was a command of practical reason.[39]

---

[36] Böckenförde (n 4) 39.

[37] Nehal Bhuta, 'The Mystery of the State: State-Concept, State-Theory and State-Making in Schmitt and Oakeshott' in David Dyzenhaus and Thomas Poole (eds), *Law, Liberty and State: Oakeshott, Hayek and Schmitt on the Rule of Law* (Cambridge University Press 2015) 23–24.

[38] Schmitt, *The Leviathan in the State Theory of Hobbes* (n 15).

[39] Ibid 32; Schmitt, 'Ethic of State and Pluralistic State' (n 29) 195. I thank Jan-Werner Müller for encouraging me to develop this section Schmitt's conception of myth.

The Value of Myth

Despite its false and ahistorical nature, myth can nevertheless explain the role, nature, and legitimacy of actual social phenomena.[40] It can also direct individuals to produce a particular social outcome.

As Müller argues, Schmitt's understanding and use of 'myth' was indebted to two of his near contemporaries: Vaihinger and Sorel.[41] In his 1911 *The Philosophy of As-If*, Vaihinger sought to show the epistemic role that 'fictions' play.[42] He argued that fictions, such as Kant's 'the thing in itself', enable or improve our apprehension of the world. In so doing, they improve our ability to pursue and realize our practical goals, despite being fictitious. Because of the practical roles they play, Vaihinger concluded that we are justified in treating fictions *as if* they were real.

Schmitt discussed Vaihinger's work in a 1913 commentary. He argued that fictions are essential to jurisprudence in particular.[43] They lay the foundations of the discipline and jurists use them regularly. Examples include 'the will' of the law and legal personhood. No one thinks that a corporation is a natural person. However, attributing personhood to a corporation (literally, a *persona ficta*) allows jurists to consider a corporation as a distinct entity under the law, one separate from its individual constitutive members. This allows jurists to, for example, directly subject that corporation to legal obligations or to attribute interests to it that are irreducible to those of its members. Schmitt argued that juristic fictions like legal personhood allow jurists and society to accomplish practical goals with the law that they might not be able to do otherwise. For that reason, he concluded with Vaihinger, we are justified in treating juridical fictions as if they were real.[44]

Analysed under Vaihinger's framework, the state is a juridical fiction *par excellence*. The state has no material reality. It exists only as an idea and an abstraction.

---

[40] Pettit's discussion of 'counterfactual genealogy' is enlightening in this context. Pettit uses the origins of money to illustrate the value of counterfactual genealogy despite its untrue or even mythical qualities. He describes how classical political economists theorized the origins of money. At first glance, their armchair anthropology may seem plausible. They argued that prehistoric human societies first relied on a system of barter for exchange. As the limits of bartering became apparent over time, societies turned to a universally acceptable commodity, such as gold, as a medium of exchange.

Pettit argues that this explanation is unsupported by evidence and it most likely never occurred. However, despite being a 'just so' story, it still has normative value. It allows members of the present to understand money's function and how vital it is for society today. The problems of an idealized counterfactual world without money can show why we, the listeners of that story, would want to live in a society that has money. The use of a mythical narrative can make its argument more accessible.

Similarly, early modern state theory often posited an idealized counterfactual world in which there was no public order, only a 'state of nature'. It uses the problems of that world to demonstrate the nature and value of the state. See Philip Pettit, *The Birth of Ethics: Reconstructing the Role and Nature of Morality* (Oxford University Press 2018) 6–7, 50–53.

[41] Jan-Werner Müller, 'Carl Schmitt's Method: Between Ideology, Demonology, and Myth' (1999) 4(1) Journal of Political Ideologies 75ff.

[42] Timothy Stoll, 'Hans Vaihinger' in Edward N Zalta (ed), *The Stanford Encyclopedia of Philosophy* (2020) <https://plato.stanford.edu/entries/vaihinger/>.

[43] Carl Schmitt, 'Juristische Fiktionen' (1913) 12 Deutsche Juristen-Zeitung.

[44] ibid 805.

It can only exist through human representations and projections of it. Yet, in this sense at least, it does exist. That existence significantly defines our social world and interactions. And that existence is possible because, as Kelly argues, we attribute legal personhood to the state and we act as if it were a corporate entity.[45] Attributing legal personhood to the state not only allows it to have agency and interests in the material world. Doing so also allows the state to represent and pursue the collective interests of a 'people', who are otherwise nothing but an unincorporated multitude of individuals.

In his 1908 *Reflections on Violence*, Sorel used the myth of the general strike to motivate proletariat class action. According to Gourgouris, Sorel thought that myth was neither fact nor an illusion.[46] Myth is not factual because it does not intend to describe reality. Myth is not mere illusion because, in depicting an imagined alternative, myth can inspire its realization. Moreover, a well-crafted myth may motivate practical action far more effectively than reasoned argument.[47] In addition, as Lara argues, a well-constructed myth can enable us to see our problems embodied in stories, and thereby translate those problems into a framework for purposive action.[48] Putting those facets together, myth can alter reality even though it is not true: first, by providing a narrative framework for understanding reality, then, by inspiring direct action to bring about the alternative reality that it depicts. Sorel's myth of 'the general strike' illustrates this function. It intertwines the social imaginary, pure praxis, and proletarian frustrations in order to paralyze and abolish the foundations of bourgeois society.[49]

As a conservative middle-class public lawyer, Schmitt was horrified by Sorel's use of myth to incite the proletariat to destabilize political order (not to mention its goal of realizing communist society).[50] Yet he recognized myth's potential to transform a multitude into a political unity and to motivate cooperation in pursuit of a political goal.[51] Rather than using myth to motivate the masses to smash the rule of law, it could instead be used to hold back the chaos and lawlessness of civil war.[52] Myth could be used to legitimate and stabilize the existing public order. Schmitt believed that the vitalism and voluntarism of myth could be used for productive ends.[53]

---

[45] I am indebted to Luke O'Sullivan for encouraging me to draw this point out. See Duncan Kelly, 'Carl Schmitt's Political Theory of Representation' (2004) 65(1) Journal of the History of Ideas 128–32.

[46] Stathis Gourgouris, 'The Concept of the Mythical (Schmitt with Sorel)' (1999–2000) 21(5–6) Cardozo Law Review 1500.

[47] Müller, 'Carl Schmitt's Method' (n 41) 76.

[48] María Pía Lara, 'Carl Schmitt's Contribution to a Political Theory of Myth' (2017) 56(3) History and Theory 381.

[49] Gourgouris (n 46) 1499.

[50] Jan-Werner Müller, 'Myth, Law and Order: Schmitt and Benjamin Read *Reflections on Violence*' (2003) 29 History of European Ideas, 464, 467.

[51] See Gourgouris (n 46) 1508.

[52] Müller, 'Myth, Law and Order' (n 50) 471; McCormick, *Carl Schmitt's Critique of Liberalism* (n 4) 112; Kelly, *The State of the Political* (n 18) 161.

[53] Müller, 'Carl Schmitt's Method' (n 41) 75.

118   DEPOLITICIZATION AND STATE AUTHORITY

Schmitt's understanding of myth combined Vaihinger's and Sorel's ideas. Despite being fictitious, myth was politically useful. It could help convey the value, function, and legitimacy of social phenomenon. Myths and fictions could enable practices that might not be possible otherwise. Their depictions can motivate individuals to realize goals and act collectively to achieve them. And because of its visceral affective qualities, myth could succeed in situations where reasoned argumentation might not.[54] A myth different from Sorel's could instead *stabilize* the modern state and correct its drift toward civil war.[55]

Hobbes' Leviathan and Political Authority

Schmitt believed that Hobbes' Leviathan was a myth capable of generating stable political authority and overcoming the centrifugal forces of mass democracy.

The principal components of the *Leviathan* narrative were all mythical: the state of nature, the act of contracting, and the state itself. Schmitt denied that *Leviathan* described some prehistoric moment in which humans inhabited a state of nature. Instead, as McCormick argues, Schmitt believed that the state of nature was a politically possible present that came about whenever and wherever political authority broke down.[56] It allegorizes the extreme case of domestic politicization: civil war.[57] Its inhabitants were actually sixteenth and seventeenth-century Europeans.[58] The state of nature depicts what happens when individual members of a single political and legislative community begin deciding for themselves who had the authority to legislate, what laws were valid, and who had the authority to enforce and interpret the law.[59]

Neither does Schmitt think that the social contract ever actually produced something like the state or constitution.[60] Schmitt argued that Hobbes did not intend to describe a historical moment in which individuals in a state of nature got together and contracted into or with a sovereign political authority. Schmitt did not think that political authority could be generated by individuals advancing their self-interest through 'business-like' demands and compromises.[61] He did not think Hobbes' state was actually generated by an aggregate of individual wills.

---

[54] Schmitt, *The Leviathan in the State Theory of Hobbes* (n 15) 81; Müller, 'Myth, Law and Order' (n 50) 467.

[55] Müller, 'Myth, Law and Order' (n 50) 466.

[56] McCormick, *Carl Schmitt's Critique of Liberalism* (n 4) 256.

[57] Schmitt, *The Leviathan in the State Theory of Hobbes* (n 15) 21.

[58] Helmut Rumpf, *Carl Schmitt und Thomas Hobbes: Ideelle Beziehungen und aktuelle Bedeutung mit einer Abhandlung über: Die Frühschriften Carl Schmitts* (Duncker & Humblot 1972) 70; Stanton (n 16) 165.

[59] Schmitt, *The Leviathan in the State Theory of Hobbes* (n 15) 48–49.

[60] ibid 33; Maschke (n 25) 200; Böckenförde (n 4) 43; Müller, 'Re-Imagining Leviathan' (n 7) 319; Galli, 'Schmitt's Political Theologies' (n 10) 38

[61] Schmitt, 'Strong State and Sound Economy' 220–21

Instead, Schmitt characterized the moment of contracting described in *Leviathan* as 'a flash [*Blitz*] of reason'.[62] Reason 'flashes' in Hobbes' mythical state of nature as its inhabitants reflect on how their natural qualities—their equality, freedom, and their self-righteousness—as well as their innate right to interpret are the cause of their collective insecurity. Reason 'flashes' as they recognize that their war of all against all is caused structurally, a consequence of when free and equal individuals act with the best of intentions based on their idiosyncratic deeply held convictions about what is right and what is true.[63] Irreconcilable differences among their most deeply held beliefs, and the competition to realize them publicly through positive law, sets individuals against one another. It made 'man a wolf to man', *homo homini lupus*. Reason 'flashes' as they recognize that, in societies characterized by pluralism, asserting law because it is 'true' or normatively 'right' will be politically divisive. Legitimate law cannot be generated by transcendent truth. Something else is needed.

In that flash of reason, individuals also recognize how to overcome the causes of domestic conflict and civil war. Because civil war is caused by competition among individuals to decide and enforce 'right' public order, each should cede their right to decide idiosyncratically to a single, public authority.[64] Hobbes' description of individuals in a state of nature ceding their natural right to the Leviathan in order to obtain peace and security is meant to instil in his contemporaries the value of the state. It also clarifies why the state ought to have the authority to enforce what is political, even if that decision does not align with one's personal values and worldview. It represents the recognition that, as long as there are multiple authorities and legislators asserting different conceptions of 'right' public order in a single territory, members will live in a miserable and existentially insecure condition.

Hobbes shows how a public order need not derive its legislative authority from some higher transcendent truth per se. Stable public order can arise when secular authority represents the lowest common denominator of its members' political identity. This is how Schmitt understands Hobbes' maxim *auctoritas non veritas facit legem (authority, not truth, makes the law)*.[65] The Leviathan myth was multifaceted, consisting of (mortal) god, (artificial) person, animal (violence), and (legislating) machine. In particular, to conceive of the state as having political authority meant conceiving of it as a juridical person who represents the political identity

---

[62] Schmitt, 'Ethic of State and Pluralistic State' (n 29) 195; Schmitt, *The Leviathan in the State Theory of Hobbes* (n 15) 33; Preuss, 'Political Order and Democracy' (n 14) 159–60, 176; Galli, 'Schmitt's Political Theologies' (n 10) 76; Loughlin (n 4) 574.

[63] Schmitt, *The Concept of the Political* (n 8) 65; Schmitt, *The Leviathan in the State Theory of Hobbes* (n 15) 45; cf Rumpf (n 58) 64–66; Preuss, 'Political Order and Democracy' (n 14) 160; McCormick, 'Teaching in Vain' (n 33) 277–78.

[64] Schmitt, *The Leviathan in the State Theory of Hobbes* (n 15) 53.

[65] Carl Schmitt, *Political Theology: Four Chapters on the Concept of Sovereignty* (University of Chicago Press 2005) 33; Schmitt, *The Crisis of Parliamentary Democracy* (n 17) 43; Carl Schmitt, *Der Begriff des Politischen: Text von 1932 mit einem Vorwort und drei Corollarien* (Duncker & Humblot 1963) 122.

120   DEPOLITICIZATION AND STATE AUTHORITY

and interests of a unified people. That representation could neutralize the political antagonisms among groups in society.[66]

Schmitt argued that Hobbes was only concerned with subjects' public, outward recognition of the legitimacy of the law and state authority in his myth.[67] Subjects had freedom of conscience, which meant the freedom to hold convictions about what was right and true contrary to the state's political identity—as long as those convictions remained within the private sphere. Privately, members were free to believe whatever they wanted—including to deny the legitimacy of the fundamental, extralegal values that defined the public order. But only privately. In public, subjects were obliged to obey the state's representation of the public order and obey its laws.

In sum, Schmitt understood Hobbes' *Leviathan* as an allegory for explaining why state authority is a command of practical reason. Despite inevitable disagreements about transcendent truth, valid and binding law could still be generated: as reason reflects on the practical problem of the corrosive effects of epistemic uncertainty and political pluralism on the ability to live at all, it pushes individuals to recognize state's authority to decide and uphold the law.

As an imaginary counterfactual, Schmitt believed that Hobbes' myth demonstrated the value of state authority over public order and the political. It also helped reconcile individuals with state authority, an authority that they were already subject to. However, Hobbes also designed his myth to convey his own fears about what he thought was the greatest evil: civil war.[68] He sought to 'frighten men in need of security', as Schmitt remarked. The state of nature, in particular its insurmountable insecurity and inevitable violent death, was intended to instil the value of the state in those who were unable to reason.[69]

Failure of a Political Symbol?

The problem was that Hobbes' state theory had broken down by the twentieth century.[70] The state was succumbing to the centrifugal forces that it was designed to overcome. Schmitt argued that Hobbes' Leviathan seemed to have run aground. Its mechanical facet had been totalized.[71] The state was conceived of only as a *machina legislatoria*, a legislating machine that transformed the will or the command

---

[66] McCormick, 'Teaching in Vain' (n 33) 272.

[67] This is the distinction between '*fides*' and '*confessio*'. Schmitt, *The Leviathan in the State Theory of Hobbes* (n 15) 55–56.

[68] Kelly, *The State of the Political* (n 18) 219.

[69] McCormick, *Carl Schmitt's Critique of Liberalism* (n 4) 265.

[70] I am indebted to Lars Vinx for pushing me to expand on Schmitt's criticism of the limits of the Leviathan myth and how, from his perspective, it contributed to the debilitation of the modern state.

[71] McCormick, *Carl Schmitt's Critique of Liberalism* (n 4) 272; Kelly, *The State of the Political* (n 18) 191; Dyzenhaus (n 18) 8; McCormick, 'Teaching in Vain' (n 33) 283–84.

of whoever controlled it into positive law, whatever that command may be. In addition, the state was conceived of as merely a contract among its constituent individuals—no more than the sum of its parts.[72]

Legally, that totalized mechanical conception meant that the state was merely the sum of the positive laws that make up its public order.[73] At most, the state was a symbol of the system of individual positive laws. But neither state nor constitution actually existed beyond them. This conception relativized the constitution by severing the relationship between higher law (as *Recht*) and whatever positive statutes happened to exist in the state—any of which could be changed via the amendment clause.

Politically, that totalized mechanical conception meant that the state's identity was defined by the aggregate of its individual members' wills, as expressed through its legislative branch. This similarly relativized the state by severing the relationship between higher law and whatever the electorate willed as legislator—which could in principle be anything at all because every member had the same formally equally chance to compete for public office, no matter what political goals they intended to pursue.

To be sure, Hobbes' state always had this mechanical and positivist facet.[74] Hobbes was a kind of positivist. But, Schmitt believed, the positivist features of the state only functioned in the way Hobbes intended when embedded within its superlegal political commitments and the state's independent authority. Schmitt thought that twentieth-century mass democracy had been disembedded because it had been designed not to have any political content at all.[75] For example, in principle and by design, every article of the Weimar constitution could be amended validly and members could pursue any political goal at all.

In a reversal, rather than neutralize internal politicization, the mechanical state ended up neutralizing itself.[76] So neutralized, the state was no longer able to hold back the politicization that Hobbes designed it to solve. To make matters worse, mass democracy had turned the state into a trophy that total parties competed over in order to impose their factional identity over all of society, exacerbating the causes of civil war that Hobbes' identified.

Despite the subtitle to his book on Hobbes' *Leviathan*, Schmitt did not really seem to believe that Hobbes' myth had failed completely. He ended that book lamenting '*Non jam frustra doces, Thomas Hobbes* [Thomas Hobbes, now you do not teach in vain]'.[77] Hobbes' state theory still had value. It just needed to be updated

---

[72] Rumpf (n 58) 66.
[73] Martin Loughlin, *Foundations of Public Law* (Oxford University Press 2010) 210.
[74] Rumpf (n 58) 68–69; McCormick, *Carl Schmitt's Critique of Liberalism* (n 4) 271, 274.
[75] McCormick, 'Teaching in Vain' (n 33) 283–85.
[76] Rumpf (n 58) 70.
[77] Schmitt, *The Leviathan in the State Theory of Hobbes* (n 15) 86. For himself, however, Schmitt remarked, 'Doceo, sed frustra' [I teach, but in vain]: Rumpf (n 58) 108; Rovira (n 35) 62.

to address the problems of modern democracy, especially legal revolution—problems that Hobbes could not have anticipated. The question was, how to do so?

Updating Hobbes's State Theory

Schmitt aimed to update Hobbes by redeploying and reinforcing its dualist distinction between the state conceived as a unity and idea, on the one hand, and the state as a reality made up of its constituent parts on the other. Schmitt focused on the dual nature of two features of the state in particular: first, 'the people' as distinct from the electorate and second, the constitution as distinct from its system of positive laws. In both cases, he theorized that the former was irreducible to the latter: 'The people' is not merely the electorate. The constitution is not merely the sum of the positive laws. By drawing those dualistic distinctions, Schmitt aimed to make explicit the limits on what democratic legal procedures could legitimately accomplish, in particular their potential for repoliticization and legal revolution. In so doing, he offered a different conception of how democracy related to the modern state.

'The People' versus the Electorate

At first glance, Schmitt's goal of restoring state authority by updating Hobbes' state theory may seem irreconcilable with modern constitutionalism's turn to democratic legitimation. In a democracy, 'the people' possesses the authority to determine its collective political identity. 'The people', not the state, has the right to decide which laws are valid and what its political identity is.

From Schmitt's perspective, if that moment of self-determination only amounts to individual members reflexively authorizing themselves *as individuals* to make political decisions, democratization fails to address the Hobbesian problem of political pluralism. It would only lead full circle and recreate the problems of a neutralized state and social politicization. At the same time, Schmitt recognized, mass democracy was a permanent feature of modern politics. It would be naïve to try to turn back the clock. The challenge that Schmitt sought to address was how to overcome and reconcile the apparent tension between the fact of democratic pluralism and the Hobbesian need for state authority.

Schmitt set about resolving that tension by considering who 'the people' is and what it means to authentically represent that 'the people'. He argued that the identity of 'the people' was paradoxical.

One the one hand, as Rubinelli has argued, there are two key elements of Schmitt's conceptualization of 'the people'.[78] First, 'the people' exists only

---

[78] Lucia Rubinelli, *Constituent Power: A History* (Cambridge University Press 2020) 115–16.

collectively. It is superior to and irreducible to the sum of its parts. Second, only as that transcendent collective entity can 'the people' exercise constituent power and decide on its political identity.

However, 'the people' does not actually exist. There is no singular 'the people', which has the agency to make political decisions.[79] It is never actually 'present'. Even if one can identify the material consequences of its decisions, 'the people' as such has no material reality. Because it is never truly present, Schmitt argued, even in its existentially most important moment, the moment of constitution when it exercises its constituent power, the political existence of 'the people' is something that must be presupposed.[80]

What Schmitt described has been called the paradox of modern constitutionalism.[81] In short, that paradox is 'the people' must already exist in order to exercise its constituent power at all. However, it is only through that constitutive act that 'the people' can come into existence at all. Loughlin suggests a solution to this paradox by describing it as a reflexive moment, in which the 'constituent power not only involves the exercise of power by a people; it simultaneously constitutes a people'.[82]

Still, it is clear from this paradox that 'the people' is immaterial. It exists only as an ideal. Even in its most existentially significant moments, 'the people' is a juridical fiction. That fiction has value, however, which explains Schmitt's interest in the concept. The fiction of 'the people' allows constitutional theorists to conceive of and ground the authority of the state and constitution and reconcile it with the normative ideal of democracy. For that reason, we are justified in acting as if 'the people' is real. Even though 'the people' never was and never is, we need the fiction of 'the people'. Without it, democratic political community and authority may not be possible at all.

Schmitt argued that, because 'the people' is never actually present, everything depends on how the will and identity of the people is formed—on who or what embodies 'the people'.[83] Without representation, 'the people' dissolves into an

---

[79] Schmitt, *Constitutional Theory* (n 9) 241; See also Rubinelli (n 78) 122–23.

[80] Schmitt, *Constitutional Theory* (n 9) 102, 240.

[81] See Simone Chambers, 'Democracy, Popular Sovereignty, and Constitutional Legitimacy' (2004) 11(2) Constellations 154; Andreas Kalyvas, 'Popular Sovereignty, Democracy, and the Constituent Power' (2005) 12(2) Constellations 238; Ulrich K Preuss, 'The Exercise of Constituent Power in Central and Eastern Europe' in Martin Loughlin and Neil Walker (eds), *The Paradox of Constitutionalism* (Oxford University Press 2007) 211; Martin Loughlin, 'The Concept of Constituent Power' (2014) 13(2) European Journal of Political Theory 219.

[82] Loughlin, *Foundations of Public Law* (n 73) 226–28.

[83] Schmitt, *The Crisis of Parliamentary Democracy* (n 17) 27; Schmitt, *Constitutional Theory* (n 9) 140–42, 239–47. This can be compared with Schmitt's remarks on the visibility of the church, in contrast with the invisibility of God. Schmitt argues that representation makes entities tangible that may otherwise exist only in a noumenal state. As the church manifests God, so too do political institutions manifest 'the people'. In neither case should we expect the represented to present itself and express its actual will and identity. It is always up to an inferior or subordinate to attempt to represent it in a fiduciary relationship.

124 DEPOLITICIZATION AND STATE AUTHORITY

unorganized multitude, incapable of deciding and acting.[84] This leads to the question: how should the identity and will of 'the people' be represented?

One answer to that question is value-neutral proceduralism, which argues that the will of the electorate—translated through democratic legal procedures and positive law—provides the most authentic representation of 'the people'. This approach effectively collapses any distinction between 'the people' and the electorate.[85] It renders them, for all intents and purposes, identical.

As discussed above, Schmitt argued that value-neutral proceduralism failed as a solution.[86] Essentially, by endowing the electorate with the constituent power of 'the people', the naturally occurring pluralism among members will politicize, as factions strive to impose their worldviews through the law. The struggle among different worldviews not only politicizes societal divisions, it also undermines the state. Competition for control over its legislative power becomes a matter of existential significance, reducing the state to just another partisan institution.

Schmitt formulates 'the people' as a combination of two principles: identity and representation. However, Bhuta highlights Schmitt's emphasis on representation—and not identity—as 'the primary means through which a status of unity and order can be effected'.[87] Representation is of something existential. The problem, Schmitt argues, is that in a *politically* plural society, the electorate cannot redecide on the identity of 'the people' without alienating members.[88] At best, the electorate merely expresses what a majority wants. Consequently, institutions should not be designed to permit the electorate to act as if it were 'the people'.

In addition, the electorate is a legally constituted and derivative power. Its composition and powers—who may participate, what powers an electoral majority has, how it is represented institutionally—are ultimately determined by the constitution.[89] These powers are conferred either directly by the constitution or by constitutionally-enacted laws.[90] The constitution thus necessarily mediates

Some interpreters have interpreted Schmitt's arguments about 'the people's' positioning itself 'above and alongside the constituted order' as a kind of radical democratic claim. However, few believe that Schmitt was genuinely interested in democratic ideals. So it is difficult to interpret Schmitt as a proponent of radical democracy. Nevertheless, Schmitt's arguments may be marshalled to develop a theory of radical democracy. Andreas Kalyvas' excellent book is an example of this: Andreas Kalyvas, *Democracy and the Politics of the Extraordinary: Max Weber, Carl Schmitt, and Hannah Arendt* (Cambridge University Press 2008).

[84] Schmitt, *Constitutional Theory* (n 9) 245ff; Preuss, 'Schmitt and the Weimar Constitution' (n 23) 476.
[85] See Schmitt, *The Crisis of Parliamentary Democracy* (n 17) 25f.
[86] Schmitt, *Constitutional Theory* (n 9) 240; Carl Schmitt, 'Freiheitsrechte und institutionelle Garantien der Reichsverfassung' in Carl Schmitt (ed), *Verfassungsrechtliche Aufsätze aus den Jahren 1924-1954. Materialien zu einer Verfassungslehre* (Duncker & Humblot 1958) 164; Preuss, 'Political Order and Democracy' (n 14) 162.
[87] Bhuta (n 37) 26.
[88] Schmitt, *Constitutional Theory* (n 9) 240–41; Preuss, 'Schmitt and the Weimar Constitution' (n 23) 483.
[89] Schmitt, *Legality and Legitimacy* (n 21) 39.
[90] Preuss, 'The Implications of "Eternity Clauses"' (n 18) 429, 434.

between the electorate and 'the people'. At most, the electorate may legitimately exercise a *secondary* constituent power, such as constitutional amendment, only as the constitution permits. Because its authority is constitutionally derived, the electorate is inherently limited in its ability to amend the constitution.[91] To attempt to turn those derivative powers against the very source of that authority would simultaneously erode its own legitimacy.

In essence, Schmitt argued that 'the people' is irreducible to the electorate.[92] Especially on fundamental political issues, the electorate was not the best representative of 'the people'. As a result, institutional constraints should be designed to reflect that normative limit, ensuring that the electorate's legal ability to represent 'the people' was appropriately circumscribed.

At first glance, distinguishing between 'the people' and the electorate may appear to be deeply undemocratic. That view challenges most prevailing intuitions about democracy. Moreover, given that view comes from Carl Schmitt, it may be tempting to dismiss his argument on an *ad hominem* basis. However, as Busk shows, this distinction is not unique to Schmitt. Many others, including even 'radical democrats' like Rancière, Mouffe, and Laclau, reject certain formally valid actions of the electorate as inauthentic expressions of 'the people'.[93] Schmitt only makes explicit what many other democratic theorists tacitly accept: the electorate is not 'the people'.[94] There is more to democracy than the immediate will of a present majority.[95]

'The People' and the Constitution

Schmitt's criticisms begs the question: what, then, is the alternative? If the electorate— with its indeterminate and artificial nature, its derivative power, and potential to repoliticize society were it to illegitimately assume full sovereign power—is an unsuitable final representative of 'the people', then who qualifies for that role?

Despite being immaterial and having no presence, 'the people' produces something that does: its constitution. Schmitt argued that the constitution concretized 'the people's' decision on the type and form of its political identity.[96] When 'the

---

[91] Schmitt, *Constitutional Theory* (n 9) 59ff. See also Preuss, 'The Implications of "Eternity Clauses"' (n 18) 434; Y Roznai, *Unconstitutional Constitutional Amendments: The Limits of Amendment Powers* (Oxford University Press 2017) 113–15.

[92] Schmitt, *Constitutional Theory* (n 9) 239.

[93] Larry Alan Busk, *Democracy in spite of the Demos: From Arendt to the Frankfurt School* (Rowman & Littlefield 2020) 51–83. Busk shows that, for those radical democrats, 'the people' could be nothing but socialist.

[94] Busk, 'Schmitt's Democratic Dialectic' (n 18) 695.

[95] See ibid 693–94.

[96] Schmitt, *The Concept of the Political* (n 8) 38–39; Schmitt, *Constitutional Theory* (n 9) 127–28, 156, 166, 248; Carl Schmitt, 'The Legal World Revolution' (1987) 72 Telos 74; see also Ulrich K Preuss, 'The Politics of Constitution-Making: Transforming Politics into Constitutions' (1991) 13(2) Law &

126 DEPOLITICIZATION AND STATE AUTHORITY

people' exercises its constitutive power, it does so in a legal vacuum. That act sublimates its political identity into a stable form. In doing so, Preuss writes, it fills that legal void and sets the identity of 'the people' beyond political contestation.[97] It establishes 'the people's' foundational narrative, explaining how a heterogeneous and divided 'multitude' coalesced around some existentially significant norms and transformed into a single political entity.

Defined in Schmitt's political sense, the constitution bridges 'the people' as a normative ideal and its material form.[98] Those defining norms may be anchored in extralegal components of the constitution, such as its preamble or its opening articles, and rooted in a concrete order.[99] Preuss argues that, given that the constitution embodies the political identity of 'the people', respecting the political authority of 'the people' equates to respect for the constitution itself.[100]

Schmitt argued that 'the people' always existed above and alongside its constitution.[101] However, because of its immateriality, he also seemed to deny that it could ever exercise its constitutive power directly. Instead, everything came down to how the will of 'the people' was formed, he wrote.[102] The will of 'the people' had to be interpreted and represented—and the legitimacy of that representation was always open to contestation.

Given that the constitution embodies the most concrete *recognized* expression of 'the people's' political will and identity, it stands as its most authoritative expression. Therefore, no other power or institution, whether a constituted or an extra-constitutional power, can legitimately claim to supersede the constitution and directly represent 'the people'.[103] Any body challenging that political identity confronts 'the people' as an other, a point elaborated on below.

Schmitt's idealized conception of 'the people' raises a question about the causal relationship between it and its constitution. If 'the people' is actually a juristic fiction, if it is never actually present and always stands in need of representation, then

---

Policy 108; Preuss, 'Political Order and Democracy' (n 14) 163; Loughlin, *Foundations of Public Law* (n 73) 212; Preuss, 'The Implications of "Eternity Clauses" ' (n 18) 438, 442; Roznai (n 91) 109.

[97] Preuss, 'The Politics of Constitution-Making' (n 96) 107.
[98] See Carl Schmitt, 'The Value of the State and the Significance of the Individual' in *Carl Schmitt's Early Legal-Theoretical Writings* (Cambridge University Press 2021).
[99] Schmitt, *Constitutional Theory* (n 9) 78–79; Schmitt, *Legality and Legitimacy* (n 21) 58; Schmitt, 'The Legal World Revolution' (n 96) 74; see also Preuss, 'The Implications of "Eternity Clauses" ' (n 18) 441; Loughlin, 'Politonomy' (n 4) 579ff; Roznai (n 91) 216.
[100] Preuss, 'The Implications of 'Eternity Clauses" (n 18) 442; see also Preuss, 'Schmitt and the Weimar Constitution' (n 23) 477–78.
[101] Schmitt, *Constitutional Theory* (n 9) 140ff; see also Preuss, 'The Implications of "Eternity Clauses" ' (n 18) 434.
[102] Schmitt, *The Crisis of Parliamentary Democracy* (n 17) 27.
[103] Preuss, 'The Politics of Constitution-Making' (n 96) 107. Because of the thorny issues surrounding the concept of constituent power, Dyzenhaus argues that constitutional theory should avoid the concept entirely. David Dyzenhaus, 'Constitutionalism in an Old Key: Legality and Constituent Power' (2012) 1(2) Global Constitutionalism.

how did its constitution come into being? Preuss provides an answer: the political identity and will attributed to 'the people' has always been the product of an organized minority, such as a constituent assembly.[104] That minority persuades a passive majority that it represents their collective interests and their representation ought to be codified and entrenched into a constitution.

Schmitt seems to rely on the juristic fiction of 'the people' to retroactively legitimate a democratic constitution. By presupposing 'the people's' prior existence, a constitution can be attributed to the will of its members after the fact, even though it was actually drafted by a constituent assembly which only presented a binary choice of 'yes or no' to the electorate. It is thanks to the integrative function of that constitutive act that members are able to have a political identity and participate as equals within that public order at all. In reality, that act brings 'the people' into existence, contrary to the traditional narrative. Drawing on Smend's constitutional theory, Schmitt argued that a constitution will ideally continue to integrate individuals into that political identity, in the process transforming them into conscious members of that collective.[105] By attributing the constitutive act to the fictional 'people', members can conceive of their constitution as a reflection of their own political public self, thereby validating it as a genuine expression of their political identity.

The Absolute Constitution and Relative Constitution

Paralleling the distinction between 'the people' and the electorate, Schmitt distinguished the constitution from individual constitutional law. He conceived of the constitution proper as an idealized, coherent whole; the latter as the material aggregate of individual positive laws. He describes those two conceptions of the constitution using the Hegelian terms 'absolute' and 'relative'. By adopting that dualist approach, Schmitt underscored that a constitution is more than the sum of its parts. The absolute constitution, albeit a juridical fiction, is nevertheless essential for grounding state authority. Neglecting the absolute constitution could compromise the legitimacy of the state.

Böckenförde noted that Schmitt wrote his *Constitutional Theory* and *The Concept of the Political* contemporaneously, and he emphasized that their axial concepts, the absolute constitution and the political, complement one another.[106] Kennedy observes that 'What *Der Begriff des Politischen* understands as a problem, *Verfassungslehre* attempts to resolve, relating the political to the constitutional'.[107]

---

[104] Preuss, 'The Implications of "Eternity Clauses" ' (n 18) 444; see my discussion of the generative paradox in Schupmann, *Carl Schmitt's State and Constitutional Theory: A Critical Analysis* (n 3).
[105] Schmitt, *Constitutional Theory* (n 9) 61–62.
[106] Böckenförde (n 4) 44–45.
[107] Ellen Kennedy, *Constitutional Failure: Carl Schmitt in Weimar* (Duke University Press 2004) 95–96.

128   DEPOLITICIZATION AND STATE AUTHORITY

If internal politicization leading to civil war is the problem that *The Concept of the Political* raises, the dualism of *Constitutional Theory* is Schmitt's solution to that problem. It aims to reveal the unity that undergirds a seemingly fragmented and chaotic legal reality.

The absolute constitution enshrines the political identity of 'the people'.[108] More precisely, it is through the absolute constitution that 'the people' articulates the goals or values that define it as a political community, which transmuted a multitude of individuals into political unity. In Schmitt's framework, 'the people', the absolute constitution, and the political are thus intimately related concepts and receive their meaning from their interrelationship. In contrast to the absolute constitution, the relative constitution designates the series of individual constitutional laws, typically found within a written constitution.

As Cristi argues, Schmitt conceived of a healthy public order as one in which those positive laws were anchored in the substance of the absolute constitution.[109] Positive law is an essential part of the absolute constitution. It is neither the entire story nor, from a political perspective, the most important part of the story, however. To the contrary, as Preuss argues, Schmitt defended the substantive commitments of the absolute constitution as normatively and lexically prior to its positive laws.[110]

However, the constitution becomes relativized when its positive, written constitution is conceived of as unmoored from the substantive commitments of the absolute constitution, severing the public order from its underlying political identity and aims.[111] When constitutional law is unmoored in that way, no particular laws or values seem to be constitutive of the state or 'the people'. Any aspect of the public order could be amended or abrogated. Schmitt used Hegel's term 'relative' to emphasize its dependent and derivative nature: in this case, the law was dependent on the will of the legislator. It has no independent validity. When the constitution is conceived of as nothing more than a series of positive laws, the only basis by which to distinguish legitimate from illegitimate legal change is whether the legislator has adhered to the formal procedures for legislation.

In opposition to a relativized conception of the constitution, Schmitt argued that every public order was in fact grounded on an absolute constitution, recognized or not.[112] The absolute constitution defined an implicitly unamendable core

---

[108] Schmitt, *Constitutional Theory* (n 9) 59–66; cf Preuss, 'The Critique of German Liberalism' (n 28) 99; Renato Cristi, 'The Metaphysics of Constituent Power: Schmitt and the Genesis of Chile's 1980 Constitution' (1999–2000) 21 Cardozo Law Review 1751–54; Loughlin, *Foundations of Public Law* (n 73) 211–12; Roznai (n 91) 109, 117.

[109] Cristi, 'The Metaphysics of Constituent Power' (n 108) 1750.

[110] Preuss, 'Political Order and Democracy' (n 14) 169.

[111] Schmitt, *Constitutional Theory* (n 9) 67ff; Cristi, 'The Metaphysics of Constituent Power' (n 108) 1755; Kumm (n 22) 342.

[112] Claude Klein, 'On the Eternal Constitution: Contrasting Kelsen and Schmitt' in Dan Diner and Michael Stolleis (eds), *Kelsen and Schmitt: A Juxtaposition* (Bleicher Verlag 1999) 67.

of the constitution.[113] As Preuss notes, that argument made Schmitt a pioneer of the intellectual movement to limit the power of constitutional amendment.[114]

A theory of implied limits to constitutional amendment holds that the power of amendment is merely a constituted power (exercised by the legislature, another *constituted* power) and is therefore qualitatively distinct from the constitutive power of 'the people'. Roznai argues that, conceived in this way, constitutional amendment is at best a kind of derived or secondary constituent power.[115] Its subordinate status limits its range of legitimate application.

Within Schmitt's constitutional theory, the absolute constitution defines the legitimate range of the amendment clause: amendments are valid 'only under the presupposition that the identity and continuity of the constitution as an entirety is preserved'.[116] They cannot legitimately alter the political identity of 'the people'. As a constituted power, the legislative branch lacks the authority to exercise constitutive power and alter the identity of the existing 'the people' or introduce a new one. Any effort to transform that constitutive decision would effectively eliminate that 'the people', and drag society back towards a state of nature. For that reason, the only legitimate changes that a constituted power can make are non-political ones—even if the amendment clause is formally unlimited in its range of application. Schmitt defines unconstitutional constitutional amendments as when the legislature or any other constituted power exploits legal procedures, like the amendment clause, to annihilate the political identity of the constitution and, by extension, of the people.

Although Schmitt's Weimar writings, such as *Constitutional Theory* and *Legality and Legitimacy*, focus on implicit unamendability, that focus seems to be due to the concrete situation in Weimar. The amendment clause was the supreme clause of the Weimar Constitution positively. According to the written text of the constitution, every article sat under the reservation of its exercise and could be amended or abrogated validly. In that juridical context, the only way to defend its absolute core was through implicit unamendability.[117] Using positive statutes to threaten to revolutionize the absolute constitution created a state of exception. Were the absolute constitution so threatened, Schmitt argued, the guardian of the constitution

---

[113] Cristi, 'The Metaphysics of Constituent Power' (n 108) 1757–58; Roznai (n 91) 137, 142.

[114] Preuss, 'The Implications of "Eternity Clauses"' (n 18) 436.

[115] Roznai (n 91) 113–17.

[116] Schmitt, *Constitutional Theory* (n 9) 150. See also Klein (n 112) 66; Kumm (n 22) 343–44.

[117] Schmitt develops this approach by building on the work of Hauriou. Schmitt's intellectual debt to Hauriou has gone mostly unappreciated. A notable exception is the work of Croce and Salvatore, who thoroughly analyse Schmitt's relationship to Hauriou, as well as other French institutionalists, through the lens of Schmitt's institutional theory. See Mariano Croce and Andrea Salvatore, *The Legal Theory of Carl Schmitt* (Routledge 2013); Mariano Croce and Andrea Salvatore, *Carl Schmitt's Institutional Theory: The Political Power of Normality* (Cambridge University Press 2022). They unfortunately do not confront the practical legal and political implications of his institutional theory, such as the relationship between Schmitt's institutional theory and constitutional unamendability. Another notable exception is Martin Loughlin's analysis of Schmitt's work on nomos and concrete order thinking. Martin Loughlin, 'Nomos' in Dyzenhaus and Poole (n 37).

130 DEPOLITICIZATION AND STATE AUTHORITY

should defend it by declaring an emergency and suspending those positive statutes for the sake of the constitution.[118]

Deformalizing the rule of law brings its own challenges and rests on the assumption that the guardian of the constitution will suspend the public order in good faith, specifically in order to uphold the superlegal absolute constitution and defend the political identity of 'the people'. Scheuerman analyses the dangers inherent in relying on Schmitt's thought to justify deformalizing the rule of law.[119] Deformalization, coupled with an unchecked executive acting as guardian of the constitution, paves the way to authoritarianism. It is imperative that democrats approach these ideas with caution.

Still, there is something to Schmitt's concern: positive procedures of legal change can be abused to undermine democracy. Legal revolution is a real problem. In Weimar, this is exactly what both the Nazi and Communist parties, the two principal enemies of Weimar democracy, publicly promised to do. Both used the legal revolution of Weimar democracy as campaign slogans and party platforms. In parliament, they kept their promises. Both exploited democratic legal procedures to undermine Weimar democracy. This example shows how, even if his motivations are suspect, it would be foolish to ignore Schmitt's diagnosis of how positive legal norms can be used to create a state of exception and illegitimately but legally overturn an absolute democratic constitution. The challenge is avoiding the pathologies of positive democratic proceduralism without veering into an authoritarian solution.

A way to avoid the complete deformalization of the rule of law may involve grounding the absolute constitution in positive constitutional law. This can be achieved through explicit unamendability, which entrenches and signals the constitution's core principles in positive constitutional law. Explicit unamendability can align the absolute and relative constitutions. Moreover, explicit unamendability sets normative limits on the discretionary power of any guardian by establishing the laws that must be defended, rather than leaving it up to the guardian's discretion to interpret and decide which extralegal principles were unamendable.

Because of the intersection of legality and legitimacy in constitutional democracies, so long as the amendment clause is the supreme clause legally, it creates an ambiguity or even indecision about the legitimate range of its exercise. Can a supermajority, elected into office by the electorate through free and fair elections, exercise the legal powers of its office to their fullest, as defined by the positive law and constitution—even if that exercise includes legal revolution?

Even in Weimar, Klein argues, Schmitt thought it outrageous that there were no formal limits on the amendment clause.[120] Far better to take those articles that

---

[118] Preuss, 'Political Order and Democracy' (n 14) 169.
[119] William E Scheuerman, *The End of Law: Carl Schmitt in the Twenty-First Century* (Rowman & Littlefield International Ltd 2019) 19–39.
[120] Klein (n 122) 66.

positively enact the absolute constitution off the legislative agenda entirely, in order to preserve and guarantee the substantive normative foundation of the entire public order against its possible legal revolution.

Schmitt's arguments had an impact in the post-War context. Preuss argues that the architects of the Article 79.3 'Eternity Clause' of the German *Basic Law* consciously incorporated Schmitt's argument that the substantive values of the constitution may not be legitimately amended under any circumstances.[121] The Eternity Clause positively entrenches the substantive normative commitments of the *Basic Law*. Schmitt, in kind, endorsed the enactment of the Eternity Clause as a valid adaptation of his Weimar constitutional theory in post-War writings.[122]

Constitutional Revolution

Because 'the people' is a juristic fiction, abrogating the political constitution will not somehow resurrect 'the people' and give it another chance at redefining its existential-political identity. Legal revolution is not an act that can be attributed to 'the people'. Nor does it create a constitutional void out of which 'the people' can re-emerge. Instead, as Preuss argues, revolutionizing the constitution only unleashes the potentially violent ambitions of politicized factions vying to constitutionalize their own beliefs about the identity of 'the people'.[123]

Revolution occurs when members fundamentally alter the public order, defined by the substantive commitments of the absolute constitution.[124] It is a preliminary step to creating a new constitution, a new political identity, and a new 'the people'.[125] Because their actions attempt to negate the currently existing 'the people', revolutionaries set themselves in opposition to whatever 'people' currently exists—even if they do so to realize a different, more legitimate 'the people'.[126]

Revolution is most often associated with violent and illegal means, evoking images of events like the French Revolution or a military coup d'état.[127] But what defines a revolution is its aim of dismantling an existing public order to realize a new one. Recognizing legal revolution is particularly important today because, as recent findings suggest, military coups play an increasingly rare role in the death

---

[121] Preuss, 'The Implications of "Eternity Clauses"' (n 18) 439.
[122] Schmitt, *Legality and Legitimacy* 95–96; see also Schmitt, 'The Legal World Revolution' (n 96) 75–76.
[123] Preuss, 'The Implications of "Eternity Clauses"' (n 18) 445.
[124] Schmitt, *Constitutional Theory* (n 9) 81, 122, 141–42; Schmitt, 'Freiheitsrechte und institutionelle Garantien der Reichsverfassung' (n 86) 165–66. See also Ivan Ermakoff, *Ruling Oneself Out: A Theory of Collective Abdications* (Duke University Press 2008) 23, 36; Gary Jeffrey Jacobsohn and Yaniv Roznai, *Constitutional Revolution* (Yale University Press 2020) 59ff.
[125] Schmitt, *Constitutional Theory* (n 9) 61, 108.
[126] Schmitt, *The Concept of the Political* (n 8) 27–28.
[127] Ermakoff (n 124) 23.

132   DEPOLITICIZATION AND STATE AUTHORITY

of democracy.[128] In fact, since 1990, almost 80 percent of democratic revolutions were the result of internal legal revolutionary methods. Understanding revolution as the dissolution of the basic commitments or identity of the constitutional order and 'the people' is an essential preliminary step to containing it, whether it takes a legal or illegal form.[129]

As discussed in chapter 1, legal revolution has two distinct forms. First, it can occur directly, when enemies of the constitution use the amendment clause and other positive legal procedures to subvert the absolute constitution itself. Second, it can occur indirectly, when enemies of the constitution leave the written constitution intact but use their possession of state power to prevent its legal practice.

For Schmitt, totalizing the mechanical face of Leviathan collapsed several interrelated state-theoretical distinctions. First, it had collapsed legitimacy into legality: the only criterion for legitimacy was positive procedural validity. Second, it had collapsed the constitution into constitutional laws: from a legal perspective, whatever positive laws happened to exist were the public order. And they could be changed through positive legal procedures, culminating in the supremacy of the amendment clause. Finally, it had collapsed 'the people' into the electorate: it implied that its will and identity was whatever a prevailing majority or supermajority dictated at that moment. Blurring those distinctions made legal revolution inconceivable in juridical terms—and thus impossible to recognize, let alone prevent.

During Schmitt's time, Thoma had argued that the essence of the constitution lay in democratic legal procedures. He believed that as long as voters adhered to the procedures in effect, their actions were inherently democratic. He simply could not conceive of the electorate using democratic procedures to pursue illegitimate ends, so he saw no reason to entrench Weimar democracy against internal threats.

Countering views like Thoma's, Schmitt argued that designing a democratic state so that its political identity could be continuously reshaped through democratic procedures, inadvertently paved the way for 'total' parties to emerge. They had every incentive to compete for the legal possession of state power, which would allow them to use the state apparatus to impose their worldviews. The battle for control over the state became existential. In the process, the state and public law themselves were delegitimated among its members. They became seen as mere instruments for advancing factional interests. As a result, public order broke down and the threat of civil war loomed.

Drawing inspiration from Hobbes, Schmitt argued that containing politicization meant reasserting state authority. To effectively do so, Hobbes' state theory needed to be updated to account for modern constitutionalism's turn to democratic legitimacy. That required correcting relativized, mechanical conceptualizations of 'the people' and the constitution as merely the sum of their constituent parts by

---

[128] Milan W Svolik, 'Polarization versus Democracy' (2019) 30(3) Journal of Democracy 20–21.
[129] Schmitt, *Constitutional Theory* (n 9) 108.

asserting the priority of the political identity of 'the people', as defined by the absolute constitution, over and possibly against the will of its individual members.

Schmitt's concept of the absolute constitution defined the normative limits of legal change and implied that the state was authorized by 'the people' to prevent constitutionally relativized laws from being turned against its political identity. Dualism thus allows legal revolution to be recognized as a threat to public order and justifies the state responding to it—in terms consistent with modern constitutionalism's turn to democratic legitimation.[130]

Schmitt believed that the myth of Leviathan helped members to reconcile themselves with this aspect of state authority. It showed how, even in a democracy, certain matters must be taken off the political agenda and constitutionally entrenched. Furthermore, it showed how the state should have the authority to defend those matters because they were the identity of 'the people'—even if that meant limiting the will of the electorate.

The Uses and Limits of Schmitt for Militant Democracy

The uses and limits of Schmitt's state and constitutional theory must be unpacked. Taking the uses first, Schmitt's state and constitutional theory defends the state's authority to entrench its political identity from subversive threats. This includes addressing threats from popular actors using legal revolutionary methods. By clarifying the state authority's over 'the political', Schmitt's approach shows how, pace Rawls, the defence of liberal democracy is *not* a practical dilemma. It is something that philosophy can resolve. Schmitt thus lays a cornerstone for an alternative, liberal normative theory of militant democracy: the legitimacy of state authority and its right to deploy militant defensive measures.

As for its limitations, although Schmitt grounded state authority, he did not address whether any constitutional norms in particular were authoritative and binding. He offered no reason to privilege liberal democracy over any other political identity. Moreover, Schmitt only got as far as justifying a kind of collective existentialism: each 'people' ought to have the space to posit and live by its own idiosyncratic values—whatever those values happened to be. Driven by that belief, Schmitt defend the state's authority unconditionally, regardless of whether it was the Second Empire, the wartime *Oberste Heeresleitung*, the Weimar Republic, the Third Reich, or the Bonn Republic.

Schmitt's worldview offers insights into some aspects of his persona that seem paradoxical at first glance. Although he appears to be an occasionalist—someone with no values or loyalties of his own—in Hobbesian fashion, Schmitt did 'confess'

---

[130] Kumm (n 22) 344–45.

134   DEPOLITICIZATION AND STATE AUTHORITY

his loyalty to the prevailing public order.[131] That conservatism helps explain his initial efforts to defend the Weimar state, despite his reservations about its democracy, followed by his about face just months after the Nazis took power. Schmitt's belief in the overriding importance of stable public order provides continuity to his otherwise seemingly incoherent actions.

Schmitt's state and constitutional theory, because of its conservatism and *völkisch* cultural relativism, only provides the *militant* dimension of a normative theory of militant democracy. It explains the state's authority to guarantee essential constitutional norms, justifying why the constitutionality of overriding the electorate's legally expressed will. However, it fails to provide the *democratic* dimension of that normative theory. Schmitt's theory does not even attempt to explain why democratic constitutional norms ought to be entrenched.

Democrats should be troubled by any defence of state authority ungrounded in liberal democratic norms, and this hold especially for Schmitt's theory. To stop with Schmitt—and accept that the state has the authority to uphold its constitutional identity, whatever that identity might be—would yield an emaciated normative theory. In Rawls' terms, Schmitt provides no way to distinguish between *de facto* stability and stability for the right reasons.[132] We know that 'peace' under a totalitarian regime is no more legitimate than the violence of the state of nature. In this regard, Hallowell was absolutely correct when he observed that Schmitt's formalism mirrors that of the neo-Kantian Weimar positivists he often criticized.[133]

Democrats do not need to limit themselves to Schmitt's formal theory of state authority, however. Complementing Schmitt's state and constitutional theory with the content of Rawls' political liberalism yields a liberal normative theory of militant democracy. While Rawls demonstrates how practical reason generates the authority of liberal norms, Schmitt establishes the state's authority to defend those norms. Rawls provides the substantive underpinnings of a liberal theory of militant democracy, Schmitt justifies its formal mechanisms, thereby overcoming what Rawls believed was the practical problem of democracy's self-defence by bridging democratic norms and militant measures.

---

[131] See Hasso Hofmann, *Legitimität gegen Legalität: der Weg der politischen Philosophie Carl Schmitts* (Duncker & Humblot 1992) 106, 147.

[132] I'm indebted to Alessandro Ferrara for this suggestion.

[133] John H Hallowell, *The Decline of Liberalism as an Ideology with Particular Reference to German Politico-Legal Thought* (Kegan Paul, Trench, Trubner & Co., Ltd. 1946) 106.

PART III

5
Unamendability

Introduction

So far I have analysed how the combination of Rawls's political liberalism with Schmitt's state theory can provide the normative foundation for a liberal theory of militant democracy. The next step is to analyse the measures it makes available to entrench its constitution and defend against legal revolution. The introduction argued that there are three principal mechanisms: explicit unamendability, political rights restrictions, and a guardian of the constitution (typically a constitutional court). The following three chapters examine each of these mechanisms in turn, beginning with unamendability.

The doctrine of unamendability holds that basic constitutional principles are inviolable. It defines otherwise duly enacted laws that conflict with those principles as 'unconstitutional' and therefore invalid. Unamendability supersedes and binds the will of even the highest constituted powers of the state, subordinating them to those basic constitutional principles. Liberal theory asserts that, because basic liberal rights are essential to democracy, they are normatively inviolable. Constitutionally, they should not be subject to alteration through democratic legal procedures. That requires installing mechanisms, such as an eternity clause, that defend them against positive constitutional amendment.

In addition to its primary role of legally entrenching democratic constitutional essentials, explicit unamendability serves a second purpose. By explicitly identifying which norms are democratic constitutional essentials, it provides a legal anchor for a definition of antidemocratic political goals, which serves as a normative basis for applying political rights restrictions. This second purpose helps address and mitigate some criticisms of militant democracy, in particular criticisms concerning its legal indeterminacy and discretionary authority.

The 1949 German *Basic Law* exemplifies explicit unamendability in practice through Article 79.3, the 'Eternity Clause'. Article 79.3 absolutely entrenches the most democratically essential articles of the *Basic Law*, including human dignity and basic rights (Article 1); the definition of Germany as 'a democratic and social federal state', whose authority is derived from 'the people' and which is bound by the constitution (Article 20); and the division of the Federation into *Länder* (states). The explicit unamendability of Article 79.3 was designed to prevent another legal revolution of German democracy, based on the founders'

Democracy despite Itself. Benjamin A. Schupmann, Oxford University Press. © Benjamin A. Schupmann 2024.
DOI: 10.1093/9780191975950.003.0006

138 UNAMENDABILITY

experience of the Nazi rise to power by exploiting Weimar's value-neutral democratic procedures.[1]

Multi-Track Constitutionalism

Unamendability might seem normatively unattractive or practically unfeasible because democratic theory tends to conceive of legislation in terms of a dual-track model: law is categorized as either ordinary or constitutional. Ordinary law has a simpler procedure, with lower thresholds for successful enactment, for example requiring only a simple 51 per cent majority to pass. Constitutional law has a more demanding and complex procedure, with higher thresholds, such as requiring a 67 per cent supermajority, because it deals with more important institutions and values.

Constitutions designed according to that dual-track legal conception encounter both normative and practical challenges. It imposes the same amendment procedure on every article of the constitution, disregarding any qualitative differences between them.[2] For example, dual-track constitutionalism does not recognize any legal difference between an article prohibiting the establishment of a state religion and an article requiring that the legislative branch meet on the first Monday of December. Yet there is clearly a qualitative difference between them: changing the former degrades democracy, changing the latter does not. When a constitution is designed according to the dual-track model, both are formally identical because both are subject to the same amendment procedure.

Because dual-tracked constitutionalism treats all constitutional law as formally identical, it creates a constitution that is either too rigid or too malleable. On the one hand, if it makes constitutional amendment too difficult, then every article of the constitution could be entrenched against legal change, locking in trivial norms and past mistakes. It may stifle the will of the electorate. For example, amending the US Constitution can be arduous. Constitutional provisions that are extremely contentious from the perspective of democratic theory and arguably constitute historical anachronisms, such as the Second Amendment, are given the same constitutional weight as democratic fundamentals and seem like an ineradicable blight on US public order. Yet because of the legitimacy that constitutional legality

---

[1] Günter Dürig, 'Zur Bedeutung und Tragweite des Art. 79 III des Grundgesetzes (ein Plädoyer)' in Hans Spanner and others (eds), *Festgabe für Theodor Maunz zum 70 Geburtstag am 1 September 1971* (CH Beck 1971) 46; Hermann Huba, 'Das Grundgesetz als dauerhafte gesamtdeutsche Verfassung: Erinnerung an seine Legitimität' (1991) 30(3) Der Staat 372–73; Martin Klamt, 'Militant Democracy and the Democratic Dilemma: Different Ways of Protecting Democratic Constitutions' in Fred Bruinsma and David Nelken (eds), *Explorations in Legal Cultures* (Elsevier 2007) 137; Markus Thiel, 'Germany' in Markus Thiel (ed), *The 'Militant Democracy' Principle in Modern Democracies* (Ashgate 2009) 127–28.

[2] Andrew Arato, 'Multi-Track Constitutionalism beyond Carl Schmitt' (2011) 18(3) Constellations 324–25.

implies, many Americans consider gun rights to be a cornerstone of democracy, if not the most important freedom. Meanwhile, the Equal Rights Amendment, aimed at enacting basic sexual equality, floundered due to insufficient ratification by individual state legislatures despite passing with a supermajority in US Congress. As a result of the US Constitution's design, it is as challenging to remove democratically trivial articles as it is to add democratically essential ones.

On the other hand, if thresholds for amendment are too low, then an opportunistic majority fearful of losing the next election might abuse constitutional amendment in order to kick the ladder to state power down entirely, undemocratically consolidating its own power and values. If essential norms are too easy to change, then there is no meaningful entrenchment. For example, a change to the Hungarian *Fundamental Law* requires only a two-thirds majority in its single legislative chamber.[3] This relatively low threshold enabled the Fidesz-dominated government to successfully weaken several democratic constitutional essentials, including the independence of the judiciary and other instances of the separations of powers, freedoms of expression and religion, and the independence of government agencies and civil society.[4]

Dual-track constitutionalism cannot recognize a political constitution. Constitutional essentials are at best implicit and rely on a constitutional guardian to define them. This relationship is problematic because it leaves the identification and guarantee of these essentials up to the discretion and will of that guardian, depending on their good faith and a broader social consensus to remain in effect over time. In addition, militant democracy, as a mechanism of constitutional entrenchment, presupposes a clear demarcation between inviolable democratic constitutional essentials and amendable constitutional laws.

Arato's concept of 'multi-track constitutionalism' offers a model that delineates those categories.[5] It holds that public law should be divided along at least three tracks: regular statutory law, amendable constitutional law, and essential constitutional law.[6] Each track is associated with a specific type of legislative power: ordinary legislative power, the amending power as a derived constituent power, and the constituent power that rests with 'the people'. In addition, that model reinforces two important distinctions—between the electorate and 'the people', and between

---

[3] See Kim Lane Scheppele, 'Constitutional Coups and Judicial Review: How Transnational Institutions can Strengthen Peak Courts at Times of Crisis (With Special Reference to Hungary)' (2014) 23 Journal of Transnational Law & Contemporary Problems; Laurent Pech and Kim Lane Scheppele, 'Illiberalism Within: Rule of Law Backsliding in the EU' (2017) 19 Cambridge Yearbook of European Legal Studies.

[4] Marc F Plattner, 'Illiberal Democracy and the Struggle on the Right' (2019) 30(1) Journal of Democracy 13.

[5] Andrew Arato, *The Adventures of the Constituent Power: Beyond Revolutions?* (Cambridge University Press 2017). See also Sharon Weintal, 'The Challenge of Reconciling Constitutional Eternity Clauses with Popular Sovereignty: Toward Three-Track Democracy in Israel as a Universal Holistic Constitutional System and Theory' (2011) 44(3) Israel Law Review.

[6] Arato, 'Multi-Track Constitutionalism beyond Carl Schmitt' (n 2) 324.

140 UNAMENDABILITY

politics and 'the political'. Those distinctions are crucial for the liberal normative theory of militant democracy, as discussed in earlier chapters.

Multi-track constitutionalism thus achieves a delicate but important balance in constitutional design. It allows for the absolute entrenchment of constitutional essentials while still permitting amendments to other parts of the constitution. Because it realizes that distinction through positive law, it ensures that constitutional entrenchment is more consistent with the principles of the rule of law.

Although multi-track constitutionalism prevents changes to a narrow subset of constitutional articles, it does so to safeguard them as democratic constitutional essentials. At the same time, it allows other, less essential articles to be amended more easily. Because the majority of constitutional articles are not locked in and may be changed through comparatively lower thresholds, the electorate has more freedom to add, amend, and abolish its constitution.

That two-pronged approach—entrenching constitutional essentials absolutely while including lower barriers for other constitutional change—enhances the overall democratic quality of the state. Except for basic liberal rights, the electorate has broad discretion over the law. Multi-track constitutionalism thus balances the entrenchment of democratic essentials, to prevent their regression, with the recognition that a constitution must adapt to changing circumstances, to continue to reflect that political community's unique and *authentic* identity over time.[7] In short, multi-track constitutionalism strikes a balance between the need to safeguard democratic constitutional essentials and broad public autonomy.

Absolute Entrenchment

One may wonder about the necessity of entrenching constitutional essentials absolutely by making them unamendable. Even if constitutional essentials should be, as Scheppele rightly argues, 'protected outside the playing field of normal politics', why are not significantly higher thresholds for amendment sufficient for that purpose?[8] As Albert argues, successfully exercising any amendment procedure typically requires an 'extraordinary confluence and sequence of events'.[9] It may require meeting supermajority thresholds, obtaining bicameral agreement, retaining control over the legislative across multiple election cycles, securing consent from

---

[7] On constitutional authenticity, see Bruce Ackerman, *Revolutionary Constitutions: Charismatic Leadership and the Rule of Law* (Harvard University Press 2019) 18; Alessandro Ferrara, 'Unconventional Adaptation and the Authenticity of the Constitution' in Richard Albert (ed), *Revolutionary Constitutionalism: Law, Legitimacy, Power* (Hart 2020) 157–68; Alessandro Ferrara, *Sovereignty Across Generations: Constituent Power and Political Liberalism* (Oxford University Press 2023) 157–63. On the broader significance of authenticity to modernity, see Alessandro Ferrara, *Modernity and Authenticity: A Study of the Social and Ethical Thought of Jean-Jacques Rousseau* (SUNY Press 1992).
[8] Kim Lane Scheppele, 'Autocratic Legalism' (2018) 85(2) The University of Chicago Law Review.
[9] Richard Albert, 'Constitutional Handcuffs' (2010) 42(3) Arizona State Law Journal 668.

legislatures below the federal level, or, with a popular referendum, mobilizing and amassing sufficient support directly from the electorate. These thresholds are not easy to meet. If they are met, it presumably signals robust support for the proposed changes. So why insist on unamendability as a necessary protective measure for democratic constitutional essentials, as a liberal theory of militant democracy does?

Recent constitutional history reveals the answer: high thresholds to constitutional change do not prevent constitutions from being revolutionized legally and degraded democratically. The abuse of amendment procedures and referenda to revolutionize democratic fundamentals has become unfortunately common since the end of the twentieth century. In states such as Venezuela (1999), Ecuador (2008), Bolivia (2009), and Hungary (2011), democratically elected governments have used amendment procedures to entirely replace the existing constitution.[10] Others, such as Colombia (2005), Sri Lanka (2011), and Turkey (2017), have taken a more incremental approach and only amended the existing constitution.[11] In these cases, amendment was used to backslide democracy, usually by diluting the constitutional separation of powers (to consolidate executive power) or weakening basic liberal rights. As chapter 1 discussed in greater detail, the constitutional supremacy of the amendment clause opens the door for these kinds of abuses, enabling antidemocrats to legally revolutionize a democratic constitution directly. In addition, indirect forms of legal revolution can be used to make constitutional change easier, as the case of Hungary demonstrates. There is thus an obvious practical reason to seek stronger entrenchment of democratic constitutional essentials.

Beyond that practical-historical reason, there is also a normative argument for seeking the *absolute* entrenchment of democratic constitutional essentials through unamendability. If democratic essentials exist, which can be established as authoritative and binding norms that are independent of the will of the electorate, and if the continued depoliticization of society hinges on the state's guarantee of those constitutional norms—as a liberal normative theory of militant democracy argues –, then those norms ought to be entrenched absolutely. If there are normative preconditions for democracy, then they cannot be legitimately removed from the constitution. Meeting a higher quantitative threshold does not convert a substantively illegitimate amendment into a legitimate one. Insofar as a norm is democratically *essential*, it does not matter whether its elimination is supported by 67 per cent or 75 per cent of the population or if its elimination remains popular over an election cycle.[12] Meeting those quantitative thresholds will not produce a qualitative change that somehow makes their abrogation any less illegitimate. By

---

[10] See David Landau, 'Abusive Constitutionalism' (2013) 47(1) UC Davis Law Review, 189; David Landau, 'Populist Constitutions' (2018) 85 The University of Chicago Law Review 521; Aziz Huq and Tom Ginsburg, 'How to Lose a Constitutional Democracy' (2018) 78(1) UCLA Law Review 78.

[11] I do not list Israel's 2023 amendment to its *Basic Law* as an example of this phenomenon because constitutional amendment in Israel requires only a simple majority in the Knesset.

[12] Carl Schmitt, *Legality and Legitimacy* (Duke University Press 2004) 41.

definition, essential norms must persist over time. Absolute entrenchment best guarantees that persistence.

A liberal theory of militant democracy holds that no constituted power, not even a supermajority of the electorate, should have the authority to exercise 'the people's' constituent power with which it could legally eliminate democratic essentials. If used in that way, that power would not only produce a substantively less legitimate state, it risks repoliticizing society. Therefore, the amendment clause should not be installed as the supreme clause of the constitution. Absolute entrenchment through constitutional unamendability prevents positive legal procedures from being hijacked to undermine democratic constitutional essentials.

Implicit Unamendability

Roznai categorizes unamendability into two basic types: implicit and explicit.[13] It is typically enforced through judicial review of both constitutional amendments and ordinary law. Unamendability is *implicit* when the amendment clause, although enacted formally as the supreme clause of the constitution, is thought to be constrained by super-positive constitutional norms.[14] An example of implicit unamendability is the 'Basic Structure Doctrine' of The Constitution of India, which holds that the written constitution rests on more fundamental but formally unarticulated principles. When based on liberal normative theory, the content of the basic structure of a constitution is defined by liberal principles of legitimacy.

At first glance, implicit unamendability may seem to align well with a liberal normative theory of militant democracy. For some, such as Arato and Cohen, implicit unamendability appears to be the only way to reconcile the practical and normative need to entrench democratic constitutional essentials with a lingering radical democratic normative commitment.[15] However, implicit unamendability faces the same issues as existing normative theories of militant democracy.[16] In particular, because constitutional essentials are not explicitly anchored in positive articles of the constitution, implicit unamendability does not address the problem of legal indeterminacy. That in turn raises questions about the degree of discretion that the judiciary, in its capacity as guardian of the constitution, exercises as

---

[13] Yaniv Roznai, *Unconstitutional Constitutional Amendments: The Limits of Amendment Powers* (Oxford 2017) 179.

[14] ibid 6, 8.

[15] Andrew Arato and Jean L Cohen, *Populism and Civil Society: The Challenge to Constitutional Democracy* (Oxford University Press 2022) 196.

[16] See also the criticisms of militant democracy. For example, Carlo Invernizzi-Accetti and Ian Zuckerman, 'What's Wrong with Militant Democracy?' (2017) 65(1) Political Studies; Anthoula Malkopoulou and Ludvig Norman, 'Three Models of Democratic Self-Defence: Militant Democracy and Its Alternatives' (2018) 66(2) Political Studies; Anthoula Malkopoulou, 'What Militant Democrats and Technocrats Share' (2023) 26(4) Critical Review of International Social and Political Philosophy.

it decides on which articles are implicitly unamendable and what counts as an unconstitutional violation. Such ambiguities can lead to legitimation problems, making implicit unamendability a less stable mechanism for entrenching and perpetuating the essential, inviolable core of the constitution.

Indeterminacy

A problem of the doctrine of implied unamendability is that it does not formally articulate the identity or basic structure of the constitution. Although it posits that there is an unamendable constitutional core, that core is not positively established. On the contrary, from the perspective of the positive legal order, the amendment clause is still the supreme clause of the constitution and every article of the constitution sits under the reservation of its exercise. Implied unamendability instead holds that other super-legal constitutional norms take precedence over positive constitutional law, in particular the amendment clause. Those super-legal norms may not even be present in the written constitution. Still, implicit unamendability treats those super-positive norms as constraining what would otherwise be considered valid legal changes. The substantive identity of the constitution either deviates from or is not explicitly stated in its written text.

By asserting that super-positive unarticulated norms exist that can trump positive law, implied unamendability drives a wedge between constitutional legality and legitimacy. That creates the potential for an opposition between the two, which could in turn become the basis for a constitutional crisis. For example, if different representatives of the state authority have antithetical views about which norms define its basic structure or if the legal procedures of the written constitution are turned against those extralegal norms, the existing order may be seriously destabilized.

That divide between legality and legitimacy bears most on constitutional amendments that meet the procedural thresholds for legal change and (presumably) have the support of a majority or supermajority of the electorate. If the identity of the constitution is legally undefined, the question of whether an amendment is 'unconstitutional', and by extension of whether it alters the political identity of the constitution, introduces a qualitatively different element into constitutional interpretation. For example, are gun rights a part of the essence of democracy? Few democratic theorists would answer 'yes'. Yet there it is, embedded in the US Constitution, where it possesses the same formal legal status as any democratic essential. Any body with the authority to interpret the constitution, for example the US Supreme Court, has a textual basis to argue that it is in fact part of the basic structure of American democracy.

In this way, implied unamendability grants considerable latitude to authorities to define what is a constitutional essential and by extension inviolable. It reduces the issue to a matter of political will—exactly the scenario that unamendability is

144 UNAMENDABILITY

intended to avoid. Implied unamendability does not stably determine which principles or articles are the political constitution and its democratic fundamentals. That instability affects the other two principle mechanisms of militant democracy, political rights restrictions and a guardian of the constitution.

Judicial Authority over the Constitution

Unamendability is not self-enforcing and requires a guardian to protect those constitutional essentials. When unamendability is only implicit, the judiciary typically asserts that it has the authority both to interpret what principles are constitutional essentials and to defend its interpretation against that of other branches of government. For example, the constitutional court may act to invalidate an amendment duly passed by the legislature if it decides that amendment undermines the constitution's basic structure.

However, implicit unamendability weakens the judiciary's claim to that interpretative authority. After all, according to positive constitutional law, those norms may be changed validly. If its interpretation of that inviolable core were challenged legally, the judiciary could find itself in the uncomfortable position of having to oppose positive constitutional law in order to assert its authority, all while judging its own cause. Examples of the difficulties involved in asserting the court's authority to interpret and uphold principles not otherwise grounded in positive law are playing out in Israel and India, which model implicit unamendability and the basic structure doctrine.

In Israel, the Netanhayu government was actively clawing back the Supreme Court's power to interpret Israel's *Basic Law*—until this was interrupted by the attack Hamas mounted on 7 October 2023.[17] Netanyahu's conservative coalition intended to legislatively restrict the Supreme Court's power of judicial review to only procedural matters. Its goal was to use normal statutory legislation to establish that Court lacked the competence to decide on the substantive constitutionality of changes to the *Basic Law*. Although many citizens believed the Knesset's actions were substantively undemocratic and troubling, the combination of the fact that Netanyahu took power legally through free and fair elections and that those changes were themselves legal left no clear legal basis on which oppose them.

India's once fiercely independent judiciary is gradually becoming more subservient to the government, failing to protect the basic rights thought to be a part of its basic structure in high profile cases.[18] In some of those cases, the judiciary has

---

[17] See Amichai Cohen and Yuval Shany, *Reversing the 'Constitutional Revolution': The Israeli Government's Plan to Undermine the Supreme Court's Judicial Review of Legislation* (2023).

[18] Šumit Ganguly, 'India's Endangered Democracy' (2021) 32(4) Journal of Democracy; Šumit Ganguly, 'An Illiberal India?' (2021) 31(1) Journal of Democracy; Ashutosh Varshney, 'How India's Ruling Party Erodes Democracy' (2022) 33(4) Journal of Democracy.

allowed the basic structure to weaken because it has sought to avoid clashing with the government, for example by outright refusing to hear cases dealing with *habeas corpus* petitions from jailed citizens in Kashmir. In others, the judiciary has actively abetted government actions to weaken the basic structure, such as through its approval of India's biometric identification project. Khosla and Vaishnav write that this change is not because of judicial capture, as in other 'illiberal democracies', but through a combination of more subtle curbs and the judiciary's 'self-abrogation'.[19] By avoiding exercising its power to review altogether, the judiciary does not force the government to limit its power or to attempt to amend the constitution to get its way.

In both Israel and India, a popularly elected government has sought to override what were thought to be the implicitly unamendable basic structures of a democratic constitution. Facing the legislature's actions, the constitutional court finds itself in a precarious situation. Its authority to counter and invalidate unconstitutional legislative acts relies on its extralegal assertion of an implicitly unamendable basic structure.[20] Were it to try to oppose the legislature's actions, the court might ignite a constitutional crisis. So although the court can claim that the legislative may only amend the constitution but cannot eliminate its basic structure, the ambiguities of implicit unamendability make it difficult to enforce that claim in practice.

Conversely, a strong and activist judiciary that acts in bad faith could exploit the weakness of implicit unamendability as a guarantee of democratic constitutional essentials. Since the judiciary defines the basic structure of democracy and upholds it, an activist court could overstep its authority to interpret the constitution by assuming 'the people's' constituent power.[21] Essentially, it could unilaterally dictate norms unrelated to democratic principles as if they were part of the basic structure and invalidate attempts to change its decision. While no concrete examples exist to illustrate this threat, the ambiguity of an implicit constitutional identity can be seen in disagreements among Indian Supreme Court Justices in *Kesavananda Bharati v. State of Kerala* about which values defined the basic structure of Indian democracy.[22] Without a material legal basis, fixed in a written constitution for example, the room for interpretative disagreement is significant.

Judicial capture offers a way to exploit that shortcoming of implicit unamendability in order to undermine democracy.[23] If the only guarantee of an inviolable democratic core rests on the good will of the guardian of the constitution— rather than explicitly unamendable articles –, then the legal revolution of that core only requires capturing the guardian. Both the content of the implicitly

---

[19] Madhav Khosla and Milan Vaishnav, 'The Three Faces of the Indian State' (2022) 32(1) Journal of Democracy 116–17.

[20] Roznai (n 13) 69.

[21] Gary Jeffrey Jacobsohn and Yaniv Roznai, *Constitutional Revolution* (Yale University Press 2020) 158.

[22] On this, see Ackerman (n 7) 67–68.

[23] I am indebted to Samuel Issacharoff for suggesting that I take up judicial capture in this context.

unamendable constitution and the guarantee of those articles depend on the will of the guardian. Although this tactic has not yet been used by antidemocrats against a basic structure, the antidemocratic potential for capturing the judiciary has been demonstrated well in states such as Poland. In short, by capturing the judiciary, antidemocrats could abuse its authority over the implicitly unamendable constitution to redefine the identity of the state and constitution.

Overall, judicial authority to interpret and safeguard constitutional essentials is less stable when limits to legal change are only positively implicit.[24] When confronting the uncertainties and normative problems that indeterminacy creates, many constitutional courts conclude, as Singapore's did, that 'had a constitution's framers intended to prohibit certain amendments, one would reasonably expect them to have included a provision to that effect'.[25]

Political Rights Restrictions

As discussed in earlier chapters, unamendability and political rights restrictions are complementary and mutually presupposing forms of constitutional entrenchment. Implicit unamendability directly impacts both the legitimacy and limits of political rights restrictions. It is particularly relevant to what Rijpkema calls the detection problem.

The detection problem of militant democracy asks how a state can identity antidemocratic threats accurately and in time.[26] Correctly identifying a political organization as an antidemocratic threat is the precondition for legitimately deploying political rights restrictions against it. By defining democracy, the inviolable core of the constitution also determines the criteria for detecting an antidemocratic threat. An actor who substantively opposes and seeks to abrogate or weaken those constitutional essentials is a threat to the state's democratic identity.

Implicit unamendability muddies the waters when it comes to detection, however. The inviolable core of the constitution is not positively defined. It is instead an extralegal assertion, usually by the constitutional court. This supports critics' concerns, described in chapter 2, that the constitutional court has excessive discretionary power to determine who qualifies as an enemy of the constitution and to act to repress that threat.[27] This is a normative issue because the constitutional court may define and interpret the unamendable core of the constitution too narrowly, so it will appear overly cautious when it comes to detecting antidemocratic threats and thereby overlook genuine enemies of democracy.

---

[24] Roznai (n 13) 209.
[25] Quoted in ibid.
[26] Bastiaan Rijpkema, 'Militant Democracy and the Detection Problem' in Anthoula Malkopoulou and Alexander S Kirshner (eds), *Militant Democracy and Its Critics: Populism, Parties, Extremism* (Edinburgh University Press 2019) 169.
[27] See Invernizzi-Accetti and Zuckerman (n 16); Malkopoulou and Norman (n 16).

Alternatively, the constitutional court may define and interpret that unamendable core too broadly, including non-essential principles in its definition of democracy, so the constitutional court will appear overzealous when it comes to detecting antidemocratic threats and restrict the political rights of organizations that actions do not pose a threat to democracy. In either case, the absence of a positive definition of democratic constitutional essentials means that decisions about the constitutionality of an organization's goals or acts will be super-positive. Political rights restrictions will not be deployed on the basis of reasonably clear or definite, known general statutes, abandoning basics of the rule of law.

Arato argues that, as long as there are no positive procedural limits on constitutional change—that is, as long as the amendment clause is the supreme clause of the constitution—political rights restrictions lack a stable constitutional foundation.[28] The uncertainty that political rights restrictions may be deployed against organizations who obeyed the positive law can undermine democracy if for no other reason than resulting in actors self-censoring.[29] From the perspective of an actor in civil society, the use of political rights restrictions may genuinely be legally arbitrary.

In the end, implicit unamendability is an unsatisfactory normative basis for entrenching democratic constitutional essentials. Were a liberal normative theory of militant democracy to adopt the doctrine of implicit unamendability to entrench constitutional essentials, it would inherit problems criticized in existing normative theories of militant democracy.

Explicit Unamendability

Unamendability is *explicit* when specific articles or clauses in the written constitution are legally unalterable through positive entrenchment mechanisms.[30] Explicit unamendability anchors the fundamental values and identity of the constitution in positive law.

The paradigmatic example of explicit unamendability is the 'eternity clause' of Article 79.3 of the German *Basic Law*. That clause absolutely entrenches the principles laid out in Articles 1 and 20 as well as the federal structure of Germany. From the perspective of liberal theory, Article 1 plays an essential role in democratic constitutionalism because it establishes the inviolability of human dignity and lays the foundation for other human rights. Article 1 reads:

(1) Human dignity shall be inviolable. To respect and protect it shall be the duty of all state authority.

---

[28] Arato, 'Multi-Track Constitutionalism beyond Carl Schmitt' (n 2) 336–37.
[29] Nancy Rosenblum, 'Banning Parties: Religious and Ethnic Partisanship in Multicultural Democracies' (2007) 1(1) Law & Ethics of Human Rights 53–55; Malkopoulou and Norman (n 16) 447.
[30] Roznai (n 13) 16.

(2) The German people therefore acknowledge inviolable and inalienable human rights as the basis of every community, of peace and of justice in the world.

(3) The following basic rights shall bind the legislature, the executive and the judiciary as directly applicable law.

The rights that follow Article 1 concretize human dignity, clarifying how state authorities can fulfil their duty to respect and protect it.[31] Those rights are the canonical basic liberal rights, such as free development of one's personality, the right to life and physical integrity, equality before the law, religious liberty, freedom of conscience, freedom of expression, freedom of assembly and association, and an inalienable right of citizenship.[32] Article 19.2 further emphasizes that the essence of those basic rights cannot be encroached on.[33]

The use of legal revolutionary methods by antidemocrats, especially constitutional replacement, underscores the need for explicit unamendability. It is a vital defence against legal revolutionary threats. Thiel suggests that explicit unamendability works by stripping 'the mask of legality' from antidemocrats' revolutionary activities, thereby forcing them to pursue their undemocratic goals overtly.[34] While antidemocrats might still find ways to overthrow constitutional democracy, they will not be able to do so by making democracy cannibalize itself.

The normative theory laid out in the preceding chapters lays the justificatory foundation to do so, by establishing that basic liberal rights are democratic constitutional essentials and that a democratic state may legitimately entrench them in order to guarantee its constitutional identity. Explicit unamendability resolves the limitations of implicit unamendability described in the preceding section. In

---

[31] Dieter Grimm, 'Dignity in a Legal Context: Dignity as an Absolute Right' in Christopher McCrudden (ed), *Understanding Human Dignity* (The British Academy 2013) 386; Christoph Goos, 'Würde des Menschen: Restoring Human Dignity in Post-Nazi Germany' in Christopher McCrudden (ed), *Understanding Human Dignity* (The British Academy 2013) 88–89.

[32] These rights roughly map onto the rights enumerated in Articles 3–20 of the *Universal Declaration of Human Rights*, which I suggested in chapter 3 might be the constitutional core of Rawls' political liberalism.

[33] In the context of German constitutionalism, human dignity is regarded as an absolute right that cannot be restricted or infringed upon. It is usually conceived in terms of Kant's object formula, which argues that human dignity requires treating a person as an end in itself, never merely as a means. Aharon Barak, 'Human Dignity: The Constitutional Value and the Constitutional Right' in Christopher McCrudden (ed), *Understanding Human Dignity* (The British Academy 2013) 369; Grimm (n 31) 384.

Conversely, other basic liberal rights are considered relative rights. They may be infringed according to the principle of proportionality. Kumm writes that the proportionality principle is at the center of contemporary human rights jurisprudence because it offers a way of balancing competing rights claims as well as legitimate public and private interests. Mattias Kumm, 'Who's Afraid of the Total Constitution? Constitutional Rights as Principles and the Constitutionalization of Private Law' (2006) 7(4) German Law Journal 348; the Constitutional Court, as guardian of the constitution, has final authority over whether proportionality has been met. Werner Heun, *The Constitution of Germany: A Contextual Analysis* (Hart Publishing 2011) 43, 196.

[34] Thiel (n 1) 128.

contrast with implicit unamendability, it legally clarifies and signals through the medium of law the democratic political identity of the constitution.

That clarity also reinforces the practice of the other two principal mechanisms of militant democracy, political rights restrictions and constitutional guardianship. By forcing antidemocrats to act illegally and criminally, it may either dissuade them from pursuing their goals at all, buying the state time to respond to their concerns, or open them up to a wider set of criminal sanctions as they act overtly against democracy.

Circumscribing and Signalling the Identity of the Constitution

Explicit unamendability better protects the political identity of the constitution by circumscribing the legally valid exercise of the amendment clause.[35] Unlike with implicit unamendability, the amendment clause is not positively the supreme clause of the constitution. Its scope is legally limited, so that no constituted power can amend the constitution's political identity. Addressing this issue resolves problems arising from two collapsed distinctions, discussed in the first chapter.

First, as long as the amendment clause is the supreme clause, any procedurally valid change to the constitution appears also to be democratically legitimate. There is no legal basis to identify a procedurally valid change as revolutionary. At best, a guardian can identify revolutionary change on the basis of extralegal values. However, as the preceding section discussed, this is a fraught approach that risks instigating a constitutional crisis. Explicit unamendability avoids this issue by subordinating democratic legal procedures to articles of the constitution that enact democracy's most fundamental values.

Second, as long as the amendment clause is supreme, it collapses the distinction between the constituent power of 'the people' and the constituted power of the electorate or their elected representatives. A positively unlimited amendment clause for all intents and purposes just formalizes the constituent power of 'the people'. Limiting the valid use of the amendment clause resolves that problem by restoring a legal distinction between constituent power and constituted power.

Explicit unamendability positively delineates revolutionary changes to the constitution. By anchoring illegitimate change in the violation of specific articles of the constitution, explicit unamendability reduces the chance that legality and legitimacy will be opposed to one another and in the process better defends against the problem of direct legal revolution.

Explicit unamendability should be interpreted restrictively, focusing on guaranteeing constitutional essentials against their abrogation. The German

---

[35] Roznai (n 13) 22.

150   UNAMENDABILITY

Constitutional Court interprets unconstitutional changes in this way. It defines changes as unconstitutional only when they abandon the enumerated principles of democracy.[36] Other acts that impact or modify them are permissible. That narrow focus thus ensures that explicit unamendability deals only with the highest levels of constitutionalism, namely that a democratic constitution must include democratic essentials in its text.[37]

Besides its circumscribing function, explicit unamendability also serves an invaluable signaling function.[38] It grounds the political identity of the constitution materially and positively in the written text of the constitution. This more clearly communicates that identity than implicit unamendability. By using positive law to specify which issues are 'political', and thus off the legislative agenda, and which are 'depoliticized', and open to contested through politics and legislation, explicit unamendability reduces ambiguities about constitutional essentials.

Beyond Judicial Authority

As discussed above, implicit unamendability is a weak guarantee of the constitution because of its reliance on the guardian's discretionary authority, both to posit and to uphold implicitly unamendable values. If captured by antidemocrats, that discretionary authority can be abused to posit a different set of values as the implicitly unamendable core. In contrast, explicit unamendability minimizes that risk by anchoring the constitution's political identity in its written text. It restricts the scope for antidemocratic forces to abuse judicial authority by redefining what norms are constitutionally essential and implicitly unamendable.

Under explicit unamendability, the judiciary does not have the authority to determine which articles are unamendable. They are already laid out in the written constitution. Unless it is overturned illegally, the political constitution remains in effect. It establishes a bedrock for Kelsen's democratic hope that 'even when the ship [of state] is sinking, and can take with democrats into the depths only the hope that the ideal of freedom is indestructible and that the deeper it has sunk, the more passionately will it revive.'[39] Should all else fail, the political constitution can serve as a restoration point for democracy because it remains in effect.

---

[36] Thiel (n 1) 128.

[37] I am indebted to Samuel Moyn for pushing me to clarify the scope and limits of unamendability.

[38] Carl Schmitt, 'Freiheitsrechte und institutionelle Garantien der Reichsverfassung' in Carl Schmitt (ed), *Verfassungsrechtliche Aufsätze aus den Jahren 1924-1954 Materialien zu einer Verfassungslehre* (Duncker & Humblot 1958) 153–55, 173; Jon Elster, 'Constitutionalism in Eastern Europe: An Introduction' (1991) 58(2) The University of Chicago Law Review 447; Arato, 'Multi-Track Constitutionalism beyond Carl Schmitt' (n 2) 334; Roznai (n 13) 26.

[39] Hans Kelsen, *Verteidigung der Demokratie* (2006), quoted from Clemens Jabloner, 'Introduction to Hans Kelsen' in Arthur J Jacobson and Bernhard Schlink (eds), *Weimar: A Jurisprudence of Crisis* (University of California Press 2002) 74.

In addition, Roznai argues, explicit unamendability strengthens the case for constitutional guardianship through judicial review, a topic taken up in greater depth in chapter 7.[40] The reasoning is intuitive. Unlike implicit unamendability, which necessitates the guardian appeal to extralegal norms, under explicit unamendability the guardian only assesses whether actions or actors violate fixed clauses of the constitution.

This difference between implicit and explicit unamendability can be illustrated using the example of a practical juridical syllogism. In the case of implicit unamendability, the judiciary has the discretion to decide both what the major premise is (what is unamendable) and, based on the minor premise (the case at hand), draw its conclusion (judge whether a particular law or policy conflicts with that unamendable provision). With explicit unamendability, the major premise is already set, narrowing the judiciary's role to issuing a judgment based on the facts at hand.

A Legal Foundation for Political Rights Restrictions

Just as explicit unamendability reinforces the constitutional basis for judicial guardianship, it also lays a stronger foundation for using political rights restrictions. As long as an unlimited legal right to amend the constitution exists, the moral and legal justification for disenfranchising actors who exercise that right is problematic.[41] By absolutely entrenching constitutional essentials and limiting the right to amend them, explicit unamendability offers a definite, textual basis for identifying unconstitutional political goals. This in turn provides a more solid legal foundation for applying political rights restrictions, because it links political repression to opposition to specific articles of the constitution. That anchoring function of explicit unamendability resolves the normative problems that affect existing theories of militant democracy, including the paradox of democracy's self-defence, the discretionary potential for abuse, and the practical paradox that militant measures cannot save a struggling democracy.

Positively defining the constitution's political identity can thus reinforce the other two mechanisms of militant democracy and provides them with a stronger constitutional foundation. When it comes to political rights restrictions, explicit unamendability narrows the judiciary's role to assessing whether a party's actions are in opposition to positively entrenched norms. The criteria for 'what is unconstitutional?' is set out in the text, which narrows the guardian's task to evaluating and interpreting whether a specific actor's goals conflict with those entrenched norms.[42]

---

[40] Roznai (n 13) 203.
[41] Arato, 'Multi-Track Constitutionalism beyond Carl Schmitt' (n 2) 336.
[42] See also Otto Kirchheimer, *Political Justice: The Use of Legal Procedure for Political Ends* (Princeton University Press 1961) 136.

152   UNAMENDABILITY

This shifts the role of the guardian from positing the existence of extra-legal constitutional essentials to the task of interpreting whether particular actions are at odds with the legal established constitutional framework.

Aligning Legality and Legitimacy

Explicit unamendability narrows the gap between legality and legitimacy, particularly when it comes to constitutional essentials. It avoids the problem of value-neutral democratic legal procedures appearing to have the same (if not greater) normative significance as substantive democratic principles. That misalignment can create situations in which legal procedures can turned against democracy.

Chapter 1 discussed two ways that antidemocrats can exploit oppositions between legality and legitimacy to advance their legal revolutionary goals. First, when presented with the dilemma between obeying a legally valid command and upholding substantive democratic norms, many choose legality. This can be true especially of segments of society typically committed to 'law and order', such as the military, social conservatives, and the middle class. Antidemocrats exploit this tendency. The Weimar Republic presents a classic example of this.[43] After the Nazis rose to power, they took over state ministries. Ordinary bureaucrats and administrators, including many committed to Weimar's democratic ideals, faced a difficult decision of whether to continue working for the NSDAP. Those who did not resign immediately may have facilitated the Nazi consolidation of state power simply by lawfully executing their duties, albeit inadvertently and indirectly.

Second, when presented with a dilemma between upholding democratic fundamentals and satisfying their partisan interests, many ordinary voters in polarized societies choose their partisan interests.[44] The problem of democratic backsliding is not necessarily one of antidemocratic elites bamboozling decent but naïve voters. Antidemocrats are often transparent about their political goals. For example, voters in Venezuela, Hungary, and Turkey consciously chose antidemocratic candidates because they were more interested in satisfying their immediate factional interests—if they were not already themselves antidemocrats.

---

[43]   Karl Dietrich Bracher, 'Nachwort und Ausblick' in Karl Dietrich Bracher, Gerhard Schulz, and Wolfgang Sauer (eds), *Die nationalsozialistische Machtergreifung Studien zur Errichtung des totalitären Herrschaftssystems in Deutschland 1933/34* (Springer Fachmedien Wiesbaden 1960) 971; Karl Dietrich Bracher, 'The Technique of the Nationalist Seizure of Power' in *The Path to Dictatorship, 1918-1933; Ten Essays* (Anchor Books 1966) 126; Hans-Ulrich Thamer, *Verführung und Gewalt: Deutschland 1933-1945* (Siedler 1986) 272; Ivan Ermakoff, *Ruling Oneself Out: A Theory of Collective Abdications* (Duke University Press 2008) 22.

[44]   Milan W Svolik, 'Polarization versus Democracy' (2019) 30(3) Journal of Democracy.

EXPLICIT UNAMENDABILITY 153

Antidemocrats exploit the opposition between legality and legitimacy to subvert democracy. A democratic public order designed to prioritize its value-neutral procedures is particularly vulnerable to this. When any political goal at all can in principle become law, members may believe that all political choices are equally legitimate. Not even well-intentioned democrats are safe from advancing antidemocratic outcomes when legality and legitimacy can be set against one another.

Conversely, by aligning legality and legitimacy, antidemocrats may struggle to mobilize support for their political goals. The infamous Trump–Raffensperger phone call from the 2020 US Presidential election may help illustrate this point.[45] Georgia Secretary of State Brad Raffensperger voted for Trump in both 2016 and 2020 and has said that he would vote for him again. He was clearly not troubled by Trump's antidemocratic but legal policies. (In fact, Raffensperger has been accused of supporting measures to disenfranchise Georgians.) However, when Trump demanded he commit a crime, pressuring him 'to find, uh, 11,780 votes', Raffensperger refused.

This example suggests that the tables can be turned on antidemocrats. Aligning legality and legitimacy presents a dilemma to would-be antidemocrats and their supporters: they are forced to choose either to act legally, thereby upholding democratic essentials, or persist in their antidemocratic goals. In that dilemma between normative orders, some will choose legality, especially traditionally conservative segments of the electorate, in the process depriving antidemocratic movements of their base.

Legality has its own normative power. Explicit unamendability brings legality and legitimacy into constitutional alignment by taking democratic essentials off the political agenda. That reduces the normative dissonance, i.e., the internal moral conflict, that committed democrats in value-neutral democracies may experience when legality and substantive democratic values collide. Alignment clarifies to partisans, as any member of the community, that antidemocratic choices are neither legally nor democratically valid. Instead, by aligning legality and legitimacy, the dilemma of choosing between legality and legitimacy can be shifted onto antidemocrats, helping to safeguard democracy.

To be sure, explicit unamendability is no panacea for democratic decay. If enough citizens are committed to democratic suicide, they may resort to illegal or even violent revolutionary tactics, such as staging a coup d'état. Still, explicit unamendability has an important role to play. Besides preventing the abrogation of democratic constitutional essentials, it forces antidemocrats rather than

---

[45] Rusty Bowers may be another example. Although he described Trump's request to illegally discard the votes of Arizonans and appoint an alternate slate of electors as 'fascism', Bowers has also announced that he will vote for Trump again in 2024. His attitude suggests that the issue is not one of antidemocratic substance per se but formal illegality.

154 UNAMENDABILITY

democrats to confront the choice between legality and their political goals. At least with regard to constitutional change, it prevents antidemocrats from masking their political goals in the guise of legality. Without that veneer of legality, ordinary citizens may be more reluctant to get behind antidemocratic goals. And with its base narrowed, an antidemocratic movement may struggle to realize its goals by any means.

6

Political Rights Restrictions

Introduction

Political rights restrictions are an effective complement to unamendability because they deny antidemocrats the opportunity to engage in direct and indirect legal revolution. They deny antidemocrats the legal possession of state power, reinforcing constitutional unamendability in the process. They are important for militant democracy because, although explicit unamendability may prevent the most flagrant forms of democratic legal revolution, it cannot protect against its more indirect forms.

Recent examples, such as the cases of Poland and India discussed in chapter 1, demonstrate how antidemocrats can erode democratic essentials without actually amending the constitution. Kirshner argues further that focusing solely on preventing antidemocratic legislation through unamendability would overlook a critical reality: antidemocrats, not just antidemocratic legislation, threaten democracy.[1] Even if they lack the strength to amend the constitution, the mere presence of antidemocrats within democratic institutions can weaken and corrupt democracy.

The 1949 German *Basic Law* offers an example of political rights restrictions in constitutional practice. First, although it recognizes the central role that parties play in the democratic process in Article 21.1, the *Basic Law* allows for the dissolution of parties that aim to undermine or abolish the free democratic basic order in Article 21.2. That article constitutionalizes the party ban. The *Basic Law* also permits the dissolution of antidemocratic associations through Article 9.2.[2]

The *Basic Law* also provides for restrictions on the rights of individual antidemocrats through Article 18, although this measure has never been used and is now thought to be merely symbolic. Finally, the *Basic Law* also helps prevent negative majorities from governing by restricting political rights in a different complementary way. Article 67 requires that any vote of no confidence be 'positive' and simultaneously appoint a new Chancellor. It was designed to prevent

---

[1] Alexander S Kirshner, *A Theory of Militant Democracy: The Ethics of Combatting Political Extremism* (Yale University Press 2014) 4.

[2] Until now in Germany, only two parties have been successfully banned under Article 21.2. In contrast, over 500 associations have been banned under Article 9.2 of the *Basic Law*. Jan-Werner Müller, 'Individual Militant Democracy' in Anthoula Malkopoulou and Alexander S Kirshner (eds), *Militant Democracy and Its Critics: Populism, Parties, Extremism* (Edinburgh University Press 2019) 20.

Democracy despite Itself. Benjamin A. Schupmann, Oxford University Press. © Benjamin A. Schupmann 2024.
DOI: 10.1093/9780191975950.003.0007

156   POLITICAL RIGHTS RESTRICTIONS

antidemocrats from obstructing the government and, by extension, the democratic process itself.

This chapter defends the legitimacy of political rights restrictions, building on the liberal normative theory of militant democracy developed in chapters 3 and 4. A liberal normative theory of militant democracy sets political rights restrictions on a significantly firmer constitutional foundation, allowing them to be deployed against antidemocratic threats more effectively.

Limits of Existing Normative Theories

Chapter 2 discussed some of the normative and practical problems of existing normative theories of militant democracy. To recap, some of the principal normative and practical that advocates and critics have raised include the paradox of democracy's self-defence, abuses due to discretionary authority and legal indeterminacy, the detection problem, and the practical paradox that democracy will already beyond saving when it becomes legitimate to actually deploy militant measures.

The paradox of democracy's self-defence occurs because a party ban, or any political rights restriction, deprives members of their political rights, which existing normative theories of militant democracy consistently argue are the *sine qua non* of democratic legitimacy. Existing normative theories of militant democracy thus advocate the use of a measure that they recognize to be antidemocratic, because it deprives members of their most fundamental and indefeasible rights.

That paradox is compounded by the detection problem, which Rijpkema defines as the difficulty of identifying an antidemocratic threat both accurately and in time in order to justify the effective deployment of political rights restrictions.[3] Because of their narrow focus on defending political rights, existing normative theories of militant democracy are unable to detect other threats to democracy, including the prevailing threat to democracy today: so-called 'illiberal democrats' whose attack on democracy focuses on liberal constitutionalism and leaves political rights sufficiently intact.

Another criticism of existing normative theories of militant democracy is that the trigger for the deployment of their measures rests on legally indeterminate criteria. The more unclear norms regarding antidemocratic behaviour are, the more discretionary authority powerholders wield in the exercise of measures of militant democracy. They can abuse that authority to repress actors who do actually threaten democracy or simply to consolidate their hold on state power. Even

---

[3] Bastiaan Rijpkema, 'Militant Democracy and the Detection Problem' in Anthoula Malkopoulou and Alexander S Kirshner (eds), *Militant Democracy and Its Critics: Populism, Parties, Extremism* (Edinburgh University Press 2019) 169.

if powerholders do not abuse their authority, uncertainty about what will trigger a militant response can still deformalize the rule of law and degrade democracy. Actors will be more likely to 'self-censor' by abstaining from certain goals to avoid potential sanctions.

Another limitation of existing normative theories of militant democracy is that normative theories of militant democracy tend to discuss the legitimacy of only one mechanism: the party ban. This tendency is common enough that the terms 'militant democracy' and 'party ban' are used synonymously in the literature. Yet political rights restrictions can take other forms.[4] Parties can be restricted in less severe ways, short of an outright ban. Political rights restrictions can also target individuals directly or limit how elected representatives can exercise their powers in the legislature.

Another problem with existing normative theories is a practical paradox. Because of the above issues, even many advocates of militant democracy are not confident in the legitimacy of political rights restrictions. As a result, they treat political rights restrictions as a last resort, to be used only against parties that pose an immediate and existential threat to democracy. This gives rise to a practical paradox, which Müller summarizes as 'countries that can have militant democracy probably do not need it; whereas those that need it, cannot have it'.[5] The concern is that, by the time a party hits the normative threshold for a ban, it will be too strong to stop. If so, political rights restrictions can play no positive role in defending democracy; they can only degrade it by depriving members of fundamental rights.

Unamendability and the Legitimacy of Political Rights Restrictions

Liberal normative theory addresses the normative and practical problems of restricting political rights described above. It defends a conception of basic liberal rights as the foundation of democratic legitimacy and a precondition for democratic legal procedures and, because of their essential role in democratic constitutionalism, it also defends their unamendability. Unamendability places the use of political rights restrictions on a significantly more solid constitutional foundation.

As discussed in the introduction, unamendability and political rights restrictions are not just mutually reinforcing mechanisms, they are *co-implicating*.[6] Restricting the exercise of political rights in a democracy presupposes that some parts of the constitution are inviolable and cannot be validly changed. Restricting

---

[4] I am indebted to Jan-Werner Müller pushing me to address this.
[5] Jan-Werner Müller, 'Militant Democracy and Constitutional Identity' in Gary Jacobsohn and Miguel Schor (eds), *Comparative Constitutional Theory* (Edward Elgar 2018) 419.
[6] Rivka Weill, 'On the Nexus of Eternity Clauses, Proportional Representation, and Banned Political Parties' (2017) 16(2) Election Law Journal; Benjamin A Schupmann, 'Constraining Political Extremism and Legal Revolution' (2020) 46(3) Philosophy and Social Criticism.

158   POLITICAL RIGHTS RESTRICTIONS

political rights can be constitutionally valid only thanks to a superior constitutional norm justifying their infringement. Such restrictions are justified because of the unconstitutionality of the goal those rights are used to pursue. If a political goal is unconstitutional and a party can be banned for pursuing it, there must be a correlative unamendable constitutional norm. From the opposite perspective, the co-implication of unamendability implies that the exercise of formal political rights with regard to certain norms can be validly limited by the state. A party ban is the extreme form of such limitations.

Explicit unamendability not only legally defines and signals the political identity of the constitution; it also provides the constitutional foundation for political rights restrictions. It provides an explicit textual basis for defining unconstitutional political behaviour and goals. Unamendability thus clarifies what kinds of political goals and actions are beyond the pale and may accordingly be sanctioned through political rights restrictions.

Circumventing the Paradox of Democracy's Self-Defence

By defining basic liberal rights as the unamendable core of the constitution, liberal normative theory circumvents the paradox of democracy's self-defence. To clarify how, exactly, requires unpacking a fundamental distinction between political rights and basic liberal rights.[7]

Basic liberal rights guarantee an individual's *private* autonomy. They guarantee that one has the means to pursue their idiosyncratic conception of the good in the private sphere, to use Rawls' language. They aim to legally protect an individual's negative liberty from the external interference of public power. They only create a claim on the state to react and restore that sphere of liberty if they have been violated.

Political rights, on the other hand, guarantee an individual's formally equal share in *public* autonomy. They permit an individual to demand the state allow them to contribute to the formation of the community's political will, for example by voting and entering the competition for public office. The state must create those opportunities for individuals in order for the right to be effective at all.

Although it recognizes that both types of rights are important for a democracy, liberal normative theory clarifies that basic liberal rights are lexically prior to political rights. The phenomenon of democratic legal revolution reinforces the need to institutionalize that hierarchy. By distinguishing the two types of rights and arguing that basic liberal rights are more fundamental, liberal theory establishes normative grounds for limiting political rights. Restricting the rights of political

---

[7] See the typology in Carl Schmitt, *Constitutional Theory* (Duke University Press 2008) 209; see also Benjamin A Schupmann, *Carl Schmitt's State and Constitutional Theory: A Critical Analysis* (Oxford University Press 2017) 182–85.

organizations, for example through a party ban, can be legitimate and constitutional when done to guarantee members' more fundamental basic liberal rights. Basic liberal rights are a precondition for any sensible conception of democracy. Conversely, on that same liberal normative basis, political rights are neither a legitimate nor a legal-constitutional means by which to abrogate basic liberal rights.

Multi-track constitutionalism, discussed in previous chapters, embeds the hierarchical relationship between those types of rights in the constitution. The first and highest constitutional track entrenches basic liberal rights absolutely while also signalling their status as democratic constitutional essentials. Setting the rest of the constitution in the second track establishes the widest possible range of public autonomy, through the exercise of political rights, without allowing that exercise to trample on its own preconditions. Designed in this way, multitrack constitutionalism thus guarantees democracy's duelling commitments to both public and private autonomy.

Although any limitation on political rights harms members of a democracy, multi-track constitutionalism nevertheless ensures that their more fundamental rights remain intact. That is, the multi-track design guarantees all members' basic liberal rights when political rights are opposed to those more fundamental rights. To be sure, repressing a political organization is a very serious affair. Guaranteeing members have the least restricted exercise of their political rights is essential for a legitimate democratic order. However, limiting the exercise of political rights by removing candidates from the ballot does not necessarily compromise that order's legitimacy as such, nor do such limitations deprive members of all opportunities to participate meaningfully.

In fact, constitutions often include many mechanisms that restrict the electoral choices available to voters, which may take voters' first choice off the ballot entirely. For example, the Twenty-Second Amendment of the US Constitution limits the number of Presidential terms to two. Despite the considerable popularity of former Presidents Reagan and Obama at the end of their second terms and the likelihood that they were the preferred choice for many in the next election, no one describes the Twenty-Second Amendment—or the elections of 1988 or 2016—as 'undemocratic'.

Of course, there does seem to be a qualitative difference between the formal restrictions imposed by the Twenty-Second Amendment and substantive restrictions on unconstitutional political goals. To prevent the abuse of substantive restrictions, it is important to have procedural safeguards in place. Issacharoff notes how, in all cases in which a democratic state has formalized the power to restrict the rights of political organizations, the judiciary acts as an independent authority that adjudicates an accusation or charges that a party is an antidemocratic threat.[8]

---

[8] Samuel Issacharoff, *Fragile Democracies: Contested Power in the Era of Constitutional Courts* (Cambridge University Press 2015) 103–04.

160   POLITICAL RIGHTS RESTRICTIONS

Here, Germany again models how militant democracy can work.[9] The government or the public prosecutor initiates a charge against a party and brings evidence of its anticonstitutional activities. The judiciary then steps in as an independent arbiter, acting according to the principle of *nemo judex in causa sua* or 'one should not judge their own case'. It reviews the evidence and evaluates the legitimacy of the government's charge. Both the separation and balance of state powers and the court's role as the guardian of the constitution are vital procedural safeguards on the practice of political rights restrictions. Chapter 7 discusses this in greater depth.

Restricting the political rights of an antidemocratic organization can be distinguished from the complete disenfranchisement and criminalization of members.[10] Of course, removing an antidemocratic party from the political arena does reduce the number of options available to voters. However, as Müller argues, banning a particular party really only deprives voters of *one* public representative of their political preferences and goals.[11] Yes, some members may not have their first choice for elected office. But they will still have opportunities to advance their *legitimate* political interests by choosing among the available parties who are not openly undemocratic and who pursue constitutional goals. Compromising on their political goals is something that every democratic citizen must do to some degree if they hope to have any share in legislative power.[12]

The blow of restricting the political rights of an organization can be further softened by being sensitive to how that organization's aims and form evolve over time. Political rights restrictions can be designed to be reversible, through the same rule of law-based juridical procedures that validated the original restrictions. This grants organizations the opportunity to reform and be rehabilitated into normal democratic politics.

---

[9] See Jan-Werner Müller, 'The Problem of Peer Review in Militant Democracy' in Uladzislau Belavusau and Aleksandra Gliszczyńska-Grabias (eds), *Constitutionalism under Stress* (Oxford University Press 2020) 263; Max Steuer, 'The Role of Judicial Craft in Improving Democracy's Resilience: The Case of Party Bans in Czechia, Hungary and Slovakia' (2022) 18(3) European Constitutional Law Review 445. The Office for the Protection of the Constitution (*Bundesamt für Verfassungsschutz*) plays an additional preliminary role in this process by surveilling and gathering evidence about a potential organizational threat. Besides becoming the basis for a parliamentary referral, the office will also share that evidence with the public, in order to inform it directly of an organization's antidemocratic agenda. See Franziska Brandmann, 'Radical-Right Parties in Militant Democracies: How the Alternative for Germany's Strategic Frontstage Moderation Undermines Militant Measures' (2022) 18(3) European Constitutional Law Review 422–23.

[10] Issacharoff, *Fragile Democracies* (n 8) 98. See the section 'Political, not Criminal'.

[11] Jan-Werner Müller, 'Protecting Popular Self-Government from the People? New Normative Perspectives on Militant Democracy' (2016) 19 Annual Review of Political Science 257–58.

[12] As Kelsen has argued, it is naïve to believe that a party should advance a single ideological interest because the entire function of the party system, and more broadly the legislative branch, is to create compromises by incorporating and blending the views of all members. In so doing, democratic processes are inherently moderating. Hans Kelsen, 'On the Essence and Value of Democracy' in Arthur J Jacobson and Bernhard Schlink (eds), *Weimar: A Jurisprudence of Crisis* (University of California Press 2002) 100–02.

Finally, although restricting a party or candidate by banning it or preventing it from holding office may deprive members of the opportunity to pursue their antidemocratic goals in the public sphere, it does not infringe on members' more fundamental rights, including the rights to hold illiberal beliefs, values, and interests privately.[13] On the contrary, that deprivation guarantees those more fundamental rights—including those of antidemocrats. To put the extreme case bluntly, in a militant democracy, members will still have the right to hold whatever morally abhorrent beliefs they want, such as Nazism or any other form of bigotry. Militant democracy only limits members' ability to *publicly* institute antidemocratic beliefs by constraining parties and candidates' ability to run for public office.

As many recognize, there is a *sociological* need for popular support for the importance of basic liberal rights. Basic liberal rights will never be secure without popular acceptance.[14] But this sociological need is distinct from the normative question of which rights are prior. That sociological foundation can be generated through civic education that integrates individual members into the democratic life and spirit of their political community.

In any case, if we recognize with liberal theory that basic liberal rights are a prior condition for legitimate public order, then it follows that political rights can be legitimately circumscribed to guarantee that precondition. And, because of that lexical hierarchy and the distinction between the types of rights, infringing on political rights does not infringe on basic liberal rights. Liberal normative theory thus does not run aground on the paradox of democracy's self-defence. For that reason, liberal theory provides a more coherent normative foundation for political rights restrictions.

Redefining Detection

Explicit unamendability helps solve a different but related normative challenge in the use of political rights restrictions. In establishing the positive procedural limits of constitutional change, multi-track constitutionalism simultaneously makes legally explicit and signals what constitutional values are constitutive of democracy.[15] The articles that are locked in through unamendability should be the constitutional

---

[13] Of course, private beliefs, values, and interests would continue to be subject to all of the regulations and qualifications to which they are currently subject in liberal democracies. For example, even in the United States, biased or hate crimes can be proscribed legally when they involve violent conduct, rather than (constitutionally protected) expressive conduct. Entrenching basic liberal rights against constitutional amendment procedures and against illiberal political parties does not guarantee that a racist can abuse others with impunity.

[14] I am indebted to Jan-Werner Müller pushing me to address this issue.

[15] Andrew Arato, *The Adventures of the Constituent Power: Beyond Revolutions?* (Cambridge University Press 2017) 336–37.

162 POLITICAL RIGHTS RESTRICTIONS

norms most essential to democracy. This eliminates ambiguity about what goals or actions are inimical to democracy. It establishes what goals are beyond the pale and, if pursued, may expose a party to political rights restrictions.

Kirchheimer discussed how the German Constitutional Court, the body in Germany with final authority to decide on political rights restrictions, relied on the democratic essentials of the *Basic Law* to detect when an antidemocratic organization threatens the constitution and, by extension, becomes a candidate for repression.[16] In determining whether to restrict an organization's political rights, the Court relies on evidence of a relationship between (antidemocratic) political goals and strategic doctrines promoted by that organization, on the one hand, and its members' concrete actions to realize those goals, on the other. It asks questions such as the following: Did an organization's strategic doctrines for pursuing its goals have a demonstrable practical effect? Can the motivation of actors attempting to harm the democratic constitutional order be tied back to that organization? Did that organization adopt or promote strategies that motivated its members to act to undermine the existence of a free democratic state?

Its approach suggests that the criteria for detecting a revolutionary organization should be based on whether affiliates were sufficiently inspired by its goals to seek to realize them—no matter how vague that organization's own advocacy of antidemocratic actions or how embryonic its own strategic plans for revolution may be. Although it may be possible to make an academic case that an antidemocratic organization's goals and strategy were too abstract to possibly aid in any serious revolutionary attempt, Kirchheimer argues that such a distinction has 'no meaning in actual life'.[17] What mattered, he argued, was whether its ideals, however abstract or concrete, motivated its members to act against the constitution. In his view, the relevant criterion for detecting a threat is evidence of a relationship between an organization's antidemocratic political goals and the acts members demonstrably their pursuit.

In addition, Kirchheimer argued that, although an organization may mask its revolutionary intentions, it will become more and more difficult to disown or camouflage unconstitutional aims as that organization grows and becomes more prominent in public affairs.[18] For any political organization to organize at a scale large enough and efficient enough to successfully compete for power in a modern democracy, its goals cannot be mysteries restricted to an elite internal cabal. The need to gather, indoctrinate, and motivate members, not to mention operate a sizeable bureaucratic apparatus, requires transparency about those political goals.

---

[16] Otto Kirchheimer, *Political Justice: The Use of Legal Procedure for Political Ends* (Princeton University Press 1961) 143, 146–47.

[17] ibid 144.

[18] ibid 141–42.

To be sure, an organization may engage in what Brandmann calls 'frontstage moderation,' i.e. when its public face either disavows antidemocratic political goals or claims to be fighting against internal extremist factions.[19] This tactic can open a gap between the public's perception of the organization and the state's allegations. Weakening public support for political rights restrictions can delay or even delegitimize the use of political rights restrictions. However, downplaying extremists' goals and actions eventually cedes them greater influence within the organization.[20] Over time, an organization that moderates or hides its political objectives will lose control over its 'backstage' extremists, who will move to the front of the stage and undermine its moderate self-presentation. 'Frontstage moderation' thus appears to be an unstable long-term practice.

Moreover, 'illiberal democrats' tend to be proud of their illiberal beliefs. Leaders like Orbán, Modi, Trump, Netanyahu, and Bolsonaro flaunt their illiberalism, using it both to rally their base and to hold their governing coalition together. In Germany, despite the very real possibility of the party ban and a history of its practice, the *Alternative für Deutschland* (AfD) now has difficulty hiding its antidemocratic goals. The party's radicalization after 2015 began the debate about whether a militant response should be adopted. In 2019, the Federal Office for the Protection of the Constitution (*Bundesamt für Verfassungsschutz*) found reasonable indications that the AfD was working against the free democratic basic order.[21] Although it tried to mask its political goals for a time, there is little uncertainty today about the AfD's political orientation. Small scale political organizations may be able to fly under the radar and organizations may be able to moderate their 'frontstage' rhetoric enough to mislead the public for a time. But neither practice can be sustained over the long term.

Complementing the above arguments, Kirchheimer also emphasized the responsibility that individual members had for their organization's political goals. He argued that an organization's revolutionary political goals may be imputed to all of its members validly, including to members whose (superficially) isolated actions do not obviously contribute to advancing those political goals practically.[22] Modern complex bureaucratic organizations coordinate individuals' actions purposively through a complex division of labour, which can insulate members from one another and appear to grant them plausible deniability of any involvement in more overt revolutionary actions.

Kirchheimer countered that, even if an individual does not openly advance an organization's broader revolutionary goals, he or she nevertheless chose to be

---

[19] Brandmann 414–15.
[20] ibid 425–26.
[21] ibid 430; Katrin Bennhold, 'Germany Places Far-Right AfD Party Under Surveillance for Extremism' *The New York Times* (3 March 2022) <https://www.nytimes.com/2021/03/03/world/europe/germany-afd-surveillance-extremism.html>.
[22] Kirchheimer (n 16) 147.

164   POLITICAL RIGHTS RESTRICTIONS

a member of that voluntary political organization. Contributing toward the organization on any level renders them morally responsible for its goals, which they must have some awareness of. Recognizing that moral responsibility helps prevent an organization from compartmentalizing a revolutionary wing, in order to deny culpability for its actions. To defend itself, an organization should provide some evidence that a revolutionary faction within it was operating autonomously when that faction adopted unconstitutional goals. Otherwise, the organization as a whole should be a candidate for political rights restrictions.

A liberal theory of militant democracy will not successfully detect every antidemocratic threat.[23] A party may successfully mask its antidemocratic political goals. It may turn to illiberalism only after successfully obtaining power. No measure of militant democracy is fool proof. But the advantage of a liberal normative theory is that it does not rely on a single mechanism to entrench democratic constitutional essentials. Even if an organization successfully evades detection, unamendability presents another barrier to legal revolution. Antidemocratic parties that legally possess state power may be able to 'breach' the constitution by passing laws that derogate constitutional essentials. Still, they will not be able to amend them.

This ensures those democratic constitutional essentials remain in effect, even if a government abuses its powers. If antidemocrats successfully evade detection and obtain state power, unamendability by itself will not be able to prevent all abuses of power. But the continuity of the constitution can provide a foundation for restoring democracy. It can also act as a mechanism for holding antidemocrats legally accountable after the crisis is resolved. Because of its multifaceted approach, a liberal normative theory of militant democracy has greater potential to withstand challenges and preserve democratic governance, even in the face of sophisticated antidemocratic threats.

Reducing Abuses of 'Democracy' and Discretionary Authority

A liberal normative theory of militant democracy mitigates concerns about the misuse of political rights restrictions because it anchors the detection of antidemocratic threats in opposition to specific articles of the constitution. This approach prevents the transformation and expansion of militant democracy into 'militant secularism'—an issue that has dogged normative theorizing about militant democracy so far.

Critics of militant democracy worry that cultural conservatives who hold state power may abuse political rights restrictions. By exploiting ambiguity in the definition of 'democracy' or simply redefining democracy in excessively broad

---

[23] I am indebted to Jan-Werner Müller pushing me to address this issue.

substantive terms, they can disenfranchise religious parties that pose no genuine threat to democracy.[24]

The 1998 decision to ban the Refah party, discussed in chapter 2, is a paradigmatic case of that kind of abuse.[25] Turkish authorities alleged that Refah intended to adopt a constitution based on Shariah law. Arguing that secularism was integral to the *democratic* identity of the Turkish Constitution, those authorities acted to ban Refah. Their actions were later supported by the European Court of Human Rights.

Democratic theorists broadly agree that the Refah party itself posed no serious threat to Turkish democracy. They also agree that the decision to ban Refah harmed, rather than defended, Turkish democracy. The religiosity of a party presents no a priori threat to secular society, let alone democratic institutions.

Cultural conservatives seem to have drawn inspiration from cases such as Refah. Some right-leaning parties have sought to collapse the distinction between democracy and secularism in order to argue that new minority groups threaten democracy because of their religious identity.[26] This dynamic plays out across Europe between cultural conservative parties and Muslim minorities, for example.

In such circumstances, critics of militant democracy worry that a militant democratic constitution, which authorizes the use of political rights restrictions against antidemocratic threats, carries too great a potential for abuse and that Western states will see similar cases to Refah. If they can make the case that a minority group is somehow inherently antisecular, conservatives can try to dissolve parties that represent that minority's interests. In this context, Macklem, Müller, and others reasonably worry about how some European states have justified so-called repressive measures, such as 'burka bans,' by using clothing as a symbol of its wearer's antidemocratic intentions. In France, some argue that the burka and niqab are a 'sectarian manifestation of a rejection of the values of the Republic.'[27]

Paraphrasing Macklem's discussion about the ECHR's conferral of a significantly wider margin of appreciation to states, the broader theoretical problem that Refah illustrates is that the narrow and primarily procedural latitude that states traditionally enjoyed to decide on rights limitations for 'democracy' has swollen. States now defend extremely robust conceptions of democracy, including the repression of

---

[24] See Nancy Rosenblum, 'Banning Parties: Religious and Ethnic Partisanship in Multicultural Democracies' (2007) 1(1) Law & Ethics of Human Rights 17, 31; Patrick Macklem, 'Guarding the Perimeter: Militant Democracy and Religious Freedom in Europe' (2012) 19(4) Constellations, 581.

[25] Rosenblum (n 24) 62–64; Jan-Werner Müller, 'Militant Democracy' in Michel Rosenfeld and András Sajó (eds), *The Oxford Handbook of Comparative Constitutional Law* (Oxford University Press 2012) 1264–65; Macklem (n 24) 579–81.

[26] Today, the French right-wing populist party *Rassemblement National and other conservative French organizations appeal to laïcité to argue that immigrants do not belong in France. See* Anne Sa'adah, 'After the Party: Trump, Le Pen, and the New Normal' (2017) 35(2) French Politics, Culture & Society 43 *Were Rassemblement National to obtain power, it is not inconceivable that it would use a conservative interpretation of laïcité as a basis to dissolve minority religious organizations that it deemed 'political'.*

[27] Quoted from Müller, 'Militant Democracy and Constitutional Identity' (n 5) 422.

religious freedom.[28] A normative theory of militant democracy should be able to explain how it avoids providing a justificatory basis for that kind of pathological expansion of militancy. Militant democracy should not become a tool for promoting illiberalism.

A liberal normative theory of militant democracy offers a solution to those problems. It recognizes basic liberal rights, including religious freedom and non-establishment, as constitutional essentials. Liberalism further recognizes that religious liberty is not just an essential property of democracy but one of the oldest and most important basic liberal rights.

Because liberal theory defines basic liberal rights as lexically prior to the exercise of political rights, the use of political rights restrictions under liberal normative theory requires a different justification than existing normative theories of militant democracy do. For liberal theory, a party becomes a valid candidate for dissolution when its political goals include the abrogation or derogation of basic liberal rights and acts to realize those goals in the public order.[29] This can apply to a religious party or association, such as those seeking to institute a state religion.

Liberal democrats are rightly concerned about abusing the state to impose the 'right' comprehensive doctrine on society (regardless of whether it is religious or atheistic). However, liberal theory addresses that concern by refraining from identifying religious organizations or individuals as potential threats to the public order until they make the leap to pursuing illiberal constitutional goals. This ensures better protection for religious individuals under liberal theory compared to existing normative theories of militant democracy. In fact, the concerns preventing the overexpansion of 'democracy' into secularism may be a reason to insist that basic liberal rights be defined as constitutional essentials and, as such, to entrench them against procedures of legal change. Liberal theory better circumscribes when political rights restrictions can be validly deployed, preventing their undue expansion into illiberal forms, such as the repressions of parties with a religious affiliation.

Political, Not Criminal

The use of political rights restrictions should centre on an organization's opposition to the values and political identity of a constitution, rather than just merely targeting illegal or criminal activities. The Weimar Republic's experience with the 1922 *Gesetz zum Schutze der Republik* (RSG) and its subsequent downfall helps demonstrate this lesson. Under the RSG, restrictions on the political rights of organizations were only triggered by overt criminal acts. Because of the RSG's narrow

---

[28] Macklem (n 24) 587.
[29] See Schupmann (n 7).

focus, antidemocratic organizations quickly adapted their revolutionary methods so that they remained within the bounds of legality or could at least plausibly deny any involvement in individually criminal acts. Weimar had no mechanisms that allowed it to defend itself against legal revolutionary attacks.

The RSG was developed in response to the Scheidermann and Rathenau assassinations. As it investigated them, the Weimar government discovered that right-wing antidemocratic organizations had financed, directed, and institutionally supported the assassins.[30] Parliament drafted the RSG to counter that threat by holding organizations as a whole accountable for members' criminal activities aimed at achieving their political goals. The RSG allowed the state to ban and seize the assets of organizations opposing 'the constitutionally established republican form of the state [*verfassungsmäßig republikanische Staatsform des Reichs*]'.[31] For a brief time, the RSG rather effectively repressed antidemocratic parties and associations. Shortly after it went into effect, 120 right wing political organizations had been banned—including the NSDAP.[32]

However, the RSG was only effective against antidemocratic organizations tied to overt criminal acts—such as political assassinations or ham-fisted beer hall putsches. Among its limitations and problems was that antidemocrats quickly learned to remain within the bounds of the law or maintain plausible deniability of any link to illegal acts.[33] Weimar antidemocrats just shifted their tactics. They realized that, by abusing its value-neutral democratic procedures, Weimar democracy could be a suicide pact. After serving five months in prison for his failed 1923 uprising, Hitler made a claim that epitomized that realization: 'the constitution dictates the method, but not the goal'.

Jasper noted that Weimar's defenders, who focused on putsches and violent revolutions, failed to recognize that the threat now came from an entirely different direction.[34] That focus on criminality, detached from any value-based defence of democracy, left Weimar defenceless against legal revolution. It also allowed radical demagogues to manipulate public opinion against democracy.[35] Complicating matters further, Weimar republicans generally believed that laws like the RSG were

---

[30] Gotthard Jasper, *Der Schutz der Republik: Studien zur staatlichen Sicherung der Demokratie in der Weimarer Republik 1922-1930* (J.C.B. Mohr (Paul Siebeck) 1963) 108–13.

[31] ibid 114–15; See also pp 295–96.

[32] ibid 128ff.

[33] Public prosecutors, the police, and the judiciary in Weimar tended to have a conservative bias, due to the government's Imperial legacy. After Weimar stabilized around 1924 and the antidemocratic right shifted its efforts to legal revolutionary action, the government and courts refocussed their attention on the political left, in particular the communist party and its affiliates. As a result, the RSG was not really used against the right after that time. Moreover, it was abused to repress the left. In particular, federal courts tended to extend the police significant latitude when it came to organizations on the left, such as the KPD and its affiliates. That bias explains, for example, the absurd contrast between the relatively light treatment of Hitler, Ludendorff, and the NSDAP for the Beer Hall Putsch and the harsh sentence of 'high treason' for a communist who recited some revolutionary poems. ibid 127, 181–82.

[34] ibid 285.

[35] ibid 290–91.

168   POLITICAL RIGHTS RESTRICTIONS

inherently undemocratic.[36] When it became time to renew the RSG in 1929, they significantly watered it down, transforming it from a mechanism that could defend the constitution into one that merely defended state representatives.[37]

Article 21 of the *Basic Law* was designed to respond to the limits of the RSG.[38] Besides explicitly recognizing parties (the Weimar *Constitution* did not mention parties), thereby affirming their importance to modern democracy, Article 21 empowered the Federal Constitutional Court to regulate the *substance* of parties' political goals as well as the form of their organization. That shift in focus, from criminality to substantive political opposition, models the constitutionality of political rights restrictions in other militant democracies today.

The German *Basic Law*'s response to Weimar's shortcomings also highlights the importance of recognizing *political* opposition to the constitution and distinguishing it from criminality. By focusing on the underlying political goals of an organization, rather than its criminality, threats to democracy can be addressed with political sanctions rather than criminal sanctions. The value of doing so can be demonstrated by contrasting political rights restrictions in German public law with the United States.

In essence, the United States collapses political opposition to the constitution into criminal opposition. The lack of a distinction stems from the legal precedents set during the McCarthy Era, in particular *Dennis v. United States*, and the US Constitution's lack of clarity on the constitutionality of political parties and their limitations. In *Dennis*, the US Supreme Court elided the distinction between prohibited political agitation and criminal agitation. In its ruling, it decided that if speech posed a danger that merits any kind of sanction, it must be because that speech falls within the scope of criminal law.[39] That ruling became the basis for the broader conclusion that political actions can be regulated only because they are criminal. In the United States, political rights restrictions are intertwined with the standards of criminal prosecution. Political threats in the United States are, consequently, addressed solely through criminal law, employing sanctions such as imprisonment.[40]

Political rights restrictions need not be tied to criminality, however. Rather as it distinguishes political opposition to the constitution from criminality, German public law distinguishes political sanctions from criminal sanctions.[41] It uses political rights restrictions primarily as a special type of regulation limiting the ability of parties to enter the political arena, focusing on the constitutionality of organization's goals. Political right restrictions for unconstitutional goals (or an

---

[36] ibid 277.
[37] ibid 284.
[38] ibid 144.
[39] Issacharoff, *Fragile Democracies* (n 8) 21–22.
[40] ibid 23.
[41] ibid 106, 113.

unconstitutional organizational form) fall outside of criminal law in Germany. That distinction minimizes the broader impact that political sanctions have on an organization or its members. Although the organization itself may be restricted or dissolved, its members can continue to pursue their private interests freely. In addition, they retain the use of their individual political rights and can still choose among parties that do not have unconstitutional goals.

Of course, restricting an organization's political rights may lead to confrontations with disgruntled members and supporters. If a confrontation turns violent or criminal, it may require a police response. For that reason, Issacharoff argues, a corollary of political rights restrictions must be a willingness to enforce that decision with police authority.[42] That reluctance is another reason to distinguish antidemocratic behaviour from criminal behaviour and to keep criminal sanctions in reserve.

In sum, by focusing on the political goals of an organization, democracies can deploy political rights restrictions in more nuanced and effective manner. That distinction also helps soften the impact that political rights restrictions might have on members while still helping to guarantee the integrity of the democratic process. Recognizing a distinction between the political and criminality better grounds political rights restrictions normatively.

The Timing of Restrictions

Tethering sanctions for unconstitutional goals to explicitly unamendable articles and identifying them as *political*, rather than criminal, allows reconsideration of when political rights restrictions can be legitimately deployed. Liberal theory shifts the assessment of the validity of political rights restrictions from the imminence of an existential threat, as normative theories of militant democracy require today, to whether a relationship exists between the goals, doctrines, and demonstrable acts of that organization. Liberal theory supports restricting an organization's political rights sooner.

Acting Sooner

Pech and Scheppele argue that recent experiences with antidemocrats in Hungary and Poland demonstrate the importance of prompt action against antidemocrats.[43] Democrats may prefer to wait, in the hope that cooler heads will prevail or

---

[42] ibid 114.
[43] Laurent Pech and Kim Lane Scheppele, 'Illiberalism Within: Rule of Law Backsliding in the EU' (2017) 19 Cambridge Yearbook of European Legal Studies 7.

170   POLITICAL RIGHTS RESTRICTIONS

democratic institutions will hold the line. But they do not always succeed. Antidemocrats exploit hesitation to consolidate their possession of state power and continue rolling back democratic essentials. Studies show that, once the process of backsliding begins, it is unlikely to be reversed.[44] Speed and timing matter in defending democracy.

In his analysis of early German Constitutional Court debates about Article 21, Kirchheimer justifies the early deployment of political rights restrictions. The section above discussed Kirchheimer's argument that the criterion for detecting whether an organization potentially warranted restrictions should be the relationship between its antidemocratic political goals and actions rather than the immediacy of the threat it poses.[45] He argued that demonstrating that causal link was more important for assessing the nature of the threat than whether the organization was 'efficient' in the pursuit of its goals.[46] He posed the question of why should a democracy tolerate an antidemocratic organization inimically opposed to its existence if the main reason that organization does not act to advance its goals is because it presently lacks the means? What mattered was whether members pursued antidemocratic goals at all, not whether they were actually any good at realizing them.

Empirical research shows how organizations that express antidemocratic goals tend to act on them in power. Lührmann, Medzihorsky, and Lindberg demonstrate that antidemocratic speech acts are a solid indication of what a party will do in office.[47] So there is good reason to take an organization at its word. This supports the idea that democrats should focus on an organization's expressed political goals rather than on the imminence of an existential threat. Kirchheimer's argument supports re-evaluating the relationship between an organization's goals and its members' actions more broadly. An individual act that only seems to pose a remote threat to democracy may actually be a part of a broader strategy executed by that organization.[48] Members might not even fully understand the implications of their actions. Kirchheimer argues that it is valid to impute the organization's broader antidemocratic agenda to members' superficially marginal acts.

Conversely, an organization may not expressly direct some members' subversive acts, claiming that they acted on their own initiative. However, insofar as that organization promotes the pursuit of antidemocratic political goals, then it may be liable for members' acts even if it did expressly condone them. Antidemocratic

---

[44] Tore Vincents Olsen, 'Citizens' Actions against Non-Liberal-Democratic Parties' (2022) 18(3) European Constitutional Law Review 467; see also Anna Lührmann, Juraj Medzihorsky, and Staffan I Lindberg, 'Walking the Talk: How to Identify Anti-Pluralist Parties' (2021) V-Dem Working Paper 116.

[45] Kirchheimer (n 16) 143, 146–47.

[46] ibid 137.

[47] Lührmann, Medzihorsky, and Lindberg.

[48] Kirchheimer (n 16) seems to have had in mind something like an insurrectionary cell or fifth column acting to realize a narrowly defined objective, the broader implications of which may not have been explained to the members of that cell.

organizations tend to be functioning bureaucracies, meaning individual members' acts can be imputed to the broader structure and vice versa. If a larger organization can be connected to individual antidemocratic actions, it should be judged as a potential threat even if those individual acts pose only a remote threat.

'Tactical' Considerations

There are other 'tactical' considerations that support taking action sooner against organizations substantively opposed to democracy, even if the threat appears 'marginal' or 'remote.' Reasons to take action sooner mainly stem from the consequences of treating antidemocrats as if they were a normal party and allowing them access to state institutions.

If antidemocrats are allowed to take office legally, they will obtain a significant temporal advantage to initiate legal processes. With that temporal advantage, they can enact legislation and policy that will take time to reverse through normal institutional checks and balances. It can make reversing antidemocrats' abuses of power extremely difficult. In effect, it allows them to create sweeping legislative *fait accomplis* that advance their antidemocratic goals, which may remain on the books and in force while institutional counterpowers challenge them.[49]

Electoral victory grants representatives of an antidemocratic party all the benefits and immunities of being an elected official, which in some states may include immunity from prosecution for certain actions—for example, against being charged with criminal incitement for a public speech.[50] Antidemocrats can weaponize those immunities to either avoid or delay being prosecuted for crimes committed prior to holding their current office, as Berlusconi and Netanyahu have been accused of, or even to commit new crimes, as Trump has been accused of.

Many states provide financial support and other material resources to legally constituted parties.[51] Treating an antidemocratic party as if it were a normal democratic party grants it access to those resources, which it can then use to finance its operations and consolidate and grow its base. In addition, if an antidemocratic party is the legal or political wing of an underground organization, it may be able to divert state-provided financial resources to feed illicit activities.

Even if an antidemocratic party is too weak to realize its political goals directly, participation in parliament—including the right to vote on legislation, set policy, participate in committees, direct agencies, and so on—creates opportunities to interfere with essential government processes. Antidemocrats may obstruct crucial votes or introduce poison pills into bills. If a coalition depends on a handful of

---

[49] Carl Schmitt, 'The Legal World Revolution' (1987) 72 Telos 74.
[50] Kirchheimer (n 16) 151–54.
[51] ibid 151.

172   POLITICAL RIGHTS RESTRICTIONS

antidemocrats to hold onto power, that small group may wield outsize control over policy or be able to demand appointment to key ministerial positions. For example, both elements of Israel's controversial judicial reforms and controversial appointments, such the appointment of Itamar Ben-Gvir as Minister of Security, are due to Netanyahu's dependence on extremists to maintain his governing coalition.

Electoral victory also grants representatives the opportunity to speak in parliament and the public sphere as a normal government representatives. An antidemocratic party can exploit that opportunity to test, tinker with, and hone its antidemocratic messaging, which allows it to broadcast its goals more effectively and expand its base.[52] Simply by presenting and repeating an antidemocratic party platform, the media inadvertently engages in 'amplifiganda': simultaneously propagating antidemocratic values through uncritical repetition and amplifying them by making them seem to be everywhere.[53] It may 'expand the Overton window' on what the public considers reasonable and acceptable, normalizing extremist views.[54] In short, treating a fringe antidemocratic party as if it were just another party gives it a veneer of legitimacy and helps to normalize its antidemocratic goals.

In addition, Kirchheimer notes that a tactical consideration for acting earlier is that, by confronting a marginal organization, the steps needed to decide on repression—the investigation and collection of evidence, trial and prosecution, deliberation on decision, and (if the court authorizes it) execution of the repression—can all be conducted with normal legal procedures, by normal police, and at a normal pace.[55] Conversely, if a party is allowed to metastasize and become an imminent and existential threat, the response will require extraordinary procedures in the context of an emergency or constitutional crisis, which denies the time needed to put together a fair and measured trial. In addition, executing repressive action against a marginal organization is practically easier and is unlikely to have destabilizing social repercussions.

Resolving the Practical Paradox of Restrictions

Deploying political rights restrictions sooner may address a practical objection to militant democracy: that militant measures cannot save a democracy in genuine distress. Some point to the case of Weimar Germany, arguing that by 1932 banning the NSDAP would not have saved Weimar Republic because the Nazis already had

---

[52] Samuel Issacharoff, 'Fragile Democracies' (2007) 120(6) Harvard Law Review, 1410.
[53] Renée DiResta, 'It's Not Misinformation. It's Amplified Propaganda', 9 October 2021, The Atlantic <https://www.theatlantic.com/ideas/archive/2021/10/disinformation-propaganda-amplification-amp liganda/620334/>.
[54] Issacharoff, 'Fragile Democracies' (n 52) 1426–29.
[55] Kirchheimer (n 16) 151–54.

a plurality with 37 per cent of the vote.[56] That objection highlights another fundamental paradox of militant democracy: if a regime could *successfully* deploy political rights restrictions, then antidemocrats may be too weak to seriously threaten democracy anyway and militancy is unnecessary.[57] Conversely, once a party becomes strong enough to pose a real threat, legal action will be likely to be ineffective and may just drive antidemocrats toward violent revolution.

As discussed earlier, existing normative theories are not confident about the democratic legitimacy of political rights restrictions. For that reason, they tend to circumscribe their use temporally and treat them as a last resort. Using the example above, they could not justify banning the Nazi party before 1932. They could only consider the ban when it was at the height of its power and posed the gravest threat. Delays not only allow antidemocrats to better threaten democracy, it can also weaken democratic parties' ability to coordinate an effective response.[58]

By shifting the criteria for detecting antidemocrats and justifying measures sooner, as a liberal theory of militant democracy allows, it becomes possible to circumvent that practical paradox. For instance, instead of asking whether banning the Nazi party in 1932 might have saved Weimar democracy, we should instead ask whether the 1923 ban of the Nazi party should have remained in place. Although the threat from antidemocratic organizations may have seemed remote during Weimar's stable middle years, many antidemocratic organizations never abandoned their political goals. Some even enlarged them. Moreover, organizations like the NSDAP had already demonstrated their willingness to act to realize them.

Antidemocratic organizations tend not to emerge already strong enough to take power. They slowly build their base, testing and refining their message. The NSDAP, for example, progressively expanded its base through rigorous campaigning after the ban was lifted in 1925. Its share of the vote grew, from 3 per cent in 1928, to 18 per cent in 1930, finally reaching 37 per cent in 1932. Although a complex series of factors led to the NSDAP's assumption of power, early intervention in 1925 might have prevented them from becoming an unstoppable political force.

Liberal theory provides a normative basis for intervening early against antidemocrats. An earlier intervention can have positive normative and practical effects. It stops antidemocratic organizations before they can damage democracy from within government, before they have the chance to persuade or propagandize the electorate or normalize their political goals, before they can obtain public funding and other forms of material support to grow themselves. It also provides democracies with the chance to respond to them with normal institutions of government. It may prevent them from becoming so powerful that no measures can

---

[56] Müller, 'Militant Democracy' 1263–64; Melissa Schwartzberg, *Democracy and Legal Change* (Cambridge University Press 2007) 157–58.
[57] Müller, 'Militant Democracy and Constitutional Identity' 419.
[58] Giovanni Capoccia, *Defending Democracy: Reactions to Extremism in Interwar Europe* (Johns Hopkins University Press 2005) 16–19.

174   POLITICAL RIGHTS RESTRICTIONS

stop them from assuming power. Timing matters when it comes to defending democracy. While the infringement of political rights must always be taken seriously and should only be enacted after careful consideration, liberal normative theory defends the legitimacy of early intervention against threats to democratic constitutional essentials.

Alternative Forms of Political Rights Restrictions

Political rights restrictions of organizations can take forms besides an outright party ban. An antidemocratic organization's political rights can be limited without dissolving it outright. Issacharoff and Capoccia have both described some of the less severe forms that rights restrictions of organizations take, which balance a sanction that defends democracy against the crucial role that organizations play in political life.

Issacharoff discusses how a democracy can defend itself first by restricting an organization's ability to act antidemocratically, for example by restricting a party's access to the electoral arena rather than dissolving it immediately.[59] Where that distinction is made, Israel and India for example, parties may be subjected initially to a less rigorous standard and instead just disqualified from running for office for a single election cycle—holding a more serious sanction like dissolution in reserve in case the party continues its antidemocratic activities.[60] Because the party persists, it has the opportunity to consider attempting to reform itself in order to participate in the next election.

Capoccia explores other less extreme forms of political rights restrictions, citing examples from Belgium, Czechoslovakia, and Finland during the interwar period.[61] Rather than seeking to eliminate a party outright, a democracy can defend itself by restricting messages in the public sphere intended to delegitimize democracy.[62] These can include measures to curb the spread of misinformation and false news, laws against the glorification of political crimes, and restrictions on foreign political propaganda to prevent symbolic support for antidemocrats. In addition, a democracy can adopt measures to preserve the public order.[63] Those measures could include laws against the militarization of political parties—for example, by restricting the use of uniforms, militaristic iconography, weapons, and militias—as well as limits on the freedom of assembly and public demonstrations.

---

[59] Issacharoff, *Fragile Democracies* (n 8) 83, 94, 113.
[60] For more detail, see Issacharoff's analysis. Issacharoff, 'Fragile Democracies' (n 52) 1447–51 and Issacharoff, *Fragile Democracies* (n 8) 83–93.
[61] Capoccia 203ff.
[62] ibid 59–60.
[63] ibid 57.

The decision on what kinds of political rights restrictions should be imposed on an antidemocratic organization can be assigned to the guardian of the constitution, since which measures are appropriate will require an *ad hoc* decision particular to the occasion. In any case, less severe restrictions on organizations will be justifiable along the same lines as a party ban under a liberal normative theory. In addition to restrictions on organizations akin to a party ban, it is important to assess the legitimacy of two other forms of rights restrictions that bolster democracy's defence against legal revolution: individual militant democracy and limits on 'negative majorities'.

Individual Militant Democracy

While organizations are the primary focus of militant democracy, some constitutions allow for restricting the rights of *individuals* who threaten democracy. Article 18 of the German *Basic Law* allows for the restriction of certain individual rights if they are abused to combat the free democratic basic order: freedom of the press (paragraph (1) of Article 5), the freedom of teaching (paragraph (3) of Article 5), the freedom of assembly (Article 8), the freedom of association (Article 9), the privacy of correspondence, posts and telecommunications (Article 10), the rights of property (Article 14) and the right of asylum.[64] Müller defines this type of restriction as 'individual militant democracy'. However, since these restrictions have never successfully been applied against individuals in Germany (the Constitutional Court has denied a total of four applications since 1949), Müller argues that they really only have *symbolic* value today, as a warning to would-be antidemocrats.[65]

Still, measures like those of Article 18 reflect the recognition that an exceptionally resourceful individual could pose a threat to democracy *as an individual*. Individual militant democracy provides a legal avenue to prevent individuals with a demonstrable pattern of anti-constitutional behaviour from acquiring state power legally. A prime example of an exceptionally resourceful individual is an oligarch. Arlen defines an 'oligarch' as an individual with discretionary access to significant concentrated wealth.[66] Oligarchs wield tremendous socio-economic power. That power grants them significant and disproportionate influence over public policy and even the ability to control or capture democratic institutions, such as political parties and the media.

Sheldon Adelson's influence over the Republican Party in the United States and Rupert Murdoch's domination of the media are both prominent examples of

---

[64] See Müller, 'Individual Militant Democracy' 19; Jan-Werner Müller, *Democracy Rules* (Farrar, Straus and Giroux 2021) 161.

[65] Müller, 'Militant Democracy' (n 25) 1258.

[66] Gordon Arlen, 'Oligarchy as a Problem for Normative Theory: A Geography', Unpublished Manuscript. Presented at APSA 2022, 4–5.

176   POLITICAL RIGHTS RESTRICTIONS

oligarchic control over essential intermediary powers of democracy.[67] However, a resourceful individual may not be an oligarch. It could instead be someone capable enough with digital technology to effectively bypass or short circuit the traditional media, for example. Such an individual could use their direct conduit to society to promulgate an antidemocratic agenda, build a political base, secure their candidacy, and even fund their campaign. They could pose as grave a threat to democracy as traditional oligarchs.

The underlying issue is that certain individuals can exploit a mix of socioeconomic power and media influence to threaten democracy. Müller cites both Silvio Berlusconi and Donald Trump as figures who combine both individual resourcefulness and an antidemocratic position, making them potential candidates for restrictions of their individual political rights. It has been argued that Trump violated his oath to defend the US Constitution by refusing to accept the outcome of the 2020 election and attempting to overthrow its results. In the process, disqualifying himself from running for future public office under Section 3 of the Fourteenth Amendment.[68] This debate matters because it provides evidence that many on both the political left and right are actively considering individual militant democracy to be a legitimate aspect of democracy's self-defence.[69]

Still, infringing on an *individual's* political rights presents a unique moral challenge compared to targeting an organization. Banning a party is one thing; targeting an individual, even temporarily, is another.[70] It undermines their equal standing as a democratic citizen. For this reason, Müller argues convincingly that rights restrictions should affect an individual's autonomy as little as possible.[71] In addition, based on a liberal normative theory of militant democracy, only political rights may be restricted. Basic liberal rights must remain untouched. Article 18 of the *Basic Law*, for example, is far too broad in its scope of restrictions. Given both Müller's concerns and the limits of liberal theory, individual militant democracy should be limited to restricting an individual's eligibility for public office. If used, individual militant democracy should be limited to denying antidemocratic

---

[67] On intermediary powers, see Müller, *Democracy Rules* (n 64) 90–139.

[68] The Fourteenth Amendment disqualifies former office holders in the United States who 'shall have engaged in insurrection or rebellion against the same' from holding office again.

[69] William Baude and Michael Stokes Paulsen, 'The Sweep and Force of Section Three' (2023) 172 University of Pennsylvania Law Review; J Michael Luttig and Laurence H Tribe, 'The Constitution Prohibits Trump from Ever Being President Again' (19 August 2023), The Atlantic <https://www.theatlantic.com/ideas/archive/2023/08/donald-trump-constitutionally-prohibited-presidency/675048/>.

[70] Müller, 'Individual Militant Democracy' (n 5) 14.

[71] ibid 16–17. Müller also argues that rights restrictions should be temporary, recognizing that antidemocratic actors may reform and reform should rewarded; see ibid 26; Müller, *Democracy Rules* (n 64) 170. Müller is sceptical, however, that it would be possible to come up with a rational test for reform. The reason is simple: when an actor's political rights are restricted, then the abuse of those political rights will cease the moment rights restrictions are imposed. There will not be any evidence of reform until rights are restored. This is not to say that reform is impossible. But there may not be any rational basis to determine whether it has happened.

individuals the legal possession of state power, balancing a minimal impact on their political rights while preserving their basic liberal rights.

It is important to differentiate between the types of threats that warrant the rights restrictions of individual militant democracy and those that do not. Müller argues that oligarchs could also be subject to political rights restrictions if they misuse public institutions to advance their private interests, such as by seeking to profit financially from their public power.[72] While such behaviour is morally wrong, as long as it does not directly threaten legal revolution of democracy, it would not qualify for the political rights restrictions under individual militant democracy. It seems more appropriate to treat such acts as financial crimes, assuming they violate existing laws. Measures to entrench democracy must be careful to avoid overreach.

While organizations more often threaten democracy, some legitimate provision for particularly resourceful antidemocratic individuals can also be made. Under exceptional circumstances, liberal normative theory justifies limiting an individual's rights to pursue public office. By doing so, it allows democracies to strike a balance between preserving constitutional integrity and respecting individual autonomy.

Limiting Negative Government

Even if an antidemocratic party is too weak to enact its political goals directly through legislation, it may abuse the opportunity to participate in government in order to govern 'negatively', that is, to engage in deliberate obstructionism and prevent law and policy from being enacted. Negative governance typically takes the form of a 'negative majority', which occurs when the political goals and worldviews of a majority of legislators are radically opposed and they cannot advance any positive legislative agenda. They are united, however, by their substantive opposition to democracy.

Although a negative majority does not govern in any meaningful sense, they will use their legal possession of state power to deliberately obstruct the everyday operations of government. They may attempt to systematically bring down the government. Negative governance burdens state institutions and the public with the costs of a decapitated and idle government. They use obstructionism as a legal cudgel against parties genuinely committed to democracy. Their broader goal may be to discredit democracy and nudge the electorate toward more radical alternatives.

Schmitt first theorized the problem of a negative majority in his analysis of antidemocrats' deliberate obstruction of the Weimar government in its final

---

[72] Müller, 'Individual Militant Democracy' (n 24); Müller, *Democracy Rules* (n 64) 169–70.

178 POLITICAL RIGHTS RESTRICTIONS

days.[73] Once they held a majority of seats in the *Reichstag*, the NSDAP and the KPD cooperated at times in an extremely unlikely alliance. The most disruptive mechanism they used was Article 54 of the Weimar Constitution, which authorized the *Reichstag* to withdraw its confidence from the Chancellor and other members of the governing cabinet and compel them to resign.[74] Although it was designed to be the first step in putting together a new government, Schmitt recognized early on that antidemocrats could instead use it as the only step.[75] And that concern was borne out in practice. Despite their diametrically opposed political goals, the NSDAP and KPD cooperated to use the vote of no confidence of Article 54 to decapitate the Weimar government, accelerate the social and economic collapse of German society, and discredit liberal democracy in the process.[76] Each party hoped that, if they succeeded in bringing Weimar down, it would emerge on top and be able to dictate Germany's political future.

Although their political goals obviously differ radically from those of early twentieth century antidemocrats, some members of the US Republican party use similar tactics of negative government today. When they do not possess a majority that would allow them to legislate, they sometimes use legal procedures to try to bring down the government. The most egregious example is their repeated refusal to pass appropriations bills. Republicans threated to use this tactic in 2011 and successfully used it in 2013 in the hopes of forcing the government to repeal the Affordable Care Act. That was part of their broader goal of 'ungoverning', as Muirhead and Rosenblum aptly describe it, by dismantling the administration.[77]

It is important to distinguish negative government from isolated negative legislative acts, such as vetoing a specific bill, voting against a law, or invalidating unconstitutional legislation. Negative government is distinctive because it shuts the government down. And that is often its goal. It holds the state hostage and may even deliberately undermine the capacity of the state to function at all. By undermining and discrediting democracy, it indirectly abets legal revolution.

Schmitt argued that negative governance could be prevented legally by requiring that a vote of no confidence be accompanied by a complementary positive or constructive act by that majority to appoint a successor.[78] Parliament could still withdraw its confidence from a government but it first needed to have a viable alternative in hand. True, a majority may find its political rights constrained

---

[73] Schmitt, *Constitutional Theory* (n 7) 364; Carl Schmitt, *Der Hüter der Verfassung* (Dunker & Humblot 1931) 115–21; Carl Schmitt, 'Reichstagsauflösungen' in Carl Schmitt (ed), *Verfassungsrechtliche Aufsätze aus den Jahren 1924-1954 Materialien zu einer Verfassungslehre* (Duncker & Humblot 1958).
[74] Schmitt, *Der Hüter der Verfassung* (n 73) 87–91.
[75] Schmitt, 'Reichstagsauflösungen' (n 73).
[76] Schmitt, *Constitutional Theory* (n 7) 364; Lutz Berthold, *Carl Schmitt und der Staatsnotstandsplan am Ende der Weimarer Republik* (Duncker & Humblot 1999) 59.
[77] Russell Muirhead and Nancy L Rosenblum, 'The Path from Conspiracy to Ungoverning' (2022) 89(3) Social Research 517.
[78] See Schupmann (n 7).

because it was stuck with a government or Chancellor that it did not choose. But no 'people' would choose to abdicate all responsibility for governing. Schmitt's argument against negative majorities became the normative foundation for the current 'constructive' vote of no confidence of Article 67 of the German *Basic Law*.[79]

Article 67 provides one model for how democratic legislators should approach potential negative government. Unfortunately, the laws that create opportunities for negative government need to be identified and dealt with on an ad hoc basis. Not every case can be dealt with by a constructive vote of no confidence. Some pathways should never be installed, such as appropriations bills. In any case, the use of legal procedures for negative governance and 'ungoverning' can be more than merely an annoyance. Antidemocrats use it to bring down democratic states. Those opportunities are particularly dangerous when a democracy faces a crisis. In such circumstances, it may make sense to authorize the Constitutional Court in its role as guardian of the constitution, the subject of chapter 7, to invalidate acts that would result in negative governance.

---

[79] Lutz Berthold, 'Das Konstruktive Misstrauensvotum und seine Ursprünge in der Weimarer Staatsrechtslehre' (1997) 36 Der Staat 81.

7

The Guardian of the Constitution

Introduction

A guardian of the constitution is the final authority on constitutionality and defends the constitution against its violation by other constituted powers. The guardian of the constitution serves as the third principal mechanism of militant democracy. Kelsen, arguably its first modern theorist, conceived the guardian as a limit on the abuse of state power.[1] Based on the experience of the democratic suicide of states such as Weimar Germany, post war constitutional jurists designed the constitutional court to be that final authority on constitutionality. It has the power to check the abuse of legislative power and halt the legal revolution of democracy. Invested with the powers of guardianship, constitutional courts have played an essential role in the post war rise of militant democracy.[2]

Among post war militant democracies, Germany's Federal Constitutional Court serves as the paradigmatic example of a constitutional guardian. Article 93 of the 1949 German *Basic Law* establishes the Federal Constitutional Court as an independent institutional check on the active governing powers of the legislature and the executive. Because it has the last word on constitutionality, commentators argue that the Constitutional Court is the epicentre of German democracy.[3]

This chapter theorizes and defends the legitimacy of installing an independent guardian of the constitution as the *pro tempore* ultimate authority over the constitutionality of both the law and political organizations. A guardian may invalidate legislation by striking it down as unconstitutional, ideally defending the unamendable core of the constitution against its direct legal revolution through abrogation or derogation. It decides on whether a political organization's goals threaten constitutional essentials and, accordingly, on whether its political rights should be restricted. The other two principal mechanisms of militant democracy

---

[1] Hans Kelsen, 'The Nature and Development of Constitutional Adjudication' in Lars Vinx (ed), *The Guardian of the Constitution: Hans Kelsen and Carl Schmitt on the Limits of Constitutional Law* (Cambridge University Press 2015) 71–73; Lars Vinx, *Hans Kelsen's Pure Theory of Law: Legality and Legitimacy* (Oxford University Press 2007) 155.

[2] Markus Thiel, 'Germany' in Markus Thiel (ed), *The 'Militant Democracy' Principle in Modern Democracies* (Ashgate 2009) 121, 137; Jan-Werner Müller, *Contesting Democracy: Political Ideas in Twentieth-Century Europe* (Yale University Press 2011) 147.

[3] Donald P Kommers and Russell A Miller, *The Constitutional Jurisprudence of the Federal Republic of Germany* (Duke University Press 2012) 38.

Democracy despite Itself. Benjamin A. Schupmann, Oxford University Press. © Benjamin A. Schupmann 2024.
DOI: 10.1093/9780191975950.003.0008

depend on an institution like the guardian for their execution. A liberal normative theory of militant democracy establishes the legitimacy of guardianship.

The Ideal of the Guardian

A constitution remains valid only as long as its contents are both observed and complied with. Even the highest constituted powers must be subject to its regulations and limitations.[4] However, law is neither self-enforcing nor self-implementing, including those laws designed to entrench and defend the constitution.[5] In addition, the meaning of law is also open to interpretation, making it subject to disagreement. For those reasons, there should be some final authority on constitutionality to resolve disputes.[6] If the constitution does not recognize some institution or body with final authority to decide and interpret the constitution, then the stage is set for a constitutional crisis, as various constituted powers may compete over that right.[7]

Political and legal theorists define that final authority over constitutionality as 'the guardian' of the constitution. For instance, Kelsen conceptualized the guardian as an institution that 'protects the constitution against violation' by those authorized to 'execute' it.[8] It ensures that the legal actions of constituted powers correspond to the higher law of the constitution as they create, apply, and execute the law.[9] Böckenförde and Freeman similarly conceive of the guardian as the institutional location of the final authority to decide on constitutionality and locate it in the constitutional court.[10] In addition, Freeman differentiates it from the traditional branches of government, namely the legislature, the executive, and the judiciary, emphasizing that it is both a delegated and institutional power. What distinguishes the guardian's function, as a constituted power, is how it guarantees the constitution against incursions by other constituted powers. Its power is typically

---

[4] Samuel Issacharoff, *Democracy Unmoored: Populism and the Corruption of Popular Sovereignty* (Oxford Univesity Press 2023) 133.

[5] Andrew Arato, *The Adventures of the Constituent Power: Beyond Revolutions?* (Cambridge University Press 2017) 368.

[6] Andrew Arato and Jean L Cohen, *Populism and Civil Society: The Challenge to Constitutional Democracy* (Oxford University Press 2022) 196, 199.

[7] See Vinx (n 1) 151.

[8] Kelsen, 'Who Ought to be the Guardian of the Constitution?' in Lars Vinx (ed), *The Guardian of the Constitution: Hans Kelsen and Carl Schmitt on the Limits of Constitutional Law* (Cambridge University Press 2015) 174.

[9] Kelsen, 'The Nature and Development of Constitutional Adjudication' (n 1) 25–30; cf Stanley L Paulson, 'Hans Kelsen and Carl Schmitt: Growing Discord, Culminating in the "Guardian" Controversy of 1931' in Jens Meierhenrich and Oliver Simons (eds), *The Oxford Handbook of Carl Schmitt* (Oxford University Press 2014) 524.

[10] Ernst-Wolfgang Böckenförde, 'Constitutional Jurisdiction: Structure, Organization, and Legitimation' in Mirjam Künkler and Tine Stein (eds), *Constitutional and Political Theory: Selected Writings*, vol I (Oxford University Press 2016) 187–88; Samuel Freeman, 'Constitutional Democracy and the Legitimacy of Judicial Review' (1990) 9 Law and Philosophy 357.

negative: it defends the constitution by negating actions that threaten the integrity of the constitution.

In a constitutional democracy, the guardian guarantees constitutional essentials against pathologies arising from democratic legal procedures. For example, Kumm argues that a guardian enforces a constitution's democratic political identity by preventing changes to essentials, in particular basic liberal rights.[11] Similarly, Issacharoff argues that the guardian's role is to prevent active branches of government from abusing majoritarian legal procedures.[12] Ferrara elaborates on this idea, arguing that a constitutional court ensures 'the people's' democratic identity, including its interest in political autonomy and basic human rights.[13] In doing so, it represents 'the people' as a continuous transgenerational entity. Zurn adds that a guardian protects the institutions and rights that raise democracy above mere majoritarianism, which allow members to understand themselves also as authors of the law.[14] In summary, a guardian defends democratic constitutional essentials, in particular as a countermajoritarian limit on democratic legal procedures.

In a militant democracy, the scope of the guardian's power includes final authority on the execution of the other two principal measure of militant democracy: unamendability and political rights restrictions. The decision to deploy either is, in the end, a judgement of constitutionality, either of a law or an association. To be effective, the guardian must have the power to nullify statutes when they violate democratic principles, even if they are otherwise valid procedurally. In other words, the guardian must have the power of judicial or constitutional review. In addition, the guardian must have the power to impose political rights restrictions, by judging that an association holds fundamentally unconstitutional goals and will attempt to realize them. Because of its critical role in interpreting and executing those principal mechanisms of militant democracy, the guardian is the third pillar of militant democracy.

Although it has final authority over constitutionality, Kelsen argued that the guardian's power is distinctive because it is both *passive* and *negative*—in contrast with the active and creative power of the legislature and executive.[15] The meaning of the guardian's passive and negative power is unpacked in greater detail below. Briefly, Kelsen distinguishes between the active and open-ended power of the

[11] Mattias Kumm, 'Who's Afraid of the Total Constitution? Constitutional Rights as Principles and the Constitutionalization of Private Law' (2006) 7(4) German Law Journal 343–45, 362.

[12] Samuel Issacharoff, *Fragile Democracies: Contested Power in the Era of Constitutional Courts* (Cambridge University Press 2015) 9, 12, 275.

[13] Alessandro Ferrara, *Sovereignty Across Generations: Constituent Power and Political Liberalism* (Oxford University Press 2023) 208, 215–16.

[14] Christopher F Zurn, *Deliberative Democracy and the Institutions of Judicial Review* (Cambridge University Press 2009) 254, 264.

[15] Kelsen, 'The Nature and Development of Constitutional Adjudication' (n 1) 47; Vinx 153–54. Kirchheimer makes a similar argument about the role of the judiciary in democracy's self-defence. See Otto Kirchheimer, 'Politics and Justice' in Frederic S Burin and Kurt L Shell (eds), *Politics, Law, and Social Change: Selected Essays of Otto Kirchhimer* (Columbia University Press 1969) 409.

legislature and the reactive and limited power of the judiciary. The power that the legislative exerts through democratic legal procedures is in principle open-ended and unlimited in its range. These procedures allow the legislature to transform its will—whatever that will may be—into law, as long as it adheres to the procedures in effect for enacting valid law.

On the other hand, the power that the guardian exerts is passive because it is interpretative and reactive, focused on responding to the actions of other branches. In addition, its power is negative because it only strikes down legislation that contradicts the higher law of the constitution. It does not create new statutes, even if its interpretations can change the way that existing statutes are understood. In this sense, the guardian is another institutionalization of the power of surveillance that Rosanvallon theorized as a 'counter-power' essential for ensuring the fundamental interests of 'the people'.[16]

For the guardian's role in entrenching the constitution to be practicable, that final authority over constitutionality must reside in a body that both stands above all other constituted powers and exists independently of them. It must exclusively possess the authority to regulate the constitutionality of the active law-creating powers.[17] If another body can override the guardian's decision on constitutionality—if the powers of the guardian sit under the reservation of another body's powers—then it is a guardian in name only. (The next section takes up objections to this authority, including concerns about juristocracy.)

Kelsen specifically warned against investing guardianship in an active power because doing so would undermine any meaningful checks and balances on the exercise of state power.[18] He believed this to be particularly true in the case of granting the legislative guardianship, arguing that it would be politically naïve to concentrate so much power in that one branch.[19] Zurn also emphasizes the importance of the guardian's independence, both from active branches of government and the electorate, in order to guard against its capture and the subversion of its protective role.[20]

Since 1945, the role of the guardian has typically been allocated to the highest court in the judicial branch, resulting in an expanded influence of courts over other branches of government.[21] Because guardianship is associated with constitutional courts, the following section focuses on the role of the court and its power of judicial review.

---

[16] Pierre Rosanvallon, *Counter-Democracy* (Cambridge University Press 2008).
[17] Böckenförde (n 10) 198.
[18] Kelsen, 'The Nature and Development of Constitutional Adjudication' (n 1) 44–47; Kelsen, 'Who Ought to be the Guardian of the Constitution?' (n 8) 211.
[19] Kelsen, 'Who Ought to be the Guardian of the Constitution?' (n 8) 175.
[20] Zurn (n 14) 269–70, 276–77.
[21] Böckenförde (n 10) 186; Yaniv Roznai, 'Introduction: Constitutional Courts in a 100-Years Perspective and a Proposal for a Hybrid Model of Judicial Review' (2020) 14(4) ICL Journal 355, 356ff; Martin Loughlin, *Against Constitutionalism* (Harvard University Press 2022) 128.

184 THE GUARDIAN OF THE CONSTITUTION

As with the other principal mechanisms of militant democracy, the model for guardianship by the constitutional court originated in Germany. Issacharoff describes how that model emerged out of a recognition of the 'categorical failure' of the executive and legislative branches to prevent the downfall of Weimar democracy through legal revolution.[22] In addition, the Weimar Constitution did not provide for a constitutional court. After the war, jurists concluded that a constitutional court could have played an important role in preventing Weimar's legal revolution. To avoid a repeat of the failures of Weimar, they designed the German Federal Constitutional Court to guarantee German democracy against both governmental overreach and popular extremism. That model has proven effective. Armed with the powers of guardianship, the Federal Constitutional Court oversaw the successful transition to stable democracy, including the reform of state institutions that had been thoroughly compromised by Nazism.[23]

The allocation of guardianship to the constitutional court can be understood by examining similarities with the judiciary.[24] Both are designed to be independent counterbalances to active governmental power. Members of both institutions should enjoy security for the length of their terms, in order to maintain their functional autonomy. Neither the guardian nor the judiciary may initiate its legal actions. Instead, their powers are only activated when a case is brought by an external party, such as a plaintiff. Neither actively legislates, for example by producing statutes. And both make their arguments empirically verifiable by publicising the reasoning that led them to their conclusions, as an extended practical syllogism. By giving reasons for their conclusions, they help create a science of law.[25] According to Rawls, they model public reasoning by resolving disputes based on established principles.[26]

Although the guardian shares some functions with the judiciary, the two also differ in some important ways. Unlike ordinary courts, the guardian possesses a 'conserving power', which allows it to regulate other constituted powers and judge whether their actions align with the constitution.[27] Because it is authorized to interpret the fundamental identity as inscribed in the constitution and state, the guardian is political in a way that ordinary courts are not. Its decisions shape and even normalize decision-making procedures by determining the possibilities and limits to how ordinary, constituted powers may acquire, possess, and exercise state power.[28] In addition, the guardian differs because its interpretation of the constitution is subject only to its own authority. Only the guardian may revise and correct

---

[22] Issacharoff, *Fragile Democracies* (n 12) 143–44.
[23] ibid 138.
[24] Kelsen, 'The Nature and Development of Constitutional Adjudication' (n 1) 47; Böckenförde (n 10) 190–91.
[25] Zurn (n 14) 278.
[26] John Rawls, *Political Liberalism* (Columbia University Press 1996) 231–40.
[27] Freeman (n 10) 359.
[28] Böckenförde (n 10) 191.

its past decisions, whereas ordinary courts' decisions may be overturned by higher authorities.[29]

Finally, there is no higher statutory law to resolve or illuminate ambiguities within the constitution or the guardian's interpretation of it. In this sense, the guardian's decisions are immanent because they emerge out of the constitution rather than by appeal to higher legal norms. As Böckenförde argued, the only real 'yardstick' for interpretation is the text of the constitution itself because there is no broadly recognized and reliable method of constitutional interpretation available, which compounds the difficulty of constitutional interpretation.[30] The guardian's decisions will have an element of 'creative determination', as he put it, which sets them apart from ordinary courts' rulings. Therefore, despite some important overlaps with the judiciary, a guardian is really a distinctive branch that does not fit neatly into the traditional separation of powers.[31]

Although the judiciary is the default institution that acts as the guardian, this is partly due to historical accident.[32] Because of that distinctive nature, some constitutional theorists discuss alternative forms that it might take. Freeman discusses Rousseau's tribunate as a potential alternative form of the guardian.[33] Several others have instead used the model of the ephorate.[34] Kelsen noted that constitutional guardianship first emerged in the *nomothétai* (νομοθέται), an ancient Athenian institution that had to approve any proposed changes to Athens' laws.[35]

Modern guardianship, Loughlin has suggested, took shape in Benjamin Constant's writings.[36] Constant's view was that the head of state, the monarch at that time, should be invested with a neutral, preservative power (a *pouvoir neutre*) that was distinct from and superior to the traditional three branches.[37] Its function was to preserve order and liberty by mediating among the other constituted powers. Issacharoff discusses the ombudsman as an alternative guardian.[38] The ombudsman monitors, investigates, and challenges institutional misconduct and

---

[29] ibid 193.

[30] ibid 192.

[31] Zurn (n 14) 264.

[32] Kelsen, 'The Nature and Development of Constitutional Adjudication' (n 1) 47.

[33] Freeman (n 10) 332 (note 6).

[34] Johannes Althusius, *Politica: Politics Methodically Set Forth and Illustrated with Sacred and Profane Examples* (Liberty Fund, Inc. 1995) 99–108; Carl Schmitt, 'The Value of the State and the Significance of the Individual' in Lars Vinx and Samuel Garrett Zeitlin (eds), *Carl Schmitt's Early Legal-Theoretical Writings* (Cambridge University Press 2021) 215–16; Carl J Friedrich, *Constitutional Reason of State: The Survival of the Constitutional Order* (Brown University Press 1957) 68, 72–73.

[35] Kelsen, 'Who Ought to be the Guardian of the Constitution?' (n 8) 194.

[36] Loughlin (n 21) 124–25.

[37] Benjamin Constant, *Political Writings* (Cambridge University Press 2007) 184ff. Schmitt's uses Constant's theory of the monarch's *pouvoir neuter* to develop his own argument that the President of the Reich should be the guardian. See Carl Schmitt, 'The Guardian of the Constitution' in Lars Vinx (ed), *The Guardian of the Constitution: Hans Kelsen and Carl Schmitt on the Limits of Constitutional Law* (Cambridge University Press 2015) 151–57; Benjamin A Schupmann, *Carl Schmitt's State and Constitutional Theory: A Critical Analysis* (Oxford University Press 2017) 153ff.

[38] Issacharoff, *Democracy Unmoored* (n 4) 204.

maladministration when it results in violations of basic human rights.[39] The ombudsman could complement the work of a constitutional court by creating additional channels for redressing rights violations, either through its own oversight powers or by bringing them before the constitutional court.

While the role of the guardian in contemporary times is often conflated with the judiciary and the role of guardian is typically played by the constitutional court, it is important to distinguish the unique conserving power of the guardian from the powers of ordinary courts.[40] This distinction remains important, even if today's constitutional democracies typically merge the powers of the guardianship with the judiciary. The guardian could instead assume a different institutional form.

Against the Guardian

At first glance, installing a constitutional court as the guardian of the constitution might appear to be at odds with democratic principles. Critics argue that a democracy in which there is a guardian risks becoming a juristocracy, which is to say a government of judges. The problem is that constitutional courts tend to be comprised of a small group of unelected elites. They are no less fallible than the members of any other constituted power. The court seems to have a weaker claim to democratic legitimacy than any elected branch. The normative problem of guardianship, as theorized above, becomes especially apparent when a court overturns laws enacted by democratically elected representatives, thus apparently undercutting a fundamental commitment of democracy: that 'the people' have control over the laws it is subject to.

The core of the problem has to do with the very qualities that make the judiciary distinct from other branches. Loughlin, for example, questions whether it makes sense for a democracy to grant final authority on constitutionality to a branch that is neither representative of the electorate nor clearly accountable to it, given the more expansive role that some courts have assumed as a result of that authority.[41]

---

[39] The Polish ombudsman, whose title is actually just 'Commissioner for Human Rights', plays an important role still in preventing further democratic backsliding of Polish democracy. It acts as an institutional constraint on the PiS regime's regressive actions. See Wojciech Sadurski, *Poland's Constitutional Breakdown* (Oxford University Press 2019) 184, 268.

[40] Freeman (n 10) 359. As Vile has argued, the pure doctrine of the separation of power, which implies that government functions could be neatly divided among distinctive branches of government is misleading. It has 'never been achieved, nor indeed is it desirable': MJC Vile, *Constitutionlism and the Separation of Powers* (Liberty Fund, Inc. 1998) 349. For that reason, it is not surprising nor should it be cause for concern that one function, guardianship, is held by a body invested with different functions and powers. It only becomes a problem if those powers somehow compromise the underlying ideal of the separation of powers, to moderate and limit governmental power in order to protect its individual constituent members' freedom from arbitrary rule. ibid 347.

[41] Loughlin (n 21) 129.

This seems especially concerning when courts interpret an unwritten, 'invisible' constitution.

There is something to this concern. Unlike the legislative and executive branches, whose members are at least held accountable to the electorate through routine elections and irregular mechanisms such as recalls, the judiciary tends not to be directly accountable to the electorate at all.[42] Judges are not typically elected. Rather, they are appointed by elected representatives after ascending through a highly professionalized ladder. In addition, the composition of a constitutional court may not reflect the demographic makeup of broader society. The judiciary tends to epitomize the very elitism that alienates the electorate and against which populists rail in their rhetoric. Finally, judges frequently serve lengthy if not lifetime tenures.

All in all, the electorate seems to have little direct recourse against judicial power—which starkly contrasts with its significantly greater influence over other branches of government. While these issues affect the judiciary as a whole, they are all the more acute when it comes to the constitutional court because it deals with existential issues.

A principal argument for adopting judicial review is that it can check the tyranny of the majority, or at least of their elected representatives in the legislative. However, this argument loses traction in light of the fact that the judges are politically motivated human beings and not mere 'mouthpieces of the law' as Montesquieu once described them.[43] Critics, including Levinson, Schwartzberg, and Loughlin, worry that the judiciary can easily cross from legal interpretation into a kind of legislative power, even if it differs from the law-creating powers of other branches.[44] To reiterate an argument from the section above, Böckenförde also argues that a constitutional court interprets the constitution without the guidance of any recognized canon of interpretative methods, suggesting that there is an insurmountable element of arbitrariness to whatever the court decides.[45] Combined with the problems that, first, interpretation is immanent and arises out of the constitution's own content because there is no higher law and that, second, a constitution also tends to contain the least concrete law, including broad principles. The court's interpretation thus becomes an essential aspect of the constitution itself. For those reasons,

---

[42] Hirschl, cynically, explains that the move to constitutionalize rights and to safeguard them is not for the sake of justice. Instead, both are reducible to an elite minority's power grab (contrary to justice). Ran Hirschl, *Towards Juristocracy: The Origins and Consequences of the New Constitutionalism* (Harvard University Press 2004) 11–12, 212–14. Hirschl unfortunately does not engage with the normative arguments for basic human rights or judicial review, not even the seminal arguments of a thinker like Rawls, in making that claim.

[43] Baron de Montesquieu, *The Spirit of the Laws* (Hafner Publishing Company 1959) 159.

[44] Sanford Levinson, 'How Many Times Has the United States Constitution Been Amended? (A) 26; (B) 26; (C) 27; (D) >27: Accounting for Constitution Change' in Sanford Levinson (ed), *Responding to Imperfection* (Princeton University Press 1995); Melissa Schwartzberg, *Democracy and Legal Change* (Cambridge University Press 2007) 106–07; Loughlin (n 21) 140, 201.

[45] Böckenförde (n 10) 194.

188 THE GUARDIAN OF THE CONSTITUTION

Loughlin argues, what appears as merely an interpretative role may actually be a means to 'master' the constitution.[46]

Loughlin argues further that, because of that power, there is a risk of courts politicizing and using their interpretative power to advance their own narrow values and interests.[47] The court's merely negative power allows it to enter into a kind of dialogue with the legislative and executive branches over policy and legislation. Doerfler and Moyn argue that concern goes beyond mere theoretical speculation.[48] They demonstrate empirically that the US Supreme Court behaves in a partisan fashion no less than the legislative and executive branches. When combined with the judiciary's unrepresentative nature, judicial review could inadvertently invest sovereign power in a small elite beyond democratic government, validating the concerns of populists, radical democrats, and civic republicans alike.

In light of these concerns, Waldron insists that the 'masses' do not uniquely threaten democracy with the spectre of tyrannical rule.[49] Every branch of government is potentially tyrannical. Critics like Waldron are not naïve about the pathologies of democratic legal procedures. They recognize that democratic legal procedures can be, and are, tyrannical because they can be manipulated to advance a faction's narrow interests or to consolidate a faction's control over state power. However, they remind us, this is a pathology of the possession of power in itself, one that the judiciary is no less susceptible to. For that reason, the case for judicial review cannot rest on the enlightenment or neutrality of the judiciary or the need to defend against the tyranny of the majority and counter the pathologies of mass democracy. It needs to demonstrate how investing the judiciary with final authority over constitutionality produces qualitatively better governance than mere majoritarianism.

Another criticism of judicial review targets the appeal to the maxim, *nemo judex in causa sua*, a principle that undergirds the ideal of a separation and balance of powers. *Nemo judex in causa sua* translates as 'one should not judge their own case'. In this case, appeal to that principle means that the legislative branch should not have the authority to judge the constitutionality of its own legislation. That would be self-defeating. As Kelsen argued, it would make guardianship an institution in name only, for the legislature obviously already believes in the constitutionality of its legislation—otherwise it would not have just passed that law. If guardianship is to have any meaning, some other power ought to oversee and have the power to check the legislative process.

---

[46] Loughlin (n 21) 140.

[47] ibid 148.

[48] Ryan D Doerfler and Samuel Moyn, 'The Ghost of John Hart Ely' (2022) 75(3) Vanderbilt Law Review 769.

[49] Jeremy Waldron, 'Judicial Review and the Conditions of Democracy' (1998) 6(4) The Journal of Political Philosophy 351–52.

Critics counter that invoking the principle of *nemo judex* does not actually make a case for judicial review. On the one hand, when it comes to deciding on constitutional essentials in a democracy, no member is disinterested in the outcome because all are equally subject to the law. So the judiciary is hardly a body without bias or prejudice. Its members are no less invested in the outcome of a fundamental decision on constitutionality than any other member. If we were to apply *nemo judex* equally to every constituted power, then the judiciary would also seem to be disqualified. Following that reasoning, critics suggest, adopting judicial review to rein in the potential tyranny of the legislative branch actually just exchanges one interested and potentially tyrannical branch for another.[50] Any branch has the potential to be a tyrant. Seen thought this critical lens, the principle of *nemo judex in causa sua* does not appear to be a solid foundation for guardianship.

On the other hand, critics argue that the democratic *bona fides* of the legislature justify its final authority in interpreting constitutionality. Waldron argues that the principle of *quod omnes tangit ab omnibus decidentur*, 'what concerns all should be decided by all', should instead guide the assignment of final authority constitutionality—not *nemo judex*.[51] Because decisions on constitutionality impact all members, everyone has a formally equal stake in them. Every member that can contribute to a decision about a disputed constitutional issue should have a formally equal chance to participate in making that decision—at least within the limits of what is practically possible.[52]

The most appropriate way to resolve disputes about constitutionality is through democratic legal procedures, mediated by the legislative branch. To adopt a different procedure would betray a fundamental commitment of democracy.[53] Overall, given the potential for bias within the judiciary, the superior democratic *bona fides* of the legislative, and the fact that issues of constitutionality affect all members, critics reject *nemo judex* as a justification for judicial supremacy on constitutionality.

Waldron acknowledges that his criticism of judicial review rests on four presuppositions, presuppositions that other critics seem to also adopt at least implicitly.[54] The first two—that democratic institutions are in reasonably good working order and that judicial institutions are based on nonrepresentative principles— are not immediately relevant for this discussion. However, his third and fourth

---

[50] Richard Bellamy, *Political Constitutionalism: A Republican Defence of the Constitutionality of Democracy* (Cambridge University Press 2007) 79; Jeremy Waldron, *Law and Disagreement* (Oxford University Press 1999) 247.

[51] Waldron, 'Judicial Review and the Conditions of Democracy' (n 49) 350; Waldron argues in *Law and Disagreement* that 'the people whose rights are in question have the right to participate on equal terms in that decision'. Waldron, *Law and Disagreement* (n 50) 244.

[52] Waldron, *Law and Disagreement* (n 50) 252ff, 300–01; Bellamy (n 50) 4ff.

[53] Bellamy (n 50) 40.

[54] Jeremy Waldron, 'The Core of the Case against Judicial Review' (2006) 115(6) The Yale Law Journal 1346, 1359–68.

190   THE GUARDIAN OF THE CONSTITUTION

presuppositions are critical. The third assumes that society is generally committed to the idea of individual and minority rights, based on a worldwide consensus about human rights, and that illiberalism is an outlier.[55] The fourth presupposition acknowledges that, although disagreements about rights will inevitably occur, members will work to settle their disagreements 'reasonably and in good faith' because of their shared fundamental commitment to the legitimacy of individual and minority rights.[56]

When these latter presuppositions hold, Waldron argues, the role of the judiciary can be reduced to upholding and concretizing members' common belief in the value of human rights and other liberal constitutional fundamentals.[57] In this way, Waldron aligns with Rawls and other liberals in recognizing that equal political rights and democratic procedures alone do not constitute a democracy. Their disagreement is not about whether basic liberal rights are preconditions for democratic legal procedures. It is about who should have the final authority to interpret and define basic liberal rights, with Waldron arguing for the supremacy of legislative authority.

If those presuppositions fail, Waldron admits, then so does his criticism of judicial review.[58] Unfortunately, he does not discuss his rationale for drawing that conclusion. But his argument might run as follows: if a critical mass of members is unreasonable and they systematically use democratic legal procedures in bad faith, then leaving democratic legal procedures and formally equal political rights unchecked institutionally will not produce legitimate and binding outcomes. Instead, unchecked democratic legal procedures will reproduce and aggravate existing fissures within society. In that case, democratic legal procedures will add a false veneer of legitimacy to what is actually just an exercise of power. Under such conditions, however, decisions lack legitimacy. They may allow for the 'unreasonable' to triumph and cannibalize democracy.

Waldron cautions, though, that a critical mass of unreasonability and the bad faith usage of democratic legal procedures does not make a case for judicial review either. He argues that if a majority or supermajority of the electorate is no longer committed to democracy, as he defines it, then 'a practice of judicial review cannot do anything for the rights of the minority'.[59] On the one hand, he thinks that the judiciary cannot effectively guard against an antidemocratic majority. On the other hand, Waldron suggests, if the electorate and legislature are substantively undemocratic, then the judiciary is likely to be as well.[60] This last argument is structurally

---

[55] ibid 1364–65.
[56] ibid 1367–68.
[57] ibid 1366.
[58] ibid 1403.
[59] ibid 1404. Vinx also makes this argument in his analysis of Kelsen's jurisprudence. Lars Vinx, 'Introduction' in Lars Vinx (ed), *The Guardian of the Constitution: Hans Kelsen and Carl Schmitt on the Limits of Constitutional Law* (Cambridge University Press 2015) 21.
[60] Waldron, 'The Core of the Case against Judicial Review' (n 54) 1405.

similar to the practical paradox of militant democracy Müller developed, discussed in chapter 6: if a democracy depends on a cabal of elite judges to survive, then it is already too far gone to be saved.

In Defence of the Guardian

Although critics raise valid concerns about a tension between democratic legitimacy and the constitutional guardianship of judicial review, guardianship can still be an essential feature of democratic constitutionalism. The core of this argument lies in the notion that the will and identity of 'the people' should be represented in various ways that extend beyond the will of a majority or supermajority of the current electorate. The will of the electorate, channelled through elected representatives and democratic legal procedures, is only one imperfect method for representing 'the people'—just like the guardian or any other representation.

Recognizing the imperfect nature of representation creates the space to re-evaluate the purpose of the *nemo judex* principle in democracy: if there can be no perfect representative of 'the people', then no single representative of 'the people' should have the unchecked or unlimited authority to decide on the validity of its representation of the political will and identity of 'the people'. Although the guardian is an imperfect representative of 'the people', its method of representation can serve as a check on the legislative's imperfect method of representing 'the people'. The guardian is effective as a check because it represents 'the people' in a radically different way: it does not delegate or represent the will of the present electorate, but instead represents the political identity of 'the people' as expressed through its fundamental laws. Designing it to be a passive and negative power realizes that particular representative ideal, in contrast to the legislative's active and positive power.

Critics' concerns about the guardian's unaccountability to the electorate can be mitigated through institutional design, which can limit its ability to assume constituent power. Given the very real and sometimes pressing need to guarantee democracy against legal revolution, a guardian is not only an institution compatible with democracy, it is essential to militant democracy.

The Electorate and Imperfect Representation

Democratic legal procedures, which channel the will of the electorate, often do represent the political identity of 'the people' and uphold fundamental democratic values. However, they are only one means of representing 'the people'. Moreover, they are limited in their ability to do so. To trust any single representative body with an unchecked, derived constituent power, as Waldron argues democrats

192 THE GUARDIAN OF THE CONSTITUTION

should, seems to be a high stakes gamble on the inherent reasonability of whoever actually holds that power.[61] As phenomena like populism and 'illiberal democracy' demonstrate, that gamble is not a sure thing.

Earlier chapters discussed *conceptual* limitations to the electorate's ability to represent 'the people'. Theorists such as Rawls and Freeman argue that 'the people' is an ideal of democratic politics, which cannot be located in any material body. It would be a category error to collapse the distinction between 'the people', as a sovereign constituting power, and the electorate, as those subjects who presently happen to have the right to vote—and treat the latter as if it were identical to the former. As other chapters discuss, 'the people' is a juridical fiction. It is a sovereign that cannot exercise its sovereignty. Moreover, democratic theory shows that, although each 'people' may have its own authentic identity, there are widely agreed upon features that must be a part of a public order for it to be democratic. Those features can be determined, at least at the level of the constitution. As chapter 3 argued, Rawls offered one of the most compelling ways to do so, that satisfies the requirements of modern constitutionalism. He generated them by following how practical reason plays out in a hypothetical procedure.[62] In any case, the point is that there is no necessary relationship between the will of the electorate, expressed through majoritarian procedures and positive legislation, and *reasonable* democratic constitutional essentials.

Complementing that conceptual limitation, Ferrara highlights a second *temporal* limitation on the electorate's ability to represent 'the people'. In *Sovereignty across Generations*, Ferrara criticizes the 'serial' representation of 'the people', which is the idea that first 'the people' can be represented by temporally divided segments, each segment made up of the present electorate, and second that each independent segment should hold *pro tempore* constitutional authority, which justifies its right to exercise 'the people's' derived constituent power unchecked.[63] The core of Ferrara's concern is that designing a democracy according to this conception allows a present generation to neglect the interests of other generations of 'the people', past and future. Most importantly, it allows a present generation to neglect 'the people's' fundamental interest in democracy. Every generation of 'the people' has a right to democracy and democratic representation.

Moreover, the boundaries defining who counts as a member of 'the people' are continually contested. Few would argue today that the 1860 US electorate represented 'the people'. The democratic ideal obviously existed then, but exclusions stemming from racism, slavery, and gender bias created a vast distance between 'the people' and the electorate. Designing a constitution according to a conception

---

[61] Ferrara (n 13) 68–69.
[62] John Rawls, 'Kantian Constructivism in Moral Theory' in Samuel Freeman (ed), *Collected Papers* (Harvard University Press 1999); Sharon Street, 'What is Constructivism in Ethics and Metaethics?' (2010) 5(5) Philosophy Compass.
[63] Ferrara (n 13) 211.

of 'serial sovereignty' risks that present electorate will privilege their short-term and immediate interests over and against those of the democratic 'people'.[64] It leaves them room to undermine the future democratic political identity of 'the people', as evidenced by the many examples of antidemocrats pursuit of legal revolutionary goals.

Ferrara argues that constitutions should instead be designed according to a 'sequential' conception of 'the people'.[65] Sequential sovereignty conceives of the present electorate as one legitimate but imperfect method of representing 'the people' among others. And it accordingly denies that the present electorate can unilaterally embody 'the people', particularly when it comes to making decisions that impact future generations. Because every generation of 'the people' deserves equal consideration on fundamental questions, Ferrara suggests constitutions adopt a norm he calls 'vertical reciprocity'.[66] That norm requires that the electorate abide by 'constitutionally defined terms of cooperation that all generations of the same people as free and equal can presumably accept'. Because of its imperfections, the electorate's representation of 'the people' should be counterbalanced by constituted powers that represent 'the people' using different methods.

Democratic 'realists', like Achen and Bartels, identify some of the most important limitations of the capacity of the electorate to represent the democratic identity of 'the people' in practice. They show that the average member of the electorate is often disinterested in and uninformed about political issues.[67] Such voters are neither very good at thinking about politics nor, distracted by quotidian demands, are they very interested in doing so. They tend to choose a party based on their group identity and uncritically mirror its political goals.[68] This tendency allows both political and socio-economic elites to manipulate them in order to advance their own interests.[69] Elites may also exploit group identity and partisan interests to help consolidate their power, at the expense of democratic ideals.[70] Achen and Bartels conclude that these dynamics undercut the prevailing 'folk' theory of democracy that most citizens are reasonable and will advance and maintain democratic values in good faith.[71]

The imperfections in the electorate's representation of 'the people' become most egregious when it seeks to revolutionize democracy legally, betraying 'the people's' democratic political identity. Those kinds of acts cast doubt on the a priori

---

[64] ibid 274–75.
[65] ibid 7.
[66] ibid 12–13.
[67] Christopher H Achen and Larry M Bartels, *Democracy for Realists: Why Elections Do Not Produce Responsive Government* (Princeton University Press 2016) 14–18.
[68] ibid 299.
[69] Larry M Bartels, *Unequal Democracy: The Political Economy of the New Gilded Age* (Princeton University Press 2017).
[70] Milan W Svolik, 'Polarization versus Democracy' (2019) 30(3) Journal of Democracy 20.
[71] Achen and Bartels (n 67) 301.

194   THE GUARDIAN OF THE CONSTITUTION

reasonableness and good faith of the electorate. These are two qualities that theorists like Waldron consider essential presuppositions for investing the electorate with unchecked constitutional authority, a point I will return to in a moment. While there can be reasonable disagreements about constitutional essentials, the electorate cannot always be relied on to demonstrate democratic integrity. For example, just as the present electorate sometimes prioritizes short-term economic interests over long-term environmental sustainability, so too can it prioritize immediate political gains and narrow factional interests over democratic constitutional essentials. This kind of behaviour underscores the risks of relying on one imperfect representative to bear the democratic interests and identity of 'the people' faithfully and over time.

In summary, due to their ideational and temporal limits, both the electorate and the branches of government that are directly accountable to it, such as the legislature, are imperfect representatives of the political will and identity of 'the people'. Those limitations have existential implications: an imperfect representative of 'the people' can turn against it, misusing or abusing its legal powers to compromise or even cannibalize 'the people's' basic commitment to democracy. The imperfections of the electorate thus highlight the need to counterbalance it with other methods and safeguards.

Tyranny and *Nemo Judex in Causa Sua*

In his criticism of judicial review, Waldron correctly observes that the problem of tyranny is not unique to majority rule: any powerholder, from a majority of the electorate to a constitutional court, has the potential to become tyrannical.[72] That potential for tyranny occurs when 'the people's' constituent power is vested unchecked in any imperfect representative.

However, Waldron's conclusion, that majoritarian democratic legal procedures should go unchecked because they are essentially the lesser evil of two evils, does not follow. He seems to present a false dilemma. Constitutional designers face a choice between two potential tyrants, one of whom must ultimately possess the unchecked constituent power of 'the people'. Given that dilemma, it should be vested in the will of the electorate, mediated through elected representatives, because that would include every member of the electorate equally in decision-making, at least in principle.

Considering that any constituted power has the potential for tyranny and that none can perfectly represent 'the people', it becomes apparent that relying on a system of institutional checks and balances to minimize any constituted power's

---

[72] Waldron, 'Judicial Review and the Conditions of Democracy' (n 49) 350–51.

ability to unilaterally assume and exercise derived constituent power is the more reasonable approach.[73] It mitigates the flaws of any single branch's representation of 'the people'.

Recognizing the imperfection of representation demands the re-evaluation of the objection to *nemo judex in causa sua*, as well as a reconsideration of whether *quod omnes tangit ab omnibus decidentur* actually stands opposed to it. As discussed above, critics like Waldron challenge the *nemo judex* principle by arguing that no member and no body can be unbiased with regard to decisions on democratic constitutional essentials; every member is affected by the outcome of a decision on constitutionality. Due to this perceived partiality, critics argue that *nemo judex* essentially justifies the transfer of final authority from the entire electorate to an elite minority, thereby undermining democracy's core commitment to equal freedom. In other words, it illegitimately shifts the locus of sovereign power. For that reason, Waldron introduced the counter-principle *quod omnes tangit ab omnibus decidentur*: 'whatever touches all, should be decided by all'.

The appeal to *quod omnes tangit ab omnibus decidentur* indeed captures the democratic ideal that 'the people' in its entirety has the right to decide on any and all questions, especially questions of constitutionality. However, the collective will of the present electorate, channelled and organized through democratic legal procedures, is just another imperfect representation of the will and political identity of 'the people'. It can misrepresent or even betray the political identity of 'the people'.

In light of representatives' imperfect representations of 'the people'. *nemo judex in causa sua* appears to complement *quod omnes tangit ab omnibus decidentur*, rather than oppose it. That is, because of the limits of any constituted power to represent 'the people', not everyone impacted by constitutional decisions will be able to participate in making them. It is not possible to realize *quod omnes tangit ab omnibus decidentur* in practice.

Given this practical limitation, *nemo judex* serves as a corrective. It justifies denying any constituted power the right to represent 'the people' unilaterally.[74] Critics are wrong to present *nemo judex* as empowering an omniscient and omnipotent judge to decide constitutional questions from some Archimedean point, *sine ira ac studio*. Rather, it addresses pragmatic concerns about limiting abuses of state power and about limiting tyranny, while still maintaining effective governance. Shklar famously argued that courts are the forum in which members confront the organized power of the state.[75] Whether courts offer individuals a defence against the abuse of state power, or instead merely reproduce it, depends on whether courts are designed to be independent. Only as independent powers

---

[73] Cristina Lafont, *Democracy without Shortcuts: A Participatory Conception of Deliberative Democracy* (Oxford University Press 2020) 235.

[74] Ferrara (n 13) 7.

[75] Judith N Shklar, 'The Liberalism of Fear' in Stanley Hoffmann (ed), *Political Thought and Political Thinkers* (University of Chicago Press 1998) 18.

196   THE GUARDIAN OF THE CONSTITUTION

can they effectively check the powers of active branches like the legislative and executive.

Ferrara argues that, given the limits of representation, no constituted power should be able to judge *for itself* the quality of its representation of 'the people'—especially when it comes to democratic constitutional essentials.[76] This holds especially for those that exercise the active and creative power of legislation. Neither should any constituted power have the unbridled authority to simply assert its will as if it were that of 'the people' and, on that basis, exercise 'the people's' constituent power. In the context of democratic constitutionality, the *nemo judex* principle is thus intended to serve as a check on the tyrannical exercise of state power. It holds that a distinct and independent body should safeguard the constitution by having final interpretative authority over representations of 'the people' that would otherwise be unchecked. This is the idea of a guardian.

Constitutional guardianship works to better guarantee the constitution in part because there are different legitimate modes of representing 'the people'. Those differences can be harnessed to address the limits and flaws of any single mode. The guardian's principal guarantee of constitutionality, judicial review, is designed to represent the political identity of 'the people' *holistically*, by making it responsible for upholding the integrity of 'the people's' constitutional project as expressed by the written constitution.[77] This helps mitigate problems such as internal legal pressures to short-circuit checks on the immediate will of the electorate.[78] Creating a system of checks and balances among different modes of representing 'the people' increases the likelihood that its underlying identity will be sustained over time. In this regard, democracy is more firmly founded when its constitution invests an independent guardian with the authority to oversee how the electorate, and its elected representatives, represents 'the people'.

The Guardian as a Different Imperfect Representative

Although installing a guardian can prevent the imperfections of elected branches from undermining democracy, the guardian's representation of 'the people' is itself imperfect—as any representation must be. Moreover, no matter how well-designed and well-instituted it may be, it cannot guarantee an ideal democratic outcome. Could not the guardian abuse its final authority to interpret constitutionality to assume a derived constituent power and thereby legally degrade democratic constitutional essentials? Does this not just create an infinite regression, raising once more the question *quis custodiet ipsos custodes*—who guards the guardians?

---

[76] Ferrara (n 13) 221, 276.
[77] Lafont (n 73) 226; Ferrara (n 13) 204–07.
[78] Issacharoff, *Democracy Unmoored* (n 4) 130–31; Ferrara (n 13) 215–16.

The guardian can be designed to mitigate concerns about its potential to assume a derived constituent power and itself threaten democracy. As Kelsen originally theorized it, the guardian's powers of oversight can and should be designed both to be *passive*, by requiring that some other body initiate its assessment of the constitutionality of a law or organization, and to be *negative*, by limiting its power to negating the actions of other branches of government. Designing it to be passive and negative counterbalances the guardian's final authority over constitutionality.

The limits of the *passive power* of the guardian stands in contrast with the active power of the legislative and executive.[79] An active power can exercise its power as it wills. For example, the legislative branch can initiate the legislative process on its own. How it uses that process tends to be open-ended because the content of legislation is up to the will of the legislator. In contrast, a passive power cannot exercise its powers independently. For example, the review of legislation is initiated by an external body and is restricted to only those issues that have been brought before it.

Lafont articulates this idea of passivity in her analysis of the democratic legitimacy of judicial review. She argues that both advocates and critics of judicial review tend to misframe the institution as an unelected elite body that imposes its will on 'the people' unaccountably from above, breaking down the democratic commitment to equality in the process. She argues that this misframing entirely obscures the role that citizens play in the process of constitutional review.[80] In reality, the review of legislation's constitutionality is initiated from below, when affected or concerned members of the electorate bring cases before a constitutional court.

Ferrara expands on this point, arguing that because every member has a formally equal right to initiate a review in response to unconstitutional legislation, guardianship actually upholds the basic democratic ideal of equality.[81] That equal chance to initiate review is strongest when any member can do so through an *actio popularis* petition.[82] The need for an external body to initiate its process of review underscores how guardianship is not actually an unaccountable power but one that responds to real fractures and oppositions within the electorate.

In light of the heterogeneity within the electorate, Lafont argues that guardianship can indeed pose a countermajoritarian difficulty—just not the one that critics believe it does. The opposition is not necessarily between an unelected elite and 'the people'. It can be between a politically marginal minority and a majority, or

---

[79] Kelsen, 'Who Ought to be the Guardian of the Constitution?' (n 8) 179.
[80] Lafont (n 73) 225.
[81] Ferrara (n 13) 223.
[82] Kelsen, 'The Nature and Development of Constitutional Adjudication' (n 1) 64–65. In order to degrade the Hungarian Constitutional Court's ability to function as the guardian of the constitution and prevent its series of legal revolutions, Fidesz specifically targeted the *actio popularis* petition in the 1989 Hungarian Constitution. Kim Lane Scheppele, 'Understanding Hungary's Constitutional Revolution' in Armin von Bogdandy and Pál Sonnevend (eds), *Constitutional Crisis in the European Constitutional Area: Theory, Law and Politics in Hungary and Romania* (Hart/Beck 2015) 114–16; Gary Jeffrey Jacobsohn and Yaniv Roznai, *Constitutional Revolution* (Yale University Press 2020) 83; Arato and Cohen (n 6) 168.

even supermajority, regarding the constitutionality of the latter's actions.[83] Not directly accountable to the will of the electorate, the guardian can address questions of constitutionality and the interests of 'the people' that might otherwise be lost or buried—because they do not align with the will of the majority for example. In this way, the guardian's different mode of representation provides a channel for the most vulnerable minorities within the electorate to be heard institutionally. It can achieve something that democratic legal procedures cannot guarantee because of their majoritarian design: the right of individuals and minorities to demand that the constitutionality of a statute be demonstrated through public and empirically verifiable juridical reasoning.[84] Thus, a guardian appears to be an essential institutional guarantor of basic liberal rights.

Importantly, the passivity of the guardian's power of judicial review should extend into its authority to decide on measures of militant democracy. Although the power to activate a ban of a political party should rest with the guardian, it should not have the power to initiate that process. It should not be able to decide unilaterally, all by itself, to investigate and repress a party.[85] Challenges to the constitutionality of a political organization that can result in the restriction of their political rights must be initiated by other 'political' bodies, that is, elected bodies such as parliament, an upper house, or the executive, or the public prosecutor. In Germany, for example, the power of initiative rests with the government, namely parliament.[86] This turns the decision to initiate the process into a process akin to peer review, as Müller describes it.[87] The government initiates the process by flagging a party as a potential threat based on evidence of its antidemocratic behaviour. However, because the power to regulate political parties is so dangerous, Issacharoff argues, the final authority over rights restrictions must rest with a body whose members are not in political competition with those they may judge.[88] Investing the power to initiate the process of restricting political rights with elected representatives reins in the guardian's power and renders it accountable indirectly.[89]

[83] Lafont (n 73) 227.

[84] ibid 231–32.

[85] Jan-Werner Müller, 'The Problem of Peer Review in Militant Democracy' in Uladzislau Belavusau and Aleksandra Gliszczyńska-Grabias (eds), *Constitutionalism under Stress* (Oxford University Press 2020) 263.

[86] See Max Steuer, 'The Role of Judicial Craft in Improving Democracy's Resilience: The Case of Party Bans in Czechia, Hungary and Slovakia' (2022) 18(3) European Constitutional Law Review 445.

[87] Jan-Werner Müller, 'Militant Democracy and Constitutional Identity' in Gary Jacobsohn and Miguel Schor (eds), *Comparative Constitutional Theory* (Edward Elgar 2018) 421.

[88] Issacharoff, *Fragile Democracies* (n 12) 50, 101–06.

[89] See Müller, 'The Problem of Peer Review in Militant Democracy' 263. Another indirect step in this process is the initial gathering of evidence, which is done in Germany by the Office for the Protection of the Constitution (*Bundesamt für Verfassungsschutz*). The government can task it to surveil a party and gather evidence of its antidemocratic actions, which parliament can use to build its case. However, the Office for the Protection of the Constitution should also inform the public of its observations. See Franziska Brandmann, 'Radical-Right Parties in Militant Democracies: How the Alternative for Germany's Strategic Frontstage Moderation Undermines Militant Measures' (2022) 18(3) European Constitutional Law Review 422–23.

In particular, it is imperative that the final judge have the legal training to assess whether the evidence brought against that party has been marshalled in a manner prescribed by the rule of law. Investing that authority in an independent body prevents parties from using rights restrictions to punish or eliminate their legitimate competitors. In Germany, for example, only the Federal Constitutional Court can decide on a party's constitutionality, which ensures that parties do not 'start outlawing their competitors'.[90] A further safeguard requires that, as long as a decision is pending on a party's constitutionality, it may be put at no political disadvantage.

In summary, the idea of passivity entails that, although the constitutional court should hold the final authority to decide on the constitutionality of a party, it should not possess the power to initiate an investigation into the constitutionality of a party.[91] If other parties believe that a particular party poses a threat to democratic constitutional essentials, they can advance a case for the constitutional court to adjudicate. That passive design thus mitigates the guardian's ability to abuse this potentially dangerous power. It gives new meaning to Rawls' assertion that 'the constitution is not what the court says it is. Rather it is what the people acting constitutionally through the other branches eventually allow the court to say it is'.[92] Depriving the guardian of the power of initiative installs an indirect check on its final authority that minimizes the risk of its abuse.

Besides passivity, the guardian's power to decide on unconstitutionality can also be designed to be *negative*, in order to limit concerns about its potential to form a juristocracy or to engage in legal revolution itself. In contrast to positive power, as we saw above, negative power is defined by the inability to create statutes. Kelsen defined positive power as 'bound by the constitution only with respect to its procedure' (at least, in the absence of a guardian's oversight).[93] It can produce new statutory laws and is unconstrained in terms of the substance of its final product. Kelsen contrasted this with the guardian's negative power, which is limited to striking down the positive legislative actions of other branches when they conflict with the constitution.[94] In addition, this negative power is limited because it is bound to the text of the constitution.[95]

The guardian's negative power, combined with the other two principal mechanisms of militant democracy, serves to protect constitutional essentials from their

---

[90] Jan-Werner Müller, 'Militant Democracy' in Michel Rosenfeld and András Sajó (eds), *The Oxford Handbook of Comparative Constitutional Law* (Oxford University Press 2012) 1258. Müller adds that, according to Article 9.2. of the German *Basic Law*, 'other associations deemed unconstitutional can be dissolved by the interior ministries'. Because of the central role that political parties play in democracy, they are privileged when it comes to political rights restrictions.

[91] Jan-Werner Müller, *Democracy Rules* (Farrar, Straus & Giroux 2021) 165–68.

[92] Rawls, *Political Liberalism* (n 26) 237.

[93] Kelsen, 'The Nature and Development of Constitutional Adjudication' (n 1) 47.

[94] Vinx, *Hans Kelsen's Pure Theory of Law: Legality and Legitimacy* (n 1) 153–54.

[95] Kelsen, 'Who Ought to be the Guardian of the Constitution?' (n 8) 194.

200 THE GUARDIAN OF THE CONSTITUTION

simple repeal and reversal. Yet, as Rawls suggested, the amendment process can still reform the constitution when the active and passive branches all agree that those reforms will bring it closer to its original promise.[96] Constitutional change thus occurs only when the different representatives of 'the people' cooperate and agree. That combination of negativity and passivity prevents the scheme of a guardian from becoming the basis for a juristocracy.

One could still argue that the guardian creates new legal norms by invalidating laws or through its interpretations. Even so, there is a qualitative difference between the positive power to enact new statutes and the negative power to invalidate other branches' exercise of their positive power. A guardian cannot, for example, abrogate or rewrite articles of the constitution, which limits it ability to assume the constituent power of 'the people'.[97] Although bad faith constitutional interpretation can distort the public order, its power cannot produce the same revolutionary effect as active powers. For this reason, Kumm describes the judiciary as strictly a 'veto player', which functions as an editor and holds other branches accountable 'at the behest of affected individuals claiming that their legitimate interests [in democratic constitutionalism] have not been taken seriously'.[98]

Nevertheless, while recognizing the limits of that negative power, even advocates acknowledge its transformative potential.[99] Despite the blurred distinction between interpretation and transformation, Ferrara argues that judgments made during this process are nevertheless *reflective* rather than conclusive.[100] When a guardian engages in constitutional interpretation, it relies on a constellation of factors that exist independent of its will, including constitutional principles and essentials, past decisions, and the history of the constitution. A court can make its reasoning empirically verifiable by presenting a practical syllogism to the public. That 'proof' does not, however, compel its conclusions in the same way that a geometric syllogism does. Its reasoning only demonstrates its interpretation of the law, which it presents publicly as a way to convince others of its correct reasoning. There is an element of uncertainty in its interpretation—what Cavell referred to as the 'whirl of organism'. The absence of any final closure in adjudication means that society may believe the guardian has crossed from interpretation to transformation. It may reject its reasoning. So, in the end, no single mechanism of constitutional entrenchment is fool proof, reinforcing again the importance of installing multiple defensive layers against legal revolutionary actions and actors.

---

[96] Rawls, *Political Liberalism* (n 26) 238–39. See also Ferrara (n 13) 244–46.
[97] Loughlin (n 21) 134–39.
[98] Kumm (n 11) 368.
[99] Zurn (n 14) 257–61.
[100] Ferrara (n 13) 237.

Accountability and Checks through Institutional Design

Designing the guardian's power to be both negative and passive serves as a significant internal check on its potential to abuse its final authority over constitutionality. Lingering concerns about the undemocratic potential of the guardian can be addressed through institutional design. Specifically, those concerns can be addressed by increasing the guardian's accountability to the electorate indirectly. Böckenförde recommended designing the guardian to minimize its potential to 'gain uncontrolled superiority over the other powers' and effectively become unaccountable.[101] He recommended four features in particular.[102] First, members of the guardian should be legitimated through some democratic procedure. Second, unilateral influences of the appointment of members should be avoided. Third, in agreement with Kelsen, membership should be professionalized.[103] Finally the length of members' terms in office must be regulated. Taken together, these measures can further mitigate concerns over the ability of the guardian to illegitimately assume a negative constituent power without compromising its ability to check the imperfections of other, active constituted powers.

Giving elected representatives control over the appointment process of the guardian grants the electorate indirect oversight. The German and Israeli models of appointment illustrate how to avoid the unilateral selection of members while simultaneously allowing eligibility to be regulated also by professional standards. In the German model, each major party has a 'right of nomination' for the same quota of seats (three) on the constitutional court along with an additional two unassigned seats whose appointees must receive support from all major parties.[104] Nominated candidates are appointed when they receive a two-thirds supermajority vote from both chambers of the legislature.

The Israeli model uses a nine-member Judicial Selection Committee to appoint members of its Supreme Court. Members of the Judicial Selection Committee are two government ministers (one of whom is the minister of justice, who also serves as chair of the committee), two members of the Knesset, three Supreme Court Justices, and two members of the Israeli Bar Association. That design ensures that legal professionals, judges, and lawyers, constitute a majority of the committee, limiting partisan influence over the composition of Supreme

---

[101] Böckenförde (n 10) 200–05.

[102] Issacharoff, *Democracy Unmoored* (n 4) 174–75. Professionalization and selection based on objective merit are a cornerstone of the effective administrative state. To be sure, the standards used to evaluate judges may not be as fine-grained or precise as those used to evaluate medical professionals, for example. But jurisprudence can and does aspire to objective and independently verifiable standards in its methods.

[103] See Kelsen, 'The Nature and Development of Constitutional Adjudication' (n 1) 48.

[104] Minor parties in a governing coalition can negotiate for the right to appoint a judge from the quota of the majority party.

202   THE GUARDIAN OF THE CONSTITUTION

Court.[105] Appointments require a seven-member majority, which ensures the acceptability of appointments to both the Supreme Court itself as well the governing coalition.

However, it is as imperative that accountability not be allowed to become an avenue for parties to capture or otherwise compromise the guardian. Besides taking measures to ensures its independence and its distinctive mode of representing 'the people', another crucial way to prevent its capture is by constitutionalizing the number of judges. Although the number of judges may itself be somewhat arbitrary, that number ought to be fixed by the constitution in order to prevent the court's capture through packing.

Although members of the guardian should be insulated against partisan political pressures from elected officials by having longer terms in office, it raises the danger of unaccountability due to what Böckenförde called 'fossilization', which occurs when judges themselves decide on their retirement, become decrepit in office, and are entirely unaccountable after their appointment.[106] Judicial terms in general should be long enough, however, to insulate members from the popularity of their decisions. Issacharoff notes that longer terms de-synchronize members from election cycles, which obstructs antidemocrats' ability to colonize nearly every branch of government at once.[107] Those delays preserve the guardian's ability to institutionally constrain antidemocrats' consolidation of power. In addition, and perhaps counterintuitively, longer terms can help the guardian better represent the transgenerational 'people' by turning it into a kind of lagging indicator of the will of the electorate.

Böckenförde ends his analysis of the guardian with a caution, however.[108] Regulations and normative considerations can only achieve so much. The success of a guardian in guaranteeing democracy ultimately depends on who exercises its power. For that reason, the utmost care must be taken in deciding who to appoint. So much hinges on character. The law is just an institution, in the end. And while it can guide the exercise of power and determine the standards and norms by which power is exercised, it can only offer that structure.

Entrenchment through Guardianship

A guardian of the constitution is an independent branch of government holding final interpretative authority over constitutionality. It represents the political

---

[105] Amichai Cohen and Yuval Shany, *The Fight Over Judicial Appointments in Israel* (16 February 2023) Lawfare <https://www.lawfaremedia.org/article/the-fight-over-judicial-appointments-in-israel>.
[106] Böckenförde (n 10) 203.
[107] Issacharoff, *Democracy Unmoored* (n 4) 122.
[108] Böckenförde (n 10) 205.

identity of 'the people', as expressed through its written constitution. It does so by exercising negative and passive powers to entrench constitutional essentials. It thus serves as a counterpower to the active and positive powers directly accountable to the electorate, ideally checking pathologies arising from their imperfect representation of 'the people'.

Democracy must include countermajoritarian institutions. Even critics of countermajoritarian institutions recognize that democracy presupposes reasonable behaviour and good faith disagreements among its members. When those presuppositions fail in practice—unfortunately, a regular enough occurrence—and members seek to turn majoritarian legal procedures against basic liberal rights and other constitutional essentials, democracy's survival may depend on whether a guardian possesses the power to defend the constitution by upholding its unamendable provisions and by barring antidemocratic actors from the public sphere.

Because unamendability and political rights restrictions are not self-enforcing, constitutional guardianship is the third principal mechanism of militant democracy. The decision to deploy either is in the end a decision on constitutionality—of a law or an organization. The guardian's final authority over constitutionality naturally includes the decision of how to execute the other two pillars of militant democracy.

To be sure, nothing can offer an absolute guarantee against legal revolutionary forces aiming to subvert democracy. The additional check of the guardian will not create a perfect democratic state. Neither will unamendability or political rights restrictions. However, a guardian may forestall democratic backsliding. Law is a normative order that is distinct from but overlaps with other normative orders and values, including those that might motivate antidemocrats. By closing off legal pathways to revolutionizing democracy and forcing would-be revolutionaries to turn instead to illegal methods, revolutionaries will hopefully lose momentum as supporters are forced to choose between legality and other norms. Ideally, they will find themselves unable to pursue their antidemocratic goals at all. In this way, militant democracy's suppression of legal revolution may buy a democracy enough time to address the underlying problems that give rise to antidemocratic sentiments and movements in the first place.

Conclusion

The epigraph of this book, taken from a fragment of Heraclitus, reads 'The people must fight for the law as for the city wall'.[1] For the Ancient Greeks, just as the city wall demarcated the boundaries of the city-state physically and helped in its defence against external enemies, the law demarcated that state politically and helped in its defence against internal strife.[2] The very existence of the city depended on both. To abandon the laws to attack or decay was no different than abandoning the walls. It would be to give up on the state and its identity. For that reason, Heraclitus argued in another fragment 'one must quench lawlessness [*hubris*] quicker than a blazing fire'.[3] Upholding the law was even more urgent than putting out a raging fire because of its constitutive role.

Echoing Heraclitus' sentiments, Carl Severing, an SPD politician and Weimar's Minister of Interior Affairs, asserted in a 1929 speech that 'a state that abandons its own defence gives up on itself' and urged the Weimar government to adopt more militant measures to entrench its constitution.[4] Severing understood well that political communities have enemies. The distinctive threat facing democracy is that its enemies can attack it using its own laws. The legality of their attacks complicates democracy's self-defence. Their attacks blur normative lines, making it unclear whether legal revolution is even democratically illegitimate.

---

[1] Fragment DK 22 B 44. I am indebted to Christina Tarnopolsky for her help with the translation and analysis of Heraclitus' fragments.

[2] Kurt A Raaflaub, 'Shared Responsibility for the Common Good: Heraclitus, Early Philosophy, and Political Thought' in Enrica Fantino and others (eds), *Heraklit im Kontext* (Walter de Gruyter GmbH 2017) 107; Thanos Zartaloudis, *The Birth of Nomos* (Edinburgh University Press 2019) 208.

[3] Fragment DK 22 B 43. Hubris refers to transgression of and disrespect for normative limits. Tyrant, which originally just meant a ruler in Ancient Greek, became a pejorative term in part because tyrants exhibited hubris. They governed without limits, unconstrained by either the law or institutional counterbalances.

[4] Severing made that remark while advocating for the renewal of the 1922 *Gesetz zum Schutze der Republik* (RSG). Severing was a lifelong member of the SPD. He served as Weimar's Minister of Interior Affairs [*Reichsinnenminister*] from 1928 to 1930. During that time, Severing sought to ban antidemocratic parties on both the left and the right. His efforts united the KPD and NSDAP in portraying him as an arch-antidemocrat and an enemy of the Republic. See Gotthard Jasper, *Der Schutz der Republik: Studien zur staatlichen Sicherung der Demokratie in der Weimarer Republik 1922-1930* (JCB Mohr (Paul Siebeck) 1963) 139–45.

In his 1929 speech, Severing urged parliament to renew and extend the powers of the RSG. The RSG was eventually renewed, but significantly watered-down. In addition, it retained all the weaknesses of the 1922 version, which included the absence of a mechanism to address legal revolutionary threats: ibid 290.

Democracy despite Itself. Benjamin A. Schupmann, Oxford University Press. © Benjamin A. Schupmann 2024.
DOI: 10.1093/9780191975950.003.0009

The history of modern democracy demonstrates that democratic cannibalism is a perennial problem. It is a question of when, not if, popular antidemocratic movements will erupt from within and try to use legal revolutionary methods to devour democracy. Democratic constitutions should be designed to provide democrats with the means to defend it and themselves.

This book has developed a normative theory of militant democracy capable of responding to the gravity of the problem posed by legal revolution—a more robust and confident theory that aims to defend democracy without compromising its identity as a democracy in the process. Adopting militant methods to defend democracy today requires rethinking what exactly is being defended and how.

Above all, it means putting liberalism first, recognizing it as a constitutive feature of democracy. It requires recognizing the state's authority to use proactive measures to guarantee that identity, in particular the explicit unamendability of constitutional essentials, restrictions on the political rights of organizations opposed to those essentials, and an independent guardian of the constitution to oversee and execute that defense. This book has shown how the divergent and in some ways opposed ideas of John Rawls and Carl Schmitt nevertheless converged in providing the normative foundations for a liberal theory of militant democracy.

The term 'militant democracy' is now firmly entrenched in the literature. However, it can be misleading and at times unhelpful—particularly when we define 'democracy' in the broader and more robust sense of liberal democracy or constitutional democracy. Every aspect of 'militant democracy' is deliberately countermajoritarian. It entrenches constitutional essentials, thereby *constraining* democracy—at least in its minimal or narrow proceduralist conception. For these reasons, a more accurate term could be 'militant constitutionalism', as András Sajó suggested in 2019.[5] But that term lacks the impact and history that 'militant democracy' has.

Regardless of which term we use, democrats should guard against what Zakaria calls 'the Weimar syndrome', that is, believing that constitutional design will not make much of a difference in maintaining and defending democracy.[6] The difficulty of constitutional design is that the opportunity to design a constitution in practice comes about rarely. For that reason, normative theorizing of the kind undertaken here may seem like an armchair fantasy. However, it is important to be ready with ideas for when the need does arise. It will.

Normative theory can also help us to appreciate our roles as members of a democratic political community, to recognize and perhaps reconcile ourselves to

---

[5] András Sajó, 'Militant Constitutionalism' in Anthoula Malkopoulou and Alexander S Kirshner (eds), *Militant Democracy and Its Critics: Populism, Parties, Extremism* (Edinburgh University Press 2019).

[6] Fareed Zakaria, 'The Rise of Illiberal Democracy' (1997) 76(6) Foreign Affairs 41.

206 CONCLUSION

the legitimacy of institutions that might seem to disadvantage us at first glance, and finally to understand the practical limits of our political ideals.

In its fiftieth anniversary report in 2023, Freedom House warned that global freedom had been declining systematically for the better part of two decades. This regression will stop eventually. When that moment comes and the dust settles, it is important for democrats to be clear about what the fundamentals of democracy are and how to redesign democratic institutions to better prevent the problems that have caused democracy's regression.

An essential element of that response is the adoption of measures rooted in sound normative theory that can cut through the dilemma of defending itself against internal legal revolutionary threats. By developing its liberal normative theory, this book has argued that democrats can be more confident about *militant* forms of constitutional entrenchment. To be sure, no measure is fool proof. As long as the underlying issues that cause members to turn to antidemocratic extremism go unaddressed, a democracy will continue to face the prospect of legal revolution.

Militant democracy must be paired with long-term legislative solutions that improve the overall quality of democracy, such as the advancement of social democracy and the promotion of civic education. A layered approach to the defence of democracy that can both address the grievances of members who might be inclined to support antidemocrats and entrench essentials against antidemocrats' attacks offers democracy the best fighting chance. In that spirit, this book has laid out a normative foundation that justifies the adoption of three principal 'militant' measures of constitutional entrenchment, to provide democracy with the tools to halt its own cannibalization.

Bibliography

Achen CH and Bartels LM, *Democracy for Realists: Why Elections Do Not Produce Responsive Government* (Princeton University Press 2016).

Ackerman B, *The Future of Liberal Revolution* (Yale University Press 1992).

Ackerman B, *Revolutionary Constitutions: Charismatic Leadership and the Rule of Law* (Harvard University Press 2019).

Albert R, 'Constitutional Amendment by Constitutional Desuetude' (2014) 62(3) American Journal of Comparative Law 641.

Albert R, 'Constitutional Handcuffs' (2010) 42(3) Arizona State Law Journal 663.

Althusius J, *Politica: Politics Methodically Set Forth and Illustrated with Sacred and Profane Examples* (Liberty Fund, Inc 1995).

Anschütz G, 'Three Guiding Principles of the Weimar Constitution' in Jacobson AJ and Schlink B (eds), *Weimar: A Jurisprudence of Crisis* (University of California Press 2002).

Arato A, *The Adventures of the Constituent Power: Beyond Revolutions?* (Cambridge University Press 2017).

Arato A, 'Multi-Track Constitutionalism Beyond Carl Schmitt' (2011) 18(3) Constellations 324.

Arato A, *Post Sovereign Constitution Making* (Oxford University Press 2016).

Arato A, 'Regime Change, Revolution, and Legitimacy' in Tóth GA (ed), Constitution for a Disunited Nation: On Hungary's 2011 Fundamental Law (Central European University Press 2013) 35.

Arato A and Cohen JL, *Populism and Civil Society: The Challenge to Constitutional Democracy* (Oxford University Press 2022).

Arditi B, *Politics on the Edges of Liberalism: Difference, Populism, Revolution, Agitation* (Edinburgh University Press 2007).

Azmanova A, 'The Populist Catharsis: On the Revival of the Political' (2018) 44(4) Philosophy and Social Criticism 399.

Badano G and Nuti A, 'Under Pressure: Political Liberalism, the Rise of Unreasonableness, and the Complexity of Containment' (2018) 26(2) The Journal of Political Philosophy 145.

Bagnoli C, 'Constructivism in Metaethics' in Zalta EN (ed), *The Stanford Encyclopedia of Philosophy* (Metaphysics Research Lab, Stanford University 2021).

Balkin JM and Levinson S, 'Understanding the Constitutional Revolution' (2001) 87(6) Virginia Law Review 1045.

Bánkuti M, Halmai G, and Scheppele KL, 'From Separation of Powers to a Government without Checks: Hungary's Old and New Constitutions' in Tóth GA (ed), *Constitution for a Disunited Nation: On Hungary's 2011 Fundamental Law* (Central European University Press 2013) 35.

Bánkuti M, Halmai G, and Scheppele KL, 'Hungary's Illiberal Turn: Disabling the Constitution' (2012) 23(3) Journal of Democracy 138.

Barak A, 'Human Dignity: The Constitutional Value and the Constitutional Right' in McCrudden C (ed), *Understanding Human Dignity* (The British Academy 2013).

Bárd P and Pech L, How to Build and Consolidate a Partly Free Pseudo Democracy by Constitutional Means in Three Steps: The 'Hungarian Model' (RECONNECT 2019).

208 BIBLIOGRAPHY

Bartels LM, *Unequal Democracy: The Political Economy of the New Gilded Age* (Princeton University Press 2017).

Baude W and Paulsen MS, 'The Sweep and Force of Section Three' (2023) 172 University of Pennsylvania Law Review.

Baynes K, 'Constructivism and Practical Reason in Rawls' (1992) 14 Analyse & Kritik 18.

Bellamy R, *Political Constitutionalism: A Republican Defence of the Constitutionality of Democracy* (Cambridge University Press 2007).

Bennhold K, 'Germany Places Far-Right Afd Party under Surveillance for Extremism' The New York Times (3 March 2022) <https://www.nytimes.com/2021/03/03/world/europe/germany-afd-surveillance-extremism.html>.

Bermeo N, 'On Democratic Backsliding' (2016) 27(1) Journal of Democracy 5.

Berthold L, *Carl Schmitt und der Staatsnotstandsplan am ende der weimarer Republik* (Duncker & Humblot 1999).

Berthold L, 'Das konstruktive Misstrauensvotum und seine Ursprünge in der weimarer Staatsrechtslehre' (1997) 36 Der Staat 81.

Bhuta N, 'The Mystery of the State: State-Concept, State-Theory and State-Making in Schmitt and Oakeshott' in David Dyzenhaus and Thomas Poole (eds), *Law, Liberty and State: Oakeshott, Hayek and Schmitt on the Rule of Law* (Cambridge University Press 2015).

Blokker P, 'Populism as a Constitutional Project' (2019) 17(2) International Journal of Constitutional Law 535.

Bourne AK and Rijpkema B, 'Militant Democracy, Populism, Illiberalism: New Challengers and New Challenges' (2022) 18(3) European Constitutional Law Review 375.

Böckenförde E-W, 'The Concept of the Political: A Key to Understanding Carl Schmitt's Constitutional Theory' in David Dyzenhaus (ed), *Law as Politics: Carl Schmitt's Critique of Liberalism* (Duke University Press 1998).

Böckenförde E-W, 'The Constituent Power of the People: A Liminal Concept of Constitutional Law' in Mirjam Künkler and Tine Stein (eds), *Constitutional and Political Theory: Selected Writings* (Oxford University Press 2016).

Böckenförde E-W, 'Constitutional Jurisdiction: Structure, Organization, and Legitimation' in Künkler M and Stein T (eds), *Constitutional and Political Theory: Selected Writings* (Oxford University Press 2016).

Böckenförde E-W, 'Der deutsche Katholizismus im Jahr 1933. Eine kritische Betrachtung' (1961) Hochland 215.

Bracher KD, 'Nachwort und Ausblick' in Bracher KD, Schulz G, and Sauer W (eds), *Die nationalsozialistische Machtergreifung. Studien zur Errichtung des totalitären Herrschaftssystems in Deutschland 1933/34* (Springer Fachmedien Wiesbaden 1960).

Bracher KD, 'The Technique of the Nationalist Seizure of Power' in *The Path to Dictatorship, 1918-1933; Ten Essays* (Anchor Books 1966).

Brandmann F, 'Radical-Right Parties in Militant Democracies: How the Alternative for Germany's Strategic Frontstage Moderation Undermines Militant Measures' (2022) 18(3) European Constitutional Law Review 412.

Brunkhorst H, *Critical Theory of Legal Revolutions: Evolutionary Perspectives* (Bloomsbury Academic 2014).

Busk LA, *Democracy in Spite of the Demos: From Arendt to the Frankfurt School* (Rowman & Littlefield 2020).

Busk LA, 'Schmitt's Democratic Dialectic: On the Limits of Democracy as a Value' (2021) 47(6) Philosophy & Social Criticism.

BIBLIOGRAPHY 209

Canovan M, 'Trust the People! Populism and the Two Faces of Democracy' (1999) 47(1) Political Studies 2.

Capoccia G, *Defending Democracy: Reactions to Extremism in Interwar Europe* (Johns Hopkins University Press 2005).

Capoccia G, 'Militant Democracy: The Institutional Bases of Democratic Self-Preservation' (2013) 9 Annual Review of Law and Social Science 207.

Chambers S, 'Democracy and Constitutional Reform: Deliberative Versus Populist Constitutionalism' (2019) 45(9-10) Philosophy and Social Criticism 1116.

Chambers S, 'Democracy, Popular Sovereignty, and Constitutional Legitimacy' (2004) 11(2) Constellations 153.

Choudhry S, 'Will Democracy Die in Darkness? Calling Autocracy by Its Name' in Graber MA, Levinson S, and Tushnet M (eds), *Constitutional Democracy in Crisis?* (Oxford University Press 2018).

Cohen A and Shany Y, 'The Fight over Judicial Appointments in Israel' Lawfare (16 February 2023) <https://www.lawfaremedia.org/article/the-fight-over-judicial-appointments-in-israel>.

Cohen A and Shany Y, 'Reversing the 'Constitutional Revolution': The Israeli Government's Plan to Undermine the Supreme Court's Judicial Review of Legislation' Lawfare (15 February 2023) <https://www.lawfaremedia.org/article/the-fight-over-judicial-appoi ntments-in-israel>.

Constant B, *Political Writings* (Fontana B ed and trans, Cambridge University Press 2007).

Corrias L, 'Populism in a Constitutional Key: Constituent Power, Popular Sovereignty, and Constitutional Identity' (2016) 12 European Constitutional Law Review 6.

Cristi R, *Carl Schmitt and Authoritarian Liberalism: Strong State, Free Economy* (University of Wales Press 1998).

Cristi R, 'The Metaphysics of Constituent Power: Schmitt and the Genesis of Chile's 1980 Constitution' (1999-2000) 21 Cardozo Law Review 1749.

Croce M and Salvatore A, *Carl Schmitt's Institutional Theory: The Political Power of Normality* (Cambridge University Press 2022).

Croce M and Salvatore A, *The Legal Theory of Carl Schmitt* (Routledge 2013).

Darwall S, Gibbard A, and Railton P, 'Toward Fin De Siècle Ethics: Some Trends' (1992) 101(1) The Philosophical Review 115.

Dahl RA, 'Procedural Democracy' in Goodin RE and Pettit P (eds), *Contemporary Political Philosophy: An Anthology* (John Wiley & Sons, Inc. 2019).

Dannemann G, 'Legale Revolution, Nationale Revolution. Die Staatsrechtslehre zum Umbruch von 1933' in Böckenförde E-W (ed), *Staatsrecht und Staatsrechtslehre im Dritten Reich* (CF Müller 1985) 3.

DiResta R, 'It's Not Misinformation. It's Amplified Propaganda' (9 October 2021) The Atlantic <https://www.theatlantic.com/ideas/archive/2021/10/disinformation-propaga nda-amplification-ampliganda/620334/>.

Doerfler RD and Moyn S, 'The Ghost of John Hart Ely' (2022) 75(3) Vanderbilt Law Review 769.

Dürig G, 'Zur Bedeutung und Tragweite des Art. 79 III des Grundgesetzes (Ein Plädoyer)' in Spanner H, Lerche P, Zacher H, Badura F, von Campenhausen P, and von Freiherr A (eds), *Festgabe für Theodor Maunz zum 70. Geburtstag am 1. September 1971* (CH Beck 1971).

Dyzenhaus D, 'Constitutionalism in an Old Key: Legality and Constituent Power' (2012) 1(2) Global Constitutionalism 229.

210 BIBLIOGRAPHY

Dyzenhaus D, "'Now the Machine Runs Itself'": Carl Schmitt on Hobbes and Kelsen' (1994-1995) 16(1) Cardozo Law Review 1.

Dyzenhaus D, 'The Politics of the Question of Constituent Power' in Martin Loughlin and Neil Walker (eds), *The Paradox of Constitutionalism* (Oxford University Press 2007).

Ehmke H, 'Verfassungsänderung und Verfassungsdurchbrechung' (1953) 79(4) Archiv des öffentlichen Rechts 385.

Eilperin J, Dennis B, and Dawsey J, '"A Factory of Bad Ideas": How Scott Pruitt Undermined His Mission at Epa' The Washington Post (21 April 2018) <https://wapo.st/2Hg8EJh>.

Elster J, 'Constitutionalism in Eastern Europe: An Introduction' (1991) 58(2) University of Chicago Law Review 447.

Ely JH, *Democracy and Distrust: A Theory of Judicial Review* (Harvard University Press 1980).

Ermakoff I, 'Law against the Rule of Law: Assaulting Democracy' (2020) 47(1) Journal of Law and Society 164.

Ermakoff I, *Ruling Oneself Out: A Theory of Collective Abdications* (Duke University Press 2008).

Esen B and Gumuscu S, 'How Erdoğan's Populism Won Again' (2023) 34(3) Journal of Democracy 21.

Feisel FM, 'Thinking EU Militant Democracy Beyond the Challenge of Backsliding Member States' (2022) 18(3) European Constitutional Law Review 385.

Ferrara A, 'Can Political Liberalism Help Us Rescue "the People" from Populism?' (2018) 44(4) Philosophy & Social Criticism 463.

Ferrara A, *Modernity and Authenticity: A Study of the Social and Ethical Thought of Jean-Jacques Rousseau* (SUNY Press 1992).

Ferrara A, *Sovereignty Across Generations: Constituent Power and Political Liberalism* (Oxford University Press 2023).

Ferrara A, 'Unconventional Adaptation and the Authenticity of the Constitution' in Albert R (ed), Revolutionary Constitutionalism: Law, Legitimacy, Power (Hart 2020).

Ferrara A and Michelman FI, *Legitimation by Constitution: A Dialogue on Political Liberalism* (Oxford University Press 2021).

Fox GH and Nolte G, 'Intolerant Democracies' (1995) 36(1) Harvard International Law Journal 1.

Freedom House, 'Freedom in the World 2023' (March 2023) <https://freedomhouse.org/sites/default/files/2023-03/FIW_World_2023_DigtalPDF.pdf>.

Freeman S, 'Constitutional Democracy and the Legitimacy of Judicial Review' (1990) 9 Law and Philosophy 327.

Freeman S, 'Political Liberalism and the Possibility of a Just Democratic Constitution' (1994) 69(3) Chicago-Kent Law Review 619.

Freeman W, 'Sidestepping the Constitution: Executive Aggrandizement in Latin America and East Central Europe' (2020) 6 Constitutional Studies 35.

Friedrich CJ, *Constitutional Reason of State: The Survival of the Constitutional Order* (Brown University Press 1957).

Galli C, *La Genealogia della Politica: Carl Schmitt e la Crisi del Pensiero politico moderno* (Il Mulino 1996).

Galli C, 'Schmitt's Political Theologies' in *Janus's Gaze: Essays on Carl Schmitt* (Duke University Press 2015).

Galli C, 'Schmitt and the State' in *Janus's Gaze: Essays on Carl Schmitt* (Duke University Press 2015).

Ganguly Š, 'An Illiberal India?' (2021) 31(1) Journal of Democracy 193.

Ganguly Š, 'India's Endangered Democracy' (2021) 32(4) Journal of Democracy 177.

BIBLIOGRAPHY   211

Ginsburg T and Huq A, *How to Save a Constitutional Democracy* (University of Chicago Press 2018).

Giovanola B and Sala R, 'The Reasons of the Unreasonable: Is Political Liberalism Still an Option?' (2022) 48(9) Philosophy and Social Criticism 1226.

Gourgouris S, 'The Concept of the Mythical (Schmitt with Sorel)' (1999-2000) 21(5-6) Cardozo Law Review 1487.

Greenawalt K, 'The Rule of Recognition and the Constitution' (1987) 85(4) Michigan Law Review 621.

Grimm D, 'Dignity in a Legal Context: Dignity as an Absolute Right' in McCrudden C (ed), *Understanding Human Dignity* (The British Academy 2013).

Goos C, 'Würde des Menschen: Restoring Human Dignity in Post-Nazi Germany' in McCrudden C (ed), *Understanding Human Dignity* (The British Academy 2013).

Grzymala-Busse A, 'Conclusion: The Global Forces of Populism' (2019) 51(4) Polity 718.

Gutmann A, 'Rawls on the Relationship between Liberalism and Democracy' in Freeman S (ed), *The Cambridge Companion to Rawls* (Cambridge University Press 2003).

Habermas J, 'On the Internal Relation between the Rule of Law and Democracy' in *The Inclusion of the Other: Studies in Political Theory* (The MIT Press 1998).

Hallowell JH, *The Decline of Liberalism as an Ideology with Particular Reference to German Politico-Legal Thought* (Kegan Paul, Trench, Trubner & Co., Ltd. 1946).

Halmai G, 'A Coup against Constitutional Democracy? The Case of Hungary' in Graber MA, Levinson S, and Tushnet M (eds), *Constitutional Democracy in Crisis?* (Oxford University Press 2018).

Halmai G, 'Populism, Authoritarianism and Constitutionalism' (2019) 20 German Law Journal 296.

Hawkins KA and Kaltwasser CR, 'Introduction: The Ideational Approach' in Hawkins KA, Carlin RE, Littvay L, and Kaltwasser CR (eds), *The Ideational Approach to Populism: Concept, Theory, and Analysis* (Routledge 2019).

Hertweck F, Kisoudis D, and Giesler G (eds), *'Solange das Imperium da Ist': Carl Schmitt im Gespräch mit Klaus Figge und Dieter Groh 1971* (Duncker & Humblot 2010).

Heun W, *The Constitution of Germany: A Contextual Analysis* (Hart Publishing 2011).

Hillgruber C, 'Deutsche Revolutionen – "Legale Revolutionen"? Über den legitimatorischen Mehr- oder Minderwert (des Anscheins) verfassungskontinuierlicher Legalität' (2010) 49(2) Der Staat 167.

Hirschl R, *Towards Juristocracy: The Origins and Consequences of the New Constitutionalism* (Harvard University Press 2004).

Hofmann H, *Legitimität gegen Legalität: Der Weg der politischen Philosophie Carl Schmitts* (Duncker & Humblot 1992).

Huba H, 'Das Grundgesetz als dauerhafte gesamtdeutsche Verfassung: Erinnerung an seine Legitimität' (1991) 30(3) Der Staat 367.

Huq A and Ginsburg T, 'How to Lose a Constitutional Democracy' (2018) 78(1) UCLA Law Review 78.

Irfan U, 'Scott Pruitt Is Slowly Strangling the Epa' Vox (8 March 2018) <https://www.vox.com/energy-and-environment/2018/1/29/16684952/epa-scott-pruitt-director-regulations>.

Invernizzi-Accetti C and Zuckerman I, 'What's Wrong with Militant Democracy?' (2017) 65(1) Political Studies 182.

Issacharoff S, *Democracy Unmoored: Populism and the Corruption of Popular Sovereignty* (Oxford University Press 2023).

Issacharoff S, 'Fragile Democracies' (2007) 120(6) Harvard Law Review.

212 BIBLIOGRAPHY

Issacharoff S, *Fragile Democracies: Contested Power in the Era of Constitutional Courts* (Cambridge University Press 2015).

Jabloner C, 'Introduction to Hans Kelsen' in Arthur J Jacobson and Bernhard Schlink (eds), *Weimar: A Jurisprudence of Crisis* (University of California Press 2002).

Jacobsohn GJ, 'Constitutional Identity' (2006) 68 The Review of Politics 361.

Jacobsohn GJ and Roznai Y, *Constitutional Revolution* (Yale University Press 2020).

Jain A, 'Citizenship by Religion: The Indian Citizenship Regime 1947–2019' Verfassungsblog (12 December 2019) <https://verfassungsblog.de/citizenship-by-religion/>.

Jasper G, *Der Schutz der Republik: Studien zur staatlichen Sicherung der Demokratie in der weimarer Republik 1922-1930* (JCB Mohr (Paul Siebeck) 1963).

Jasper G, *Die Gescheiterte Zähmung. Wege Zur Machtergreifung Hitlers, 1930-1934* (Suhrkamp 1986).

Jellinek G, 'Constitutional Amendment and Constitutional Transformation' in Jacobson AJ and Schlink B (eds), *Weimar: A Jurisprudence of Crisis* (University of California Press 2002).

Johnson TR, 'The New Voter Suppression' (16 January 2020) <https://www.brennancenter.org/our-work/research-reports/new-voter-suppression>.

Jovanović M, 'How to Justify 'Militant Democracy': Meta-Ethics and the Game-Like Character of Democracy' (2016) 42(8) Philosophy and Social Criticism 745.

Kaltwasser CR, 'Militant Democracy Versus Populism' in Malkopoulou A and Kirshner AS (eds), *Militant Democracy and Its Critics: Populism, Parties, Extremism* (Edinburgh University Press 2019).

Kalyvas A, *Democracy and the Politics of the Extraordinary: Max Weber, Carl Schmitt, and Hannah Arendt* (Cambridge University Press 2008).

Kalyvas A, 'Popular Sovereignty, Democracy, and the Constituent Power' (2005) 12(2) Constellations 223.

Kelly D, 'Carl Schmitt's Political Theory of Representation' (2004) 65(1) Journal of the History of Ideas 113.

Kelly D, *The State of the Political: Conceptions of Politics and the State in the Thought of Max Weber, Carl Schmitt, and Franz Neumann* (Oxford University Press 2003).

Kelsen H, 'Foundations of Democracy' (1955) 66(1) Ethics 1.

Kelsen H, *General Theory of Law & State* (Transaction Publishers 2008).

Kelsen H, 'The Nature and Development of Constitutional Adjudication' in Lars Vinx (ed), *The Guardian of the Constitution: Hans Kelsen and Carl Schmitt on the Limits of Constitutional Law* (Cambridge University Press 2015).

Kelsen H, 'On the Essence and Value of Democracy' in Jacobson AJ and Schlink B (eds), *Weimar: A Jurisprudence of Crisis* (University of California Press 2002).

Kelsen H, *The Pure Theory of Law* (Max Knight tr, University of California Press 1970).

Kelsen H, 'Who Ought to Be the Guardian of the Constitution?' in Lars Vinx (ed), *The Guardian of the Constitution: Hans Kelsen and Carl Schmitt on the Limits of Constitutional Law* (Cambridge University Press 2015).

Kennedy E, *Constitutional Failure: Carl Schmitt in Weimar* (Duke University Press 2004).

Khosla M and Vaishnav M, 'The Three Faces of the Indian State' (2022) 32(1) Journal of Democracy 111.

Kirchheimer O, 'Politics and Justice' in Burin FS and Shell KL (eds), *Politics, Law, and Social Change: Selected Essays of Otto Kirchheimer* (Columbia University Press 1969).

Kirchheimer O, *Political Justice: The Use of Legal Procedure for Political Ends* (Princeton University Press 1961).

Kirshner AS, *Legitimate Opposition* (Yale University Press 2022).

Kirshner AS, 'Militant Democracy Defended' in Malkopoulou A and Kirshner AS (eds), *Militant Democracy and Its Critics: Populism, Parties, Extremism* (Edinburgh University Press 2019).

Kirshner AS, *A Theory of Militant Democracy: The Ethics of Combatting Political Extremism* (Yale University Press 2014).

Kirişci K and Sloat A, 'The Rise and Fall of Liberal Democracy in Turkey: Implications for the West' Brookings (2019) <https://www.brookings.edu/research/the-rise-and-fall-of-liberal-democracy-in-turkey-implications-for-the-west/>.

Klamt M, 'Militant Democracy and the Democratic Dilemma: Different Ways of Protecting Democratic Constitutions' in Fred Bruinsma and David Nelken (eds), *Explorations in Legal Cultures* (Elsevier 2007).

Klein C, 'On the Eternal Constitution: Contrasting Kelsen and Schmitt' in Diner D and Stolleis M (eds), *Kelsen and Schmitt: A Juxtaposition* (Bleicher Verlag 1999).

Kommers DP and Miller RA, *The Constitutional Jurisprudence of the Federal Republic of Germany* (Duke University Press 2012).

Korioth S, 'Rettung oder Überwindung der Demokratie - Die weimarer Staatsrechtslehre im Verfassungsnotstand 1932/33' in Gusy C (ed), *Demokratisches Denken in der weimarer Republik* (Nomos Verlagsgesellschaft 2000).

Kumm M, 'Who's Afraid of the Total Constitution? Constitutional Rights as Principles and the Constitutionalization of Private Law' (2006) 7(4) German Law Journal 341.

Kyle J and Mounk Y, 'The Populist Harm to Democracy: An Empirical Assessment' Tony Blair Institute for Global Change (26 December 2018) <https://www.institute.global/insights/geopolitics-and-security/populist-harm-democracy-empirical-assessment>.

Lafont C, *Democracy without Shortcuts: A Participatory Conception of Deliberative Democracy* (Oxford University Press 2020).

Levinson S, 'How Many Times Has the United States Constitution Been Amended? (a) 26; (B) 26; (C) 27; (D) >27: Accounting for Constitution Change' in *Responding to Imperfection* (Princeton University Press 1995).

Landau D, 'Abusive Constitutionalism' (2013) 47(1) UC Davis Law Review 189.

Landau D, 'Populist Constitutions' (2018) 85 The University of Chicago Law Review 521.

Lara MP, 'Carl Schmitt's Contribution to a Political Theory of Myth' (2017) 56(3) History and Theory 379.

Lazar NC, *States of Emergency in Liberal Democracies* (Cambridge University Press 2009).

Lefort C, 'The Permanence of the Theologico-Political?' (David Macey trans, 1988) in *Democracy and Political Theory* (Polity Press 1988).

Lefort C, 'The Question of Democracy' in *Democracy and Political Theory* (David Macey tr, Polity Press 1988).

Lefort C, 'Reversibility' in *Democracy and Political Theory* ((David Macey tr, Polity Press 1988).

VI Lenin, 'Left-Wing Communism: An Infantile Disorder' in *Collected Works* (Progress Publishers 1974).

Levitsky S and Ziblatt D, *How Democracies Die* (Crown 2018).

Loewenstein K, 'Militant Democracy and Fundamental Rights, I' (1937) 31(3) The American Political Science Review 417.

Loewenstein K, 'Militant Democracy and Fundamental Rights, II' (1937) 31(4) The American Political Science Review 638.

Loughlin M, *Against Constitutionalism* (Harvard University Press 2022).

Loughlin M, 'The Concept of Constituent Power' (2014) 13(2) European Journal of Political Theory 218.

214 BIBLIOGRAPHY

Loughlin M, *Foundations of Public Law* (Oxford University Press 2010).

Loughlin M, 'Nomos' in David Dyzenhaus and Thomas Poole (eds), *Law, Liberty and State: Oakeshott, Hayek and Schmitt on the Rule of Law* (Cambridge University Press 2015).

Loughlin M, 'Politonomy' in Jens Meierhenrich and Oliver Simons (eds), *The Oxford Handbook of Carl Schmitt* (Oxford University Press 2015).

Loughlin M and Walker N, 'Introduction' in Loughlin M and Walker N (eds), *The Paradox of Constitutionalism* (Oxford University Press 2007).

Lührmann A, Medzihorsky J, and Lindberg SI, 'Walking the Talk: How to Identify Anti-Pluralist Parties' (V-Dem Working Paper 116 2021).

Michael Luttig J and Tribe LH, 'The Constitution Prohibits Trump from Ever Being President Again' (19 August 2023) The Atlantic <https://www.theatlantic.com/ideas/arch ive/2023/08/donald-trump-constitutionally-prohibited-presidency/675048/>.

Macklem P, 'Guarding the Perimeter: Militant Democracy and Religious Freedom in Europe' (2012) 19(4) Constellations 575–90.

Macklem P, 'Militant Democracy, Legal Pluralism, and the Paradox of Self-Determination' (2006) 4(3) International Journal of Constitutional Law 488–516.

Maschke G, 'Zum "Leviathan" Von Carl Schmitt' in Günter Maschke (ed), *Der Leviathan in der Staatslehre des Thomas Hobbes: Sinn und Fehlschlag eines politischen Symbols* (Hohenheim Verlag 1982).

Malkopoulou A, 'Militant Democracy and Its Critics' in Malkopoulou A and Kirshner AS (eds), *Militant Democracy and Its Critics: Populism, Parties, Extremism* (Edinburgh University Press 2019).

Malkopoulou A, 'What Militant Democrats and Technocrats Share' (2023) 26(4) Critical Review of International Social and Political Philosophy 437.

Malkopoulou A and Norman L, 'Three Models of Democratic Self-Defence: Militant Democracy and Its Alternatives' (2018) 66(2) Political Studies 442.

de Maistre J, 'Study on Sovereignty' in Lively J (ed), Works (Allen & Unwin 1965).

McCormick JP, *Carl Schmitt's Critique of Liberalism: Against Politics as Technology* (Cambridge University Press 1997).

McCormick JP, 'Fear, Technology, and the State; Carl Schmitt, Leo Strauss, and the Revival of Hobbes in Weimar and National Socialist Germany' (1994) 22(4) Political Theory 619.

McCormick JP, 'Teaching in Vain: Thomas Hobbes, Carl Schmitt and the Crisis of the Sovereign State' in Jens Meierhenrich and Oliver Simons (eds), *The Oxford Handbook of Carl Schmitt* (Oxford University Press 2014).

Medina V, 'Militant Intolerant People: A Challenge to John Rawls' Political Liberalism' (2010) 58(3) Political Studies 556.

Mehring R, *Carl Schmitt: Aufstieg und Fall* (CH Beck 2009).

Meyer B, 'Over-Diagnosing Democratic Decline' The Progress Network (14 March 2023) <https://theprogressnetwork.org/over-diagnosing-democratic-decline/>.

Michelman FI, 'Constitutional Authorship' in Larry Alexander (ed), *Constitutionalism: Philosophical Foundations* (Cambridge University Press 2001).

de Montesquieu B, *The Spirit of the Laws* (Hafner Publishing Company 1959).

Mouffe C, *For a Left Populism* (Verso 2018).

Moyn S, *Liberalism against Itself: Cold War Intellectuals and the Making of Our Times* (Yale University Press 2023).

Moyn S, 'The Secret History of Constitutional Dignity' in McCrudden C (ed), *Understanding Human Dignity* (The British Academy 2013).

Mudde C and Kaltwasser CR, 'Exclusionary Vs. Inclusionary Populism: Comparing Contemporary Europe and Latin America' (2013) 48(2) Government and Opposition 147.

Muirhead R and Rosenblum NL, 'The Path from Conspiracy to Ungoverning' (2022) 89(3) Social Research 501.

Müller J-W, 'Carl Schmitt's Method: Between Ideology, Demonology, and Myth' (1999) 4(1) Journal of Political Ideologies 61–85.

Müller J-W, *Contesting Democracy: Political Ideas in Twentieth-Century Europe* (Yale University Press 2011).

Müller J-W, *Democracy Rules* (Farrar, Straus and Giroux 2021).

Müller J-W, 'Individual Militant Democracy' in Malkopoulou A and Kirshner AS (eds), *Militant Democracy and Its Critics: Populism, Parties, Extremism* (Edinburgh University Press 2019).

Müller J-W, 'Militant Democracy' in Rosenfeld M and Sajó A (eds), *The Oxford Handbook of Comparative Constitutional Law* (Oxford University Press 2012).

Müller J-W, 'Militant Democracy and Constitutional Identity' in Jacobsohn G and Schor M (eds), *Comparative Constitutional Theory* (Edward Elgar 2018).

Müller J-W, 'Myth, Law and Order: Schmitt and Benjamin Read Reflections on Violence' (2003) 29 History of European Ideas 459–73.

Müller J-W, 'Re-Imagining Leviathan: Schmitt and Oakeshott on Hobbes and the Problem of Political Order' (2010) 13(2–3) Critical Review of International Social and Political Philosophy 317–36.

Müller J-W, 'Rising to the Challenge of Constitutional Capture: Protecting the Rule of Law within EU Member States' Eurozine (21 March 2014) <https://www.eurozine.com/rising-to-the-challenge-of-constitutional-capture/>

Müller J-W, 'A "Practical Dilemma Which Philosophy Alone Cannot Resolve"? Rethinking Militant Democracy: An Introduction' (2012) 19(4) Constellations 536.

Müller J-W, 'The Problem of Peer Review in Militant Democracy' in Belavusau U and Gliszczyńska-Grabias A (eds), *Constitutionalism under Stress* (Oxford University Press 2020).

Müller J-W, 'Protecting Popular Self-Government from the People? New Normative Perspectives on Militant Democracy' (2016) 19 Annual Review of Political Science 249.

Müller J-W, *What Is Populism?* (University of Pennsylvania Press 2016).

Niesen P, 'Anti-Extremism, Negative Republicanism, Civic Society: Three Paradigms for Banning Political Parties' (2002) 03(07) German Law Journal 1–32.

Niesen P, 'Banning the Former Ruling Party' (2012) 19(4) Constellations 541–61.

Nitzschner P, 'On Militant Democracy's Institutional Conservatism' Philosophy and Social Criticism 1–21.

Olsen TV, 'Citizens' Actions against Non-Liberal-Democratic Parties' (2022) 18(3) European Constitutional Law Review 466.

Orbán V, 'Speech at Conference in Memory of Helmut Kohl Budapest, 16 June 2018) <https://miniszterelnok.hu/prime-minister-viktor-orbans-speech-at-a-conference-held-in-memory-of-helmut-kohl/>.

Orbán V., 'Speech at the 29th Bálványos Summer Open University and Student Camp' (Băile Tuşnad (Tusnádfürdő), 28 July 2018) <https://visegradpost.com/en/2018/07/30/say-goodbye-to-the-entire-elite-of-68-the-new-project-of-viktor-orban-full-speech/>.

Paulson SL, 'Hans Kelsen and Carl Schmitt: Growing Discord, Culminating in the "Guardian" Controversy of 1931' in Meierhenrich J and Simons O (eds), *The Oxford Handbook of Carl Schmitt* (Oxford University Press 2014).

Paulson SL, 'Statutory Positivism' (2007) 1(1) Legisprudence 1.

Pech L and Scheppele KL, 'Illiberalism Within: Rule of Law Backsliding in the Eu' (2017) 19 Cambridge Yearbook of European Legal Studies 3.

216 BIBLIOGRAPHY

Pettit P, *The Birth of Ethics: Reconstructing the Role and Nature of Morality* (Oxford University Press 2018).

Plattner MF, 'Illiberal Democracy and the Struggle on the Right' (2019) 30(1) Journal of Democracy 5.

Preuss UK, *Constitutional Revolution: The Link between Constitutionalism and Progress* (Humanities Press International 1990).

Preuss UK, 'The Critique of German Liberalism: Reply to Kennedy' (1987) 71 Telos 97.

Preuss UK, 'The Exercise of Constituent Power in Central and Eastern Europe' in Martin Loughlin and Neil Walker (eds), *The Paradox of Constitutionalism* (Oxford University Press 2007).

Preuss UK, 'The Implications of "Eternity Clauses": The German Experience' (2011) 44(3) Israel Law Review 429.

Preuss UK, 'Political Order and Democracy: Carl Schmitt and His Influence' in Chantal Mouffe (ed), *The Challenge of Carl Schmitt* (Verso 1999).

Preuss UK, 'The Politics of Constitution-Making: Transforming Politics into Constitutions' (1991) 13(2) Law & Policy 107.

Preuss UK, 'Schmitt and the Weimar Constitution' in Jens Meierhenrich and Oliver Simons (eds), *The Oxford Handbook of Carl Schmitt* (Oxford University Press 2014).

Jonathan Quong, *Liberalism without Perfection* (Oxford University Press 2011).

Preuss UK, 'The Rights of Unreasonable Citizens' (2004) 12(3) The Journal of Political Philosophy 314.

Raaflaub KA, 'Shared Responsibility for the Common Good: Heraclitus, Early Philosophy, and Political Thought' in Enrica Fantino, Ulrike Muss, Charlotte Schubert, and Kurt Sier (eds), *Heraklit im Kontext* (Walter de Gruyter GmbH 2017).

Rawls J, 'The Domain of the Political and Overlapping Consensus' in Samuel Freeman (ed), *Collected Papers* (Harvard University Press 1999).

Rawls J, 'The Idea of an Overlapping Consensus' in Samuel Freeman (ed), *Collected Papers* (Harvard University Press 1999).

Rawls J, 'The Idea of Public Reason Revisited' (1997) 64 The University of Chicago Law Review.

Rawls J, *Justice as Fairness: A Restatement* (The Belknap Press 2003).

Rawls J, Justice as Fairness: Political Not Metaphysical' in Samuel Freeman (ed), *Collected Papers* (Harvard University Press 1999).

Rawls J, 'Kantian Constructivism in Moral Theory' in Samuel Freeman (ed), *Collected Papers* (Harvard University Press 1999).

Rawls J, *The Law of Peoples* (Harvard University Press 1999).

Rawls J, *Political Liberalism* (Columbia University Press 1996).

Rawls J, *A Theory of Justice* (Belknap Press 1999).

Reid A, 'How Can Political Liberalism Respond to Contemporary Populism?' (2022) 21(2) European Journal of Political Theory 299.

Rijpkema B, 'Militant Democracy and the Detection Problem' in Malkopoulou A and Kirshner AS (eds), *Militant Democracy and Its Critics: Populism, Parties, Extremism* (Edinburgh University Press 2019).

Rijpkema B, *Militant Democracy: The Limits of Democratic Tolerance* (Routledge 2018).

Rosanvallon P, *Counter-Democracy* (Cambridge University Press 2008).

Rosenblum N, 'Banning Parties: Religious and Ethnic Partisanship in Multicultural Democracies' (2007) 1(1) Law & Ethics of Human Rights 17.

Rosenblum N, *On the Side of Angels: An Appreciation of Parties and Partisanship* (Princeton University Press 2008).

BIBLIOGRAPHY 217

Rovira MG-S, 'On Carl Schmitt's Reading of Hobbes: Lessons for Constitutionalism in International Law?' (2007) 4 No Foundations: Journal of Extreme Legal Positivism 61.

Roznai Y, 'Introduction: Constitutional Courts in a 100-Years Perspective and a Proposal for a Hybrid Model of Judicial Review' (2020) 14(4) ICL Journal 355.

Roznai Y, 'The Straw That Broke the Back of the Constitution? When Quantity Transforms to Quality' International Journal of Constitutional Law Blog (2021) <http://www.iconn ectblog.com/2021/02/the-straw-that-broke-the-back-of-the-constitution-when-quant ity-transforms-to-quality/>.

Roznai Y, *Unconstitutional Constitutional Amendments: The Limits of Amendment Powers* (Oxford University Press 2017).

Roznai Y, '"We the People", "Oui, the People" and the Collective Body: Perceptions of Constituent Power' in Gary Jacobsohn and Miguel Schor (eds), *Comparative Constitutional Theory* (Edward Elgar 2018).

Rubinelli L, Constituent Power: A History (Cambridge University Press 2020).

Rummens S, 'Resolving the Paradox of Tolerance' in Malkopoulou A and Kirshner AS (eds), *Militant Democracy and Its Critics: Populism, Parties, Extremism* (Edinburgh University Press 2019).

Rummens S and Abts K, 'Defending Democracy: The Concentric Containment of Political Extremism' (2010) 58 Political Studies 649.

Rumpf H, *Carl Schmitt und Thomas Hobbes: Ideelle Beziehungen und aktuelle Bedeutung mit einer Abhandlung über die Frühschriften Carl Schmitts* (Duncker & Humblot 1972).

Sa'adah A, 'After the Party: Trump, Le Pen, and the New Normal' (2017) 35(2) French Politics, Culture & Society 43.

Sadurski W, 'Constitutional Crisis in Poland' in Graber MA, Levinson S, and Tushnet M (eds), *Constitutional Democracy in Crisis?* (Oxford University Press 2018).

Sadurski W, *Poland's Constitutional Breakdown* (Oxford University Press 2019).

Sadurski W and Steinbeis M, 'What Is Going on in Poland Is an Attack against Democracy' Verfassungsblog (15 July 2016) <https://verfassungsblog.de/what-is-going-on-in-pol and-is-an-attack-against-democracy/>.

Saffon MP and Urbinati N, 'Procedural Democracy, the Bulwark of Equal Liberty' (2013) 41(3) Political Theory 441.

Sajó A, 'Militant Constitutionalism' in Malkopoulou A and Kirshner AS (eds), *Militant Democracy and Its Critics: Populism, Parties, Extremism* (Edinburgh University Press 2019).

Sajó A, 'Militant Democracy and Emotional Politics' (2012) 19(4) Constellations.

Sala R, 'The Place of Unreasonable People Beyond Rawls' (2013) 12(3) European Journal of Political Theory 253.

Street S, 'What Is Constructivism in Ethics and Metaethics?' (2010) 5(5) Philosophy Compass 363.

Sauer W, 'Die Mobilmachung Der Gewalt' in Bracher KD, Schulz G, and Sauer W (eds), *Die Nationalsozialistische Machtergreifung. Studien Zur Errichtung Des Totalitären Herrschaftssystems in Deutschland 1933/34* (Springer Fachmedien Wiesbaden 1960).

Scanlon TM, 'The Appeal and Limits of Constructivism' in Lenman J and Shemmer Y (eds), *Constructivism in Practical Philosophy* (2012).

Scheppele KL, 'Autocratic Legalism' (2018) 85(2) The University of Chicago Law Review.

Scheppele KL, 'Constitutional Coups and Judicial Review: How Transnational Institutions Can Strengthen Peak Courts at Times of Crisis (with Special Reference to Hungary)' (2014) 23 Journal of Transnational Law & Contemporary Problems 51.

Scheppele KL, 'How Viktor Orbán Wins' (2022) 33(3) Journal of Democracy 45.

218   BIBLIOGRAPHY

Scheppele KL, 'Hungary and the End of Politics' The Nation (6 May 2014) <https://www.thenation.com/article/hungary-and-end-politics/>.

Scheppele KL, 'The Rule of Law and the Frankenstate: Why Governance Checklists Do Not Work' (2013) 26(4) Governance: An International Journal of Policy, Administration, and Institutions 559.

Scheppele KL, 'Trump's Non-Emergency Emergency, Part II' Verfassungsblog (17 February 2019) <https://verfassungsblog.de/trumps-non-emergency-emergency-part-ii/>.

Scheppele KL, 'Understanding Hungary's Constitutional Revolution' in von Bogdandy A and Sonnevend P (eds), *Constitutional Crisis in the European Constitutional Area: Theory, Law and Politics in Hungary and Romania* (Hart/Beck 2015).

Scheuerman WE, *The End of Law: Carl Schmitt in the Twenty-First Century* (Rowman & Littlefield International Ltd 2019).

Schmitt C, *The Concept of the Political* (The University of Chicago Press 1996).

Schmitt C, *Constitutional Theory* (Duke University Press 2008).

Schmitt C, *The Crisis of Parliamentary Democracy* (The MIT Press 1988).

Schmitt C, *Der Begriff des Politischen: Text von 1932 mit einem Vorwort und drei Corollarien* (Duncker & Humblot 1963).

Schmitt C, 'Der Führer schützt das Recht' (1934) 15(39) Deutsche Juristen-Zeitung.

Schmitt C, *Der Hüter der Verfassung* (Dunker & Humblot 1996).

Schmitt C, *Der Wert des Staates und die Bedeutung des Einzelnen* (Dunker & Humboldt GmbH 2004).

Schmitt C, 'Die vollendete Reformation' (1963) 4(1) Der Staat 51.

Schmitt C, 'Ethic of State and Pluralistic State' in Chantal Mouffe (ed), *The Challenge of Carl Schmitt* (Verso 1999).

Schmitt C, 'Freiheitsrechte und institutionelle Garantien der Reichsverfassung' in *Verfassungsrechtliche Aufsätze aus den Jahren 1924-1954. Materialien zu einer Verfassungslehre* (Duncker & Humblot 1958).

Schmitt C, 'The Guardian of the Constitution' in *The Guardian of the Constitution: Hans Kelsen and Carl Schmitt on the Limits of Constitutional Law* (Cambridge University Press 2015).

Schmitt C, 'Juristische Fiktionen' (1913) 12 Deutsche Juristen-Zeitung 804.

Schmitt C, 'The Legal World Revolution' (1987) 72 Telos 73.

Schmitt C, *Legality and Legitimacy* (Duke University Press 2004).

Schmitt C, *The Leviathan in the State Theory of Hobbes: Meaning and Failure of a Political Symbol* (University of Chicago Press 2008).

Schmitt C, *Political Theology: Four Chapters on the Concept of Sovereignty* (University of Chicago Press 2005).

Schmitt C, 'Reichstagsauflösungen' in *Verfassungsrechtliche Aufsätze aus den Jahren 1924-1954. Materialien zu einer Verfassungslehre* (Duncker & Humblot 1958).

Schmitt C, 'Strong State and Sound Economy' in Renato Cristi (ed), *Carl Schmitt and Authoritarian Liberalism* (University of Wales Press 1932).

Schmitt C, 'The Value of the State and the Significance of the Individual' in *Carl Schmitt's Early Legal-Theoretical Writings* (Cambridge University Press 2021).

Schmitt C, 'Was Bedeutet Der Streit Um Den "Rechtsstaat"?' in Günter Maschke (ed), *Staat, Großraum, Nomos: Arbeiten Aus Den Jahren 1916-1969* (Dunker & Humblot 1995).

Schupmann BA, *Carl Schmitt's State and Constitutional Theory: A Critical Analysis* (Oxford University Press 2017).

Schupmann BA, 'Constraining Political Extremism and Legal Revolution' (2020) 46(3) Philosophy and Criticism 249.

BIBLIOGRAPHY 219

Schupmann BA, 'Hans Kelsen's Political Theology: Science, Pantheism, and Democracy' (2022) 51(3) Austrian Journal of Political Science 42.

Schwartzberg M, *Democracy and Legal Change* (Cambridge University Press 2007).

Scriba F, *'Legale Revolution'? Zu den Grenzen verfassungsändernder Rechtssetzung und der Haltbarkeit eines umstrittenen Begriffs* (Duncker & Humblot 2008).

Shklar JN, 'The Liberalism of Fear' in Stanley Hoffmann (ed), *Political Thought and Political Thinkers* (The University of Chicago Press 1998).

Shklar JN, 'Rights in the Liberal Tradition' (2023) 71(2) Political Studies 279.

Sottiaux S and Rummens S, 'Concentric Democracy: Resolving the Incoherence in the European Court of Human Rights' (2012) 10(1) Case Law on Freedom of Expression and Freedom of Association 106–26.

Stahl RM and Popp-Madsen BA, 'Defending Democracy: Militant and Popular Models of Democratic Self-Defense' (2022) 29(3) Constellations 310.

Stanton T, 'Hobbes and Schmitt' (2011) 37 History of European Ideas 160.

Steuer M, 'The Role of Judicial Craft in Improving Democracy's Resilience: The Case of Party Bans in Czechia, Hungary and Slovakia' (2022) 18(3) European Constitutional Law Review 440.

Stolleis M, *A History of Public Law in Germany, 1914–1945* (Oxford University Press 2004).

Stoll T, 'Hans Vaihinger' in Edward N Zalta (ed), *The Stanford Encyclopedia of Philosophy* (2020) <https://plato.stanford.edu/entries/vaihinger/>.

Street S, 'What Is Constructivism in Ethics and Metaethics?' (2010) 5(5) Philosophy Compass 363.

Svolik MW, 'Polarization Versus Democracy' (2019) 30(3) Journal of Democracy 20.

Talbot M, 'Trump, Barr, and the Rule of Law' The New Yorker (5 May 2019) <https://www.newyorker.com/magazine/2019/05/13/trump-barr-and-the-rule-of-law>.

Thiel M, 'Germany' in Thiel M (ed), *The 'Militant Democracy' Principle in Modern Democracies* (Ashgate 2009).

Thamer H-U, *Verführung und Gewalt: Deutschland 1933-1945* (Siedler 1986).

Thoma R, 'The Reich as Democracy' in Jacobson AJ and Schlink B (eds), *Weimar: A Jurisprudence of Crisis* (University of California Press 2002).

Tóth GA (ed), *Constitution for a Disunited Nation: On Hungary's 2011 Fundamental Law* (Central European University Press 2013).

Triepel H, 'Die Nationale Revolution Und Die Deutsche Verfassung' Deutsche allgemeine Zeitung (2 April 1933).

Tushnet M, 'Peasants with Pitchforks, and Toilers with Twitter: Constitutional Revolutions and the Constituent Power' (2015) 13(3) International Journal of Constitutional Law 639.

Tyulkina S, *Militant Democracy: Undemocratic Political Parties and Beyond* (Routledge 2015).

Uitz R, 'Can You Tell When an Illiberal Democracy Is in the Making? An Appeal to Comparative Constitutional Scholarship from Hungary' (2015) 13(1) International Journal of Constitutional Law 279.

Uitz R, 'Hungary' in Thiel M (ed), *The 'Militant Democracy' Principle in Modern Democracies* (Ashgate 2009).

Urbinati N, *Democracy Disfigured: Opinion, Truth, and the People* (Harvard University Press 2014).

Urbinati N, *Me the People: How Populism Transforms Democracy* (Harvard University Press 2019).

Urbinati N, 'Political Theory of Populism' (2019) 22 Annual Review of Political Science 111.

Varol OO, 'Stealth Authoritarianism' (2015) 100(4) Iowa Law Review 1673.

220 BIBLIOGRAPHY

Varshney A, 'How India's Ruling Party Erodes Democracy' (2022) 33(4) Journal of Democracy 104.

Vergara C, 'Populism as Plebeian Politics: Inequality, Domination, and Popular Empowerment' (2020) 28(2) Journal of Political Philosophy 222–46.

Verovšek PJ, 'Caught between 1945 and 1989: Collective Memory and the Rise of Illiberal Democracy in Postcommunist Europe' Journal of European Public Policy (2020) 840–57.

Verovšek PJ, *Memory and the Future of Europe: Rupture and Integration in the Wake of Total War* (Manchester University Press 2020).

Verovšek PJ , '"The Nation Has Conquered the State": Arendtian Insights on the Internal Contradictions of the Nation-State' (2023) Review of International Studies 1–18.

Vile MJC, Constitutionalism and the Separation of Powers (Liberty Fund, Inc. 1998).

Vinx L, 'Democratic Equality and Militant Democracy' (2020) 27(4) Constellations 685.

Vinx L, *Hans Kelsen's Pure Theory of Law: Legality and Legitimacy* (Oxford University Press 2007).

Vinx L, 'Introduction' in Lars Vinx (ed), *The Guardian of the Constitution: Hans Kelsen and Carl Schmitt on the Limits of Constitutional Law* (Cambridge University Press 2015).

Waldron J, 'A Right to Do Wrong' in *Liberal Rights: Collected Papers 1981-1991* (Cambridge University Press 1993).

Waldron J, 'The Core of the Case against Judicial Review' (2006) 115(6) The Yale Law Journal 1346.

Waldron J, 'Judicial Review and the Conditions of Democracy' (1998) 6(4) The Journal of Political Philosophy 335.

Waldron J, *Law and Disagreement* (Oxford University Press 1999).

Weber M, *Economy and Society: An Outline of Interpretive Sociology*, Roth G and Wittich C (eds), 2 vols (University of California Press 1978).

Weill R, 'On the Nexus of Eternity Clauses, Proportional Representation, and Banned Political Parties' (2017) 16(2) Election Law Journal 237.

Weill R, 'Secession and the Prevalence of Both Militant Democracy and Eternity Clauses Worldwide' (2018) 40(2) Cardozo Law Review 905.

Weinar L, 'John Rawls' *The Stanford Encyclopedia of Philosophy* (2021) <https://plato.stanford.edu/archives/win2013/entries/rawls/>.

Weintal S, 'The Challenge of Reconciling Constitutional Eternity Clauses with Popular Sovereignty: Toward Three-Track Democracy in Israel as a Universal Holistic Constitutional System and Theory' (2011) 44(3) Israel Law Review 449.

Weyland K, 'Latin America's Authoritarian Drift: The Threat from the Populist Left' (2013) 24(3) Journal of Democracy 18.

Willms B, 'Politics as Politics: Carl Schmitt's 'Concept of the Political' and the Tradition of European Political Thought' (1991) 13(4) History of European Ideas 371–83.

Zakaria F, 'The Rise of Illiberal Democracy' (1997) 76(6) Foreign Affairs 22.

Zartaloudis T, *The Birth of Nomos* (Edinburgh University Press 2019).

Zurn CF, *Deliberative Democracy and the Institutions of Judicial Review* (Cambridge University Press 2009).

Index

For the benefit of digital users, indexed terms that span two pages (e.g., 52–53) may, on occasion, appear on only one of those pages.

Amendment clauses see **unamendability**
Antidemocrats
    aligning legality and legitimacy 152–54
    decline of Hungary
        Constitution of 1989 7–9
        key example 7
        transformation into an 'illiberal
            democracy' 9–13
    development of new liberal normative
        theory 2
    Hungarian Constitution of 1989 7–8
    Hungary's veneer of democracy 13
    illegitimacy of restricting political rights 68
    impact on democratic parties 5–6
    inadequacies of normative theory
        focus on narrow conception of
            'democracy' 53–54
        need for a last resort 54
    legal possession of state power 49–51
    legal revolution and democracy 52
    limitation of existing normative theories 73
    measures to entrench constitutional norms 99
    need for improved civic education 76
    normative theories of militant democracy 55
    political rights restrictions as last resort 70–73
    problem of militant democracy 1
    problems of prevention and response 31
    quietist view 76–78
    role of unamendability 137
    social contract theories 69–70
    success by adopting legal revolutionary
        tactics 5
    'the paradox of democracy's
        self-defence' 60–61
    threat from legal revolution 4
    threats to democracy 29
    twenty-first century political goals 6

Balance of powers *see* **separation and balance
    of powers**

Basic liberal rights
    see also **human rights; political rights
        restrictions**
    advantage of liberal normative theory 3–4
    authoratative and binding norms *see guardians
        of the constitution* 2
    constructivism's substantive output: the
        authority of basic liberal rights 90–91
    detection problems of militant democracy 60
    effect of antidemocrats 3
    guardians of the constitution 182
    indirect legal revolution 39–41
    legitimacy of installing an independent
        guardian of the constitution 180–81
    measures to entrench constitutional norms
        overview 94–95
        political rights restrictions 99–102
        unamendability 95–99
    sine qua non of democratic
        constitutionalism 2
    threat of populism 29
    underlying arguments 24
Brazil 14–15
Breach of constitution
    indirect legal revolution 36–37
    typology of legal revolution 34

Civil society
    antidemocrats 58–59, 75–76
    Hungary's veneer of democracy 14–15
    indirect legal revolution 36, 39–41
    need for improved civic education 76
    thresholds for constitutional amendment 139
    typology of legal revolution 35
    use of political rights restrictions 147
Constitutional courts *see* **guardians of the
        constitution**
Constitutional entrenchment *see* **entrenchment**
Constitutional theory *see* **state and
        constitutional theory**

222 INDEX

Constitutionalism
advantage of liberal normative theory 3–4
authority of constitutional norms
'the people' versus the electorate 91–94
conceptual origins of legal revolution 32–33
guardian of the constitution 191–203
indirect methods of legal revolution 14–15
legal revolution and democratic legitimacy 41
measures to entrench constitutional norms
overview 94–95
political rights restrictions 99–102
unamendability 95–99
multi-track constitutionalism
political constructivism 96–97
unamendability 138–40
paradox of modern constitutionalism 42–45
political constructivism
constructivism's formal output: normative
truth 88–89
constructivism's substantive output: the
authority of basic liberal rights 90–91
foundations for any democracy 84
hypothetical 'second order'
proceduralism 85–88
'the people' and the electorate
distinguished 91–94
Schmitt's state and constitutional theory
basis to settle existential-political
disagreements about public
order 114–22
focus on dualistic distinctions 122–33
'occasionalism' in Schmitt's thought 106–7
overview 105–6
problem of politicization 107–14
uses and limits for militant
democracy 133–34
supremacy of amendment clauses 48
two basic components of liberal normative
theory 2
Containment
measures to entrench constitutional
norms 99–102
'Containment'
Rawls' ambivalence about deploying militant
measures 103
Courts *see* **guardian of the constitution**
Covid-19 pandemic 26

Democracy
see also **militant democracy**
authority of constitutional norms 84
decline of global freedom 206

decline of Hungary
Constitution of 1989 7–9
key example 7
transformation into an 'illiberal
democracy' 9–13
democratic cannibalism as a perennial
problem 205
development of new liberal normative
theory 2
'Freedom in the World Report' 2023 14
guardian of the constitution
criticisms of judicial review 186–91
essential feature of democratic
constitutionalism 191–203
Hungary's veneer of democracy 13–16
illegitimacy of restricting political
rights 66–68
imperfections 16
and legal revolution
difficulties of formulating a response 52
mis-use of supremacy of the amendment
clause 52
two interrelated and pressing questions 52
underlying problem 52
limitation of existing normative
theories 73–75
need for an alternative normative
theory 75–76
need for defence against legal revolution 4
need for stronger forms of constitutional
entrenchment 17
need to defend itself 1
normative theories of militant
democracy 56
post-Cold War backsliding 6
putting liberalism first 205
respect for the democratic process 30
role of institutional design 205
role of normative theory 1–2
Schmitt's state and constitutional
theory 109–12
social contract theories 68–70
'the paradox of democracy's
self-defence' 60–61
threat of antidemocratic political goals 29
unamendability and the legitimacy of political
rights restrictions 164–66
unique vulnerability of 'bourgeois'
democracy 5
unreasonable beliefs 82–84
Depoliticization
criticisms of militant democracy 61

distinction between 'the people' and the
electorate 94
liberal normative theory 166–68
liberal rights 97, 98
Schmitt's state and constitutional theory
basis to settle existential-political
disagreements about public
order 114–22
democratization and politicization 109–12
fundamental problem of modern
society 107–9
illegitimacy of state and law 112–14
'the paradox of democracy's self-
defence' 23, 54
trivialization of democracy by militant
democracy 64–66
Derogation from constitution
breach of constitution 36–37
typology of legal revolution 34
unamendability 20, 73
Desuetude
breach of constitution 36–37
typology of legal revolution 34
Detection problems
challenge to existing normative theories 78
constitutional entrenchment 16–17
illiberalism 57–60
implicit unamendability 146
militant democracy 53–54
shadow over the legitimacy of political rights
restrictions 72
'the paradox of democracy's self-defence' 22
unamendability and the legitimacy of political
rights restrictions 161–64
Dignity *see* **human dignity**
Direct legal revolution
changes to the written constitution 35
examples
changes to the written constitution 36
Ecuador 36
Hungary 35
Turkey 35–36
indirect legal revolution distinguished 35
supremacy of amendment clauses
collapsing of two conceptual
distinctions 47
constituted power 47–48
determination of validity 46
enabling of direct legal revolution 46–47
fundamental normative commitments 48
requirement of modern
constitutionalism 48

solution to the paradox 45–46
US example 46
typology of legal revolution 34
Discretionary authority
legal indeterminacy 62–63
'the paradox of democracy's self-defence' 22

Elections
absolute entrenchment 141–42
guardian of the constitution
electorate and imperfect
representation 191–94
guardian as a different imperfect
representative 196–200
unelected guardian of the
constitution 186–88
Hungary 8–9
Hungary's veneer of democracy 13
legal possession of state power 48–49
post-Cold War democratic backsliding 6
potential for the electorate to use its final
control 31
Rawls' ambivalence about deploying militant
measures 103
restrictions on electoral choice 159
'the people' and the electorate
distinguished 91–94
transformation of Hungary into an 'illiberal
democracy' 12
Electorates
guardian of the constitution
electorate and imperfect
representation 191–94
guardian as a different imperfect
representative 196–200
unelected guardian of the
constitution 186–88
political constructivism 91–94
state and constitutional theory 122–25
Entrenchment
absolute entrenchment 140–42
antidemocratic potential 16
defence measure against militant
democracy 1
development of new liberal normative
theory 2
guardians of the constitution 183, 202–3
Hungarian Constitution of 1989 7
limitation of existing normative theories 73
militant democracy as constitutional
entrenchment
courts and judiciary 21–22

224 INDEX

Entrenchment (*cont.*)
  human dignity 21
  interelatedness of unamendability and
    political rights restrictions 20–21
  need for stronger forms of constitutional
    entrenchment 17
  normative theories of militant democracy 55
  political constructivism
    overview 94–95
    political rights restrictions 99–102
    unamendability 95–99
  post-Cold War democratic backsliding 6
  Rawls' ambivalence about deploying militant
    measures 102, 105
  role of normative theory 1–2
  unamendability 137
  underlying arguments 24
Explicit unamendability
  liberal normative theory
    aligning legality and legitimacy 152–54
    beyond judicial authority 150–51
    circumscribing and signalling identity of
      constitution 149–50
    legal foundation for political rights
      restrictions 151–52
    positive entrenchment mechanisms
      147–49
  political constructivism 95–96

Fidesz 9–13

Germany
  Basic Law
    basis for future design 4
    deficiencies of existing normative
      theories 54
    explicit unamendability 95, 137–
      38, 147–48
    paradigmatic militant democratic
      constitution 2, 17–19
  concept 'legal revolution' 29–30
  conceptual origins of legal revolution
    32–34
  guardian of the constitution 180
  guardians of the constitution 184
  impact of antidemocrats on democratic
    parties 5–6
  legal possession of state power 49–50
  limitation of existing normative
    theories 73
  oppositions between legality and
    legitimacy 152
  origins of militant democracy 4

political rights restrictions
  focus on an organization's opposition to
    the values and political identity of a
    constitution 166–68
  as last resort 71–72
  resolving the practical paradox of
    restrictions 172–73
  timing of restrictions 170
  unamendability and the legitimacy of
    political rights restrictions 162
recognition of unique vulnerability of
  'bourgeois' democracy 5
Schmitt's state and constitutional
  theory 106, 130
unamendability and the legitimacy of political
  rights restrictions
  substantive restrictions on unconstitutional
    political goals 159–60
Governments
  Hungarian Constitution of 1989 7
  indirect methods of legal revolution 15–16
  post-Cold War democratic backsliding 6
  threat of populism 29
  transformation of Hungary into an 'illiberal
    democracy' 10
Guardian of the constitution
  essential feature of democratic
    constitutionalism
    accountability and checks through
      institutional design 201–2
    electorate and imperfect
      representation 191–94
    entrenchment through guardianship 202–3
    guardian as a different imperfect
      representative 196–200
    overview 191
    tyranny and *nemo judex in causa sua* 194–96
  final authority on constitutionality 180
  German Basic Law 18–19
  Hungarian Constitution of 1989 8
  implicit unamendability 95
    indeterminacy 143–44
    judicial authority over the
      constitution 144–46
    overview 142–43
    political rights restrictions 146–47
  indirect methods of legal revolution 14–15
  judiciary distinguished 184–85
  liberal normative theory
    essential feature of democratic
      constitutionalism 191–203
    explicit unamendability 150–51
    ideal of the guardian 181–86

one of three three principal mechanisms 137
    as the pro tempore ultimate
        authority 180–81
    risks to democracy 186–91
militant democracy as constitutional
    entrenchment 21–22
post-Cold War democratic backsliding 6
putting liberalism first 205
transformation of Hungary into an 'illiberal
    democracy' 11–12
underlying arguments 25

Health insurance 16
Human dignity
    explicit unamendability of German Basic
        Law 17–18, 147
    militant democracy as constitutional
        entrenchment 21
Human rights *see* also **basic liberal rights**
    explicit unamendability of German Basic
        Law 17–18
    illegitimacy of restricting political rights 68
    reducing abuses of democracy and
        discretionary authority 165–66
    Refah case 63–64
    transformation of Hungary into an 'illiberal
        democracy' 9
Hungary
    absolute entrenchment 141
    Constitution of 1989 7–9
    democratic decline 7
    example of direct legal revolution 35
    example of indirect legal revolution 39
    measures to entrench constitutional
        norms 96–97
    political rights restrictions
        as last resort 72
        timing of restrictions 169–70
    transformation into an 'illiberal
        democracy' 9–13
    unamendability 139
    veneer of democracy 13–16

Illiberal democracy
    advantage of liberal normative theory 3–4
    contradiction in terms 16
    detection problems
        narrow conception of democracy 58–59
        need to analyse whole picture 59
        theoretical acknowledgement 60
        value of existing normative theories 60
    fragility and reversibility of an overlapping
        consensus 85

Hungary's veneer of democracy 14
inadequacies of normative theory 53–54
need for an alternative normative
    theory 75–76
spotlight on democracy's imperfections 16–17
transformation of Hungary 9–13
twenty-first century political goals 6
unamendability and the legitimacy of political
    rights restrictions 163
unreasonable beliefs 84
Implicit unamendability
    guardian of the constitution 142–43
    liberal normative theory
        indeterminacy 143–44
        judicial authority over the
            constitution 144–46
        overview 142–43
        political rights restrictions 146–47
    political constructivism 95–96
Indirect legal revolution
    direct legal revolution distinguished 35
    legal possession of state power
        antidemocrats in power 49–51
        electoral victories 48–49
        undermining of democratic identity 48
    main subtypes
        breach of constitution 36–37
        breakdown of separation and balance of
            powers 37–39
        erosion of civil society and individual rights
            protections 39–41
        overview 36
    typology of legal revolution 34
Institutional design
    deeper problem of legal revolution 30
    for democrats with the means to defend
        democracy and themselves 205
    Germany's *Basic Law* as model 4
    guardians of the constitution 201–2
    Hungarian Constitution of 1989 8
    multi-track constitutionalism 138
    need for stronger forms of constitutional
        entrenchment 17
    need to redesign 206
    post-Cold War democratic backsliding 6
    pressing question raised by legal revolution
        and democracy 52
    Rawls' ambivalence about deploying militant
        measures 103
    transformation of Hungary into an 'illiberal
        democracy' 9–10, 11–12
    'Weimar syndrome' 205

226 INDEX

Judiciary *see* guardian of the constitution

Law
  see also rule of law
  for the Ancient Greek 204
  'containment' 101
  distinctive threat facing democracy 204
  ideal of the guardian 181–82
  state and constitutional theory
    constitution and individual constitutional
      law distinguished 127–31
    illegitimacy of state and law 112–14
Legal indeterminacy
  discretionary authority 62–63
  inherent arbitrariness 61
  normative theories 62
  'the paradox of democracy's self-defence' 22
Legal revolution
  conceptual origins 32–34
  deeper problem of constitutional design 30
  deleterious effect on a democratic
    constitution 83–84
  and democracy
    difficulties of formulating a response 52
    mis-use of supremacy of the amendment
      clause 52
    two interrelated and pressing questions 52
    underlying problem 52
  democratic decline of Hungary
    Constitution of 1989 7–9
    key example 7
    transformation into an 'illiberal
      democracy' 9–13
  democratic legitimacy
    dissolution of boundary 42
    populism 41
    requirements of constitutionalism 41
  distinctive threat facing democracy 204
  'Freedom in the World Report' 2023 14
  indirect methods of legal revolution 14–16
  legal procedures to effect change 1
  need for an alternative normative
    theory 75–76
  need for defence of democracy 4
  potential for the electorate to use its final
    control 31
  problems of prevention and response 31
  right to mis-use democracy's procedures and
    institutions 31
  state and constitutional theory
    constitution and individual constitutional
      law distinguished 130
    constitutional revolution 131–33

theoretical perspectives
  changes formally legal yet apparently
    substantively revolutionary 31
  positive potential for non-democracies 31–32
  regressive potential 32
threat of antidemocratic goals 4
twenty-first century political goals 6
typology
  direct and indirect legal revolution
    distinguished 35
  direct legal revolution 35–36
  five pathways that constitutional
    retrogression can take 32–35
  indirect legal revolution 36–41
underlying arguments 24
underlying concept 29–30
unique vulnerability of 'bourgeois'
  democracy 5
Legislatures *see* parliaments
Liberal normative theory
  answer to theoretical limitations 3–4
  broader value of theory 4
  centrality of Rawls' thought
    authority of constitutional norms 84–93
    focus on overlapping consensus 82–84
    measures to entrench constitutional
      norms 94–102
    overview 81
    Rawls' ambivalence about deploying
      militant measures 102–4
  development of new normative theory 23
  explicit unamendability
    aligning legality and legitimacy 152–54
    beyond judicial authority 150–51
    circumscribing and signalling identity of
      constitution 149–50
    legal foundation for political rights
      restrictions 151–52
    positive entrenchment mechanisms 147–49
  guardian of the constitution
    essential feature of democratic
      constitutionalism 191–203
    explicit unamendability 150–51
    ideal of the guardian 181–86
    one of three three principal
      mechanisms 137
    as the pro tempore ultimate
      authority 180–81
    risks to democracy 186–91
  implicit unamendability
    indeterminacy 143–44
    judicial authority over the
      constitution 144–46

overview 142–43
political rights restrictions 146–47
institutional redesign 206
legitimate measures of measures of
entrenchment 2
militant methods to defend democracy 205
political rights restrictions
focus on an organization's opposition to
the values and political identity of a
constitution 166–69
one of three three principal
mechanisms 137
overview 155–56
timing of restrictions 169–74
unamendability and the legitimacy of
political rights restrictions 157–66
putting liberalism first 205
Schmitt's state and constitutional theory
basis to settle existential-political
disagreements about public
order 114–22
focus on dualistic distinctions 122–33
'occasionalism' in Schmitt's thought 106–7
overview 105–6
problem of politicization 107–14
uses and limits for militant
democracy 133–34
two basic components 2
unamendability
absolute entrenchment 140–42
basic doctrine 137
explicit unamendability 147–54
implicit unamendability 142–47
multi-track constitutionalism 138–40
one of three three principal
mechanisms 137
underlying arguments 24
Liberal rights see **basic liberal rights**

Militant democracy
alternative approaches 75–78
as constitutional entrenchment
courts and judiciary 21–22
human dignity 21
interelatedness of unamendability and
political rights restrictions 20–21
criticisms
criteria for deploying repressive
measures 61
legal indeterminacy 61
normative problems 61
risk of depoliticizing issues 61
defence against legal revolution 53

defence measures 1
deficiencies of existing normative theories
failure to discuss key issues 54
focus on narrow conception of
'democracy' 53–54
need for a last resort 54
'the paradox of democracy's
self-defence' 54
depoliticization 61–62
detection problems
narrow conception of democracy 58–59
need to analyse whole picture 59
theoretical acknowledgement 60
value of existing normative theories 60
German Basic Law
explicit unamendability 17–18
'objective order of values'. 18
paradigm of militant democracy 17
political rights restrictions 19
role of Federal Constitutional Court 18–19
illegitimacy of restricting political
rights 66–68
inadequacies of existing normative theories 3
legal indeterminacy
defining feature of the formal rule of
law 61–62
discretionary authority 62–63
inherent arbitrariness 61
normative problem 62
liberal normative theory
answer to theoretical limitations 3–4
broader value of theory 4
theoretical origins 2–4
two basic components 2
long-term legislative solutions 206
misleading and sometimes unhelpful term 205
need for stronger forms of constitutional
entrenchment 17
normative theories 54
'concentric model' of democracy's
self-defence 56–57
entrenchment 55
entrenchment of members' political
rights 57
essence of 'democracy' 56
focus on party bans 73–75
need for an alternative 78
party bans 55–56
political rights restrictions as last resort 70–73
reponses to the paradox 66–70
responses to paradox 66
value-neutral procedures 56
varied emphasis 57

228 INDEX

Militant democracy (*cont.*)
normative theory
development of new normative theory 23
doubts of scholars and policy makers 23
early stage of development 22
significant normative, practical, and
explanatory challenges 22–23
origins in Germany 4
popularity of 'illiberal democracy' 16
quietist view 76–78
Rawls' ambivalence about deploying militant
measures 102–4
role of normative theory 1–2
sC0Pe of the guardian's power 182
'the paradox of democracy's self-defence' 60–61
'the Weimar syndrome' 205
underlying arguments
basic liberal rights 24
challenge of legal revolution 24
courts and judiciary 25
entrenchment 24
minimisation of legal revolutionary
threats 25–26
normative foundations for an alternative
theory 24
political rights restrictions 25
supremacy of amendment clauses 25
three principal militant mechanisms for
entrenchment 25
underlying paradox 1
uses and limits of state and constitutional
theory 133–34
Militant secularism
case of Refah 63–64
liberal normative theory 164–66
Poland 37
weakening of constitutional
commitments 9–10
Multi-track constitutionalism
political constructivism 96–97
unamendability 138–40
Myth
Hobbes' Leviathan 118–20
Schmitt's state and constitutional theory 116–18

Negative republicanism 67
Nemo judex in causa sua 188–89, 191, 194–96
Normative theories
see also **liberal normative theory**
deployment of militant measures 1–2
focus on party bans 73–75
illegitimacy of restricting political
rights 66–68

inadequacies when dealing with militant
democracy
failure to discuss key issues 54
focus on narrow conception of
'democracy' 53–54
need for a last resort 54
overview 3
'the paradox of democracy's
self-defence' 54
legal indeterminacy 62
militant democracy
'concentric model' of democracy's
self-defence 56–57
development of new normative theory 23
doubts of scholars and policy makers 23
early stage of development 22
entrenchment 55
entrenchment of members' political
rights 57
essence of 'democracy' 56
party bans 55–56
responses to paradox 66
significant normative, practical, and
explanatory challenges 22–23
value-neutral procedures 56
varied emphasis 57
need for an alternative 78
political rights restrictions as last resort
70–73
pressing question raised by legal revolution
and democracy 52
problems with political rights
restrictions 156–57
reponses to the paradox
illegitimacy of restricting political
rights 66–68
overview 66
social contract theories 68–70
'the paradox of democracy's
self-defence' 60–61
understanding our political ideals 205–6

Parliaments
Hungarian Constitution of 1989 7
indirect methods of legal revolution 14–16
post-Cold War democratic backsliding 6
transformation of Hungary into an 'illiberal
democracy' 7–8, 10
Party bans
deficiencies of existing normative
theories 54, 157
limitation of existing normative
theories 73–75

normative theories of militant
democracy 55–56
Schmitt's state and constitutional theory 106
synonymous with militant democracy 1
'the paradox of democracy's
self-defence' 60–61
underlying paradox 1
Philippines 14–15, 31
Poland
indirect methods of legal revolution
14–15, 38
legal possession of state power 51
political rights restrictions
as last resort 72
timing of restrictions 169–70
Police power
antidemocratic potential 16
Political constructivism
authority of constitutional norms
constructivism's formal output: normative
truth 88–89
constructivism's substantive output: the
authority of basic liberal rights 90–91
foundations for any democracy 84
hypothetical 'second order'
proceduralism 85–88
'the people' and the electorate
distinguished 91–94
basis for new liberal normative theory 81
focus on overlapping consensus 82–84
measures to entrench constitutional
norms 94–95
overview 94–95
political rights restrictions 99–102
unamendability 95–99
Rawls' ambivalence about deploying militant
measures 102–4
theoretical origins of liberal normative
theory 2–3
Political rights restrictions
see also **party bans**
advantage of liberal normative theory 3–4
basic component of liberal normative
theory 2
deficiencies of existing normative
theories 54
German Basic Law 19
implicit unamendability 146–47
indirect legal revolution 39–40
interelatedness of unamendability 20–21
as last resort 70–73
liberal normative theory
explicit unamendability 151–52

focus on an organization's opposition to
the values and political identity of a
constitution 166–69
implicit unamendability 146–47
one of three three principal
mechanisms 137
overview 155–56
timing of restrictions 169–74
unamendability and the legitimacy of
political rights restrictions 157–66
limitation of existing normative
theories 73–75
measures to entrench constitutional
norms 99–102
normative theories of militant
democracy 57
normative theory's response to paradox 66
overview of existing normative
theories 156–57
post-Cold War democratic backsliding 6
sine qua non for a legitimate democracy 75
social contract theories 68–70
threat of populism 29
timing of restrictions
importance of prompt action 169–71
overview 169
resolving the practical paradox of
restrictions 172–74
tactical considerations 171–72
unamendability and the legitimacy of political
rights restrictions
circumventing 'the paradox of democracy's
self-defence' 158–61
co-implicating mechanisms 157–58
redefining detection 161–64
reducing abuses of democracy and
discretionary authority 164–66
underlying arguments 25
Politicization *see* **depoliticization**
Populism
detection problems 59
fragility and reversibility of an overlapping
consensus 85
Hungary's veneer of democracy 13
inadequacies of normative theory 53–54
legal revolution and democratic
legitimacy 41
need for an alternative normative
theory 75–76
threat to both new and consolidated
democracies 29
twenty-first century political goals 6
unreasonable beliefs 84

230 INDEX

Proceduralism
democratic theory 30
hypothetical 'second order'
proceduralism 85–88
paradox of modern constitutionalism 44–45
Rawl 2

Quietism 76–78
Quis custodiet ipsos custodes 196
Quod omnes tangit ab omnibus
decidentur 189, 195

Rawls, J. *see* political constructivism
Refah case 63–64
Rule of law
for the Ancient Greek 204
'containment' 101
legal determinacy 61–62
state and constitutional theory 130
transformation of Hungary into an 'illiberal
democracy' 9–10

Schmitt, C. *see* state and constitutional theory
Secularism *see* militant secularism
Self-determination
transformation of Hungary into an 'illiberal
democracy' 9–10
Separation and balance of powers
Hungarian Constitution of 1989 8
indirect legal revolution 36, 37–39
indirect methods of legal revolution 14–119
nemo judex in causa sua 188–89
transformation of Hungary into an 'illiberal
democracy' 11–12
typology of legal revolution 34–35
Social contract theories 68–70
Sovereignty
supremacy of amendment clauses 47–48
transformation of Hungary into an 'illiberal
democracy' 9–10
State and constitutional theory
basis to settle existential-political
disagreements about public order
failure of Hobbes' theory 120–22
Hobbes' Leviathan and political
authority 118–20
need for authoritative basis 114–15
role of myth 116–18
focus on dualistic distinctions
constitution and individual constitutional
law distinguished 127–31
constitutional revolution 131–33
overview 122
'the people' and the constitution 125–27

'the people' and the electorate
distinguished 122–25
'occasionalism' in Schmitt's thought 106–7
overview 105–6
problem of politicization
democratization and politicization 109–12
fundamental problem of modern
society 107–9
illegitimacy of state and law 112–14
theoretical origins of liberal normative
theory 2–3
uses and limits for militant
democracy 133–34
Supremacy of amendment clauses see
unamendability

'The paradox of democracy's self-defence'
critical arguments 75–76
deficiencies of existing normative theories 66
depoliticization 23, 54
detection problems 22
discretionary authority 22
legal indeterminacy 22
liberal normative theory 158–61
normative theories
illegitimacy of restricting political
rights 66–68
social contract theories 68–70
normative theories of militant
democracy 60–61
problems with political rights restrictions 156
responses to paradox 66
'The people'
political constructivism 91–94
state and constitutional theory
and the constitution 125–27
the electorate distinguished 122–25
Triepel, H. 32–34

Unamendability
basic component of liberal normative
theory 2
basic doctrine 137
collapsing of two conceptual distinctions 47
constituted power 47–48
defence measure against militant
democracy 1
deficiencies of existing normative theories 54
determination of validity 46
enabling of direct legal revolution 46–47
explicit unamendability of German Basic
Law 17–18
fundamental normative commitments 48
Germany's Basic Law 137–38

Hungarian Constitution of 1989 7
interelatedness of political rights
   restrictions 20–21
legal anchor for a definition of antidemocratic
   political goals 137
legal revolution and democracy 52
legitimacy of political rights restrictions
   circumventing 'the paradox of democracy's
     self-defence' 158–61
   co-implicating mechanisms 157–58
   redefining detection 161–64
   reducing abuses of democracy and
     discretionary authority 164–66
liberal normative theory
   absolute entrenchment 140–42
   explicit unamendability 147–54
   implicit unamendability 142–47
   multi-track constitutionalism 138–40
   one of three three principal
     mechanisms 137
limitation of existing normative
   theories 73, 74–75
measures to entrench constitutional
   norms 95–99

multi-track constitutionalism 138–40
requirement of modern constitutionalism 48
Schmitt's state and constitutional theory 106
solution to the paradox 45–46
underlying arguments 25
US example 46
United States
implicit unamendability 143
indirect methods of legal revolution
   breakdown of separation and balance of
     powers 38–39
   erosion of civil society and individual rights
     protections 39–40
   overview 14–15
measures to entrench constitutional
   norms 96–97
political rights restrictions
   focus on an organization's opposition to
     the values and political identity of a
     constitution 168
   restrictions on electoral choice 159
unamendability 138–39

'Weimar syndrome' 205